ISBN 978-1-331-90622-3
PIBN 10252333

1 MONTH OF
FREE
READING

at
www.ForgottenBooks.com

By purchasing this book you are eligible for one month membership to ForgottenBooks.com, giving you unlimited access to our entire collection of over 700,000 titles via our web site and mobile apps.

To claim your free month visit:

Similar Books Are Available from
www.forgottenbooks.com

BY
H. NOEL WILLIAMS
AUTHOR OF
"A PRINCESS OF ADVENTURE"

WITH SEVENTEEN ILLUSTRATIONS

NEW YORK
CHARLES SCRIBNER'S SONS
1912

PREFATORY NOTE

THE principal authorities, both contemporary and modern, which I have consulted in the preparation of this volume are mentioned either in the text or the footnotes. I desire, however, to acknowledge my obligations to the following works by modern writers : Duc d'Aumale, "Histoire des Princes de Condé;" M. Édouard Barthélemy, "La Princesse de Condé: Charlotte Catherine de la Trémoille;" M. Henri Bouchot, "Les Femmes de Brantôme;" Victor Cousin, "La Jeunesse de Madame de Longueville;" Comte Jules Delaborde, "Éléonore de Roye, Princesse de Condé (1535-1564);" M. I. Henrard, "Henri IV. et la Princesse de Condé;" MM. Homberg and Jousselin, "La Femme du Grand Condé;" Comte Hector de la Ferrière, "Trois Amoureuses au XVIᵉ siècle;" and M. H. Thirion, "Madame de Prie (1698-1727)."

H. NOEL WILLIAMS

CHAPTER I

CHAPTER II

CHAPTER III

CHAPTER IV

CHAPTER V

CHAPTER VI

CHAPTER VII

CHAPTER VIII

CHAPTER IX

CHAPTER X

CHAPTER XI

CHAPTER XII

CHAPTER XIII

CHAPTER XIV

CHAPTER XV

CHAPTER XVI

CHAPTER XVII

CHAPTER XIX

CHAPTER XX

CHAPTER XXI

CHAPTER XXII

LIST OF ILLUSTRATIONS

THE
LOVE-AFFAIRS OF THE CONDÉS

CHAPTER I

Origin of the House of Condé—Louis de Bourbon, first prince of the name—His modest *début* at the Court—His personal appearance and character—Enmity between the Bourbons and the Guises—Condé attaches himself to the party of the Connétable Anne de Montmorency, and marries the latter's niece, Éléonore de Roye—Noble character of Éléonore—Gallantries of Condé—His early military career—Death of Henry II.—Progress of the Reformation in France—Condé embraces Protestantism and places himself at the head of the opposition to the Guises—He is arrested at Orléans, brought to trial for high treason and condemned to death—But is saved by the opportune death of François II.

THE Condés and the Bourbons have a common origin. Both families descend from Robert de France, Comte de Clermont, youngest son of St. Louis. An ancient barony, the inheritance of that prince's wife, was erected into a dukedom in favour of Louis, his son, and gave to his descendants the name which they have retained, that of France being reserved for the royal branch.

After the death, without issue, of the Connétable de Bourbon at the assault of Rome in May 1527, his brother, Charles, Duc de Vendôme, became first Prince of the Blood, though, owing to the profound mistrust with which François I. now regarded the Bourbons, he never acquired either the authority or influence that so high a position ought to have given him. Nor did he succeed in recovering any of the vast possessions of the Constable, which were definitely alienated from his House, and, on his death in 1538, he left but a scanty fortune. This was the more at the siege of Rouen.

2. François, Comte d'Enghien, born 23 September, 1519; commanded the French army in the great victory of Ceresole, 14 April, 1544; died 23 February, 1546, from the result of what was probably an accident, but was by many attributed to deliberate intent.[1]

3. Charles, Cardinal de Bourbon ("*le cardinal des bouteilles*"), who was proclaimed King of France by the League after the death of Henri III.); born 22 December, 1523; died 9 May, 1590.

4. Jean, Comte de Soissons, and, after the death of his brother François, Comte d'Enghien; born 6 July, 1526; killed at the battle of Saint-Quentin, 15 August, 1557.

[1] The Court was staying at the Château of la Roche-Guyon, not far from Mantes. As there had been a heavy fall of snow, François I. suggested that the younger members of the Court should organize a snowball-fight. Sides were accordingly formed; one led by the Dauphin and François de Lorraine, afterwards Duc de Guise, defending a house; the other, led by Enghien, besieging it. "During the combat," says Martin du Bellay, "some ill-advised person threw a linen-chest out of the window, which fell on the Sieur d'Enghien's head, and inflicted such injuries that he died a few days later." Du Bellay does not give the name of the "ill-advised person," but certain writers, less reticent, name François de Guise, and have even gone so far as to assert that he acted by orders of the Dauphin, who was jealous of Enghien's military fame, while others say that he was a certain Conte di Bentivoglio, an Italian noble in the service of the Guises, whom they accuse of having instigated the deed. It is probable, however, that the death of Enghien was due merely to one of those acts of brutal horse-play so common at this epoch, and that the culprit, whoever he may have been, was innocent of any homicidal intention. See on this matter the author's "Henri II.: his Court and Times" (London, Methuen; New York, Scribner, 1910).

The earliest recorded mention of him occurs in the Domestic Roll of Henri II. for the year 1549, where he appears under the name of "Louis Mr de Vendôme, gentleman of the chamber to the King, at a salary of 1200 livres."

The precise time and occasion of his assuming the title which he and his descendants were to render so illustrious are likewise involved in obscurity. The Duc d'Aumale asserts that the earliest official document in which it is given, is in the *procès-verbal* of the Bed of Justice held on 15 January, 1557 ; [1] but since the duke wrote it has been discovered that he is thus qualified in at least half-a-dozen other deeds previous to that date, the earliest being an *acte seigneurial* of 30 March, 1553 ; while Henri II., in a letter to the Duc de Nevers written on 12 June, 1554, refers to the duke's youngest brother-in-law as "My cousin, the Prince de Condé." [2]

Equal uncertainty prevails as to whether he derived the title from Condé-sur-l'Escaut or Condé-en-Brie, both of which lordships seem to have been owned by his father, Charles, Duc de Vendôme. "The best known of the chroniclers of the family, Désormeaux," observes the Duc d'Aumale, "declares it to be beyond all doubt that the first prince derived his name from

[1] "Histoire des Princes de Condé."

[2] Comte Jules Delaborde, "Éléonore de Roye, Princesse de Condé, 1535-1564."

Condé-en-Brie. Indeed, in the marriage-contract of Louis I., the lordship of Condé-en-Brie appears in the list of the prince's possessions. He owned a château there, at which he often resided, and executed various deeds, whereas there is no official document relating to him known to exist in which any mention is made of Condé-sur-l'Escaut. But another historian of the family, l'Hullier, who, though a tedious and very dull writer, has left in MS. many historical and genealogical memoirs, of which Désormeaux has often made use, declares himself in favour of Condé-sur-l'Escaut; and the Convention appeared to be of the same opinion, by its naming that place " Nord-libre." The illustrious author modestly " leaves to more learned historians the task of solving the question," but the majority of modern writers are inclined to favour the claims of Condé-sur-l'Escaut, though, apparently, for no better reason than because it is the more important of the two places.

Few Princes of the Blood have made a more modest *début* at the Court of France than the first of the Condés. Since the treason of the Connétable de Bourbon his family had fallen into a sort of discredit, and, though, in the last years of the previous reign, the partiality shown by François I. for the young Comte d'Enghien had seemed a promise of returning favour, the untimely death of the count, followed by that of the King, soon dissipated their hopes. When the head of the house, Antoine, Duc de Vendôme, was hard put to maintain a position in accordance with his rank, there was little enough for his younger brothers ; and Louis de Bourbon made his appearance at Court so quietly dressed and with so modest a suite as to provoke no small merriment at his expense among the gorgeous butterflies of both sexes who adorned the salons of the Louvre and the gallery of the Tournelles.

Nor was there anything in the personal appearance of this youth of nineteen to suggest the great part that he was to play in after years. Unlike his ancestors, who had been tall men of imposing presence, he was short and slightly built, and some anecdote-mongers even represent him as hump-backed. Admitting however, that he may have been round-shouldered, the

Moreover, if somewhat diminutive in stature, he was "nimble and vigorous, and as adroit at martial exercises, both on foot and on horseback, as any man in France."[1] His features, too, were pleasing without being regular, and illuminated by a pair of very bright eyes; he had excellent natural abilities, and had not neglected to cultivate them, being exceptionally well-informed and a good conversationalist, with a touch of sarcasm, which, however, his good-humour deprived of its sting, and "agreeable, accessible, and amiable."[2]

The young prince was, therefore, not without qualifications to ensure advancement at Court, but in the two most essential wealth and influence—he was conspicuously lacking. The absence of the first might have mattered little had he possessed the second, but the cloud under which the Bourbons had lain for a quarter of a century showed no sign of lifting. Henri II., who had ascended the throne two years before Condé's arrival at Court, was a well-meaning man, who sincerely desired to do his duty and promote the interests of his subjects, but he was "born to be governed, rather than to govern,"[3] and was surrounded by ambitious and greedy favourites, who thought only of exploiting him for their own selfish ends. In the early days of the new reign, the favour of the King had been divided between his mature mistress, Diane de Poitiers, Duchesse de Valentinois, and his old friend, the Connétable Anne de Montmorency, who, disgraced by François I. in 1543, had, on the death of that monarch, been recalled to Court and entrusted with the direction of affairs. Diane, however, jealous of the influence of the Constable, formed an alliance with the Guises, those able and ambitious Lorraine princes who were to play so conspicuous a part in all the troubles of the latter half of the

[1] Brantôme.   [2] Ibid.   [3] Beaucaire.

sixteenth century; François de Lorraine, who succeeded his father as Duc de Guise in the spring of 1550, and his brother, Charles, the second Cardinal de Lorraine, became two of the King's most trusted advisers; and they and their younger brothers were loaded with honours and benefits. Henri II.'s favourites stood like a bodyguard around the throne to prevent any one else approaching it; their greed was insatiable; "estates, dignities, bishoprics, abbeys, offices, no more escaped them than do the flies the swallow; there was not a choice morsel that was not snapped up in a moment." [1]

For the Bourbons to have attempted to break through this bodyguard and insinuate themselves into the good graces of their Sovereign would have been a hopeless task; and they soon recognized that their only chance of bettering their fallen fortunes was to follow the example of the other courtiers and attach themselves to one or other of the favourites who governed the King, in the hope that some scraps of the royal bounty might be passed on to them. From the party of Diane de Poitiers and the Guises they had nothing to expect, for, though the two families were closely connected,[2] their relations were exceedingly strained. In both Court and camp their paths crossed; and the sinister rumours to which the death of the young victor of Ceresole had given rise is an eloquent testimony to the jealousy which existed between them. Since the death of François I., who had regarded the Guises with profound mistrust, and in his last hours had warned his son to be on his guard against them, since "their aim was to strip him to his doublet, and his people to their shirts," [3] the Lorraines had plainly shown their determination to keep the Bourbons in the background, and not content with enjoying the privileges of foreign princes, had profited by the impotence of their kinsmen to usurp those of the Princes of the Blood.

Policy and inclination therefore both prompted the Bourbons

---

[1] Vincent Carloix, "Mémoires sur le maréchal de Vieilleville."

[2] Antoinette de Bourbon, sister to Charles de Bourbon, Duc de Vendôme, Condé's father, had married Claude de Lorraine, Duc de Guise, and was the mother of Duc François de Guise and his brothers.

[3] De Thou.

nobility than did that of the Duchesse de Valentinois and the Guises, was supported by the bulk of the provincial noblesse, and Montmorency's great wealth and official position—he was Grand Master of the King's Household as well as Constable of France—enabled him to dispense extensive patronage. He had five sons and seven daughters, besides numerous nephews and nieces, and he did his duty nobly by them all, and allowed no opportunity to pass of advancing the importance of his family and enriching his relatives and friends. Condé, more ambitious than his brothers, determined to establish claims on the great man's favour which it would be difficult for him to overlook, and, towards the end of the year 1550, demanded in marriage the hand of Éléonore de Roye, eldest daughter and heiress of Charles, Seigneur de Roye and de Muret, Comte de Roncy, an alliance which would unite him with the two great Houses of Montmorency and Châtillon. For Éléonore de Roye's mother, Madeleine de Mailly, was the daughter of Louise de Montmorency, sister of the Constable ; [1] and Louise de Montmorency, by her second marriage with the Maréchal de Châtillon, was the mother of the future Admiral, Gaspard de Coligny, and of his two brothers, Odet, Cardinal de Châtillon, and François, Seigneur d'Andelot.

The consent of the young lady's parents was readily given. They could not, indeed, fail to be flattered by such a proposal from a Prince of the Blood, besides which they felt that this young man, frank, brave, chivalrous, and amiable, was a husband of whom any girl might well be proud, and ought to have a brilliant future before him. It is possible that the rumours of their prospective son-in-law's addiction to feminine society which had reached them may have occasioned them some mis-givings ; but Gaspard de Coligny, who had negotiated the affair, assured them that marriage would change all that, and that he had no doubt that, once in possession of the prince's affections, Éléonore would be able to fix them permanently. This, in view

---

[1] By her marriage with Fery II. de Mailly, Baron de Conty.

inclined to judge others by himself; while the political advantages of a match which would unite the Houses of Montmorency, Bourbon and Châtillon, and counterbalance the exorbitant credit of the Guises, may well have disposed him to regard the young prince's gallantries with a lenient eye.

After being accepted by the Comte and Comtesse de Roye, the project was submitted to the Constable, who was graciously pleased to approve of it, and promised to obtain the sanction of the King. This proved far from an easy task, as Diane de Poitiers and the Guises did everything possible to persuade his Majesty to refuse his consent; but, in the end, Montmorency triumphed over their opposition, and on June 22, 1551, the marriage was celebrated at the Château of Plessis-lès-Roye, by the Cardinal de Bourbon, the bridegroom's uncle.

This marriage added little to Condé's fortune, but it brought him "an inexhaustible treasure of affection and devotion." "If ever, in fact," writes an enthusiastic biographer, "a young girl, pure and loving, entered married life with the energetic resolution to consecrate all the living forces of her soul to the practice of the most holy duties, and raised herself by her piety and her virtues, by the generosity of her soul and the heroism of her character, to the rank of a *femme d'élite*, it was this incomparable Éléonore de Roye, who, from the day of her union with Louis de Bourbon, became for this prince, and remained up to the day when she succumbed prematurely to the cruel attacks of disease, a tender and submissive companion, a faithful friend, an immovable support in time of trial."[1]

Amidst that band of noble Huguenot ladies, who in the evil days to come so bravely upheld their persecuted faith against the overwhelming forces arrayed against it, and inspired their disheartened co-religionists with fresh energy and enthusiasm to maintain the unequal struggle, there is no nobler figure than that of Éléonore de Roye. Less capable, less ambitious, than Jeanne d'Albret, she is infinitely more attractive, for she

[1] Comte Jules Delaborde, "Éléonore de Roye, Princesse de Condé."

yielded to none of her sex in beauty, in grace, in intelligence and in chastity, and that she "surpassed every one in knowledge, in courage, and in magnanimity."[2]

Condé could not be indifferent to the devotion of such a woman, and there can be no doubt that, for a long time, he reciprocated her affection and that he always entertained for her a sincere regard. Nevertheless, his marriage did little to subdue his taste for gallantry, and his attentions to the light beauties of the Court must often have caused her the keenest pain. "The good prince," observes Brantôme, "was as worldly as his neighbour and loved other people's wives as much as his own, partaking largely of the nature of the Bourbons, who have always been of a very amorous complexion."

If, however, Condé shared his family's weakness for the fair sex, he shared also its taste for a military career, and, for some years after his marriage, it was the camp rather than the Court which claimed the greater part of his time. The long and bitter struggle between the Houses of France and Austria, closed for a time by the Peace of Crépy, broke out afresh in the early summer of 1551, in Italy, where Henry II. and Charles V., though still nominally at peace, intervened in the dispute between Pope Julius III. and his vassal Ottavio Farnese, Duke of Parma. Condé, though only a few days married, at once demanded and obtained permission to serve as a volunteer in the Army of Italy, commanded by the Maréchal de Brissac, and set out for Piedmont.

[1] "Additions aux Mémoires de Castelnau."
[2] "Histoire de la Maison de Bourbon."

When Louis Joseph de Bourbon, Prince de Condé, went to the wars, two centuries later, he took with him an immense retinue of servants, and a long procession of carts and carriages, to transport which over two hundred horses were required ; [1] while a whole regiment had to be detached for the protection of his precious person. His ancestor must have started on his first campaign in very different fashion ; indeed, there was probably little to distinguish him from the crowd of gentlemen volunteers whom the prospect of some hard fighting had drawn across the Alps ; and he evidently did not disdain to perform the work of the humblest soldier, since we hear of him toiling for two whole nights at the task of dragging the guns up the steep heights which commanded the Castle of Lantz. At the conclusion of the campaign, in which he had given abundant proof that he possessed all the courage of his race, although his general had found him "a little difficult to manage," he reappeared for a brief interval at Court, and then, in the spring of 1552, took part in the "Austrasian expedition," that military promenade through the Rhine country which gave to France, almost without striking a blow, Metz, Toul, and Verdun.

In the autumn of the same year, when Charles V., freed from his Germanic embarrassments by the agreement of Passau, laid siege to Metz, Condé and his brother, the second Comte d'Enghien, were among the young nobles who received permission "to take their pleasure at the siege." The two Bourbon princes were entrusted with the defence of a part of the ramparts, and acquitted themselves with courage and capacity.

The summer of 1553 found Condé in Picardy, sharing with the Duc de Nemours the command of the light cavalry. In an engagement with the Imperialist cavalry at Doullens, he brought up four squadrons at a critical moment, and, by a brilliant charge on the enemy's flank, decided the day. In the following year, he commanded the light cavalry on the Meuse and distinguished himself at the combat at Renty, and in 1555 he returned to the Army of Italy, in which he rendered excellent service on several occasions, notably at the siege of Vulpiano.

[1] "Mémoires du Duc de Luynes."

soon broken, and at the beginning of 1557 the dogs of war were again slipped. In the summer, the Spaniards invaded Picardy and laid siege to Saint-Quentin, on the Somme, one of the bulwarks of Paris. Realizing the importance of saving a town the fall of which would open the road to the capital, the Constable hurried northwards with all the troops he could muster, and Condé accompanied him. The overwhelming superiority of the enemy in numbers, however, decided Montmorency not to risk an engagement, but merely to make a feint against the besiegers' lines, and, under cover of this movement, to throw reinforcements and provisions into the town, after which he intended to retire. But the non-arrival of the boats required to transport the reliefs across the Somme caused a delay of more than two hours; and, when Montmorency began to retire, he found that the enemy had crossed the river by a ford of which he appears to have been in ignorance, seized the only road by which he could retreat, and cut his army right in two.

Surprised and hopelessly outnumbered, the French were routed with terrible loss. Condé's brother, the gallant Comte d'Enghien, was among the slain, while the Constable and the Maréchal de Saint-André were taken prisoners. Condé himself, who was stationed with part of the light cavalry on the extreme right wing of the army, displayed the most admirable courage and presence of mind amid the general panic, and, keeping his men together, succeeded in cutting his way through the victorious Spaniards and reaching La Fère. He lost no time in taking the field again and kept it throughout the autumn, continually harassing the enemy and attacking their foraging-parties and convoys. So much activity and vigour on the morrow of a great

¹ A *compagnie d'ordonnance* was composed of from seventy-five to three hundred men, one third being men-at-arms, or heavy cavalry, the rest foot-soldiers.

defeat undoubtedly merited some substantial recognition; but when, at the beginning of the following year, he solicited the post of colonel-general of the light cavalry which he had so gallantly led, he was, to his intense mortification, passed over in favour of the Duc de Nemours, the candidate of the Guises. It is true that, by way of compensation, he was nominated colonel-general of the Cisalpine infantry, that is to say, of the infantry stationed in Piedmont; but, since France had lately withdrawn all her troops from Piedmont with the exception of a few garrisons, the appointment was regarded as an affront rather than an honour.

The Peace of Cateau-Cambrésis, which was concluded in the following spring, prevented Condé from acquiring any further military distinction in the service of his country, and henceforth whatever laurels fell to his share were gained on fields where Frenchmen were opposed to Frenchmen. If, however, the life of Henri II. had been prolonged only a little while, it is almost certain that the prince's faithful services would not have remained unrewarded; for both the King and Diane de Poitiers were becoming seriously alarmed at the growing power and arrogance of the Guises, and the latter had broken with them and formed an alliance with Montmorency. But before the summer was over, Henri II. slept with his fathers at Saint-Denis; Diane and the Constable had been disgraced, and the Guises, thanks to the marriage of their niece, Mary Stuart, to the new King, had become the masters of France.

Condé's patience had been severely tried during the reign which had just terminated; and it was scarcely to be expected that a young prince of his ambitious and energetic character would resign himself to the sight of the royal authority concentrated in the hands of those whose aim it had always been to exclude his family from their rightful share in the direction of affairs. Nor were the means for giving very effective expression to his dissatisfaction wanting.

The Reformation in France, which had made immense strides during the last years of Henri II., notwithstanding the fierce, if intermittent, persecution to which it had been subjected, had ceased to be a purely religious movement and was developing into a formidable political combination with which it was the interest of discontented and ambitious nobles to make common cause, without in any way partaking of its spiritual aspirations. Condé, with his gay and pleasure-loving nature, could have had but little sympathy with the austere tenets of Calvinism, and it is probable that the mortifications he had experienced, the hope of uniting his fortunes with the chances of success which the Reformers were able to offer, and, above all, his hatred of the Guises, contributed far more than religious convictions to decide him to embrace their faith and their cause. His elder brother, Antoine, who, on the death of his father-in-law Henri d'Albret, in 1555, had succeeded to the throne of Navarre, had already done so, but, though brave enough in war, he was irresolute and shifty to the last degree, and now, when faced with the necessity for vigorous action, he declined to compromise himself; and it was therefore to the second Prince of the Blood that the Huguenots and the swarm of disbanded soldiers and disappointed office-seekers whom the Guises had driven into the ranks of the opposition looked for leadership. How far Condé was implicated in the Conspiracy of Amboise, whether or no he was the *chef muet* who, in the event of a first success, was to place himself at the head of the movement, is a question which is never likely to be satisfactorily answered. It is sufficient that he was almost universally identified with that mysterious personage at the time, and that this belief came near to costing him his life.

Athough permitted, after his indignant denial of the charge, to withdraw from Court, he and the King of Navarre, notwithstanding the entreaties of the Princesse de Condé, most imprudently resolved to obey the summons of François II. to the States-General at Orléans. It was to place his head in the lion's mouth, for in the interval fresh evidence, or what might pass for evidence, against him had been obtained, and the Guises were resolved on his destruction. On 30 October, 1560, the two princes arrived at Orléans. The King received them with ominous coldness, and, as Condé was leaving the apartments of the Queen-Mother, where the audience had taken place, he was arrested, and conducted to a house near the convent of the Jacobins, which was immediately barred up, surrounded by soldiers, and transformed into a veritable Bastille. His wife, who, on learning of his arrest, had hastened to Orléans, was refused permission to see him ; his attendants were withdrawn, and he was kept in the most absolute solitude.

Catherine de' Medici, who at this time possessed little or no power, and had been compelled, from the instinct of self-preservation, to cling to the Guises, pretended to approve of what had been done, and replied to all who besought her not to allow the prince to be brought to trial. "It is my son's will." She confined her efforts to saving the King of Navarre, who was merely kept under surveillance in his apartments.

Although, as a Prince of the Blood, it was Condé's undoubted privilege to be tried by the Grande Chambre of the Parlement in Paris, in which the princes and peers sat, the King entrusted his examination to a commission of judges presided over by Christophe de Thou, First President of the Parlement. Condé denied the competency of this tribunal, and "appealed from the King ill-advised to the King better-advised." But his imprudence in accepting the services of two advocates gave a semblance of legality to the proceedings, and his appeals and protests having been overruled by the Privy Council, in which such was the fear inspired by the Guises that no one dared to utter a word in his defence, on 26 November, he was sentenced "to lose his head on the scaffold."

It was at first considered probable that the King's clemency would be extended to his condemned kinsman, "in consideration of his youth," and every effort was made by the Princesse de Condé, the Châtillons, and other persons of high rank to secure a remission of the sentence. But nothing less than the death of their rival would satisfy the Guises, and, though the Chancellor de l'Hôpital, under the pretext of some legal flaw in the decree, succeeded in delaying the execution, it was finally fixed for 10 December, and the scaffold on which it was to take place was erected before the royal lodging.

awaiting his fate, and actually playing cards with some of the officers who guarded him, when one of his servants, who had been permitted to attend him, approached as though to pick up a fallen card, and whispered: "*Notre homme est croqué!*" Mastering his emotion, the prince finished his game, and then, taking the man aside, learned from him that François II. was dead. The sickly young King had been taken ill on 16 November, and, though he so far recovered as to preside over the Council which passed judgment against Condé, on the following day his malady assumed a grave form, and on 5 December an abscess which had formed in the ear suddenly broke, and he died in a few minutes.

Foreseeing her eldest son's approaching end, Catherine de' Medici, on the advice of l'Hôpital, had determined to save the Bourbons, in order to use them to counterbalance the Guises and assure the independence of the royal power of which she was about to hold the reins. Scarcely had François II. drawn his last breath, when the old Connétable de Montmorency, hastily summoned by her, arrived at Orléans, at the head of eight hundred gentlemen ; and the despotism of the Lorraine princes was at an end.

The death of François II. opened the doors of Condé's prison, but the prince, who attached more importance to his honour than his liberty, refused to accept the latter until the former had been publicly vindicated, and, in the meanwhile, announced his intention of remaining where he was. In this decision he was supported by his wife, but, as his health had suffered during his imprisonment, she persuaded him, towards the end of December, to exchange the severe régime of his detention at Orléans for a mitigated captivity, more apparent than real, in the form of residence on an estate belonging to the King of Navarre, near la Fère, in Picardy. Here he remained for some weeks, when he returned to Court, where his innocence was acknowledged by a declaration of the new King, Charles IX., which was subsequently confirmed by the Parlement, and he was restored to his former position.

CHAPTER II

NEVER had the internal condition of France been more critical, never had she stood more in need of a strong and wise government, than at the moment when the imaginary majority of François II. was succeeded by the real minority of Charles IX. The danger which threatened her was no longer, as in the time of the last Sovereign of that name, a struggle between individual ambitions ; private ambitions had now identified themselves with the living forces of the nation ; the whole of the nobility and gentry were already engaged in the quarrel of the great factions which divided France, and the mass of the people only awaited the signal to follow their example.

And the person who was called upon to deal with this critical situation was Catherine de' Medici, a woman, a foreigner. During the reign of her husband, Catherine had perforce remained in the background, Henri II. being completely under the influence of his mistress, Diane de Poitiers ; under François II., the government, as we have seen, had fallen into the hands of the Guises, and she had been, politically speaking, a mere cipher. But the early death of her eldest son had given her the opportunity which she so ardently desired—for all her life she had hungered for power and influence as a starving man hungers for bread—and having persuaded the King of Navarre to resign his claims to the Regency, in consideration of receiving the title of Lieutenant-General of the Kingdom, she at once assumed a quasi-absolute authority. She brought to the task a remarkable knowledge of men and affairs—the fruit of long years of quiet study and observation—a boundless activity, an untiring vigilance, a charm of manner which few who came into contact with her could resist, and a soul depraved by a life of subjection and dissimulation. Her master-passion was to govern through her sons, and she dreaded every influence which might weaken by one iota her personal authority.

To a certain extent, she succeeded in preserving this, but, though sincerely anxious to maintain peace, she was powerless to save France from the anarchy which menaced her. For she was timid, shifty, and irresolute, and incapable of any noble aim ; while it is also probable that she failed to recognize, at any rate until matters had gone too far to be remedied, the gravity of the situation. "To divide in order to reign" was the principle upon which she acted ; to give a little encouragement to the Huguenots, to instil a little apprehension into the Catholics, and to accustom both parties to regard her as the dominating factor in the situation. The result was that she was distrusted by both alike, and hastened the very calamity she desired to avert.

And this calamity was rapidly approaching. Calvinism was not, as certain Protestant historians would have us believe, a sect which demanded nothing but the liberty to worship God in its own way ; it was violent, intolerant, propagandist, and, under the influence of the exiles who had tasted democracy in Switzerland, and of the discontented nobles who exploited it for their own ends, was becoming as much a political as a religious organisation. Thus, it deliberately provoked persecution and played into the hands of its most implacable enemies. The coalition which had been formed to check the ambition of the Guises was dissolved ; while Condé and Coligny turned openly to Protestantism, the Constable, a rigid Catholic and a

c

Triumvirate. Shortly afterwards, the vain and fickle Antoine de Bourbon, allured by what de Thou calls "the entertainment of hopes" dangled before his eyes by Philip II. of Spain, renounced both his family ties and his Protestant convictions and joined the Triumvirs.

Nevertheless, during the latter part of the year 1561 the Court was certainly rallying to the side of the Reformers, for the King of Navarre's accession to the Triumvirate had given the latter such a predominance that Catherine was obliged to seek a counterpoise. It was with her warm approval that the Colloquy of Poissy took place, in the hope of arriving at some settlement of the chief differences between the two religions. The latitudinarian Prince de la Roche-sur-Yon was appointed the young King's *gouverneur;* Coligny's brother Andelot, most stalwart of Huguenots, was admitted to the Council. The celebrated Théodore de Bèze was invited to Paris; the King and Queen-Mother went to hear him preach, and he and other eminent divines expounded Calvinistic doctrines daily in the lodgings of Condé and Coligny to the ladies and gentlemen of the Court. The Huguenots in the provinces as well as in the capital were accorded a covert toleration, and the authorities recommended "to close their eyes to what only concerned the practice of their religion."

But a much stronger hand than Catherine's was required to persuade the two religions to dwell together in even a pretence of harmony. The Huguenots were determined to be treated no longer as legal outcasts; the High Catholic party, represented by the Triumvirate, was equally resolute to allow of no equality. After three months of argument and recrimination, and, at the last, of mere invective and abuse, the Colloquy of Poissy was dissolved; daily disturbances broke out; partisan feeling became more and more embittered; the Regent was powerless to stem the fast rising tide of hatred.

One last despairing effort for peace Catherine made. In the

middle of January 1562, on the urgent advice of Condé, Coligny, and l'Hôpital, she promulgated the celebrated edict, known as the] "Edict of January," which recognized the legality of Protestant worship outside the walls of towns. The Huguenots were exultant; the Catholics correspondingly exasperated; disturbances, attended in several instances with bloodshed, occurred in the capital and in other towns; and on March 1, the Massacre of Vassy by Guise's followers kindled the long-expected conflagration.

No effort had been spared by the Triumvirate to detach Condé from the Reformers; and the means which had proved so efficacious in the case of the King of Navarre had not been omitted. But the prince was made of sterner stuff than his brother; beneath a somewhat frivolous exterior he concealed a haughty and resolute spirit, and this, joined to the influence of his noble wife, kept him true to the cause which he had espoused. When the news of the massacre reached him, he was in Paris, where every Sunday he might have been seen, pistol in hand and accompanied by several hundred gentlemen on horseback, escorting Huguenot pastors through the howling mob to their meeting-place at Charenton. Furious with indignation, he lost not a moment in sending Bèze to the Court, which was then at Fontainebleau, to demand that the *massacreur* of Vassy should not be permitted to enter Paris. "I speak," cried the divine, when the King of Navarre endeavoured to defend Guise, "for a Faith which is better in suffering than in avenging wrong; but remember, Sire, that it is an anvil which has worn out many a hammer."

Catherine, without declaring her intentions, wrote to the duke ordering him to join her "*peu accompagné*" at Monceaux, in Brie, whither she proceeded with the young King, and, at the same time, sent orders to the Maréchal de Saint-André, who was in Paris, to repair to his government. Both declined to obey, and on March 16 Guise entered the capital at the head of 2000 horse, and was hailed by the populace "*comme envoyé de Dieu.*"

There were now in Paris two hostile camps, as in the time

of the Bourguignons and Armagnacs ; and Catherine, fearing a collision, sent orders to Condé to leave Paris. Recognizing the impossibility of disputing the capital with the Catholics, he obeyed, and proceeded to Meaux, where, after some hesitation, Coligny joined him.   Catherine and the young King had returned to Fontainebleau, and the former wrote to Condé entreating him "to save the children, the mother and the king-dom." If he and Coligny had acted with energy and decision, they might have secured the person of the young Sovereign ; but they waited for reinforcements, and when at length they advanced towards Paris, they found that the Triumvirs had forestalled them, and that the King was in the hands of the enemy.

Foiled in this attempt, Condé turned southwards, with the intention of occupying Orléans, a place which, on account of its central position, would serve as an admirable base for his opera-tions, and, to some extent, counterbalance the advantage which the Triumvirs derived from the possession of the capital.

On reaching Artenay, six leagues from Orléans, on the morning of April 2, he learned that Andelot, with a handful of men, had seized one of the gates of that town, and was holding it against the garrison and a part of the citizens. " He had with him about two thousand gentlemen and their valets, and, putting himself at their head, he set off at full gallop for the gate, and the whole pack after him." Baggage, horses, and men fell and rolled over in the dust, without any one attempting to draw rein, amid shouts of laughter from the reckless cavalcade, and to the great astonishment of peaceable travellers, who, ignorant that hostilities had broken out, asked one another if it were " an assembly of all the madmen in France." But the " madmen " swept along on their headlong course, and before noon had sounded from the clocks of Orléans, they were masters of the town and " of the taps of the most delicious wines of France." [1]

" Under these joyous auspices," observed Henri Martin,

[1] La Noue, " Mémoires."

"began the most horrible civil war of modern times;" and unhappy France became the scene of a frightful orgy of massacre, rape, and pillage. At first Fortune smiled upon the Reformers, who, thanks to the organization of their churches, were better prepared for hostilities than their adversaries. The principal towns of Central France, Tours, Blois, and Bourges, declared against the Triumvirate, and admitted Huguenot garrisons; Rouen and Le Havre, in Normandy, Lyons and many cities in the South, fell into their hands. For a few weeks the movement seemed irresistible. But the Catholic party was by far the stronger. It had secured the person of the young King and forced Catherine to side with it, and thus had at its disposal the Treasury and most of the permanent forces of the realm. It appealed, also, to the Catholic States for assistance, and obtained from Phillip II. an auxiliary corps of 4000 Spaniards, which operated in Guienne and Gascony; while the Duke of Savoy sent troops into the Rhône valley. By the middle of August, all the towns seized at the outset by the Huguenots had been recovered, and the Protestant cause seemed well-nigh hopeless.

Desperately pressed, Condé turned to England for aid. Emissaries were dispatched to London, and on September 20, 1562, the Vidame de Chartres, on behalf of the prince, signed the Treaty of Hampton Court, which stipulated that Le Havre and Dieppe were to be placed in Elizabeth's hands, in return for a loan of 140,000 crowns and a contingent of 6000 men. The vidame, however, went beyond his instructions, and permitted Cecil to insert an article whereby it was agreed that the English were to remain at Le Havre, not until the termination of the war, but until Calais was restored to them.

The calling in of the hereditary enemy brought great odium upon the Huguenot leaders, nor did they derive from it the advantages upon which they had counted, since Elizabeth, desirous only of securing an equivalent for Calais, declined to allow her troops to pass beyond the lines of Le Havre and Dieppe. At the risk of incurring her anger, Sir Adrian Poynings, who commanded temporarily at Le Havre, pending the arrival of the Earl of Warwick, sent five hundred men to endeavour to make their way into Rouen, which was now closely invested by the royal troops. The majority succeeded in this desperate enterprise, but they were powerless to save the town, which was taken by assault, after a siege during which the King of Navarre received a wound from which he died a month later, "still flattering himself with the hopes raised by the King of Spain." He left as his heir a boy nine years old, who was one day to succeed to the throne of France through the common ruin of the Valois and the Guises.

The intervention of the English, if it had served no other purpose, had drawn off the Catholic army from its projected siege of Orléans, and Condé, ever sanguine, did not allow himself to be cast down by the reverses his cause had sustained. "We have lost our two castles (Bourges and Rouen)," said he, employing a chess metaphor, "but we shall take their knights"; and he was eager to stake the last chances of his party in a great battle. At the beginning of November, the news that a considerable force of German mercenaries, which Andelot had raised in the Rhineland, was on the march to join him, determined the prince to quit Orléans and advance upon Paris. At Pithiviers, on November 11, he affected his junction with the foreign levies, and, at the head of an army of some 15,000 men, more than one-third of whom were cavalry, he moved slowly towards the capital, taking and pillaging the towns on his line of march.

Paris was very weakly defended, most of its regular garrison being in the field with the Triumvirs, and, had he acted with vigour, he might have made himself master of at least a part of the city. But he allowed himself to be drawn into negotiations by Catherine, and the delay which these entailed enabled Guise to arrive with the advance-guard of the army which had been besieging Rouen.

After a skirmish beneath the walls, and two unsuccessful attempts to take the city by camisado, Condé drew off his troops and marched into Normandy, with the intention of getting into touch with the English at Le Havre. But, owing principally to the immense number of carts for the conveyance of past and future plunder which the Germans insisted on taking with them, his army made such slow progress that the Triumvirs were able to outmarch it, and on December 19 the prince found them barring his road near the town of Dreux.

The royal forces were superior in infantry and artillery to the Huguenots, but the latter had a decided preponderance in cavalry, and the battle which followed was long and obstinately contested. Condé, who had distinguished himself more by his intrepidity than his generalship, was unhorsed and taken prisoner; the Constable, who commanded the royal army, experienced a like fate; while Saint-André was killed.[1] The carnage on both sides was very great, but the Catholics remained masters of the field, though Coligny was able to draw off the beaten Huguenots in excellent order.

The Constable was dispatched, in charge of Andelot, to Orléans, where he had the Princesse de Condé for hostess; Condé was conducted by Montmorency's second son, the Baron de Damville, to whom he had surrendered, to the quarters of Guise. In these detestable wars, prisoners were often treated with great harshness and cruelty, and sometimes, as we have just seen, their lives were not even spared when they happened to fall into the hands of some personal enemy. But Guise received Condé with as much courtesy and deference as the Black Prince had shown his royal captive at Poitiers. He placed at his disposal the peasant's cottage in which he was quartered, apologizing for being compelled to give so poor a reception to so illustrious a visitor, and it was only at the prince's repeated request that he consented to share with him this humble lodging. They supped together off the same coarse fare, conversing amicably the while, and the same bundle of straw served them for a bed. The duke, however, could well afford to show magnanimity towards a fallen foe, for, now that the King of Navarre and Saint-André were dead, and

---

[1] Saint-André had also been taken prisoner, but among his captors was a Huguenot gentleman named Bobigny whom he had deeply injured, and who proceeded to revenge himself by blowing out the unfortunate marshal's brains with a pistol.

Condé and the Constable prisoners, he had no rival but Coligny to fear, and the predominance of his ambitious House seemed assured.

The day after the battle, Condé was again entrusted to the care of Damville, who had only surrendered his prisoner to Guise as an act of deference, and who was subsequently constituted his legal custodian by a special authority from the King. Damville, who naturally regarded him as a hostage for the safety of his father, the Constable, guarded him very strictly, though his servants were allowed to remain with him, and a Huguenot pastor named Pérussel, who had also been taken prisoner, was authorized to minister to his spiritual needs and conducted a long "*prêche*" in his chamber every day. After being successively conducted to Chartres, Blois, and Amboise in the wake of the Court, he was incarcerated by the Regent's orders, in the Château of Onzain, an old feudal fortress, about three leagues from the last-named town.[1] Here he succeeded in bribing two of his gaolers, and arranged with their assistance to escape in the disguise of a peasant. But one of the men betrayed the plot to Damville, and Condé learned that all had been discovered by seeing the other soldier dangling from a gibbet erected beneath his window. After this, the prince was deprived of his servants, placed in solitary confinement, and most rigorously guarded ; and a rumour began to spread, though it was probably without foundation, that the Guises intended to compel Catherine to have him again brought to trial for high treason.

Meanwhile, the Duc de Guise had laid siege to Orléans, the last stronghold left to the Reformers. The town taken, it was his intention to call out the *ban* and *arrière-ban*, for which purpose a tax had been levied on the revenues of the Church, overwhelm Coligny, who with the Huguenot cavalry was overrunning Normandy, drive the English from Le Havre and

---

[1] It was here that Lord Grey de Wilton had been incarcerated after being made prisoner at Guines, in 1558. His captor, the Comte de la Rochefoucauld, treated him most harshly, and he only recovered his liberty by the sacrifice of practically the whole of his fortune.

Dieppe, and convert his office of Lieutenant-General of the Kingdom, which the King had been obliged to confer upon him in recognition of his services at Dreux, into a dictatorship.

The defenders of Orléans, decimated by famine and the plague, were incapable of offering more than a feeble resistance ; the outworks were quickly captured, and the final assault was daily expected, when, on the evening of February 15, 1563, while returning from a reconnaissance, the duke was mortally wounded by a Huguenot fanatic, Poltrot de Méré, who fired upon him from the shelter of a copse. He expired six days later, to the undisguised joy of the Reformers and to the secret relief of Catherine, who dreaded nothing so much as the prospect of a second period of Guise ascendancy.

The death of the Duc de Guise paved the way for peace ; and, through the intervention of Catherine and the Princesse de Condé, it was arranged that the prince and the Constable should meet and discuss its conditions. On March 7, two barges, the first coming from Orléans, the second from the opposite bank of the Loire, arrived at the Ile-aux-Bœufs, situated a little below the town. In one was the Constable, under the care of his nephew, Andelot ; in the other, Condé, under that of Damville. "There was a handsome boat ready for them, laid over with planks to make it broad and chamber-like, and covered with tapestry from the sun, where they should have ' parlemented ' together." But the uncle and nephew, unwilling to risk their conversation being overheard, "liked better to walk, which they did for two hours, d'Anville (sic), l'Aubespine and d'Aussy standing by, but not within hearing." [1]

Then they parted, without having arrived at any agreement, since Condé insisted that the " Edict of January " should be re-established in its entirety, to which Montmorency absolutely declined to consent, declaring that the Catholics would refuse to observe it. The Constable was escorted back to Orléans, and the prince to the Catholic camp at Saint-Mesmin.

On the morrow, they returned to the Île-aux-Bœufs. This time the prince's barge was followed by another, in which sat

[1] Smith to Cecil, March 12, 1563, State Papers (Elizabeth), Foreign Series.

Catherine de' Medici, Condé's only surviving brother, the Cardinal de Bourbon, and the Duc d'Aumale, and two of the Queen-Mother's maids of honour. It was remarked that these two damsels were the most beautiful of the bevy of young beauties whom Catherine had collected round her, and there was a shrewd suspicion that it was for that very reason they had been chosen to attend her Majesty upon this occasion. History has not preserved the name of the elder, but that of the younger was Isabelle de Latour-Limeuil, a lady who was destined to play a very prominent part in Condé's life.

Condé was a bad subject for prison life, and the rigorous detention to which he had been subjected at the Château of Onzain had not been without its effect upon him ; he was anxious to safeguard the interests of his co-religionists, but he was still more anxious to recover his liberty. "The little man to whom I have spoken," wrote the Prince de la Roche-sur-Yon, who had had an interview with him some days before, to Catherine, "is very desirous to see the end of these troubles ; he will accommodate himself to everything." The writer had correctly judged the situation.

The conference was renewed, this time in the presence of the Queen-Mother. Catherine had always exercised a great influence over Condé, and, only a few months before, in an interview between them at Thoury, she had all but brought him to conclude peace on her own conditions, when Coligny had interfered and caused the negotiations to be broken off. Now, however, Coligny was far away, and Catherine did not fail to press her advantage home. She made an eloquent appeal to the prince's patriotism ; she flattered him ; she "insinuated that, if he were to conclude peace without being too obstinate over the conditions, he should be elevated to the rank of the late King of Navarre, his brother,[1] and might do, from that time, all that he wished for those of the Religion."

Condé was ambitious; he was far from unsusceptible to flattery, and he ardently desired to recover his freedom. He looked at the subtle diplomatist who was speaking him so fair,

[1] The post of Lieutenant-General of the Kingdom.

LOUIS I DE BOURBON, PRINCE DE CONDÉ

and forced himself to believe that she was sincere in her protestations.   He looked at Damville and his guards, and thought with a shudder of the gloomy fortress which he had lately left, and to which it would probably be his fate to return, if the negotiations were broken off.   And then his glance wandered to the maids-of-honour, standing just out of earshot, and rested on Isabelle de Limeuil ; and he felt his heart beat a trifle faster, as he noted her charming face and the graceful lines of her figure. Did she not represent all the pleasures of the Court from which he had been so long separated, but which it was now in his power to enjoy again ?

The prince was already won over, already prepared to accept important modifications of the "Edict of January," when, that same evening, with the consent of the Queen, he entered Orléans to confer with the council of the Protestant Association.   He found the council divided into two sharply defined parties ; on the one side were all the ministers, to the number of seventy-two, with Théodore de Bèze at their head ; on the other, the great majority of the Huguenot gentlemen.

"The men of war demanded only peace ; the ministers of the Holy Gospel called for the continuance of the war, at least until the "Edict of January" was re-established in its entirety, and invited the prince to require the King to mete out rigorous punishment to all 'atheists, freethinkers, Anabaptists, Servetists, and other heretics and schismatics.'   Barely escaped from the stake themselves, they demanded the right to drag other victims to it." [1]

With ill-concealed impatience, Condé listened to the demands of these intractable theologians ; then, turning from them, he invited his old companions-in-arms to express their opinion.   With one voice these gentlemen, who were heartily weary of the war and asked only to be allowed to return to their homes, declared themselves willing to accept peace on the conditions which the Court was prepared to offer.   Strong in their support, the prince felt that he could afford to defy the ministers and the democratic section of the party ; and when,

[1] Henri Martin, "Histoire de France jusqu'en 1789."

on March 23, Coligny, fresh from his victorious campaign in Normandy, arrived at Orléans to take part in the negotiations, he found that he was too late. The Edict, or Peace, of Amboise had been promulgated in that town on the 19th, and published in the royal camp on the 22nd.

The Admiral was deeply mortified at Condé's surrender, in which he suspected that personal considerations had counted for not a little, and declared, with pardonable exaggeration, that "by a stroke of the pen more churches had been ruined than the enemy could have razed in ten years." As for the Huguenot ministers, they were exasperated to the last degree against the prince, stigmatized the treaty as "that of a man who had left half his manhood in captivity," and accused him of having yielded to the seductions of Catherine's Court, and of having *halené* her maids-of-honour.[1]

Somewhat conscience-stricken, Condé joined the Admiral in a belated attempt to get the articles modified in a Protestant sense, but, though Catherine agreed to some concessions, she firmly refused to allow them to be inserted in the edict. On April 1 she made her entry into Orléans, having the Cardinal de Bourbon on her right hand, and Condé on her left. A few days later, Coligny set out for Châtillon, to seek in the bosom of his family the repose which he had so well earned. Condé would have done well to follow his example. Unfortunately, he preferred to follow the Court to Amboise.

[1] D'Aubigné, "Histoire Universelle."

CHAPTER III

THE life of the Court, which naturally possessed a great attraction for a man of Condé's temperament, was full of snares and pitfalls. It was not for the mere pleasure of beholding their pretty faces that Catherine recruited her *entourage* from the most beautiful young girls in France. During the lifetime of her husband, in the days before she had been called upon to play a political rôle, Catherine had been the most austere of queens, guarding the reputation of her ladies as jealously as she did her own, and visiting with her severe displeasure the slightest breach of decorum on their part. But when she found herself a widow, struggling in an endless web of plot and falsehood to protect her children's heritage; beset on one side by the Catholics, on the other, by the Huguenots ; often driven to her wits' end to devise means to prevent the royal authority being submerged amid the strife of contending parties, her austerity gave way before political exigencies, and, recognizing how formidable a weapon she possessed in the charms of her "*escadron volant*," she exploited them without scruple. " These maids-of-honour," writes Brantôme, "were sufficient to set fire to the whole world ; indeed, they burned up a good part of it, as many of us gentlemen of the Court as of others who approached their flames."

Catherine received not a few remonstrances concerning the havoc wrought by the *beaux yeux* of these damsels. "You ought, Madame," runs one of them, "to content yourself with a small train of maids-of-honour, and to look to it that they do not pass and repass through the hands of men, and that they are more modestly clothed." But Catherine's squadron had demonstrated its peculiar value on too many occasions for her to dream of disbanding it, or even of placing it on a peace-footing ; and so its members continued to illuminate the Court ball-rooms, "like stars shining in a serene heaven."[1] For the rest, her Majesty pretended to ignore the vices of her *filles d'honneur*, the better to make use of them when occasion for their services arose. No one could have shown more adroitness in throwing some isolated and often unconscious combatant in the path of the politicians and party-leaders whom she had reason to fear, to captivate their senses and surprise their secrets. It was against the Huguenot chiefs that this insidious mode of warfare was most frequently employed. "However austere they may wish to appear, these men are of their time, and share the weaknesses of their contemporaries. Women had, in many cases, launched them into adventures, women will check them in full career. Those who succeed without provoking scandal are highly praised and rewarded ; the maladroit will be the less supported in their difficulties in that they are never able to invoke the excuse of a definite mission."[2]

Knowing what we do of Catherine's little ways, it is not difficult to imagine the tactics adopted. The destined victim, on some pretext or other, is lured to the Court. He comes, not ill-pleased to be afforded an opportunity of airing his grievances in the royal presence, but very resolved not to allow the Queen to penetrate the secrets of his party or to obtain from him the least concession. He is very coldly received, informed that his demands are unreasonable, and that the Queen fears that it

[1] Brantôme.   [2] M. Henri Bouchot, " les Femmes de Brandôme."

his departure, without the faintest suspicion that the most accomplished actress of the sixteenth century has been playing one of her many parts. Passing through the ante-chamber, he perceives, apparently awaiting her royal mistress's summons, a demure damsel of disturbing beauty—it is always the freshest and most innocent-looking of the squadron who is detailed for this kind of service—who modestly lowers her eyes as they meet his, but not before he has had time to remark that they are in keeping with her other perfections. Our Huguenot, who, though he yawns through a long sermon each Sunday and conducts family worship every day of the week, that is to say, when he does not happen to be engaged in burning his Catholic neighbours' chateaux over their heads, is none the less a courtier of beauty, finds himself wondering who the lady can be, and goes on his way not without a lingering hope that he may see her again.

On the morrow, he returns. This time, he is informed that the Queen is giving audience to one of the foreign ambassadors, and that he will have to wait for a few minutes. A quarter of an hour passes, and he is beginning to grow impatient, when the damsel whom he has seen on the previous day enters and advances to the door of the Queen's cabinet, with something for her royal mistress in her hand. Here, however, she is stopped by the usher; Mademoiselle cannot be allowed to enter; her Majesty has given orders that she is on no account to be disturbed. And she, too, must wait. In the circumstances, Monsieur, who is, of course, a great noble, and may therefore be permitted what in others might be considered a liberty, ventures to address her. She answers with a modesty which charms him, and they converse very agreeably until presently he is summoned to the royal presence.

Here, some further pretext is invented for detaining him some days longer at the Court, but he resigns himself to the delay with a good grace, for those few minutes' conversation in the ante-chamber have not been barren of result. A few hours later, he receives a courteous note from Catherine, greatly regretting the inconvenience to which he is being subjected and inviting him to a ball which she is giving the following evening. "The Religion" looks with scant favour on such worldly pleasures, but he tells himself that it would be churlish, perhaps impolitic, to refuse. Naturally, he meets Mademoiselle, arrayed in a ravishing toilette—very probably a present from the Queen —and looking more alluring than ever. He requests to be presented to her; they dance together, and he finds her as charming as she is beautiful. Opportunities for further meetings will not be wanting, for by this time the girl has received her instructions from headquarters; and soon there will be no further need for Catherine to devise pretexts for keeping the gentleman at Court.

When our Huguenot's partisans learn what is going on, they will write letter upon letter, warning him that an ambush is being laid for him, and reproaching him with bringing discredit upon the Faith. But he is now fairly in the toils, and their warnings and reproaches will serve no purpose save to irritate him against them and loosen the ties which bind him to them. Perhaps, lured by the blandishments of his inamorata and incensed by the suspicions of his party, he will end by abandoning it altogether; at the least, a breach will be created between them which will not be easy to heal, and some very useful information, which has escaped his lips in unguarded moments, will find its way into Catherine's cabinet.

It was thus that Condé's elder brother, Antoine de Bourbon, King of Navarre, had met Louise de la Beraudière,[1] Demoiselle de Rouet—*la belle* Rouet, as the Court called her—in whom he found so refreshing a contrast to his sharp-featured and austere consort that he permitted her to lead him whither she,

---

[1] She was the daughter of Louis de la Beraudière, Sieur del' Île Rouet, in Poitou.

or rather Catherine, willed.[1] She was the cause of his death. Wounded at the siege of Rouen and scarcely convalescent, he called her to him, and "behaved as though he considered that kings were immortal," with the result that might be expected.

> "Cy-gist le corps au vers en proye
> Du roy qui mourut pour la Roye [Rouet].
> Cy-gist qui quitta Jésus-Christ
> Pour un royaum par escript,[2]
> Et sa femme très vertueuse
> Pour une puante morveuse."

So ran a Huguenot epitaph on the ill-fated Antoine. But her connexion with the King of Navarre did not prevent *la belle* Rouet from making an advantageous marriage with Robert de Gombault, Sieur d'Arcis-sur-l'Aube, *maître d'hôtel* to Charles IX., whom she presented with two daughters.

The events of the civil war had profoundly altered Catherine's views in regard to the two parties which divided the kingdom. At the opening of hostilities, she had believed that the Huguenots possessed the better chance of success, and, though constrained to lend her name to the Catholic leaders, she was careful not to allow herself to be identified too closely with their objects. But, as time went on, it became evident that, although the Huguenots were undoubtedly formidable, they were very inferior in numbers, and that the mass of the people were faithful to the Old Religion. She was compelled, therefore, to recognize that she had been mistaken, and that it would be very inadvisable for her to alienate the Catholic party. On the other hand, it would be easy to seize the direction of that party, for the King of Navarre and François de Guise were dead, the sons of Guise mere boys, the Cardinal de Bourbon absolutely incapable, the Montmorencies divided among themselves, and the Cardinal de Lorraine, deprived of the support of his brother, as humble as he had once been arrogant. She, therefore, decided

---

[1] By the King of Navarre she had had a son, Charles de Bourbon, who became Archbishop of Rouen.

[2] "Un royaume par escript," means the illusory kingdom in the South promised Antoine by Philip II. of Spain.

undermine the ramparts of Calvinism, not to carry them by assault;"[1] to take back little by little, by restrictive interpretations of the Edict of Amboise, the concessions granted the Reformers ; to disarm and dissolve their religious and military associations ; and to dishearten them by withholding the protection of the Law and assuring impunity to the violence of the Catholics. But, aware that her task would be immensely facilitated if she could begin by depriving them of their protectors in high places, she was determined to leave no means untried to seduce or discredit the Huguenot chiefs, and particularly Condé—the first Prince of the Blood, the link between the noble and democratic sections of the party, the man whom she half-suspected of aspiring to the throne.

From the time of the Peace of Amboise, it was easy for Catherine to perceive that Condé, who had just consented to such important modifications of the " Edict of January," was unlikely henceforth to show himself a very zealous champion of Protestantism, and that a considerable section of the Huguenots was disposed to question the seriousness of his conversion and the sincerity of his devotion to their cause. She knew, too, that if, on the one hand, Condé aspired, as a Prince of the Blood, to play a prominent part in affairs of State, and was ambitious to secure the title of Lieutenant-General of the Kingdom, he would be, as a man, eager to compensate himself for the ennui of his recent captivity by a round of pleasure and dissipation.

At first, Catherine's attitude towards Condé was everything that he could possibly desire ; she overwhelmed him with atten-tions ; consulted him constantly on public affairs, and showed for his opinion a deference which delighted him. But all this was merely intended to put him off his guard and foster the pleasing illusions which he had entertained since the conference on the Ile-aux-Bœufs. For, so far from having any intention

---

[1] Henri Martin, "Histoire de France jusqu'en 1789."

of sharing the direction of affairs with the prince, she had determined to detach him from his alliances with the foreign Protestants, compromise him with his own party, and reduce him to political impotence. And, to accomplish this she proposed to deal with him as she had dealt with his unfortunate brother, the King of Navarre, by encouraging his taste for those sensual pleasures which the most dissolute Court in Europe offered so many opportunities of gratifying.

To dominate Condé, Catherine had in reserve an auxiliary not less redoubtable than *la belle* Rouet. It was Isabelle de Limeuil, one of the two maids-of-honour whom she had brought to the Île-aux-Bœufs, and who had already made a very favourable impression upon the inflammable prince.

Isabelle was a member of a branch of the House of La Tour d'Auvergne, to which Madeleine de la Tour, the mother of Catherine de' Medici, had belonged, and was therefore a kinswoman of the Queen-Mother.[1] She was a blond, with beautiful blue eyes and a dazzling complexion, in figure somewhat thin, but exquisitely formed. She had been well-educated, was extremely intelligent and possessed of a mordant wit, which she used freely at the expense of those admirers who did not suit her fancy, not sparing even the most exalted personages. Brantôme relates how, one day during the siege of Rouen, she rebuffed the old Connétable de Montmorency, whose bitter tongue was dreaded by all the Court. The Constable, who, in spite of his age and gravity, did not disdain an occasional *amourette*, attempted to make love to her and addressed her, in anticipation, as " his mistress." She replied tartly that, if he supposed he would ever have the right to address her thus, he was greatly mistaken, and promptly turned her back on him. Little accustomed to such a rebuff, the old gentleman took his departure, decidedly crestfallen. " My mistress," said he, " I leave you ; you snub me cruelly." " Which is quite fitting," she retorted, "since you are accustomed to snub everybody else."

---

[1] Isabelle's father, Gilles de la Tour, Sieur de Limeuil, was the second son of Antoine de la Tour, Vicomte de Turenne. From Oilles's elder brother, François, sprang, in the fifth generation, the celebrated Maréchal de Turenne.

Her *soupirants* were legion, and included the Duc d'Aumale ; Florimond Robertet, Sieur du Fresne, one of his Majesty's Secretaries of State ;[1] Charles de la Marck, Comte de Mau-levrier ; Claude de la Châtre, afterwards *maréchal de France ;* Brantôme and Ronsard, one of whose most charming *chansons* she inspired :

> " Quand ce beau printemps je voy,
>   J'apercoy
> Rajeunir la terre et l'onde,
> Et me semble que le jour
>   Et l'amour
> Comme enfans naissent au monde.
>
> Quand le soleil tout riant
>   D'Orient
> Nous monstre sa blonde tresse,
> Il me semble que je voy
>   Devant moy
> Lever ma belle maistresse.
>
> Quand je sens, parmi les prez
>   Diapiez,
> Les fleurs dont la terre est pleine,
> Lors je fais croire à mes sens
>   Que je sens
> La douceur de son haleine.
>
> Je voudrois, au bruit de l'eau
>   D'un ruisseau,
> Desplier ses tresses blondes,
> Frizant en autant de nœus
>   Ses cheveux
> Que je verrois frizer d'ondes.
>
> Je voudrois, pour la tenir,
>   Devenir
> Dieu des ces forests désertes
> La baisant autant de fois
>   Qu'en un hois
> Il y a de feuilles vertes."

With the exception of Du Fresne, who passed for her *amant de cœur*, it is doubtful if any of the gentlemen we have named ever saw his hopes materialize, for the fair Isabelle was

---

[1] He must not be confused with his cousin, Florimond Robertet, Sieur d'Alluye, who was also a Secretary of State.

one of those sirens who have a nice appreciation of the commercial value of their charms, and who not only set an exalted price upon their favours, but do not scruple to discount it in advance and subsequently decline to meet their obligations. "Monseigneur," writes she to the Duc d'Aumale, in a letter appealing to his benevolence, "if you have not discovered how much I desired to do the thing which was agreeable to you, it was not because you had not the means, but the will." [1]

Isabelle lent herself the more readily to Catherine's plans, since the mission confided to her was one in which her inclination happened to harmonize with her interests. For she seems to have been attracted from the first by this good-humoured little man, with his pleasant face and his laughing eyes, who danced so gracefully, paid such pretty compliments to the ladies, and, notwithstanding his lack of inches, could hold his own in manly exercises with any gentleman at the Court. And, besides, he was a Prince of the Blood and one of the bravest captains in France; and his narrow escape from the scaffold three years before, his exploits in the field, and his recent captivity, all of which naturally made a powerful appeal to ladies of a romantic disposition, had greatly enhanced the favour with which he had always been regarded by the opposite sex, many of whom would have been only too willing to accept him as a "*serviteur.*"

As for Condé, flattered by the preference of a young beauty for whom some of the most fascinating gallants of the Court had sighed in vain, he never paused to consider how far this *bonne fortune* was due to his own attractions, but plunged into it with the same impetuosity with which on the battlefield he threw himself into the thick of the enemy's squadrons. He promised himself merely an agreeable adventure; he found one of those entanglements from which it is a difficult matter to escape.

Isabelle de Limeuil was very soon afforded an opportunity

[1] La Ferrière, "Trois amoureuses au xvi⁰ siècle."

of putting the devotion which her royal admirer professed for her to the test.

Coligny and the Huguenot stalwarts had not been the only allies whom Condé had offended in accepting the conditions imposed by the Court in the Peace of Amboise. It will be remembered that an article in the Treaty of Hampton Court had stipulated that the English were to retain possession of Le Havre and Dieppe| until Calais had been restored to them. Now, Condé had never officially ratified the engagements that the Vidame de Chartres had undertaken in his name ; indeed, he pretended to be unaware of their full import; and had he ever been so desirous of it, it would have been impossible for him to have made the immediate restoration of Calais, or the continued retention of Le Havre by the English as a lien upon that town, a condition of peace. As an English historian very justly remarks, such a proposal would have "enlisted the pride of France against himself and his cause and have identified religious freedom with national degradation."[1] When, there-fore, on his return to Orléans after the conference on the Ile-aux-Bœufs, he wrote to inform Elizabeth of what was taking place, he said not a word about Calais, but boldly assumed that her Majesty's motives in coming to the assistance of the Huguenots had been entirely disinterested, and that, since liberty of conscience was on the point of being secured, there was no longer any occasion for continuing the war. "Now, Madame," he wrote, "you will let it be known that none other reason than simply your zeal for the protection of the faithful who desire the preaching of the pure Gospel induced you to favour our cause."[2]

Elizabeth, however, cared very little for the protection of the faithful in comparison with Calais, and she wrote the prince a very angry letter, in which she called upon him to fulfil his promise and bade him beware "how he set an example of perfidy to the world." Her remonstrances, however, produced

[1] J. A. Froude, "History of England," vol. vii.
[2] Condé to Elizabeth, 8 March, 1563, in the Duc d'Aumale, "Histoire des Princes de Condé."

no effect, and immediately after the signing of the Peace, in accordance with an article which stipulated that the foreign auxiliaries on both sides should be sent home, the Earl of Warwick received notice that he was expected to withdraw from Le Havre.

This, however, Elizabeth firmly declined to allow him to do. In vain, Condé wrote, offering her, in the name of himself, the Regent, and the entire nobility of France, to renew formally and solemnly the clause in the Treaty of Cateau-Cambrésis for the restoration of Calais in 1567, to repay the money which she had advanced the Huguenots, and to remove all restrictions upon English trade with France. In vain, he despatched envoys to explain his position and to reason with her. In vain, the young King wrote himself, offering the ratification of the treaty, with " hostages at her choice " for its fulfilment from the noblest families in France. Bitterly mortified at having been outwitted in a transaction from which she had intended to reap all the advantage, she would listen to no terms. The Prince de Condé, she declared, was "a treacherous, inconstant, perjured villain," with whom she desired to have no dealings ; she required Calais delivered over to her and her money paid down, and until she had obtained both, Le Havre should remain in her hands.

Catherine de' Medici had viewed with complacency the obstinacy of the English Queen. Although the reduction of Le Havre, a place which could easily be revictualled from the sea and which had been furnished during the English occupation with new defences, might prove a formidable undertaking, she had no doubt of success ; and she preferred recovering it by conquest to seeing it amicably restored, since she would then be at liberty to retain Calais. Moreover, if Condé could be brought to turn against Elizabeth the army which her own money had assisted him to raise, and to take part in the war in person, an irremediable breach would be created between them, and she would have nothing more to fear from English intervention.

Inspired by Catherine, Isabelle de Limeuil employed all her

persuasions to induce the prince to break with England; but, great as was the empire which she already exercised over Condé, and deeply incensed as the latter was by the tone of Elizabeth's letters, and still more by the contemptuous manner in which she had spoken of him, he still remained undecided. There was no blinking the fact that, however great the difference between her promises and her performances, and however selfish her motives, the Queen had rendered the Huguenots material assistance in the late war; and Coligny and Andelot had so well recognized this that, while warmly approving of the refusal to surrender Calais, they had declined to bear arms against her. Condé was unwilling to show himself less scrupulous than they; and, besides, he had, while at Orléans, solemnly assured the English envoy that " his sword should never cut against the Queen's Majesty." [1]

He, therefore, urged Catherine to make a final endeavour to effect a peaceful settlement. Very reluctantly, she consented, and, towards the end of May, the Sieur d'Alluye was despatched to London with fresh propositions. D'Alluye was a young man of thirty, ignorant, conceited, and presumptuous; in fact, if it had been Catherine's intention—which it probably was—to wound the pride of Elizabeth and provoke a new and humiliating refusal, she could not have made a better choice. Condé having requested that his confidant La Haye should be joined to d'Alluye, the Regent readily consented, well aware that a refusal transmitted through him would only have the more weight. Everything fell out precisely as might have been foreseen. After several acrimonious conferences with the English Ministers, in which d'Alluye " showed nothing but pride and ignorance," [2] that gentleman haughtily informed the Queen, that " he had no commission to treat of Calais; his charge was only to demand Newhaven [Le Havre]." [3] Elizabeth lost her temper, and, red with anger, replied that, in occupying Le Havre, she had had no other purpose than to avenge the honour of England, which had been compromised by the loss of Calais.

This frank avowal stung the national pride of the French to

---

[1] Middlemore to Cecil, 30 March, 1563.
[2] Cecil to Smith, 4 June, 1563.   [3] *Ibid.*

mobilized to wrest Le Havre from the grip of the English. Catherine adroitly seized the occasion to renew, through Isabelle de Limeuil, her importunities ; the last scruples of Condé were overcome, and on 19 June the English envoy Middlemore, who, on the pretext of facilitating communications between Condé and Elizabeth, had been charged by the latter to attend the prince everywhere, writes to Cecil : " The inconstancy and miserableness of this Prince of Condé is so great, having both forgotten God and his own honour, as that he hath suffered himself to be won by the Q.[ueen] mother to go against her Majesty at Newhaven [Le Havre], and for the present is the person that, above all others, doth most solicit them of the Religion to serve in these wars against her Majesty." And he adds that the prince, " specially desiring now to have every man to show himself as wicked as he, hath sent for the Admiral and M. Andelot, his brother, to come to the Court out of hand, where, being once arrived, they think to prevail with them as to win them to like and take in hand the said enterprise." Isabelle de Limeuil had served Catherine well.

A few days later, Condé having courteously desired Middlemore, who continued to stick to him like a burr, "to retire himself," joined the army before Le Havre, where operations had already begun. The garrison had promised Elizabeth that "the Lord Warwick and all his people would spend the last drop of their blood before the French should fasten a foot in the town" ; but, unhappily, they had an enemy to contend with within the walls infinitely more formidable than the one without—an enemy whom no skill could outwit and no courage repel. In the first days of June, the plague broke out among them, and, pent up in the narrow, fetid streets, the soldiers died like flies. By the end of the month, out of seven thousand men who had formed the original garrison, but three thousand were fit for duty ; and by 11 July only fifteen hundred were left.

¹ J. A. Froude, "History of England."

Reinforcements were hurried across the Channel, only to sicken and die in their turn ; a south-westerly gale drove the English ships from the coast, and the French succeeded in closing the harbour, so that soon famine was added to pestilence.

Elizabeth, alarmed by the disastrous news from Le Havre, began to repent of her obstinacy, and offered to accept the terms which she had so indignantly rejected. But it was now too late ; the French, well aware of the condition of the garrison, refused to reopen the negotiations, and on 27 July, just as the besiegers, who had already made two breaches in the defences, were preparing for a general attack, Warwick, who, the previous evening, had received permission from the Queen to surrender at the last extremity, offered to capitulate. Terms were soon arranged, and on the 29th the town was restored to France, and the remnant of its brave defenders sailed for England, carrying with them the plague, which they spread far and wide through the land.

After long negotiations, peace was finally concluded at Troyes, in April 1564. Elizabeth lost all her rights over Calais, and had to content herself with a sum of 120,000 crowns, as the price of the freedom of the French hostages. Although she on more than one occasion pressed Condé and Coligny for the repayment of the money she had advanced the Huguenots, she does not appear to have succeeded in recovering any part of it.

CHAPTER IV

Condé is disappointed in his hopes of obtaining the post of Lieutenant-General of the Kingdom—The prince incurs the hatred of the extreme Catholics—Plot to assassinate him on the Feast of Corpus Christi—Suspicion with which he is regarded by the zealots of his own party—Condé, deceived in his ambition and mortified by the hostility of the extremists on both sides, turns to pleasure for consolation—Violent passion of the Maréchale de Saint-André for him—Indignation and alarm aroused at Geneva by the rumours of Condé's amorous adventures—Calvin and Bèze address a joint letter of remonstrance to the prince—Condé at Muret—Death of two of his children—Failing health of the Princesse de Condé—Her touching devotion to her husband—Her dignified attitude in regard to his infidelities —Return of Condé to the Court—Quarrel between him and Isabelle de Limeuil—Temporary triumph of the Maréchale de Saint-André—Refusal of the King to sanction the betrothal of the Marquis de Conti to Mlle. de Saint-André—Condé quits the Court in anger, but is reconciled to Isabelle and returns—A second honeymoon.

AFTER having broken definitely with his former allies, and even borne arms against them in person, Condé looked to receive from the hands of the Queen-Mother the post of Lieutenant-General of the Kingdom, which Catherine appears to have given him to understand would be the reward of his compliance with her wishes. But her Majesty, though she complimented him warmly on the courage he had displayed during the siege, had not the smallest intention of sharing with the prince the power of which she was so jealous ; and, by causing the Parlement of Rouen to proclaim the majority of Charles IX., who had just entered his fourteenth year, she adroitly contrived to reduce to nothing all pretension on his part to the coveted title and to retain the sovereign authority in her own hands.

The discovery that he had been the dupe of his ambition was not the only mortification which Condé had to endure. If he were at bottom but a lukewarm adherent of the Reformed Faith, if in the negotiations which had preceded the Peace of Amboise he had been not unmindful of his own interests, he was none the less sincerely anxious that the rights guaranteed to the Protestants by that treaty should be observed ; and his persistence in defending them drew upon him the hatred of the extreme Catholics. So exasperated, indeed, were the fanatical Parisians against him that for some months his friends considered it unsafe for him to appear in the capital, even in the suite of the King, and on one occasion when he did venture there, he narrowly escaped being assassinated.

In one of his despatches to Cecil, Middlemore gives the following account of the affair :—

" On the 9th inst., the King went from Bois de Vincennes to Paris, as well to keep the people from sedition as to assist at the Feast of Corpus Christi, which was the next day. Condé (who had refused to go thither) was won to accompany him, and on the morrow brought him to Our Lady Church,[1] where he left him at the door, without entering. These ceremonies passed, the King, about 7 p.m., came back to bed to Bois de Vincennes, accompanied by his mother and the Prince. As they passed the town-gates,[2] they found 600 horsemen, well-armed and mounted, who were assembled to slay the Prince and all his, if they could have taken him out of the presence of the King ; but perceiving the King, they divided themselves on both sides of the way, and suffered him to pass quietly, on whose right hand at that time the Prince was, and the Queen-Mother on his left. The Princess, his wife, coming in her coach a little after, was assailed by them, and would have been murdered had not the cochier bestirred himself ; and such gentlemen as were about her cried to them that it was not the Princess of Condé, but the Queen's maids, which kept them from shooting their pistols at her, having them ready bent, until they overtook the King, in whose presence (when they saw that they had failed of the Prince and Princess) they killed a captain of the Prince[3] at the side of his wife's coach, and took five or six of his gentlemen

---

[1] Notre-Dame.   [2] The Porte Saint-Antoine.
[3] The name of the unfortunate gentleman was Couppé.

prisoners, and retired. This outrage is greatly stomached by the Prince, who has since been assured that some of the House of Guise did 'dress' him this party; and therefore he told the Queen, before the whole Council, that he will not tarry in the Court unless the whole House of Guise retire from thence; and so has desired her to consider which of them shall do the King better service, and that the others may be commanded forthwith to dislodge."[1]

On the other hand, the zealots of Condé's own party, who had so bitterly denounced the Peace, could not forgive his want of enthusiasm, nor the very plain language in which he rebuked their insulting behaviour towards the Catholics in those districts in which the latter happened to be in a minority. They accused him of "swimming betwixt two waters," "of playing the Machiavelli," and of seeking to use both parties for his own ends.[2] "In their eyes," observes the Duc d'Aumale, "his desire for the maintenance of peace was nothing but the indifference of gratified ambition, or the forgetfulness of duty amidst the intoxication of pleasure."[3]

[1] Middlemore to Cecil, 17 June, 1563, State Papers (Elizabeth), Foreign Series. The *dénoûment* of this affair is a singular illustration of the impotence or unwillingness of the Law to punish crimes committed against the Protestants by the ferocious rabble of the capital.

On the day following the outrage, the King sent for the Provost of the Merchants and ordered him to bring the murderers to justice, under pain of answering for them himself, adding that "if any more of such insolences were done in Paris, he would send the four marshals of France there to see better order kept." The provost, trembling in his shoes, returned home, and, next day, the authorities caused one Garnier, a captain of the city militia, and another person to be arrested, on suspicion of being concerned in the crime. Whereupon "the rest of the captains and lieutenants of Paris gathered themselves together to 4000 or 5000, and made such ado that they were glad to let them go." No further attempt to execute justice was made, nor could the authorities even secure decent burial for the murdered gentleman. By a decree of the Châtelet, the body was ordered to be interred in the cemetery of the Innocents, together with that of an unknown Huguenot, "whom also on the Thursday, in the worship of that holy day, the Parisians had sacrificed and, after their manner, thrown into the water (the Seine). But certain women and boys (for they are now the judges and executioners of Paris) digged them up again; which being known, to avoid danger they were buried there again by the watch, and were again unburied, and no man knows what is done with them."—"Journal of Sir Thomas Smith," State Papers (Elizabeth), Foreign Series.

[2] Smith to Cecil, 22 May, 1563.   [3] "Histoire des Princes de Condé."

If Condé's efforts on behalf of his co-religionists should have sheltered him from such accusations, his private life, it must be admitted, was very far from being in accordance with the austere religion which he professed, and was calculated to arouse grave apprehensions among the Protestants. Deceived in his ambition, mortified by the hostility which his well-intentioned efforts had been received by the extremists of both parties, he had turned to pleasure for consolation and surrendered himself unreservedly to all the temptations of that gay and dissolute Court. His days were passed in the hunting-field, the tennis-court, and the tilt-yard ; his nights at the ball, the play, or the card-table, and often in more questionable amusements. Grave Huguenots who came to lay their grievances before him were indignant to find the chief of their party, who should have been occupying himself with the interests of religion and setting an example of godly living to those about him, mingling in all the profane diversions of the Court, as though he had not a care in the world, and in-expressibly shocked to learn that he was forgetting his devoted wife in the embraces of " Midianitish women."

For Isabelle de Limeuil, if she occupied the premier place in Condé's affections, could not claim a monopoly of them. His Highness, in point of fact, disdained few *bonnes fortunes*, and the complaisant beauties of Catherine's Court were generally ready to meet the advances of the first Prince of the Blood a good deal more than halfway.

Among those who entered the lists against Isabelle, the most redoubtable was Marguerite de Lustrac, the widow of the unfortunate Maréchal de Saint-André, so foully slain at Dreux. Although no longer in her first youth, Madame la Maréchale was still one of the most beautiful and fascinating women at the Court—"*la Marguerite de douceur*,"[1] a contemporary writer calls her. She was also extremely wealthy and gave herself the airs of a queen, being always attended by an immense retinue, which included cadets of the noblest families in France.

Feeling the need of consolation in her bereavement, the lady

---

[1] François Billon, " le Fort inexpugnable de l'honneur féminin." Paris, 1555.

cast a favourable eye in the direction of Condé, and, piqued by his indifference—he was just then in the middle of his honeymoon with Isabelle—soon conceived for him the most violent passion. Since sighs and languishing glances did not suffice to bring him to her side, she resolved to have recourse to other means. By the Maréchal de Saint-André she had had a daughter, who was one of the greatest heiresses in France. This daughter had for some time past been destined for the young Henri de Lorraine, who, by the tragic death of his father, had now become Duc de Guise, and she had even been confided to the care of the widowed duchess. But, the maréchale, having decided that the surest means of subjugating Condé was to appeal to his interests, suddenly demanded that her daughter should be sent back to her, repudiated her engagements with the Guises, and offered the girl to the prince, for his eldest son, Henri, Marquis de Conti, now twelve years old.

The prospect of an alliance which would not only bring great wealth into his family, but inflict a cruel humiliation on the hated Guises was naturally very favourably received by Condé, and the enamoured maréchale did not fail to take full advantage of the frequent interviews between her and the object of her passion which the affair, of course, necessitated. Nevertheless, she did not succeed in weaning the Prince from Isabelle, and had to rest content with the few crumbs of affection which he condescended to bestow upon her.

Rumours of his Highness's amorous adventures were not long in reaching Geneva, where they aroused both indignation and alarm. Had the delinquent been a less exalted personage, he would probably have been straightway excommunicated; but Calvin and Bèze, though exasperated by the carelessness with which he was compromising their common cause, knew very well that the first Prince of the Blood was an asset with which the party could not possibly dispense. They knew, too, that his *amour-propre* had already been deeply wounded by the reproaches that had been addressed to him at the time of the Peace of Amboise, and that it was necessary to spare his feelings as much as possible; and, accordingly, contented themselves by

addressing to him, in the name of their afflicted Church, a lette
of remonstrance, couched in studiously moderate terms:

MONSEIGNEUR,

We cannot forbear to beseech you not only to use
your endeavours in the cause of Our Lord Jesus Christ, for the
advancement of the Gospel and for the security and repose of
the poor faithful, but also to show in your whole life that you
have profited by the doctrines of salvation, and to let your
example be such as to edify the good and to close the mouths
of all slanderers. For in proportion as you are conspicuous
from afar in so exalted a position, ought you to be on your
guard lest they should find any fault in you. You cannot
doubt, Monseigneur, that we love your honour as we desire
your salvation ; and we should be traitors were we to conceal
from you the rumours that are in circulation concerning you.
We do not suppose that there is any direct offence to God; but
when it is reported to us that you make love to ladies, your
authority and reputation are seriously prejudiced. Good people
will be scandalized thereby ; the evil-disposed will make it a
subject of mockery. It involves a distraction which hinders
and retards you from attending to your duty. There must
even be some mundane vanity in it ; and it becomes you, above
all else, to take heed lest the light which God has placed in you
be quenched or grow dim. We trust, Monseigneur, that this
warning will be taken in good part, when you reflect how much
it is for your service. From Geneva, this thirteenth day of
September 1563.

> Your very humble brethren,
> JEAN CALVIN
> THÉODORE DE BESZE

Condé received this letter at the Château of Muret, in
Picardy, whither he had just arrived on a visit to his wife and
family, accompanied by his brother-in-law, the Comte de la
Rochefoucauld,[1] and his nephew, the Prince de Porcien. I

---

[1] La Rochefoucauld had married Catherine de Roye, younger sister of the
Princesse de Condé.

would not appear to have been altogether without effect, for, on 2 October, Condé's mother-in-law, the Comtesse de Roye, wrote to the Duke of Würtemberg: "The prince, my son-in-law, intends to devote himself more and more to everything which can further the reign of Jesus Christ."[1]

In the course of that same month, a domestic calamity came to add weight to the counsels of Calvin and Bèze. Two of his younger children, Madeleine, aged three, and Louis, a child of eighteen months, fell ill and died within a few days of one another, to the inexpressible grief of the Princesse de Condé, who was one of the most devoted of mothers.

The princess's relatives and friends, who probably regarded the death of the children as a direct judgment from Heaven upon the father's sins, did not fail to improve the occasion, and represented to Condé that it was his duty to withdraw, for some time at least, from the Court and remain with his bereaved wife. The poor lady, indeed, needed all the care and attention which were in his power to bestow, since she was a prey to bodily suffering as well as to anguish of mind. Always a delicate woman, the dangers and agitations of the past two years had tried her cruelly. In the spring of 1562, when on her way from Meaux to Muret with her eldest boy and a small retinue, she had been attacked by a mob of fanatical peasants, who were marching in a Catholic procession, "without any cause, unless it were that they had been incited by a malignant priest, out of hatred for the Religion."[2] The litter in which the princess was being carried was smashed to pieces by volleys of stones, and she herself narrowly escaped serious injury. She was then in an advanced stage of pregnancy, and had barely time to reach the nearest village when she gave birth to twin sons. Nevertheless, as soon as she was able to leave her bed, she insisted on setting out for Orléans to join her husband, and, during the siege of that town in the following winter, she

---

[1] Comte Jules Delaborde, "Éléonore de Roye, Princesse de Condé."
[2] Bèze. But other writers assert that the princess's attendants had provoked the attack by insulting the priests.

E

remained there, amid all the horrors of war, pestilence, and famine, to encourage its defenders by her heroic example.

Although her health had been profoundly affected by all that she had gone through during the civil war, the princess considered it her duty, so long as any physical strength remained to her, to reside at the Court with her husband, and to follow him in his journeys. Thus, when, in the early summer of 1563, Condé decided to take part in the expedition against Le Havre, she set out for Normandy, accompanied by her mother, the Comtesse de Roye. But, on reaching Gaillon, she was attacked by small-pox of so severe a type that, for some time, she was in grave danger. Scarcely was she convalescent than Madame de Roye fell ill, in her turn ; and the princess, in attending to her mother, neglected her own health, which from that moment declined steadily.

Although the dissolute life which Condé was leading had caused her the greatest grief, she had refrained from reproach-ing him. "For her," says her biographer, "the true remedy for the irregularities of the unfaithful husband and for the anguish of the outraged wife was to be found in earnest and continual prayer. She implored God to save the soul led astray, and strove, by patient efforts, discreetly directed, and loving instances, to bring back this soul into the path of duty, and to revive in it family affections."[1] She now joined her entreaties to those of her friends and relatives to persuade her husband to remain with her. But Condé's career of dissipation had stifled his better nature ; the impressions produced on his mind by the death of his children were soon effaced, and, oblivious of the duty which he owed his ailing wife, and of the many obligations under which she had placed him, in the first days of November he quitted her abruptly and returned to the Court, which was now in residence at Fontainebleau.

A most unwelcome piece of intelligence greeted him on his arrival. He was informed that, during his absence in Picardy Mlle. de Limeuil had shown herself so unworthy of the signal honour he had done her as to find consolation in the homage

[1] Comte Jules Delaborde, "Éléonore de Roye, Princesse de Condé."

of M. du Fresne, a gentleman for whom she had shown a
decided preference in the days before Condé appeared upon the
scene. The prince, who entertained a very high opinion both
of the lady and of his own powers of fascination, was at first
incredulous ; but the evidence laid before him was sufficiently
circumstantial to disturb his peace of mind very seriously. In
consequence, the reunion to which he had looked forward with
so much impatience was shorn of all its rapture, and, instead of
smiles, endearing words, and embraces, there were reproaches,
indignant denials, sarcastic rejoinders, tears, and sulks.

The Maréchale de Saint-André did not fail to profit by the
indiscretions of her rival, and delivered so vigorous and well-
timed an assault upon the prince's heart that she succeeded in
temporarily establishing herself there, and "audaciously flaunted
her conquest before the eyes of the whole Court." The
maréchale had now recovered her daughter from the Duchesse
de Guise, though not without an appeal to the law courts, and
the little girl was on the point of being formally betrothed to
the Marquis de Conti, when the Queen-Mother, who had got
wind of the project, and had no mind to see the House of
Condé thus aggrandized, suddenly intervened and persuaded
the King to inform the parents that he should refuse his
sanction to the match.

Condé could not contain his indignation. "The Prince de
Condé has left the Court in anger," runs a letter from Fontainebleau, "because they (Charles IX. and Catherine) would not
give the daughter of the late Maréchal de Saint-André to his
son. He believes that they intend to give her to Guise. The
Constable has gone to fetch him back. Others have gone to
fan the flame."[1] But it appears to have been Mlle. de Limeuil,
and not the Constable, who persuaded the prince to stomach the
affront he had received and to return to the Court. Acting
doubtless by Catherine's orders, the damsel addressed to him
eloquent and persuasive letters, assuring him that he alone
possessed her heart, and that the affair with M. du Fresne had

[1] Letter of Almerigo Bor Fadino to Pierre du Bois, merchant of Antwerp,
13 November, 1563, State Papers (Elizabeth), Foreign Series.

been no more than a harmless flirtation, which malicious persons of both sexes—woman who envied her her happiness, and gallants who could not forgive her for having preferred the prince to them —had magnified into an intrigue.   As for the matter which had caused his departure from the Court, was it worth while to sacrifice his pleasures to his *amour-propre?*   The little Mlle. de Saint-André was a sickly child, who would probably never live to a marriageable age.   Let him return, and he would find his Isabelle impatiently awaiting him.

Condé did return, forgetting for the nonce his grievances against Catherine and anxious only for a reconciliation with his mistress.   The Maréchale de Saint-André was compelled, to her intense mortification, to resign her conquest and retire temporarily from the field; and the prince and Isabelle embarked upon a second honeymoon, which was conducted with so little pretence at concealment that people were astonished that Catherine, who still insisted on the observance of some outward decorum at her Court, should permit such "goings on."   Her Majesty, however, who was fully alive to the political advantages of a passion which was, so to speak, binding her adversary hand and foot, found it convenient to be a little blind.

In the course of the month of November, Coligny and Andelot arrived at the Court, and, on learning of the manner in which Condé was parading his profligacy, expostulated with him in no measured terms.   Their remonstrances, however, had very little effect, and it was not until the following February, when the Princesse de Condé paid a brief visit to Fontainebleau, that his Highness condescended to show some respect for *les convenances.*

CHAPTER V

THE Court was very gay that winter. At the beginning of the spring, Charles IX. and Catherine were to set out on a grand progress through the kingdom, which was expected to occupy the better part of two years ; and, before their departure, Catherine wished to revive the magnificent fêtes of which Fontainebleau had been the theatre in the days of " *le Roi chevalier.*" In the vast galleries where Primaticcio has immortalized the beauty of her rival Diane de Poitiers, she entertained the *élite* of the nobility of France, Catholics and Protestants being invited without distinction. Hunting-parties, tilting-matches, mimic combats on foot and on horseback, balls, banquets and theatrical representations filled the days and nights ; the princes and great nobles vied with one another in the sumptuousness of the entertainments which they, in return, offered to their young Sovereign and his mother ; and a stranger who had been suddenly transported into the midst of all this gaiety and extravagant splendour would have found it difficult to believe that he was in a country where the ashes of a desolating civil war had scarcely had time to grow cold.

by a "*ballet-comédie*," which Catherine gave at the Vacherie. Isabelle de Limeuil figured in it, in the character of Hebe, and "attired in a tunic of transparent gauze, which permitted one to catch a glimpse of limbs which the goddess might have envied," was the cynosure of all eyes. Condé was no doubt not a little flattered by the admiration which his lady-love was arousing, and it is to be hoped that the charms which she so freely displayed sufficed to preserve him from the manœuvres of her fair colleagues in the Queen's service, who, we are told, were indefatigable in their efforts to detach him from her. At the Court of Charles IX., it was something even to be faithful in infidelity!

On 13 March, 1564, their Majesties quitted Fontainebleau, and set out on their progress through the realm. This journey had been long meditated by Catherine, who expected from it important results. In the first place, respect for the central authority had almost disappeared amid the anarchy of the civil war, and the Queen desired, by making the young King known to the nation, to re-establish the monarchical power in the interior. In the second, the crisis through which France had just passed had lowered the country immeasurably in the eyes of other States, and she flattered herself that, by means of interviews with foreign sovereigns on the frontiers, she might do much to restore the prestige of the French name. Moreover, by establishing a good understanding with them, and particularly with Philip II. of Spain, she hoped to free herself from the tutelage of the grandees of the kingdom.

The *cortège* was a most imposing one, for Catherine wished to impress the people and the sovereigns whom she was to meet by the magnificence of the royal retinue. The whole of the Court followed the King—princes, ministers, gentlemen, and ladies—and there was a veritable cohort of pages and lackeys, wearing his Majesty's livery of blue, red, and white, all the pages being dressed in velvet. The military escort was a very large one, and comprised not only all the Household troops, but several companies of men-at-arms. The Constable marshalled

27 March. In this town, where the negotiations for peace with England were finally concluded, Condé "fell sick of the palsy or apoplexy, which took him at tennis, and a fever upon it," [2] and his condition appeared sufficiently grave for his wife, who was then at the Château of Condé-en-Brie, to be summoned to nurse him. The devoted woman, although suffering herself, lost not a moment in hastening to her faithless husband's side, and in lavishing upon him the tenderest care. Thanks in a great measure to her solicitude, the prince's health was soon re-established—for his illness would appear to have been much less grave than was at first supposed—and she was able to return to her children. But the hurried journey to Troyes, and the anxiety she had suffered on her husband's account, had exhausted her slender reserve of strength, and scarcely had she reached Condé-en-Brie, than she was taken dangerously ill.

A courier, dispatched in all haste, found Condé at Vitry-le-François, whither he had followed the Court, and, though, for reasons which will presently be understood, he was extremely loath to part from Isabelle at this juncture, he felt obliged to take leave of their Majesties and return to his neglected wife. On his arrival, he found her somewhat better, but the doctors did not disguise from him that her recovery was hopeless, and that, in all probability, she had but a few weeks to live. The prince, however, an incurable optimist, declined to believe that the case was as serious as they represented, and, though he decided to remain with her, it is evident, from the following letter, written by him to his nephew, the Prince de Porcien, that he was determined to get as much amusement out of his enforced sojourn by the domestic hearth as circumstances would permit :

---

[1] F. Decrue, "Anne, duc de Montmorency, connétable et pair de France."
[2] Smith to Cecil, 14 April, 1563, State Papers (Elizabeth), Foreign Series.

"MY NEPHEW—My desire to have news of you prompts me to write you this letter, and, at the same time, to entreat that, if your convenience permits, you will come to see and console your good friend and relative, who is very wearied [*ennuyé*] by his wife's serious illness. Come with your greyhounds and your horses and arms, if that be possible, and I will promise to show you as fine hunting as you could know how to find. My horse and arms will arrive here to-day, and I hope that, if you come, we shall find means, please God, to enjoy ourselves." [1]

Meanwhile, the Court was continuing its progress. From Troyes, it proceeded to Bar-le-Duc, where Charles IX. stood sponsor to the infant son of his sister Claude and the Duke of Lorraine, and on 22 May arrived at Dijon, where it remained until the 30th, their Majesties being lodged in the palace of the old Dukes of Burgundy.

It was during the sojourn of the Court in this town that the liaison of Condé and Isabelle de Limeuil had the most scandalous *dénoûment*. At the Queen-Mother's *coucher*, according to some writers, at an audience given by their Majesties to a deputation which had come to present them with an address of welcome, according to others, Isabelle was suddenly taken ill, and carried into Catherine's wardrobe, where she gave birth to a fine boy, of whom she at once declared Condé to be the father.[2]

It was not the first casualty of its kind which had occurred in the ranks of the "*escadron volant.*" Only a little while before, a like misfortune had befallen another maid-of-honour, Mlle. de Vitry by name; but, in this case, an open scandal had been avoided. Brought to bed in the morning, Mlle. de Vitry had had the fortitude to drag herself to a ball given at the Louvre that same evening, and thus had contrived to preserve what shreds of reputation may have been left to her.[8] For a young

[1] Letter of 6 May, 1564, published by the Comte Jules Delaborde.
[2] " Which was a great infamy for the so-called Reformed Religion."—" Journal de Bruslard."
[3] La Ferrière, " Trois amoureuses au XVIᵉ siècle."

forgivable one of being found out ; but, once they were so maladroit as to be detected, they must expect no consideration at her hands.

However, since Isabelle was, after all, a soldier wounded in her Majesty's service, and had done her duty nobly until she had been placed *hors de combat*, it is probable that no worse fate would have befallen her than dismissal from the "squadron" and the Court, had not her enemies profited by her misfortune to launch against her a most formidable accusation.

Isabelle, as we have mentioned elsewhere, possessed a biting wit, which she was accustomed to exercise freely at the expense of those who were so unfortunate as to displease her, not sparing even the most exalted personages. The sharpness of her tongue, indeed, made her as many enemies as the charms of her person gained her admirers, and often those who approached her with words of devotion on their lips were so cruelly rebuffed that they retired with vengeance in their hearts.

Among those whom she had thus contrived to offend, was Charles IX.'s former *gouverneur*, the Prince de la Roche-sur-Yon,[2] an extremely dangerous person for a maid-of-honour to have as an enemy, since not only was he a Prince of the Blood, and a gentleman of a peculiarly vindictive character, but his wife[3] held the post of Grand Mistress of Catherine's Household, a position which enabled her to make things extremely unpleasant for any of the Queen's damsels of whose conduct she

[1] "Abrège chronologique de l'histoire de France."

[2] Charles de Bourbon. He and his elder brother, Louis, Duc de Montpensier, represented the younger branch of the Bourbons.

[3] Philippe de Montespidon. She had been previously married to the Maréchal de Montjean.

de Limeuil passed her time when off duty. The lady was of her husband's opinion, and, from that moment, the maids-of-honour, and Isabelle in particular, found their opportunities for clandestine meetings with their admirers seriously curtailed ; while, as time went on, the Grand Mistress began to evince an interest in Mlle. de Limeuil's health which occasioned the object of her solicitude infinite embarrassment.

The girl, who well knew whom she had to thank for these annoyances, was furious against La Roche-sur-Yon, and made no secret of the hatred which she entertained for him. One of those to whom she expressed her opinion of the prince was the Comte de Maulevrier,[1] a great admirer of hers, who had himself no cause to love his Highness. In the summer of 1560, it had happened that Maulevrier was hunting with the prince's only son, the Marquis de Beaupréau, a boy of thirteen. The marquis's horse stumbled and fell ; Maulevrier, who was close behind, was unable to stop his, and the animal came down with all its weight upon the unfortunate lad, who was so badly crushed that he died shortly afterwards. Although this calamity was obviously due to pure accident, La Roche-sur-Yon, who had been passionately attached to his son, conceived the most violent resentment against Maulevrier, and swore that he should answer for the boy's life with his own. So threatening an attitude did he assume, that the count deemed it prudent to go into hiding for some time, and though, thanks to the intervention of Catherine, the bereaved father was eventually persuaded to forego his vengeance, it was only on the

---

[1] Charles de la Marck (1538–1622). He was the second son of Robert de la Marck, Duc de Bouillon. It is singular, in view of what we are about to relate, that he afterwards married as his second wife Antoinette de la Tour, younger sister of Isabelle.

understanding that Maulevrier should never again venture to appear before him.

Maulevrier had no desire to do so, and carefully avoided the prince, until one day, in the previous summer, they happened to meet by accident. No sooner did La Roche-sur-Yon catch sight of the involuntary murderer, than he drew his sword and rushed upon him like a madman, and the count only saved himself from being spitted like a fowl by promptly taking to his heels.

Such being the relations between La Roche-sur-Yon and Maulevrier, it is not surprising that Isabelle should have expected to find in the latter a sympathetic listener, when she inveighed against the prince as the instigator of all the annoyances to which she and her colleagues were being subjected by the Grand Mistress, or that, when in his company, she should have occasionally indulged in that extravagant language in which angry and excitable women are accustomed to find an outlet for their wounded feelings, but to which, fortunately for them, sensible people seldom attach any importance. For how could she have imagined that Maulevrier, who had always expressed so much admiration for her, and who had himself been subjected to such unmerited persecution at the hands of La Roche-sur-Yon, would betray her confidences to their common enemy?

But Maulevrier, whether because he had some secret grudge against the girl, or, more probably, because he hoped that, by pretending to render a great service to La Roche-sur-Yon, he might persuade that personage to be reconciled to him, gave a most sinister interpretation to the expressions which the exasperated Isabelle permitted to escape her, and communicated them to the prince, with no doubt a good many exaggerations.

No steps, however, seem to have been taken by La Roche-sur-Yon in the matter until the occurrence of the scandal which we have just related, when, having decided that the moment for action had arrived, he persuaded Maulevrier to draw up and sign a formal information against Isabelle, which he lost no time in laying before the King and the Queen-Mother.

In this document, Maulevrier declared that Isabelle had on several occasions said to him : "If I were in your place, I should poison the prince"; that during the journey of the Court she had indulged in the most violent language against his Highness, whom she accused of inspiring all the annoyances which his wife had inflicted upon the Queen's "maids," and of having sought to injure her in a matter which closely concerned her honour ; that, one evening, she had sent for him, and told him that La Roche-sur-Yon was giving a supper-party the following night, and that it would be the last that he would ever give, warning him, at the same time, not to repeat a word of what she had said, or "he would be found dead in the corner of some ditch"; that, notwithstanding this threat, he had sent warning to the prince, who had begged him to entice Mlle. de Limeuil into further confidences; that, a few days later, the Court being at Vitry, the lady had said to him : "The coup failed ; the prince postponed his supper-party, but the opportunity will recur"; with which she drew from an envelope a white powder and gave him part of it, telling him to make his dog take it and he would see that in a short time the animal would be dead; and, finally, that on the morning of a state dinner given at Bar-le-Duc, Mlle. de Limeuil had remarked to him : "It is truly astonishing that the Queen-Mother has not been ill !"[1]

It was, of course, impossible for Charles IX. and Catherine to ignore so grave an accusation as that of having planned the poisoning of a Prince of the Blood, backed by evidence drawn up with such minuteness and precision of detail as to give it an air of probability.   At the same time, Catherine would perhaps, in ordinary circumstances, have hesitated to accept the unsupported testimony of Maulevrier, who was not a person on whose word much reliance was usually placed.   But, as La Roche-sur-Yon had, of course, foreseen, the scandal of which Isabelle had just been the cause was scarcely calculated to incline her to view the matter from a judicial standpoint; and, at her instigation, the King at once signed an order for Isabelle to be

---

[1] "Information contre Isabelle de Limeuil," cited by La Ferrièrè.

Her child was taken away from her and given into the charge of a poor woman at Dijon.

On arriving at Auxonne, Isabelle was received by M. de Ventoux, governor of the town, who conducted her to the convent. Here, she was incarcerated in a little, bare, low-ceilinged room, like a prison cell, and very strictly guarded. The unfortunate girl, though still in ignorance of the charge against her, was in despair, and, we are assured, for three days and nights did nothing but groan and weep. M. de Ventoux, a kindly man, who visited her several times, was touched with compassion, and, after vainly endeavouring to console her, despatched the most alarming reports of her condition to the Court, in one of which he declared that, if it were possible for a woman to die of melancholy, then assuredly she had not long to live.

With such rapidity and secrecy had Isabelle been carried off from Dijon, that none of her relatives or friends at the Court had the least idea what had become of her. But, on receiving Ventoux's reports, the Queen-Mother so far relented as to authorize him to transmit to the prisoner all the letters which were addressed to her, and to forward to their destination those which she wrote herself, having first taken the precaution to open and copy them, since in this way some very useful information might be obtained. Singularly enough, neither Isabelle nor her friends seemed to have had the least suspicion that their correspondence was being tampered with.

Catherine must have been disappointed if she expected to secure from these epistles any evidence in regard to the charge which had been brought against Isabelle, but, *en revanche*, they contained some interesting information concerning other matters. The first letters, for instance, which passed between the fair captive and M. du Fresne were peculiarly enlightening, and established beyond all possibility of doubt the character of their relations.

The enamoured Secretary of State begins by deploring that he had been unable to take farewell of the lady before the

Court left Dijon ; but the mere suspicion that he had done so had so enraged the Queen-Mother that to have defied her would have probably entailed his prompt disgrace. On the other hand, the Prince de Condé, whom he had taken upon himself to inform of the interesting event which had taken place at Dijon and of the subsequent disappearance of its heroine, had expressed much annoyance, because he had happened to mention that he had lent Isabelle a dressing-gown, being evidently of opinion that it was a piece of presumption for any one but himself to assist the lady. "It is very strange," he writes, "that, being abandoned, as I was able to tell him you had been by every one, the prince should take it ill that you have been visited and succoured by those who were incurring risks in order to serve you." However, he should not cease to employ his life and his property for her, "the person whom he loved and esteemed the most in the world." But, at the same time, he thinks it would be perhaps advisable for her to return the dressing-gown, "since he saw clearly that it was not agreeable to the prince [Condé] that she should make use of it." And he concludes by reminding her of the happy days they had spent together when the Court was in Normandy the previous summer, when he had received "*tant de contentement.*" In a postscript, he bids her burn his letter, which, in view of the fact that a copy was already in the hands of M. de Ventoux, seems a rather unnecessary precaution.

Isabelle's reply was calculated to satisfy the most exacting of lovers. It was impossible to tell him what pleasure his letter had given her ; words quite failed her to describe it. She did nothing all day but think of him, and he might rest assured that, whatever Fortune might have in store for her, she would never cease to love him. [The minx will write much the same to Condé a little later.] She sends him a scarf woven with her own fair hands, two pictures of saints which she has painted, a heart, and a book, the "Patience of Job," which, is "*fort à propos.*" She concludes by kissing his hands "thousands and millions of times." [1]

[1] " Information contre Isabelle de Limeuil."

It was, as we have seen, through the medium of Du Fresne that Condé, retained by the bedside of his dying wife, was informed of the misfortunes of Isabelle. To receive such news of his mistress through the courtesy of a rival occasioned him, as may be supposed, the keenest mortification ; and his jealousy reveals itself very plainly in the first letter which he addressed to the lady :

"Alas! my heart, what can I say to you, save that I am more dead than alive, seeing that I am deprived of the means of serving you, and seeing you depart [1] without knowing how I may be able to aid you ? M. du Fresne often informs me that you send him news of yourself, but I, I cannot know whither you have been conducted, and I am greatly astonished, since you have the means of writing to some persons, that I may not receive your letters also. For you know that there is not a man in the world who would be so much grieved at your distress as myself, nor who, with greater gaiety of heart, would be more determined to hazard his life to do you a useful service. I am sending you one of my dressing-gowns, which has served me and you also when we were together, begging you to believe that I should prefer you to your gown, since I should be of more service to you than a sable. Let me know that you are as anxious to retain me in your good graces, now that you are a captive as when you were at liberty ; for you know that, being accustomed not to share them with any one, but to be the first and the only one, I feel sure that you have not lost the good opinion that you have of me, but, on the contrary, that it is rather increased. It remains to make use of me and to give me the opportunity of coming to free you from the trouble in which you are, for you must acquaint me with the means of doing so. I have eyes which do nothing but weep, and strength which is inanimate, since it is not commanded by you."

If Condé had been unable at first to discover the place where his Isabelle had been incarcerated, he had succeeded in getting her son into his possession ; and, having received two

[1] The word, almost illegible, may be either *partir* or *pâtir* (to be in distress).

letters from Isabelle recommending the child to his care, he hastens to relieve her maternal anxiety :

"I shall content myself by telling you that I have our son in my hands, safe, and merry and certain to live. . . . It is true that they had left him at the house of a poor woman, who made him lie on straw for six nights, like a hound, which I thought very strange.   But if, at the beginning, those to whom he did not belong treated him like a little dog, I have taken him like a father to bring him up *en prince*. He deserves it, for he is the most beautiful creature that ever man saw."

And the lovelorn prince concludes :

"If I do not see you soon, I would as lief die as live.   I desire it as much or more than my salvation."   And, at the end of the monogram which replaces the signature, he writes : "Let us die together!"

On receiving this epistle, which confirmed the warning which Du Fresne had given her concerning the suspicions of Condé, Isabelle hastened to assure the prince that her heart was wholly his, and that henceforth she would communicate with him alone.   Meantime, however, Condé had learned that gossip was far from unanimous in attributing the paternity of the child to him, and that the general opinion at the Court was that M. du Fresne's claims to the honour were at least equal to his own.[1]   All aflame with jealousy, he writes to his mistress :

"I assure you, my heart, that I am very greatly annoyed that people are able to find in your conduct reason to ask : 'Whose is this child?' which is as much as to say that you admit two persons to a like degree of favour.   I do not tell you this because, I believe it, as I will show you ; for I will give

[1] A Latin satire of the time ran:

> "At multi dicunt quod pater
> Non est princeps, sed est alter
> Qui Regi est a secretis
> Omnibus est notus satis."

you a proof whether I love you or no in a few days. My heart, since we have gone so far, we must raise the mask, for every one knows what has passed between us. You will be honoured and esteemed by all, since you show them, as much in small things as in great, that you do not wish to address or to receive news save from him whom you have loved more than that which you prize more dearly than yourself [*i.e.* her honour]. . . . You have heard that they speak at the Court of a certain person [Du Fresne]. You must take care to silence these false reports. You need not resort to oaths to make me believe that your son is mine, for I have no more doubt of him than of those of my wife. But act in such a way that others may be able to entertain no doubt of it, and reflect that whoever sees him will say with reason that he is my son and yours, for our two faces are to be recognized in his. I implore you, my heart, to love me and never to abandon me, as you have promised ; and when you remind yourself of the occasion on which it was made, I am sure that you will keep your promise to me. I send you a fur-lined dressing-gown. I should like to be near you in its place, for I cannot be so useless as not to be of as much service to you as it will be.

"Our son is very well, and is being well taken care of, and is in my hands, which is my only consolation, since I am separated from you, and is a pledge to render me for ever assured of remaining in your good graces, which is the thing which I prize the most, and more so than I have ever done."

In a third letter, couched in equally passionate terms, the prince informs his lady-love that he has entrusted her son to a gentleman who will bring him up as one of his own children, advises her to write to the Queen-Mother to implore her clemency, and impresses upon her the importance of receiving only the servants whom he may send to her, "by which she will make it known that she loves no one save him." He concludes by assuring her that he intends to live and die with her.

F

received a commission from the King to investigate the charges against Isabelle, arrived at Auxonne. The prisoner was brought before them and very closely interrogated. She admitted that she had bitter cause to complain of La Roche-sur-Yon, who had not only egged on his wife to pester her with questions concerning her health, but had told Condé that he was "very blind and very credulous if he believed that Limeuil was with child by him." At the same time, she denied absolutely that she had ever made, or even contemplated, an attempt upon the life of the prince. Nor had she ever suggested to Maulevrier that he should poison his Highness, although, on one occasion, when she and the count were in the company of a number of other persons, she had heard some one, whom she did not name, advise Maulevrier to make away with him, "in the interests of his repose." Mlle de Bourdeille,[1] who was one of those present, would confirm her statement.

The commissioners departed for Lyons, where the Court had just arrived, taking with them a very dignified and pathetic letter from Isabelle to the Queen-Mother:

"MADAME—After having heard from the Sieurs Sarlan and Du Puy the reasons which have induced your Majesty to send them to me, it has afflicted me to such a degree that, but for the aid of God and the hope that I repose in your kindness, I should have fallen into the greatest despair that a poor creature could be in, not being so forgetful of God as to have conceived or meditated such wickedness. When it shall have pleased God to make known to you my innocence, I implore you, for the honour of those to whom I am related, to do such justice upon the false accuser as I should have deserved, had I committed such a crime."

Meanwhile Condé had not been idle. He had sent to Auxonne one of his confidential servants, who had put himself into communication with the leading Huguenots of the town,

---

[1] The sister of Brantôme.

budge and threatened to kill herself; but eventually she thought better of it, and allowed herself to be conducted to the river, where she and her escort embarked in a boat to proceed to Maçon, the first stage of their journey. Scarcely, however, had they got her on board, when she was seized with a violent attack of hysteria and gave vent to the most heartrending cries. Then, for a whole day and a night she refused either to eat or drink, until Gentil began to fear that she would never reach her destination alive. At length, however, she became more tractable, partook of some food, and, asking for writing materials, indited an appealing letter to Condé, which was intercepted by Gentil and, in due course, transmitted to Catherine. It was as follows:

"Alas! my heart, have pity upon a poor creature who suffers all things for having loved you more than herself.[1] My affliction will be only pleasure, provided, that you remember me, and that I am so happy as to be the only one to possess your love. I am so afraid that my absence has the misfortune to banish me from your good graces, which tortures me more than I can describe. My heart, help me and free me from the position in which I have no more to suffer for the rest of my life. Write

[1] From this it is evident that Isabelle had refrained from informing Condé of the charge that had been brought against her, and allowed him to suppose that the Dijon scandal was the sole cause of her imprisonment.

to the Queen in my favour and make the Maréchal de Bourdillon write."

On reaching Mâcon, Gentil decided that it was inadvisable to proceed further with so weak an escort, for the Huguenots were very strong in that part of the country, and he accordingly wrote to Catherine begging her to send reinforcements, as he was in hourly dread of being attacked and his prisoner carried off. On her side, Isabelle, more and more alarmed as to the fate in store for her, profited by the delay to write another despairing letter to Condé, which, like the first, was intercepted by the vigilant Gentil and forwarded to his mistress

"The Queen is sending me to Lyons; if you have not compassion on me, I see myself the most miserable creature in the world, in such manner do they drag me about, with soldiers for my guards, as though I were a person who had merited death. I have no hope save in God and you. It would be well for you to write to Madame de Savoie,[1] to persuade her to obtain my pardon from the Queen. I am a more faithful, a more affectionate, slave to you than ever I was, and the greater my tortures, the more I adore you. Send to this Lyonnais country to ascertain where I may be. I believe that I shall not be far away from it. Alas! my heart, remember that you have promised to be faithful to me. Place me in such a position that, at least ere I die, I may be able to see you. Have no other heart than mine, or make me die first. I kiss your hands and feet a thousand times."

On the arrival of the soldiers demanded by Gentil, Isabelle was conducted to Lyons and thence to Vienne, where she arrived on 18 July, and was incarcerated in the Château des Canoux. Here she was again examined, this time by two members of the Council, the Bishops of Orléans and Limoges, who were frequently employed in important negotiations. The two

---

[1] Marguerite de Valois, youngest daughter of Francois I., who had married, in 1559, Emmanuel Philibert X., Duke of Savoy.

warm reception, "liar," "evil liver," and "drunkard" being among the epithets which she hurled at his head. Maulevrier persisted in his charges, but could call no evidence to support them ; Isabelle reiterated her denials. Their lordships, though they pretended to look very wise, could make nothing of the affair at all ; but, since a man is not less a man because he happens to be a bishop, and Isabelle's beauty and distress had not been without its effect upon them, they left her with a promise to intercede for her with the Queen.

Their intercession, however, does not appear to have had any effect, for the months passed, and the lady still remained under lock and key.

CHAPTER VI

Death of the Princesse de Condé—Question of the prince's remarriage—
The Maréchale de Saint-André's bid for his hand—Rumours of a matrimonial
alliance with the Guises—Catherine de' Medici, alarmed at such a prospect,
resolves to set Mlle. de Limeuil at liberty—Isabelle joins Condé at Valery—
Intense indignation of the Huguenots at the scandalous conduct of the
prince—Quarrel between Condé and Coligny—The leaders of the party
take counsel together "to find a remedy for so great an evil"—The deputa·
tion of Protestant pastors—Condé declines to separate from his mistress,
but eventually breaks with her—His marriage with Mlle. de Longueville—
Condé persuaded by his wife to demand the return of the presents he has
given his mistress—Revenge of Isabelle—Her marriage—Renewal of the
civil war—Battle of Saint-Denis—Peace of Longjumeau—Flight of Condé
to La Rochelle—Third war of Religion breaks out—Battle of Jarnac—
Death of Condé.

MEANWHILE, an event had occurred which had
occasioned a great stir in both political camps.
The gloomy prognostications of the Princesse de
Condé's physicians, which her husband had at first ridiculed,
proved only too correct ; all through the remainder of the
spring and the first weeks of summer the poor lady was
gradually becoming weaker, and by the middle of July it was
plain that she had but a few days to live. To the last she
was full of consideration for the husband who had shown so
little consideration for her. "Fearing to distress him too much,
if she told him herself that she felt death approaching," writes
her biographer, "the princess charged two grave personages,
friends of her family, to go to Condé's apartments, to acquaint
him with what she foresaw must soon happen, and to ask to be
allowed to entrust him with her last wishes in an authentic
form. 'Tell the prince,' said she to these two friends, 'that,
since God is pleased so soon to separate our bodies, I trust

that at least our souls may continue to be bound inseparably together in the love that we ought to bear to our common Saviour Jesus Christ, who has delivered us so miraculously, in the eyes of all Europe, from so many enemies and dangers. Tell him also that,—to begin my will,—I constitute him the universal heir to the mass of love I have vowed to my children, and I conjure him, in loving them doubly henceforth both for himself and for me, to keep vigil in my place, so that they may be brought up in the fear of God, which I am convinced is the surest estate and patrimony that I can bequeath to them.'"[1]

Condé appeared to be profoundly affected. He declared that he had received from the princess a lesson in courage which he should strive to follow out of love for her and her children; adding that the latter would always find him faithful to the last recommendations of their mother. "God, who joined us now divides us, since it pleases Him," he exclaimed. "Oh! blessed will be the moment when He ordains that we shall be reunited in Heaven in an eternal bond!"

These pious expressions, which, though they may appear so out of place on the lips of the lover of Isabelle de Limeuil, were probably uttered in all sincerity, seem to have greatly comforted the poor princess, who then sent for two notaries and dictated to them her will.

Afterwards, she summoned her chaplain Pérussel, who, it will be remembered, had shared Condé's captivity after Dreux, and another minister, and conversed with them on spiritual matters. On their departure, Condé returned to her bedside, and spoke to her some affectionate words. "Four things," replied the dying princess, taking his hands in hers, "render me happy: the first is the assurance of my salvation, the second, the reputation of being a good wife, which, by God's grace, I have always had; the third, the certainty that you are satisfied with me, because I have always as faithfully served, loved, and honoured you as it was possible for a wife, in this world, to serve, honour, and love her husband; the fourth, my joy that

---

[1] Comte Jules Delaborde, "Éléonore de Roye, Princesse de Condé."

will bring them up in the fear of God, in accordance with my principal desire." And, after a moment's silence, she added : " And now I must finish my course to gain the prize which I see prepared for me at the end of the lists of this laborious career."

Condé then withdrew, and the princess's children entered to take farewell of her and receive her last recommendations.

Towards midnight, fearing that she would soon be too weak to make herself understood, she expressed a wish to have a final conversation with her husband. " I am sure," said she, " that the prince will not mind being awakened for this occasion, and it would not be well to wait until I could no longer declare to him the things that God has put into my heart."

On the arrival of Condé, every one present withdrew out of hearing, and husband and wife conversed together for nearly an hour.

The end came at eight o'clock the following morning (23 July, 1564). Condé, who had quite broken down, had retired to his own room, and one of the Huguenot ministers, who had been with the princess in her last moments, came to break the sad news to him. Dissolute as his life had been of late years, his heart was not quite corrupted, and the grief which he experienced was accentuated by remorse for the pain which his infidelities had so often caused the devoted companion who had just been taken from him. Now, probably for the first time, he seemed to realize her worth, and nothing could have been more touching than the terms in which he spoke of her to his weeping children. " Strive, my darling," said he to his little daughter, " to resemble your mother, that God may help you as He helped her, that every one may esteem you, and that I may love you more and more, as I shall surely do if you are as she was." Then, laying his hand on the head of the Marquis de Conti, he added : " My son, you are the first pledge of the blessing and favour of marriage which God gave to your mother and myself. See that you always give me joy and consolation, which you will do if you follow in the footsteps of your mother in the way of

ÉLÉONORE DE ROYE, PRINCESSE DE CONDÉ

virtue. Recognize the traces, for fear lest you go astray along the paths of the dangerous labyrinth of this world. Sons are usually like their fathers, but you must strive to copy the virtues of your mother. For you will be told things about your father and his life that you ought not to imitate, though there are other things in him that you must follow. But in your mother . . . you will find nothing which is not worthy to be a treasured example, as she was worthy of a place in the foremost ranks of virtuous women." [1]

Condé's grief had, for the moment, exalted him, but his impressions were always more violent than lasting, and scandal was soon to be busy again with his name.

Scarcely had the grave closed upon Éléonore de Roye than all kinds of rumours were in circulation as to her probable successor, for no one doubted that a prince in the very prime of manhood and of so "amorous a complexion" would take unto himself a second wife with as little delay as need be.

It was said that the Maréchale de Saint-André was determined to have him; and the death of the little Mlle. de Saint-André, which had occurred at the Convent of Longchamps three weeks before that of Condé's wife, whereby the little girl's immense fortune passed to her mother, was freely ascribed to a diabolical crime on the part of the maréchale, in order to facilitate her union with the prospective widower.

There would not appear to have been any foundation for so terrible a charge, though the maréchale, who, besides being desperately enamoured of Condé, was a very ambitious woman, was certainly prepared to move heaven and earth to secure her elevation to the rank of Princess of the Blood. No sooner did she learn that poor Éléonore de Roye's recovery had been pronounced hopeless than, with the object of establishing claims to the expected vacancy which it would be difficult to ignore, she made the prince a present of the estate and magnificent château of Valery, near Sens, which her luxurious husband had rebuilt and furnished with the most costly magnificence. At

---

[1] Comte Jules Delaborde, "Éléonore de Roye, Princesse de Condé."

withdrawn her objections to the marriage of the Marquis de Conti and Mlle. de Saint-André. But when, after the death of the latter had put an end to this project, the maréchale not only confirmed the gift of Valery, but added to it a considerable part of the fortune left by her daughter, it was no longer possible to disguise the motive of such unexampled generosity ; and people said very unkind things, both about the giver and the prince, who had accepted, apparently without a blush, an almost regal present from one of his avowed mistresses.

Other rumours espoused Condé to Catherine de Lorraine, daughter of the late Duc de Guise, or to her widowed mother, Anne d'Este, still very beautiful ; while others again united him to Mary, Queen of Scots.

The prince had no intention of gratifying the ambitions of the Maréchale de Saint-André, being of opinion that to become her husband would be to pay altogether too high a price for Valery. But he was not indisposed to a union with the Guises, for, though they had done him much injury in the past, the death of their illustrious head had deprived them of their influence, and he was of too generous a nature to cherish rancour against a fallen foe.

The Guises on their side, hated by the Huguenots, disliked by the Montmorencies, and distrusted by the Queen, were sincerely anxious for a union with Condé. At the end of December 1564, the Cardinal de Lorraine, returning from the Council of Trent, passed through Soissons, to which town the prince had come, on a visit to his sister, Catherine de Bourbon, abbess of the Convent of Notre-Dame. A very cordial interview took place between them, in which his Eminence suggested to Condé a marriage between him and Mary Stuart. The cardinal had already approached his niece on the subject, excusing the inconsistency of a Prince of the Church recommending a heretic as a husband on the ground that the Huguenots were so determined to compass his ruin that the marriage was absolutely necessary for his political salvation. It is true that me."[1] Nevertheless, the cardinal did not despair of ultimately obtaining her consent.

On leaving Soissons, the Cardinal de Lorraine proceeded to Paris, followed by "fifty arquebusiers and some hundreds of his friends and servants, with arms, pistols, and arquebuses." On reaching Saint-Denis, he was met by a gentleman of the Maréchal de Montmorency, governor of the Île-de-France and his personal enemy, who warned him that he could not be permitted to enter the city with an armed retinue, since the edicts forbade it. The prelate, however, thought proper to ignore this warning, and, on 8 January, 1565, he and his whole company entered Paris by the Porte Saint-Denis. Near the Church of the Innocents they were met by Montmorency, at the head of a considerable force. The marshal called upon them to lay down their arms ; one man refused and was immediately killed ; the rest obeyed, and the cardinal, never remarkable for his personal courage, took refuge in the house of a merchant, where he remained until nightfall.[2]

This affair caused a great commotion. The partisans of the Guises assembled at Meudon, under the leadership of the Duc d'Aumale, and assumed a most threatening attitude ; the Maréchal de Montmorency summoned his friends to his assistance, and, since he was known to favour the Huguenots, Coligny and a number of Protestant gentlemen hastened to Paris to offer him their services. To the general astonishment, however, Condé took the cardinal's part and openly blamed Montmorency. "If," said he, referring to the fraças by the Innocents, "this was intended for a jest, it was too much ; if it was in earnest, too little."

With the object of showing his sympathy with the cardinal

[1] Martin Hume, "The Courtships of Mary Stuart."
[2] Castelnau, "Mémoires."

reaching the Bastille, however, he received a message from Montmorency summoning him to retire immediately, which he did, though not without addressing a letter of protest to the King, which was the cause of violent dissensions in the Council, where the Cardinal de Bourbon took the part of his brother, and the Constable energetically defended the action of his son. On a second visit to the capital, which the prince paid a few weeks later, he assured the Bishop of Paris that he would protect the ecclesiastical hierarchy, and that he deplored the affront which had been offered the Cardinal de Lorraine ; and when the Parlement complained that, in contravention of the edict, *prêches* had been held at his house, he answered that he had neither authorized nor attended them.

The conduct of the prince, which seemed to foreshadow a complete change of policy on his part, and to confirm the rumours already in circulation as to a matrimonial alliance with the Guises, naturally gave the greatest umbrage to the Huguenots, and the extreme section of the party, already, as we have seen, very dissatisfied with their leader, vented their annoyance in a stream of lampoons and satires. The Duc d'Aumale, in his " Histoire des Princes de Condé," stigmatizes the Protestants as " unjust and ungrateful," and declares that " there is no proof that Condé ever contemplated a union by marriage with the House of Lorraine." "In any case," continues the royal historian, "if he did 'bind himself afresh' to his former rivals ; if he refused to take part in all the quarrels and to share all the passions which were raging around him, it was because he was sincerely desirous to obliterate the traces, and prevent the renewal, of the civil war."

The Duc d'Aumale could not, however, have been aware, at the time when this was published, of a letter written by Mary Stuart to her aunt the Duchesse d'Arschot, from which it would appear that the project of a marriage between Condé and the beautiful young widow of François II. had not only been very favourably received by the prince, but that he had actually taken some active steps in the matter. "I hear," writes Mary, "that the Prince de Condé has demanded my hand of my grandmother [1] and of the Cardinal de Lorraine, my uncle, and that he has made the most splendid offers imaginable, both in regard to religion and other matters." [2]

Whatever offers Condé may have made, they had no effect upon Mary, who was now firmly resolved to marry Darnley, and was, besides, thoroughly disgusted with the unabashed selfishness of the Cardinal de Lorraine. But the Queen of Scotland was not the only card in his Eminence's hand, and, though a match with the widowed Duchesse de Guise—whose infatuation for the fascinating Duc de Nemours was common knowledge—or with her daughter, a girl of thirteen, was not likely to prove so attractive to Condé, there was still a possibility that it might be arranged, and for months the Protestants were in a state of trepidation.

Their alarm was shared by Catherine de' Medici, to whom the prospect of so intimate a *rapprochement* between the Houses of Bourbon and Lorraine was anything but pleasing. Fully sensible though her Majesty was of the importance of detaching the first Prince of the Blood from the Protestant cause, she judged that this advantage would be too dearly purchased by the subordination of the Crown to two ambitious families, which would be the inevitable consequence of their alliance; and she was determined to use every means in her power to avert such a calamity. It was, of course, the King's prerogative to refuse to sanction a marriage of which he might happen to disapprove, but arbitrary measures seldom commended themselves to Catherine, who always preferred to gain her ends by indirect means, and shift the odium which she would! otherwise incur upon the shoulders of her agents. She therefore bethought herself of Isabelle de Limeuil, who had lately been transferred from Vienne to the Château of Tournon. Here, ready to her hand, was a woman, who, as their intercepted correspondence had shown her, had contrived, notwithstanding the infidelities of

---

[1] Antoinette de Bourbon, widow of Claude de Lorraine.
[2] Labanoff, "Lettres de Marie Stuart."

heart, by associating the most incredible expressions of tenderness with the most exaggerated flatteries. If Isabelle and her prince were brought together again, if matters could be so arranged that the latter should be compelled to offer his mistress the shelter of one of his own residences, was it not probable that, in the joy of this reunion, the question of his second marriage would be relegated, for a time at least, to the background ? And was it not probable, too, that the open scandal would provoke remonstrances from his co-religionists which would irritate Condé and widen the breach which existed between him and his party ?

Interesting indeed must have been the letters which passed at this time between the captive of Tournon and the enamoured prince, as the result of which Isabelle was not only rescued from her prison, but conducted to her lover at Valery, the château presented to Condé by her rival—a piquant revenge, in good truth, upon the Maréchale de Saint-André for the advantage which she had taken of Isabelle's enforced absence from the field ! Unfortunately, the correspondence has not been preserved, and the only light cast upon the situation is a passage in a despatch from Smith to Cecil, dated 10 April, 1565 : " The Prince de Condé has by a certain gentleman stolen Mademoiselle de Lymoel (*sic*) from Tournon, where she was kept, and has her with him." [1]

And has her with him ! Yes, under the same roof ! " *Grand Dieu !* it was enough to make Calvin rise from his grave ! " [2] cried the Huguenot pastors, holding up their hands in righteous horror. " Had the prince taken leave of his senses that he should choose to create a public scandal and make 'the Religion' a by-word in the mouths of the froward, at the very moment when Catherine and Philip of Spain were believed to be plotting its destruction ? Had not the way of salvation been made sufficiently plain to him ? Had not Bèze and Pérussel and l'Espine and Laboissière spread the choicest flowers of their

[1] State Papers (Elizabeth), Foreign Series. [2] Calvin had died on 27 May, 1564.

The politicians of the party were scarcely less indignant than the divines, and the reappearance of Isabelle upon the scene was the signal for a very pretty quarrel between them and the prince, of which a piquant account is given in an anonymous letter in Italian in the Simancas Collection

"I have seen a letter of Madame de Chelles,[1] from which she appears to entertain great hopes of friendship between her brother and the cardinal [de Lorraine]. My friend and I think that nothing can be founded upon the words or the acts of so frivolous a man as Condé shows himself to be, who is at present more than ever enamoured of his Limeuil. Paroceli [2] has been here four or five days, and has preached in private to his Huguenots. Languet learned from him that dissension has arisen, on the subject of la Limeuil, between Condé and Châtillon [Coligny], and subsequently between the aforesaid Condé and his followers, in such manner that Châtillon has parted from him, has come to Paris, and has withdrawn, some say to Châtillon, others to an abbey belonging to him, and that Condé's followers have almost all abandoned him.

"The occasion of this was that a certain letter was written to Condé from Paris, at the close of which was written: 'The young lady has come.' Châtillon, who was standing over Condé as he read the letter, saw these words, and, guessing what they meant, said to Condé: 'I can tell what young lady it is that has come to Paris.' To which Condé replied in certain words which showed that Châtillon's speech was not agreeable to him; but the matter did not go any further for the time being.

"After la Limeuil had arrived at the place to which Condé had ordered her to be conducted, and they had been seen

---

[1] Renée de Bourbon, Abbess of Chelles, sister of Condé.

[2] Presumably Condé's chaplain, Pérssel, whose name is sometimes written Pérocel.

together, certain Huguenot gentlemen went and found Condé
and began to admonish him, and, so to speak, to reprove him
on the subject of his mistress. Upon which, Condé, supposing
that his secret had been revealed to them by Châtillon, and
that it was at his instigation that they had come to reprove
him, grew angry and said many things against them, designating
them spies, and then adding that it was Châtillon who had told
them this, and had sent them to talk to him ; and with such
indignation that he went on to say much evil of Châtillon and
his whole House . . . accusing them of arrogance, of presump
tion, and of not only wishing to put themselves on a level with
princes, when they were naught but gentlemen of humble rank
but even of daring to insult him ; and that it was not in
his nature to suffer this any longer. Through these and
such-like words, and even worse, it came about that Châtillon
separated himself from Condé. The greater part of the
Huguenots have done likewise, so that he finds himself now
almost alone."

However, a little reflection sufficed to convince the
Huguenot leaders that the discredit which it was bringing upon
their Faith was not the most serious aspect of Condé's infatuation for Isabelle ; in other words, that Catherine was at the
bottom of the affair, and had deliberately thrown the two
together again, "with a view to the prince becoming what his
brother had already become by means of la Rouet." "Suspect
ing which," continues the writer of the letter already cited, "the
gentlemen of Condé's party took counsel together to find a
remedy for so great an evil, and resolved upon three courses
first, that the ministers should speak out roundly to him
representing the personal danger and disgrace of the affair, and
the scandal common to the whole Religion, since he was its
chief, and persuade him, if he could not keep continent, to take
a wife. The second remedy, if the first did not succeed, was
for the principal gentleman of the Religion, acting in common
accord, and his own intimate friends, to wait upon him and
address to him the same remonstrances, making him understand
that, if he did not separate himself from la Limeuil, they would

of Satan."

In accordance with these resolutions, a deputation selected from the most prominent Huguenot divines waited upon the backsliding prince at Valery and endeavoured to awaken him to a sense of the error of his ways. Condé received his reverend friends courteously enough, but declared that he "could not keep continent and could not take a wife, since it was difficult to find a person of his own rank belonging to the same religion, and impossible to find one of another religion."

Sadly the ministers withdrew, and the lay deputation advanced to the attack. It met with anything but a cordial reception: indeed, his Highness expressed his opinion of its interference with his private affairs in such exceedingly plain language that it was obliged to beat a precipitate retreat. Whence, we are told, "the Religion found itself in great trouble and knew not what further to do, since it feared to make matters worse by excommunicating la Limeuil, Condé being of a nature so inclined to women that there was great danger lest la Limeuil should have more power over him than the Religion."

The counsel of the more prudent members of the party was to leave things alone, and to trust to time. It proved a wise decision. Passions of this kind are more frequently nourished than overcome by opposition; while, on the other hand, the greater the facilities for enjoying the society of the enchantress, the more speedily do disillusion and lassitude arrive. After the first rapture of the reunion, Condé began to ask himself whether, after all, he was not acting very unwisely in quarrelling with his personal friends and jeopardizing his political future for the sake of a girl who had been the cause of so much scandal, and who, he had good reason to believe, had not even troubled to remain faithful to him. Isabelle, perceiving that

o

the prince had not the least intention of regularizing their connexion, and mortified by the manner in which her name was being bandied about, began to regard Condé as the author of her misfortunes. Hence arose quarrels, tears, recriminations. Condé reproached Isabelle with her intimacy with Du Fresne and others. Isabelle retorted by accusing the prince of neglecting her for the Maréchale de Saint-André, to whom, in recognition of the gift of Valery, he had felt obliged to pay some fugitive attentions, and did not fail to take advantage of the opportunity which his acceptance of the maréchale's calculating generosity afforded her for the exercise of her powers of sarcasm. Wit is a dangerous weapon for lovers to play with, and Isabelle's was sharper than a two-edged sword.

At length, the situation became so unpleasant that Condé determined to put an end to it ; and, towards the close of the spring, he broke of his own free will with Isabelle and was reconciled to the Protestants. They, needless to say, received the repentant prodigal with open arms and lost no time in setting to work to procure him a second wife. They found her in Mlle. de Longueville,[1] a young lady who joined to high rank and the profession of the Reformed faith considerable personal attractions, and, in September, Condé set off for Niort to obtain the King's sanction to his marriage, "leaving the Maréchale de Saint-André dissolved in tears and regrets for having been so foolish as to consume her substance in vain expenses to acquire the quality of the wife of a Prince of the Blood."

Catherine, though disappointed at the reconciliation between Condé and his party, was greatly relieved that the prospect of

[1] Françoise Marie d'Orléans, posthumous daughter of François d'Orléans, Marquis de Rothelin, a cadet of the House of Longueville, and Jacqueline de Rohan. The House of Longueville was a branch of the Royal House of France, descended from the celebrated Comte de Dunois—the " Bastard of Orleans "—son of Louis I., Duc d'Orléans. His nephew, Charles VII., gave him, in 1463, the county of Longueville, in the district of Caux, which had been ceded to Charles VI. by Bertrand du Guesclin, half a century earlier. Dunois's grandson, François, was created a duke in 1505, and, in 1571, his successor, Léonor, brother to the second Princesse de Condé, received from Charles IX., for himself and his descendants, the title of Princes of the Blood.

up and was, moreover, of a decidedly jealous disposition, and she was determined not to permit the souvenirs of her husband to be dragged about France by his former mistresses. No sooner married, than, following the example of the Duchesse d'Étampes when she had supplanted Madame de Châteaubriand in the affections of François I., she imperiously demanded of the prince that he should require Isabelle to restore all the presents that he had made her ; and Condé, who was one of those men who are quite incapable of resisting the caprices of the preferred of the moment, was mean enough to obey.

When the messenger sent by the prince informed Isabelle of the object of his visit, she flew into the most violent passion and made so terrible a scene that, had he not happened to be a Huguenot of a particularly inflexible type, he would doubtless have returned to Condé and reported the failure of his mission. As it was, he waited patiently until her fury had expended itself, and then repeated his request. The lady left the room and presently returned with a packet, in which she had placed all the jewels she had received from Condé and a portrait of the prince by a celebrated painter, the first token of his love that he had given her. Sitting down at the table, she placed the portrait before her and decorated it with an enormous pair of horns ; and then contemptuously tossed it and the packet of jewels to the astonished messenger. "Take them, my friend," said she, " and carry them to your master ; I send him everything that he gave me. I have neither added nor taken away anything. Tell that beautiful princess, his wife, who has importuned him so much to demand from me what he gave me, that, if a certain nobleman—mentioning him by name—had treated her mother in the same way, and had claimed and taken away all that he had given her, she would be as poor in trinkets and jewels as any demoiselle of the Court. Well, let her make use of the paste and the baubles; I leave them to her." [1]

It is to be hoped that Condé had the grace to feel ashamed of himself when his messenger returned; but since, in common with the majority of his contemporaries, he possessed a pretty thick skin, we are inclined to doubt whether such a reproof would have occasioned him more than a momentary vexation. Public opinion, we are told, however, judged him very severely, and declared that he had acted most ungenerously. "in having despoiled this poor lady, who had honestly earned such presents *par la sueur de son corps.*" [2]

In one of his despatches, written soon after the rupture between the prince and Isabelle, Sir Thomas Smith announced that "the Prince de Condé had married la Limoel (*sic*) to a gentleman of his and given them 15,000 livres a year." [3] The Ambassador had been misinformed, for Isabelle was still single at the time, nor was this project, if it really existed, ever realized. The lady, however, notwithstanding the notoriety of her relations with Condé and the criminal charge which had been brought against her, was not long in finding a husband.

There was at this time in Paris an Italian banker named Scipion Sardini, who, by the favour of Catherine de' Medici, who appears to have dipped pretty frequently into his purse, had contrived to amass an immense fortune, and "from a little sardine had grown into a big whale." He had recently acquired the estate and the beautiful château of Chaumont-sur-Loire and the title of baron to go with it, and desired to find a high-born damsel who would be willing to share his prosperity. Since however, high-born damsels were, for the most part, inclined to look askance at a suitor whose origin was shrouded in impenetrable obscurity, he cast his eyes in the direction of Isabelle,

---

[1] Brantôme. [2] Ibid.
[3] Smith to the Earl of Leicester, 5 May, 1565. State Papers (Elizabeth), Foreign Series.

condescended to accept them, and went to live at the sumptuous Hôtel Sardini, situated in the Quartier Saint-Marcel, at the corner of the Rue de la Barre. The union was not an unqualified success, for Isabelle's misfortunes had soured her temper, and the pretentious *parvenu* whom she had married had good reason to regret that he had not contented himself with a more amiable, if less aristocratic, consort. A great lady still, despite her lost reputation, she never forgave her husband his lowly origin, and permitted no opportunity to pass of allowing him to see how much she despised him ; and, whenever he had been so unfortunate as to displease her, which appears to have happened pretty frequently, she would remind the poor man of the honour which she, a woman of such noble birth, had done him in giving him her hand. To which Sardini would reply, not without reason : "I have done more for you ; I have dishonoured myself in order to restore you your honour!" Then Isabelle would hurl at him a perfect volley of invective, until, fearing that it might be followed by missiles of a more substantial kind, he would fly from her presence and take refuge in his own apartments.

These perpetual quarrels, however, did not prevent this ill-assorted couple from having three children : two sons and a daughter, of whom the latter, Madeleine Sardini, is said to have inherited not a little of her mother's beauty. Unfortunately, she appears to have inherited her quarrelsome disposition as well, as did her brothers, for, after their parents' death, they went to law over the division of the Sardini fortune and provided the gentlemen of the long robe with some very pretty pickings.

We shall pass briefly over the last three years of Condé's eventful life.

In September 1567, civil war broke out again. The Protestants, alarmed and exasperated by the refusal of the Government to disband a force of 6000 Swiss mercenaries, which had been and Coligny, at the head of a body of cavalry, to seize the person of the King, as he was on his way from Monceaux, where he had intended to pass the autumn, to Paris. But Charles IX. had had time to summon the Swiss to his aid, and, the Huguenots not being in sufficient force to risk an engagement with these valiant mercenaries, who, "lowering their pikes, ran at them like mad dogs, at full speed," he reached his capital in safety.

Condé followed, and, having been reinforced, occupied Saint-Denis and proceeded, with astonishing daring, to blockade Paris, although his army does not seem to have exceeded 6000 men and he was without a single piece of artillery; while the Constable, with a vastly superior force, lay within the city. Montmorency, however, who always carried caution to excess, was disinclined to take the offensive, and it was not until the Huguenots had committed the mistake of detaching a considerable part of their slender forces, under Andelot and Montgomery, to occupy Poissy and Pontoise that he ventured to offer battle. The royal army was 19,000 strong, that of Condé certainly did not exceed 3000 men; but the prince had no thought of declining an engagement, and ranged his little force in the plain near Saint-Denis. The Catholic attack was repulsed all along the line, and then, while Coligny fell upon the Parisian militia, who, arrayed in all their martial finery—"gilded like chalices," as a Huguenot historian puts it [1]—formed the left wing of the Royalists, and drove them in headlong rout towards the city, Condé, with the bulk of the Huguenot horse, burst suddenly upon the centre, where the Constable commanded in person. So furious was his charge that the Catholic cavalry were broken and hurled back, and the Constable himself fell mortally wounded. "If the Grand Signior," exclaimed the Turkish Ambassador, who, from the heights of Montmartre,

[1] D'Aubigné.

had witnessed the prince's onslaught, " if the Grand Signior had only two thousand men like those in white "—the Huguenots wore white surcoats—" to place at the head of each of his armies, in two years the world would be his ! "

But a complete victory against such overwhelming odds would have been in the nature of a miracle. The main body of the Catholics was unbroken ; the Maréchal de Montmorency, the Constable's eldest son, assumed the command and rallied the shattered squadrons ; and the Huguenots were being hard pressed on all sides, when the failing light came to their assistance and enabled them to fall back in tolerable order on Saint-Denis. The Royalists, disheartened by the fall of their leader, did not attempt to pursue, and, after occupying the field of battle for a few hours, in sign of victory, re-entered Paris.

Condé's position being no longer tenable, he decided to lead his little army towards Lorraine, to join John Casimir, son of the Elector Palatine, who was advancing to his assistance with a strong force of German mercenaries. After a hazardous march, he crossed the Meuse in safety, and at Pont-à-Mousson effected his junction with the Germans. Having now once more a considerable army at his disposal, he turned again towards Paris, and, at the end of February 1658, laid siege to Chartres. Negotiations for peace had, however, already begun ; and a month later (23 March) the Peace of Longjumeau, which reaffirmed the Amboise Edict, put an end to the second war.

It was merely a respite, for the Court had determined on the ruin of the Huguenots, and, at the end of August, orders were issued for the arrest of Condé and Coligny, who were at the former's château of Noyers, in Burgundy. Warned in time, they succeeded in effecting their escape with their families, traversed the whole breadth of France, and gained the sheltering walls of La Rochelle, where they were joined by Jeanne d'Albret, and her young son, Henri of Navarre.[1]

[1] It was a perilous journey, for they were hotly pursued, and had not the Loire risen in sudden flood just after they had forded it near Sancerre, and arrested the pursuit, they would certainly have been captured. The fugitives saw in this event the direct interposition of Providence in their favour, and falling on their knees, sang the Psalm : *In exitu Israel.*

autumn campaign of 1568 were favourable to the Protestants, who mastered almost all the South and West. But, with the new year, their fortunes changed. In February, Condé and Coligny with the main Huguenot army marched eastwards to meet their German allies, who were advancing from the Rhine. Finding, however, that Tavannes, who directed the Catholics, under the name of the Duc d'Anjou (afterwards Henri III.), had divined this movement and was preparing to oppose it, they turned to the South-West, with the intention of effecting their junction with the Huguenot forces from Quercy. Tavannes, however, outmarched them and barred their way, upon which they decided to turn to the North, seize one of the passages of the Loire, and join hands with the Germans. But Tavannes followed close on their heels, crossed the Charente by a stratagem, and fell upon the rearguard of the Huguenots, under Coligny, near Jarnac (13 March).

On learning that the Admiral was attacked, Condé, who had left Jarnac with the main body of the army that morning, turned back at once, and, after sending orders to the rest of his troops to follow him with all speed, hastened to his assistance, at the head of three hundred horse. "For," says Le Noue, "he had the heart of a lion, and, whenever he heard that there was fighting, he longed to be in the thick of it." On the way, he was met by a messenger from Coligny, who had sent to beg him not to make a useless effort, and to retreat. "God forbid," he replied, "that Louis de Bourbon should turn his back to the enemy!" And he hastened on.

On his arrival on the field, he found Coligny struggling against almost the entire Catholic army, and in danger of being surrounded. An immediate retreat would have been the wisest course, but to this the prince refused to consent, and drawing up the cavalry in a long line, with himself and his little band in the centre, he prepared to charge the dense columns of the enemy. A day or two before, his left arm had been badly crushed by a fall from his horse, and, now, as his helmet was being adjusted, his right leg was broken by a kick from the charger of his brother-in-law, the Comte de la Rochefoucauld. "You see," said he, mastering the pain, "that mettlesome horses are of more harm than use in an army."

Those about him urged him to dismount, but he refused to leave the saddle, and, pointing first to his injured limbs and then to his standard, which bore the device: "*Pro Christo et patriâ dulce periculum*," he cried : "Nobles of France, behold the moment so long desired ! Remember in what plight Louis de Bourbon goes into battle for Christ and country ! " [1]

Then, with his three hundred horse, he threw himself on the Catholic cavalry and drove them back in confusion on the "*bataille*," which the Duc d'Anjou led in person. But the charges of Coligny on the right, and Montgommery on the left, failed completely, and the prince's little troop was soon assailed on all sides by overwhelming numbers. Condé's horse was killed under him, and, impeded by his injuries, he was unable to mount another. His followers gathered around him and fought on heroically, but one by one they were cut down. Among these devoted men, d'Aubigné tells us, was an aged gentleman named La Vergne, who had joined Condé accompanied by twenty-five of his sons, grandsons, and nephews. "He and fifteen of his relatives were left dead on the field, all in a heap."

Soon Condé found himself almost alone, but, with his back to a tree and kneeling on one knee, he continued to defend himself. His strength, however, was failing fast, and perceiving two Catholic gentlemen, d'Argence and Saint-Jean, to whom he had once been of service, he called out to them, raised the vizor of his helmet, and handed them his gauntlets, in token of surrender. The two gentlemen sprang from their horses, and with several others formed a circle round Condé, promising to protect his life with their own. Scarcely, however, had they done so, when Anjou's guards passed by, and their captain, "a very brave and honourable gentleman, called Montesquiou," [2] learning the name of the prisoner, wheeled his horse round, galloped up to the group, and shouting : "Kill ! *Mordieu !* Kill !"

[1] D'Aubigné, "Histoire universelle."   [2] Brantôme.

head from behind, killing him instantly.[1]

Thus died—"on the true bed of honour," as Jeanne d'Albret expresses it—Louis I. de Bourbon, Prince de Condé, a man typical of his age and of his country, alike in his faults and his good qualities. If the former were, as we have seen, many and glaring, the latter were no less conspicuous. "In courage and in courtesy," writes La Noue, "no one surpassed him. His conversation was eloquent, rather from nature than from cultivation; he was generous and affable towards all; he was an excellent leader in war, yet, at the same time, a lover of peace. In adversity he bore himself even better than in prosperity."

The battle of Jarnac was little more than a skirmish, for the greater part of the Protestant army had not been engaged at all, and its losses, except among the cavalry, were inconsiderable. The death of Condé, however, created a profound impression. The Catholic chiefs fondly imagined that, with his fall, the Huguenots would cease to be formidable, and their joy, in consequence, was extreme. A solemn *Te Deum* was chanted at the Court and in every church in France; thanksgiving processions took place at Brussels and Venice, and the captured standards were sent to Rome, to be hung in St. Peter's as a perpetual memorial.

By the orders of the detestable Anjou, the body of the murdered prince was treated with the most shameful indignity. "The same night that the battle was fought, the Duc d'Anjou, pursuing the enemy, victoriously entered into Jarnac, whither the body of the prince was carried in triumph on the back of a miserable ass, to the infinite joy and diversion of the whole army, which made a joke of this spectacle, though, while he lived, they were terrified at the name of so great a man."[2] For two whole days it lay exposed to the effects of the air and

---

[1] By the orders of his master, it was generally believed. "He (Condé)," writes Brantôme, "had been very earnestly *recommended* to several of the favourites of the said *Monseigneur* (Anjou) whom I knew."

[2] Davila, cited by Mr. A. W. Whitehead, "Gaspard de Coligny."

CHAPTER VII

Henri I. de Bourbon, Prince de Condé—His personal appearance and character—Jeanne d'Albret presents Henri of Navarre and Condé to the army—The "Admiral's pages"—The "Journey of the Princes"—Battle of Arnay-le-Duc—Condé at La Rochelle—Henri of Navarre is betrothed to Marguerite de Valois, and Condé to Marie de Clèves—An awkward lover—Marriage of Condé—Massacre of Saint-Bartholomew—The King of Navarre and Condé are ordered to abjure their religion—Firmness of the latter, who, however, at length yields—Humiliating position of Condé—Intrigue between his wife and the Duc d'Anjou—Condé at the siege of La Rochelle—Anjou elected King of Poland—He offers the hand of his discarded mistress, Mlle. de Châteauneuf, to Nantouillet, provost of Paris—Unpleasant consequences of the provost's refusal of this honour.

B Y his two marriages, Louis I., Prince de Condé, had had eleven children, of whom seven—six sons and a daughter—survived him.[1] The eldest son, Henri de Bourbon, was at this time in his seventeenth year. In appearance, he was very short, like his father, and very slightly built, with a countenance which betokened an extremely sensitive nature, a nervous and delicate constitution : a high forehead, large, expressive blue eyes, a long face, a long, straight nose, and thin lips. In character, save in the matter of physical

---

[1] The surviving children by his marriage with Éléonoıe de Roye were :

(1) Henri de Bourbon, Prince de Condé ; born 27 December, 1552 ; died 5 March, 1588.

(2) François de Bourbon, Prince de Conti, born 18 August, 1558.

(3) Catherine de Bourbon.

(4) Charles de Bourbon, afterwards the third Cardinal de Bourbon, born 30 March, 1562.

Those by his marriage with Françoise d'Orléans were :

(1) Charles de Bourbon, Comte de Soissons, born 3 November, 1566.

(2) Louis de Bourbon.

(3) Benjamin de Bourbon.

Both of the two last children died young.

1e had shared with her the hardships and dangers of the civil war, and had been shut up in Orléans, amid the horrors of that :errible siege. Returning home, he had seen the poor princess, ' to whom he had plighted his boundless reverence and love," [1] slowly languish away before his eyes, worn out by sickness and sorrow. Then had come Condé's second marriage, and the lad had been left to the care of bigoted divines, who had brought 1im up in the strictest tenets of the Calvinistic faith. Finally, scarcely had he been summoned to take his place by his father's side, than that father had been foully slain. Thus, at the age of sixteen, Henri de Bourbon had experienced little of life but its sorrows, and was a thoughtful, grave, and almost melancholy youth, without any of those social qualities which had made his father so popular, but very superior to him in the earnestness of his religious convictions, and ready, as we shall see hereafter, to suffer for the truth in circumstances which overcame the courage and constancy of some even of the boldest.

On the day of Jarnac, the young prince and his cousin, Henri of Navarre, had been with the Protestant army. But they had not been permitted to take any part in the engagement, and had been ordered to retire to Saintes, where they were joined by Jeanne d'Albret, who at the first news of the defeat had left La Rochelle. Taking the two lads with her, the indomitable Queen of Navarre hastened to the Huguenot camp at Tonnay-Charente, and, in an eloquent speech, presented them to the troops, and made each of them swear " on his honour, soul, and life" never to abandon the cause. The army received them with acclamations, and the young Prince of Béarn was forthwith chosen as its leader ; while, as a mark of its respect and gratitude for the hero whom it had lost, the new Princé de Condé was associated with him in command.

For more than two years the double signature, " Henry,

[1] Comte Jules Delaborde, " Éléonore de Roye, Princesse de Condé."

Henry de Bourbon," appeared at the foot of the official documents of the Reformed party.[1]   But, though always accompanied by the two young princes, and nominally acting as their lieutenant and counsellor, Coligny had henceforward the undivided command of the Huguenot army, as well as the principal voice in determining the policy of his party ; and, by the camp-fire, the lads were commonly referred to as "the Admiral's pages."

The young Béarnais, with his good-humoured, sunburned face, his broad shoulders, and his wiry frame strengthened and developed by the manly, outdoor life which he had led amid the keen and bracing air of the Pyrenees, presented a singular contrast to his slight, delicate-looking, grave cousin.   The Queen of Navarre had charged him to love Condé as a brother and "cultivate with him an affection cemented by the ties of blood and religion which should never be severed."   But, though the prince, ever a dutiful son, seems to have made some effort to follow her instructions, and though, during the remainder of the Queen's life, an appearance of close intimacy was strictly maintained between the cousins, their characters and tastes were far too dissimilar for much sympathy to have existed between them, and, in later years, their relations became at times very strained indeed.

The summer and autumn of 1569 were disastrous to the Protestant cause.   Although, owing to the jealousy between the Court generals, in May, the Duke of Zweibrücken's German mercenaries were able to cross the Loire and join the main Huguenot army, the combined forces effected comparatively little, and at the beginning of October they experienced a crushing defeat in the bloody battle of Moncontour.

If the Royalists had followed up their success, this might have proved a fatal blow to the Protestants ; but Charles IX., jealous of the success of Anjou, the nominal commander at Moncontour, himself took command of the army, and frittered its strength away in besieging Saint-Jean-d'Angely, thus giving the Huguenots time to reorganize their forces.

[1] Duc d'Aumale, "Histoire des Princes de Condé."

of Navarre and the young Condé, started southwards from Parthenay (6 October), on that wonderful march afterwards known as the "Journey of the Princes." A month later saw him at Montauban, where he stayed for a while to rest his troops, and then, crossing the Garonne, he mercilessly ravaged the country south of that river. Recrossing to the north bank, where he was joined by Montgommery with reinforcements, he swept down on Toulouse, burned the country houses of the members of the Parlement in revenge for the judicial murder of one of the late Prince de Condé's gentlemen two years before, passed by the walls of Carcassonne and Montpellier, and entered Nimes. Here he turned to the North, and marched through Dauphiné and the Lyonnais to the very heart of France, carrying terror and devastation wherever he went.

Meanwhile, a Catholic force under the Maréchal de Cossé had gathered in the Orléannais and marched eastwards to intercept his advance. At Arnay-le-Duc, on 26 June 1570, the two armies met. The Royalists outnumbered their adversaries by more than two to one, and were well provided with artillery, whereas the Huguenots had not a single gun. But Coligny took up a masterly position, which prevented the enemy either from employing their cannon or from outflanking him, and drove them back with heavy loss.

It was in this engagement that the two young princes received their "baptism of fire." Hitherto, notwithstanding their urgent entreaties, Coligny had refused to allow them to expose themselves. Thus, though they had been with the army at Moncontour, they had been ordered to the rear before the battle actually began, accompanied by so large an escort that, according to d'Aubigné, the Huguenot forces were thereby seriously weakened. On the present occasion, however, Coligny's position was too critical for him to spare an escort, and Henri of Navarre was accordingly given the nominal command of the first line of cavalry, while Condé was at the head of the second. Both took part in several charges, and gave abundant proof that they had inherited the bravery of their warlike ancestors.

country, the exhausted finances, the enmity between the Montmorency and Lorraine factions of the Catholic party, the jealousy between Charles IX. and Anjou, and the fear of active intervention by England, had all combined to persuade Catherine that it was impossible to carry on the war much longer ; and she now decided that peace must be made with as little delay as possible. Pius V. and Philip II. made every effort to dissuade her, the former warning her that "there could be no communion between Satan and the sons of light ;" but their remonstrances were unheeded, and on 8 August, the Peace of Saint-Germain put an end to the war, and accorded the Protestants infinitely greater concessions than any which they had yet obtained.[1]

The two years which followed "*la paix boiteuse et malassise*,"[2] as the Peace of Saint-Germain was wittily called, were passed by Condé chiefly at La Rochelle, which had now become the headquarters of the Huguenots, and was one of the four towns which they were permitted to hold as security for the strict observance of the edict. The religious earnestness and gravity so far beyond his years which the young prince showed had gained him the entire confidence of Coligny, who had decided to delegate to him the direction of the Protestants of the West ; and it was Condé who, in the Admiral's absence, executed his orders in Poitou and Saintonge and kept him informed of all that was passing there.

[1] They received a general amnesty and the restoration of their confiscated estates. They were admitted upon equal terms with their Roman Catholic fellow-subjects to the benefit of all public institutions, and declared eligible to fill every post in the State. They were permitted to appeal from the judgment of the notoriously hostile Parlement of Toulouse to the Cour des Requêtes, in Paris. Finally, they were permitted to retain possession of four towns which they had conquered : La Rochelle, Cognac, La Charité, and Montauban, as a guarantee of the King's good faith, on condition that Henri of Navarre and Condé bound themselves to restore them to the Crown two years after the faithful execution of the Peace.

[2] From the two royal plenipotentiaries who concluded it, the Maréchal de Biron, who was lame, and Henri de Mesmes, Sieur de Malassise.

During the greater part of the year 1571, Jeanne d'Albret and Henri of Navarre were also at La Rochelle. If Condé had little affection for his cousin, to his aunt he was warmly attached, while she, on her side, seems to have looked upon him almost as a second son. As for his step-mother, the dowager-princess, his feelings towards her were the reverse of cordial. Not only had she never shown him any sympathy or affection, but, having recently abandoned the Reformed faith herself, she had surrendered her sons and stepsons to their uncle, the Cardinal de Bourbon, to be brought up in the Catholic religion. Her conduct, which was denounced by the Huguenots as an act of infamous treachery to her dead husband, had naturally occasioned Condé the most intense indignation, but, since it had occurred during the war, he had, of course, been powerless to interfere.

In order to flatter the Huguenots and allay their suspicions, while, at the same time, weakening their power of offence, by bringing their nominal chief directly under her own influence, Catherine de' Medici was now anxious to arrange a marriage between her only unmarried daughter, Marguerite de Valois, and Henri of Navarre; and from the beginning of 1571 active negotiations were carried on between the Court and La Rochelle, and Biron, Cossé, and Castelnau were in turn despatched thither to confer with Jeanne d'Albret and the Protestant leaders. Jeanne received the overtures of the Court with mixed feelings. She was intensely ambitious for her idolized son and desirous of doing everything in her power to promote the interests of her party. But she hated Catherine and all the Valois, and entertained the most profound distrust of their professions of friendship; and, had the decision rested with her alone, the proffered alliance would most certainly have been rejected. However, the Huguenot leaders were practically unanimous in urging her to consent; the nobility of her own little kingdom likewise pronounced for the marriage; and Henri himself added his persuasions to theirs. And so, with a very bad grace, the Queen yielded, and early in January, 1572, left Pau for Blois, to settle the preliminaries with Catherine.

H

The negotiations for the marriage of Henri of Navarre had been preceded by the arrangement by Jeanne d'Albret of a very advantageous match for the young Prince de Condé. The wife selected for him was his cousin, Marie de Clèves, Marquise d'Isles, the youngest of the three daughters of François de Clèves, Duc de Nevers, and Marguerite de Bourbon.[1] Marie de Clèves was not only a great heiress, but an extremely beautiful girl, and Condé considered himself a very fortunate young man. He had reason to think differently, however, before he had been married many weeks.

Condé and his bride-elect were both at Blois when the Queen of Navarre arrived there. It was some years since Jeanne had passed any time at the Court, and it had changed very much for the worse in the interval. In a letter to her son, she stigmatizes it, with good reason, as "the most vicious and corrupt society that ever existed." "No one that I see here," she writes, "is exempt from its evil influences. Your cousin, the marchioness,[2] is so greatly changed that she gives no sign of belonging to the Religion, if it be not that she abstains from attending Mass; for, in all else, save that she abstains from this idolatry, she conducts herself like other Papists, and my sister *Madame la Princesse*[3] sets an even worse example. This I write to you in confidence. The bearer of this letter will tell you how the King emancipates himself; it is a pity. I would not for any consideration that you should abide here. For this reason, I desire to see you married, that you and your wife

---

1 The three girls were co-heiresses to the great wealth of the Duc de Nevers, as he had left no son. The eldest, Henriette, Duchesse de Nivernais, married Ludovico di Gonzaga, brother of the Duke of Mantua ; the second, Catherine, married Antoine de Croy, Prince de Porcien, who died in 1564; and, six years after her husband's death, became the wife of Henri de Lorraine, Duc de Guise. The Prince de Porcien had been one of the leaders of the Huguenots and had entertained the most violent hatred of the Guises. On his death-bed, he is said to have thus addressed his wife : " You are young, beautiful, and wealthy ; you will have many suitors when I am gone. I have no objection to your marrying again, if only it be not the Duc de Guise. Let not my worst enemy inherit what of all my possessions I have cherished the most."

2 Marie de Clèves, Marquise d'Isles, Condé's betrothed.

3 Françoise d'Orléans, Princesse de Condé.

may withdraw yourselves from this corruption; for, although I believed it to be very great, it surpasses my anticipation. Here, it is not the men who solicit the women, but the women the men. If you were here, you would never escape, save by some remarkable mercy of God."

Although Jeanne strenuously resisted all attempts of the King and Catherine to draw her son to Blois, she felt perfectly at ease in regard to Condé's presence there, for the young prince's Calvinism was of that rigid type which made no distinction between pleasure and vice, and, unlike his cousin, he had never shown any inclination for feminine society. He had, nevertheless, quickly succumbed to the charms of his beautiful *fiancée*, though his awkward attempts at love-making must have aroused no small amount of amusement; for the Queen of Navarre wrote to her son that "if he could not make love with better grace than his cousin, she counselled him to leave the matter alone."

The marriage of Condé and Marie de Clèves took place on 10 August, 1572, at the Château of Blandy, near Melun, the seat of the Marquise de Rothelin, mother of the Dowager-Princesse de Condé, in the presence of Charles IX., Henri of Navarre, his *fiancée* Marguerite de Valois, the two queens, Catherine de' Medici and Elizabeth of Austria, and a great number of noblemen of both religions; and was celebrated "*tout-à-fait à la Huguenote.*" For the Reformers, however, it seemed to take place under somewhat mournful auspices, since she who had planned it was no more. Jeanne d'Albret had arrived in Paris in the last week in May; on 4 June she was taken ill, and on the 9th she died, at the age of forty-four. Sinister rumour were circulated concerning her death, and it was asserted that the Queen-Mother had caused her to be poisoned. But, as we have pointed out in a previous work, there can be no question that Jeanne's health had been gradually failing for some time past, and the most trustworthy evidence goes to indicate that she died a natural death.[1]

[1] See the author's "Queen Margot" (London, Harpers; New York, Scribner, 1906).

Immediately after the marriage, Condé and his bride came to Paris for the marriage of the young King of Navarre, which was celebrated with the utmost magnificence on Monday, 18 August. But the wedding festivities were of very brief duration ; for on the Friday came the attempted assassination of Coligny, and on the Sunday the terrible Massacre of St. Bartholomew, to which Catherine had been driven by the failure of the lesser crime.

Very early in the morning—the massacre had begun about two hours after midnight by the murder of Coligny at his lodging in the Rue des Fossés-Saint-Germain-l'Auxerrois—the King of Navarre and Condé, who were both lodged with their brides in the Louvre, were arrested and conducted to Charles IX.'s cabinet. "Take that *canaille* away!" cried Charles, pointing to the attendants of Navarre, who had been apprehended with their master ; and the hapless gentlemen were led out and mercilessly butchered in the courtyard of the palace. Then the half-mad King, who was beside himself with passion, informed the princes that all that was being done was by his orders ; that they had allowed themselves to be made the leaders of his enemies, and that their lives were justly forfeited. As, however, they were his kinsmen and connections, he would pardon them, if they conformed to the religion of their ancestors, the only one he would henceforth tolerate in his realm. If not, they must prepare to share the fate of their friends.

Navarre, of a more politic and wary disposition than his cousin, and, besides, somewhat indifferent on the subject of religion, assumed a conciliatory tone, begging the King not to compel him to outrage his conscience, and to consider that he was now not only his kinsman, but closely connected with him by marriage. Condé, on the other hand, courageously replied that he refused to believe the King capable of violating his most sacred pledges, but that he was accountable for his religion to God alone, and would remain faithful to it, even if it cost him his life. "Madman! conspirator! rebel! son of a rebel!" cried the infuriated monarch. "If in three days you do not change your tone, I will have you strangled!" And he dismissed them from his presence, with directions that they should be most strictly guarded.

The conversion of the two princes greatly occupied the Court. The young Queen of Navarre, a fervent Catholic, spared no effort to persuade her husband to return to the fold of the Church, and found zealous auxiliaries in the Cardinal de Bourbon, the Queen's confessor the Jesuit Maldonato, and Sureau des Roziers, an ex-Huguenot pastor, who had been converted to Catholicism by the sound of arquebuses. The astute Béarnais, who already seems to have had some presentiment of the part he was one day to play, was not the man to sacrifice a great future to his attachment to the Reformed doctrines, and accordingly feigned to lend an attentive ear to the arguments of his teachers.

Condé was the object of like solicitation, to which, however, he replied with anger and contempt. His obstinacy so enraged the King that one day, when he learned that the prince had proved more than usually contumacious, he called for his arms, swearing that he would proceed to his cousin's apartments, at the head of his guards, and slay him with his own hand. Probably, he only intended to intimidate him into submission; but his queen, the gentle and pious Elizabeth of Austria, believing that he was in earnest, threw herself at his feet, and besought him not to stain his hands with his kinsman's blood. His Majesty yielded to her entreaties and contented himself with summoning Condé to his presence, and, when he appeared, shouting in a voice of thunder: "Mass, death, or Bastille! Choose!" "God allows me not, my lord and king," replied the prince quietly, "to choose the first. Of the others, be it at your pleasure, whichever God may in His providence direct!"

Despite this bold answer, he shortly afterwards consented to abjure, "laying upon the head of Des Roziers the risk of his damnation"; the King of Navarre did likewise; and on 3 October, the "converted" princes addressed to the Pope a very humble letter, begging him to accept their submission and admit them into the fold. Condé and Marie de Cléves also expressed their regret for having allowed themselves to be united in wedlock without the rites of Holy Church.

Gregory XIII., who had just caused a medal to be struck with his own portrait on one side, and, on the other, a destroying angel immolating the Huguenots, was graciously pleased to accord the petition of the young couple, and granted them absolution and dispensation, in virtue of which they were married again, this time according to the Catholic ritual, in the Church of Saint-Germain-des-Prés (December, 1572).

Notwithstanding their abjuration, the King of Navarre and Condé were still regarded with suspicion and remained in a sort of quasi-captivity. Their position was a difficult one, and it must have needed all their self-control to prevent them from openly resenting the sneers and taunts which the nobles of the Court felt themselves safe in levelling at them. "On All Hallows' Eve," writes L'Estoile, "the King of Navarre was playing tennis with the Duc de Guise, when the scant consideration which was shown this little prisoner of a kinglet, at whom he threw all kinds of jests and taunts, deeply pained a number of honest people who were watching them play." [1]

The "kinglet," however, knew how to accommodate himself to circumstances, and was often able to turn the laugh on his own side by some lively repartée. After a while, too, Charles IX., who had always entertained a strong liking for Henri, began to treat him with kindness and even affection, in consequence of which even the Guises felt obliged to show him a certain degree of deference.

With Condé, however, it was very different. To one of his austere nature, this Court, which had degenerated to such an appalling extent, owing to the corruption of morals produced by the civil wars, that vice had become the mode, and virtue, even ordinary decency, was mocked at and derided, must have seemed the very anti-chamber of hell; and he was at no pains to conceal the disgust with which it inspired him. The King of Navarre might drink and gamble with the murderers of his

[1] "Journal du règne de Charles IX."

HENRI I DE BOURBON, PRINCE DE CONDÉ

faithful followers, and make love to the high-born courtesans who had passed obscene jests on the stripped corpses of the Huguenot nobles as they lay in the courtyard of the Louvre on that terrible morning. Policy required, he said, that he and his cousin should dissimulate their feelings. Well, let him do it! For himself, he would have no dealings with them, beyond that which ordinary courtesy demanded. And so he stood aloof, a gloomy, silent figure—an object of suspicion, dislike and derision to King and courtiers alike—with none to sympathize or condole with him in his loneliness and humiliation.

For even his wife had failed him. She was but a giddy butterfly, who, though educated in the Reformed Faith, had never professed any attachment for it, and had forsaken it without a regret. As for her husband, she appears to have married him merely because he happened to be the best match which offered itself, and because her relatives desired it. His sombre nature, embittered by the new trials to which he was being subjected, was but little to her taste, and she infinitely preferred the society of the Duc d'Anjou, who had conceived for her a most violent passion.

If we are to believe Brantôme, this affair had begun some few months before the lady's marriage to Condé, and Anjou had not been permitted to sigh in vain. "This same prince [Anjou]," he writes, "aware that she [Marie de Clèves] was about to marry a prince [Condé] who had displeased him and very much troubled the State of his brother [Charles IX.], debauched her . . . and then, in two months' time, she was given to the aforesaid prince [Condé] to wife, as a pretended virgin, which was a very sweet revenge."

We can well believe that the seduction of the promised wife of an enemy would have been just the kind of exploit to appeal to the future Henri III.; but Brantôme is too incorrigible a scandalmonger for much reliance to be placed on his unsupported testimony. However, that may be, Anjou's admiration for Marie de Clèves was now the talk of the Court, and the poet Philippe Desportes, who prostituted his muse to the services of the last Valois, as we shall see Malherbe, at a later date, minister to the amorous fancies of Henri IV., hastened to immortalize the affair in verse, and composed an elegy, in which the lovers figured under the names of Eurylas and Olympias, and the jealousy of the husband was unmercifully ridiculed.

Anjou was already provided with a mistress in the person of one of Catherine's maids-of-honour, Renée de Rieux, demoiselle de Châteauneuf—called *la belle* Châteauneuf—a ravishing blonde of twenty summers, with wonderful blue eyes, a complexion of lilies and roses, and "hair which looked like a crown of gold." She passed for the most perfect beauty of the Court, and one could pay a lady no higher compliment than to say that she resembled her.[1]

Mlle. de Châteauneuf was so proud of the distinction which his Royal Highness had conferred upon her that she was prepared to make any sacrifice rather than lose him. Anjou already showed a marked taste for the ornaments and dress proper to the other sex—a caprice which he carried to the most extravagant lengths when he became King of France[2]—and wore habitually "a double row of rings on his fingers and pendants in his ears." In the hope of retaining his wayward affections, the poor lady ruined herself in jewellery, and covered her royal lover with gold chains and costly trinkets of every description. He accepted them all with alacrity; nevertheless, the star of *la belle* Châteauneuf paled before that of the Princesse de Condé and she suffered the fate which had befallen Isabelle de Limeuil. She was not called upon to restore the presents which Anjou had made her—she had given far more than she had ever received—but, on the other hand, she had the mortification of seeing those which she had made the prince decorating the person of her triumphant rival. "In order to

---

[1] It is to her that Baïf dedicated his "Hymne de Vénus":

"Noble sang des Rieux, si mes vers ne desdaigne. . . ."

[2] After he succeeded his brother on the throne, he appeared, on one occasion at a Court ball, his face rouged and powdered, the body of his doublet cut low, like a woman's, with long sleeves falling to the ground, and a string of pearls round his neck.

"Si qu'au premier abord, chacun étoit en peine
S'il voyoit un roi femme ou bien un homme reine."

show," writes Brantôme, "that he had abandoned his former mistress for her [the Princesse de Condé], and that he desired to honour and serve her entirely, without bestowing a thought on the other, he gave her all the favours, jewels, rings, portraits, bracelets, and pretty conceits of every kind which his former mistress had given him, which being perceived by her, she was like to die with mortification, and was unable to keep silence about it, but was contented to compromise the reputation of the other by compromising her own."

The amours of Anjou and Marie de Cléves were interrupted by the outbreak of the fourth civil war. For a moment, Catherine had deluded herself into the belief that the Huguenot party was expiring at her feet, but she soon learned that religions do not die beneath the knives of assassins. Coligny, La Rochefoucauld, Soubise, Pilles, and other aristocratic leaders had perished in the St. Bartholomew ; Navarre and Condé had been constrained to renounce their faith ; Montgommery and La Noue were in exile ; the Protestant noblesse was disheartened and disorganized by the loss of its chiefs. But the popular element in the Reform party saved it, and raised the banner which was falling from the hands of the nobility. The citizens of La Rochelle, Montauban and Sancerre continued the struggle which the Bourbons and Châtillons had begun, demanding not only religious toleration, but the redress of political grievances ; and other towns in the South and West followed their example.

The Government determined on the reduction of La Rochelle, and a formidable army was despatched thither, under the command of Anjou ; and the "converted" Bourbons were ordered to accompany it. The unhappy Condé must have felt that his cup of humiliation was indeed filled to overflowing when he found himself marching against the stronghold of Protestantism—against those brave citizens amongst whom he counted so many personal friends—beneath the banner of the man who, after causing his father to be murdered, had robbed him of the affection of his wife. When the siege began, he courted danger with the eagerness of a man weary of life ; but, as not infrequently happens in such circumstances, the balls passed him by, and, though men fell fast around him, he himself remained unscathed.

La Rochelle offered an heroic resistance, and at the end of four months the royal army had lost nearly 20,000 men, including the Duc d'Aumale, and was no nearer success than when the trenches were opened. In the meanwhile, Anjou, thanks to the dexterity of his mother's diplomatic agents, had been elected King of Poland; and, on the pretext that it was undesirable that the Polish Ambassadors should find him engaged in besieging a Protestant town, acceptable terms were offered to the Rochellois, and the siege was raised. A month later (July, 1573), the Edict of Boulogne granted the Huguenots even better terms than had been promised them by the Peace of Saint-Germain.

The new King of Poland seemed in no hurry to take possession of his throne, and manifested very little enthusiasm for what he regarded as a kind of exile, far removed from the Court of the Valois and the pleasures which he held so dear. He had become so desperately enamoured of the Princesse de Condé that the prospect of parting from her was extremely distasteful to him, and he also feared, that, in the event of the death of Charles IX.—the unhappy King, who had been a changed man since the St. Bartholomew, was now in consumption, and it was obvious that he had not long to live—his absence might result in his younger brother, François, Duc d'Alençon, seizing the throne. These considerations led him to linger in Paris until the end of September; and it was only when the King informed him that, "if he did not go of his own free will, he would make him go by force," that he took his departure.

Before leaving Paris, his Polish Majesty, smitten perhaps by compunction for the shabby way in which he had treated Mlle. de Châteauneuf, sought to make amends by providing her with a husband. In this intention, he cast his eyes upon a very wealthy citizen, Duprat de Nantouillet, provost of Paris. The provost, however, showed himself very little flattered by the rôle proposed to him and peremptorily declined the lady's hand.

Transported with rage, the prince determined to be revenged, and, having taken counsel with Charles IX. and the King of Navarre, sent word to Nantouillet that they were all three coming to sup with him, and proceeded to his house, accompanied by a band of courtiers. Their visit occurred at a most inconvenient moment for the worthy provost, who happened to have selected that very day to pay off a little score of his own against some rival in love or politics, for which purpose he had concealed four bravos in his house. However, he put the best face on the matter he could, and provided his uninvited guests with a most sumptuous repast, which had such an exhilarating effect upon some of the company, that they finished up the evening by breaking open their host's coffers, and carrying off all his silver plate and about 50,000 livres in money.

Next morning, Christophe de Thou, First President of the Parlement of Paris, requested an audience of Charles IX. and told him that this nocturnal escapade had excited the greatest indignation in the city. His Majesty swore that he had had nothing whatever to do with it, and that it was a gross calumny to assert that he was responsible. " I am delighted to hear it," replied the magistrate, " and I am going to order an enquiry and punish the guilty." " No, no!" cried the King, "don't trouble yourself about this matter ; simply tell Nantouillet that, if he demands satisfaction for the loss he has suffered, he will get the worst of it."

The unfortunate Nantouillet thereupon decided to put up with the loss of his plate and money, lest a worse fate should befall him. But his troubles were not yet over, for one day, while walking in the street, he happened to meet Mlle. de Châteauneuf, on horseback. No sooner did the indignant beauty perceive the man who had dared to refuse her hand, than she rode up to him, and proceeded to belabour him soundly with her riding-whip, to the great amusement of the onlookers.

CHAPTER VIII

Departure of Anjou for Poland—Condé, compromised in the conspiracy of the "Politiques," escapes to Strasbourg, where he reverts to the Protestant faith—Death of Charles IX., who is succeeded by the King of Poland—Flight of the new King from Cracow—Death of the Princesse de Condé : extravagant grief of Henry III.—Condé invades France at the head of an army of German mercenaries—The "*Paix de Monsieur*"—Condé endeavours to establish himself in the West of France—Formation of the League and renewal of the civil war—Condé refuses the hand of Mlle. de Vaudémont, Henry III.'s sister-in-law—His second Odyssey—He commands the Huguenot forces in Poitou and Saintonge—He proposes for the hand of Charlotte Catherine de la Trémoille—Letter of Mlle. de la Trémoille to the prince—He visits her at the Château of Taillebourg—Disastrous expedition of Condé against Angers—He is obliged to take refuge in Guernsey.

THE Court escorted the King of Poland as far as La Fère, Condé accompanying it. On taking leave of the Prince, his Majesty informed him that he had obtained for him the restoration of his government of Picardy and permission to proceed thither whenever he wished. This pretended favour was really a precautionary measure, for fresh troubles were brewing, and Catherine desired to separate Condé and the King of Navarre, and deprive the latter, who was erroneously believed to be as vacillating as his father, of the support and advice of his kinsman. However, Condé was well-pleased to turn his back on the Court, where he had suffered so many humiliations, and at the end of the autumn he set out for Amiens.

The Massacre of St. Bartholomew had been not only a crime, but a blunder of the most fatal kind. It had shocked and horrified the moderate Catholic party—the "Politiques" as they had now begun to be called—and convinced their leaders, the Montmorencies, that the Queen-Mother intended their ruin after that of the Bourbons and the Châtillons. The result was a *rapprochement* between the "Politiques" and the Huguenots, which, by the beginning of 1574, had developed into a vast conspiracy enveloping nearly the whole of France. Its secret head was Catherine's youngest son, the ambitious and treacherous François, Duc d'Alençon, who had long chafed under the subjection to which his brother's dislike and his mother's indifference had relegated him, and was determined to assert himself at all hazards.

The plans of the conspirators were carefully laid. At the end of February, risings were to take place simultaneously in Normandy, Picardy, Champagne, Poitou, Dauphiné, Guienne, and Languedoc ; while a bold Huguenot chief, the Sieur de Guitry-Bertichères, with several hundred men, was to force the gates of the Château of Saint-Germain, where the Court was then residing, and carry off Alençon and the King of Navarre, who would at once put themselves at the head of the rebels.

Unfortunately for them, Guitry's enterprise, on which the success of the whole movement hinged, failed through his own precipitation. Owing to some misunderstanding, he anticipated the day, and appeared with his men in the environs of Saint-Germain some time before he was expected. Catherine's suspicions were at once aroused, and her remarkable skill in unravelling the tangled threads of even the most complicated intrigues soon placed her in possession of the whole plot. In the early hours of the following morning (23–24 February), she hurried the Court off to Paris. Charles IX., travelling in a litter, surrounded by the Swiss in battle-array, as during the retreat from Meaux, while she herself followed in her coach with Navarre and Alençon, whom she was determined not to allow out of her sight.

Meanwhile, the rebels had risen in arms and issued a manifesto demanding various reforms, though it was obvious that these were only a cloak for their real intentions, and that, should the rising prove successful, its effect would be to deprive the King of Poland of the succession to the throne, which must speedily become vacant, in favour of the more accommodating

Alençon.   Catherine, however, invested with full powers by the illness of the King, took prompt and energetic measures to meet the danger.   Three armies were despatched against the rebels of Normandy, the South, and Central France ; Navarre and Alençon, who were found to be planning an attempt at escape, with the connivance of two of the latter's favourites, La Môle and Coconnas, were shut up in the keep of the Château of Vincennes, and a commission appointed to examine them ; while the two gentlemen were brought to trial on a charge of high treason, condemned and executed ; the Maréchaux de Montmorency and de Cossé, who had had the temerity to come to Court to endeavour to justify their conduct, were seized and thrown into the Bastille, and orders were sent to Amiens for the arrest of Condé.

Condé had not yet been guilty of any overt act of rebellion ; but he had been compromised by the avowals of the pusil- lanimous Alençon, who had made a full confession, and also by those wrung from Coconnas in the anguish of torture.[1] Warned in time, however, he succeeded in affecting his escape, and fled to Strasburg, where he lost no time in returning publicly to the faith from which in his heart he had never wavered.   His wife, to whom he had been reconciled, and who was three months pregnant, he left behind him.   They were never to meet again.

On 31 May of that year, the unhappy Charles IX. expired, " rejoicing that he left no heir in such an age, since he knew of his own sad experience how wretched was the state of a child- king, and how wretched the kingdom over which a child ruled." On the previous day, he had publicly declared the King of Poland his lawful heir and successor, and his mother Regent until his return to France ; and Catherine wrote, urging her favourite son to return without delay and take possession of his birthright.

[1] The Duc d'Aumale (" Histoire des Princes de Condé ") asserts that he was also compromised by the confessions of La Môle, but, in justice to that unfortunate gentleman, we must observe that such was not the case.   La Môle, though most horribly tortured, exhibited remarkable fortitude, and compromised no one, with the exception of Guillaume de Montmorency, who had already compromised himself by taking to flight.

The latter needed no pressing. Although he had only occupied the throne of Poland a few months, he was already heartily tired of his kingdom, both the people and the customs of which were utterly distasteful to one of his indolent and luxurious temperament; and he was impatiently awaiting the event which should recall him to France—and the Princesse de Condé. Absence, so far from diminishing, had only served to increase his devotion to that lady. "I love her so greatly, as you know," he wrote to one of his confidants at the Court, "that you must certainly inform me of everything that befalls her, for the sake of the tears that I shed for her. But I will speak no more of her, for love is intoxicated." And he employed a good part of his time in inditing to her passionate letters, written in his own royal blood!

So soon as the news of his brother's death reached him, he quitted his sombre palace at Cracow, secretly, in the middle of the night, accompanied by some of his French attendants, and rode without drawing rein until he reached the Moravian frontier, hotly pursued by his indignant subjects, who, singularly enough, had conceived for him a great affection, and wished to compel him to remain their ruler. The explanation he subsequently condescended to give of this 'escapade, was that the condition of France was so disturbed that even a week's delay might imperil his succession. Nevertheless, having once shaken the dust of his adopted country off his feet, he seemed in no hurry to return to his own; he preferred to travel by way of Vienna and Turin, where he extravagantly rewarded the hospitality of the Duke of Savoy by the restoration of Pinerolo, the gate of Italy; and it was not until the beginning of September that he turned his steps towards France.

At Bourgoin, he was met by Catherine and the greater part of the Court. The Queen-Mother brought with her the King of Navarre and Alençon, whom she had set at liberty, having first extracted an oath from them that they would "neither attempt nor originate anything to the detriment of his Majesty the King and the state of his realm." They were still, however, kept under very close observation by her Majesty, and treated very much like naughty schoolboys.

After a short stay at Bourgoin, the Court proceeded to Lyons, where it remained for several weeks, its sojourn being marked by splendid festivities. In the middle of October, a sad event came to interrupt these rejoicings : news arrived that, on the 13th, the Princesse de Condé had died in Paris, in giving birth to a daughter.[1]

Brantôme assures us that Henri III. had fully resolved to petition the Pope to annul the marriage of Marie de Clèves and Condé—" which he would not have refused, since he was so great a king, and for divers other reasons that one wots of "—and to make the lady his queen ; and it would seem that the princess was not indisposed to such an arrangement. However that may be, his Majesty exhibited the most extravagant grief at the death of his inamorata. On opening the letter which contained the fatal news, he instantly fell down in a dead faint, and was carried to his apartments, which he caused to be draped in black velvet, and where he remained shut up for several days, for the first two of which he persistently refused to touch either food or wine. When he, at length, reappeared, he was clad in the deepest mourning, and the points of his doublet and even the ribbons of his shoes were garnished with little death's-heads. From that moment little death's-heads in gold, coral, or crystal became the trinket *à la mode.*

From being the life and soul of every fête and pleasure-party, the grief-stricken King now plunged into the most extravagant devotion, and at Avignon, to which the Court had removed, with the idea of affording him some distraction from his sorrow, nothing would content him but to join the Flagellants, a sect very strong in the Papal city, who, dressed in sackcloth, nightly paraded the streets by torchlight, chanting the *Miserere* and scourging one another with whips. The Court and the Royal Family were compelled to follow suit ; and the Cardinal de Lorraine, unaccustomed to such mortification of the flesh, caught a chill which caused his death.

[1] Catherine de Bourbon, Marquise d'Isles. She died unmarried in 1592.

have the body of the Princesse de Condé removed from the vaults of Saint-Germain-des-Prés, in which it had been temporarily deposited, the King refusing to enter the abbey, as long as those precious remains were there. Even his marriage to the sweet and charming Louise de Lorraine,[1] which took place at Rheims, in February, 1575,[2] three days after his *Sacre*, seems to have been a tribute to the memory of his lost love, for the young lady, whom he had met at Nancy, on his way to Poland in the autumn of 1573, had first attracted his attention by the resemblance she bore to the Princesse de Condé.

Condé was still a fugitive in Germany when the news of his

---

[1] Daughter of Nicolas, Comte de Vaudémont, and Marguerite d'Egmont.

[2] It was on the occasion of his marriage that his Majesty made another attempt to provide Mlle. de Châteauneuf with a husband. This time, however, he flew at much higher game than a provost of Paris, his vassal, François de Luxembourg, being his quarry. Luxembourg had been a suitor for the hand of Louise de Lorraine, and his addresses had been very favourably received by the lady, until the appearance of the King of France in the field had put an end to his hopes. The prince had attended the *Sacre* and the marriage, and, a day or two after the latter ceremony, his suzerain drew him aside and said : " Cousin, I have married your mistress ; but I desire that, in exchange, you should marry mine." And he offered him the hand of Mlle. de Châteauneuf. Luxembourg, making, very naturally, a distinction between the two senses attached to the word " mistress," thanked the King for his thoughtfulness, but begged him to give him time to think the matter over. "I desire," replied his Majesty, " that you should espouse her immediately." The unfortunate prince then "begged very humbly that the King would grant him a week's respite." To which the King answered that he would give him three days only, at the expiration of which, if he were not prepared to marry the damsel, something exceedingly unpleasant would probably befall him. Before another day had dawned, Luxembourg was riding for the frontier as hard as his horse could gallop.

Soon after this episode, Mlle. de Châteauneuf was expelled both from Catherine's squadron and the Court, for impertinence towards the young Queen. Having thus fallen into disgrace, she condescended to espouse a Florentine named Antinoti, who was intendant of the galleys at Marseilles. The marriage, however, had a tragic termination, for, "having detected him in a compromising situation with another demoiselle, she stabbed him bravely and manfully with her own hand." Shortly afterwards, she married another Florentine, Alloviti by name, who called himself the Baron de Castellane ; but, a few months later, the baron was killed in a brawl by Henri d'Angoulême, Grand Prior of France, a natural son of Henri II., by Mary Stuart's governess, Lady Fleming, though not before he had succeeded in mortally wounding his antagonist.

bereavement reached him. It can scarcely have failed to cause him pain, for, notwithstanding her relations with Henri III., he had remained attached to his wife; but the reflection that now that her royal admirer had reappeared upon the scene, she would, had she lived, most certainly have brought fresh scandal upon his name, must have served to temper his grief. In the previous July, he had been proclaimed chief of the confederates by a Huguenot-Politique assembly which had met at Milhaud; but he made no attempt to return to France, but wandered about Germany and Switzerland, negotiating with the Protestant princes and enlisting soldiers. With the aid of English gold, he finally succeeded in raising a small army, and, in the early autumn of 1575, he despatched part of it, under the command of Montmorency-Thoré, to the assistance of Alençon, who had just succeeded in effecting his escape from the Court and had placed himself at the head of the confederates.[1] But this force was too weak to effect anything, and was defeated by the Duc de Guise at Dormans.[2]

Having levied fresh troops to replace those he had lost, in the following April, Condé himself re-entered France, after an absence of two years, crossed the Loire, near La Charité, and effected a junction with the troops of Alençon in the Bourbonnais. Henri III. and Catherine were obliged to negotiate, and on 6 May another hollow peace—the "*Paix de Monsieur*"—was signed at Beaulieu. The Protestants obtained greater concessions than any which they had yet enjoyed; the Massacre of St. Bartholomew was formally disavowed and the property of Coligny and other prominent victims restored to their heirs; and eight fortresses were handed over to the Reformers, as security for the due observance of the treaty. Alençon received the addition to his appanage of Anjou, Berry, Touraine and Maine, and assumed the title of Duc d'Anjou, which had been that of Henri III. before his accession to the throne; while the

---

[1] In February, 1576, the King of Navarre also made his escape, and promptly reverted to the Protestant faith, but he took no active part in the remainder of the war.

[2] It was in this engagement that the duke received the wound in the face which earned him, like his celebrated father, the name of "*le Balafré.*"

governor of Péronne, a friend of the Guises, refused to deliver that fortress into his hands and formed a confederacy between the partisans of the Guises and the bigoted Catholics to oppose him.

Deeply irritated by this breach of faith, Condé determined to seek compensation in the west, and proceeded to take possession of Cognac and Saint-Jean-d'Angely, and to purchase, from the Sieur de Pons, the government of the important fortress of Brouage. Then he went to La Rochelle, where, "by a succession of very able orations," he succeeded in convincing the citizens, who were at first inclined to regard his pretensions with suspicion, that their mayor and bailiffs were quite unworthy of their confidence, and that they could not do better than entrust themselves to his protection, with the result that in a few weeks he was virtually master of the town.

But the concession granted the Huguenots at the "*Paix de Monsieur*" had aroused, as had been the case after the Peace of Saint-Germain, the most violent resentment among the more zealous Catholics, who regarded them in the light of a betrayal of their faith; and the efforts of Condé to consolidate his position in the West stimulated the growth of that confederacy which had already been formed against him in Picardy. The movement spread with astonishing rapidity, especially among the fanatical population of Paris, and soon grew into a general "Holy League," or association of the extreme Catholic party throughout the kingdom.

The formation of the League, whose members were binding themselves to regard as enemies all who refused to join it, greatly alarmed Henri III., and, after an unsuccessful attempt to obtain a promise from the Guises that they would do nothing calculated to lead to a breach of the recent peace, he decided that the only course open to him was to place himself at its head. This decision rendered a new war inevitable, and early in 1577 it duly broke out.

In the South, the Huguenots contrived to hold their own, but Condé, who commanded in Poitou and Saintonge, with the title of the King of Navarre's Lieutenant-General, fared badly, largely, it would seem, through his own want of military capacity, and was soon obliged to take refuge in La Rochelle, and look on helplessly while the enemy conquered the whole of the surrounding country. Finally, he made his; way into Guienne and joined his cousin, upon whom he, very unfairly, endeavoured to throw the blame of his ill-success in the West. In September, the Peace of Bergerac, another ineffectual treaty, which granted in the main what that of the previous year had already promised, nominally put an end to the war, though private hostilities—storming of châteaux, assassinations, and pillage—still continued.

At the end of the following year, Marguerite de Valois joined her husband at Nérac. Catherine, whom the King left free to intrigue as she pleased, accompanied her daughter, bringing with her her "squadron," whose charms wrought much havoc among the gentlemen of Henri's little Court. She remained there several months, but the results of her visit fell very far short of her expectations, and, on her return to Paris, she made overtures to Condé, who, since the last war, had been on far from cordial terms with the King of Navarre. With a view to separating him entirely from his cousin, she offered him the hand of the Queen's sister, Mlle. de Vaudémont, together with a considerable pension and the restoration of his government of Picardy. Condé declined the marriage, on the plea of difference in religion, and the next thing Catherine heard about him was that he had made his way in disguise into Picardy, and seized the town of La Fère, by means of a stratagem (November, 1579).

The prince was left in peaceable possession of La Fère for some months, though his efforts to extend his influence through the rest of the province were unsuccessful. But when, in the somewhat futile operations.

The Treaty of Fleix was followed by four years of anarchic peace, which were passed by Condé chiefly at Saint-Jean-d'Angely. He had been reconciled to the King of Navarre, and the two cousins visited one another on several occasions ; but this reconciliation was never really sincere, for Condé was not a little jealous of the military reputation which Henri had acquired in the last war, and he and the more fanatical section of the Protestants disapproved of the moderation shown by the young king, and sometimes endeavoured to compel him to adopt measures which his good sense condemned.

On 11 June, 1584, the Duc d'Anjou died of consumption at Château-Thierry. His death made the King of Navarre heir-presumptive to the French crown, and, as Henri III. had, for some time past, abandoned all hope of leaving children behind him, the question of the succession at once became of paramount importance. But the accession of a heretic to the throne was repugnant to the whole Catholic population, and was certain to be violently opposed by a considerable section of it. For the intimate connexion of the State and the orthodox Church was held to be a fundamental law of the monarchy ; and even men of moderate views, who were willing enough that the Huguenots should be tolerated, were alarmed at the prospect of their domination.

Very intelligent, whenever he could contrive to free himself for a time from his idle and voluptuous habits, Henri III. had

foreseen this, and, about the middle of May—that is to say,
about three weeks before Anjou's death—had despatched one
of his favourites, the Duc d'Épernon, to the King of Navarre,
"bearing him letters in which he admonished, exhorted, and
entreated him, seeing that the life of the Duc d'Anjou, his
brother, was despaired of, to come to Court and go to Mass,
because he desired to recognize him as his true heir and
successor, and to give him such rank and dignity near his
person as his qualification of brother-in-law and heir to the
throne deserved." The Protestants testified the greatest
uneasiness at these overtures, and began to approach Condé,
with a view to his adoption as the leader of the party, in the
event of the King of Navarre again renouncing their faith.
But their alarm was groundless, for, though Henri held but
lightly by his creed, and all the Catholics about him besought
him to remove the one obstacle to his succession, he felt that
the time had not come when he could afford to offend the
Huguenots. And so, with many protestations of gratitude
and loyalty, he declared himself unable to accede to his
Majesty's wishes.

The fact that the legitimate heir to the throne was a heretic
made the renewal of the civil war inevitable, and, on the death
of Anjou, the Guises and the League at once began to organize
their forces for the coming struggle. The wretched, vacillating
King was intimidated into giving them his countenance and
support ; and, on 15 July, 1585, signed the Treaty of Nemours,
which promised the revocation of all the edicts in favour of
toleration, and placed at the disposal of the League all the
resources of the Crown. Having secured the assistance of the
temporal power, they next summoned the spiritual to their aid,
and persuaded the new Pope, Sixtus V., to launch against the
two princes a Bull of Excommunication, wherein he declared
them "degraded from their fiefs and baronies, and incapacitated
from succession to the Crown of France." The cousins issued
a scornful response, a copy of which was posted up even in
Rome itself, and war began.

Condé again received the command of the Huguenot forces

before the renewal of hostilities, he had decided to propose for the hand of Charlotte Catherine de la Trémoille, only daughter of Louis III., Duc de Thouars, Prince de Tarente and de Talmont, and Jeanne de Montmorency.

Charlotte de la Trémoille's father, who, by the way, had been a fanatical Catholic and a determined opponent of Condé in Poitou, of which province he was lieutenant-general, had died some years before, since which the girl had lived with her mother at the Château of Thouars, in Anjou. She was now seventeen, very pretty, very intelligent, and of a highly romantic disposition, for the Duchesse de Thouars, who appears to have had little affection for her daughter, had left her very much to her own devices, and she was accustomed to spend a good deal of her time in the perusal of the " Amadis " and other fashionable works of imagination.

Condé despatched one of his officers to the Duchesse de Thouars to make the first overtures on his behalf. They were favourably received, and the duchess hastened to send her daughter to the Château of Taillebourg, a fortress of some importance on the banks of the Charente, whither she intended to follow her, so that his Highness might have an opportunity of paying his addresses to the young lady, and she of discussing with him the financial side of the affair. The alliance of the first Prince of the Blood, one of the leaders of the Huguenots, was very flattering to the pride of the La Trémoilles, who did not share the prejudices of the late head of the family ; indeed,

On learning of the favourable reception of his overtures, Condé, who was besieging Brouage, lost no time in addressing to the Duchesse de Thouars a formal request for her daughter's hand. The duchess informed Charlotte, who wrote to the prince the following letter ·

"MADAME,[1]
"I am not able, it seems to me, to thank you as I should wish for the honour that it pleases you to do me by your letter, and for the good-will which it appears you entertain for me, which oblige me to serve you in such fashion that I shall esteem myself very happy all my life if I am favoured by your commands, which I shall execute with as much fidelity as any creature in the world. And, since I know that Madame de la Trémoille, my mother, is replying to what you have been so good as to write to her, I shall say nothing on this subject, save that my intention has ever been to conform to her will, and that it will remain so eternally, and to assure you again Mons' (*sic*) that my little merit must prevent me from believing what it pleases you to express for me. . . I thank you very humbly for the honour which I receive from your suit, although I know that I am in no way worthy of it, which places me under a very great obligation to you. I shall leave to Madame de la Trémoille, my mother, to reply on the subject of the journeys of the bearer of this, for all that I have desired my whole life, is to follow these

[1] The young lady, of course, intended to write "Monsieur."

commands, in which I shall never fail, and, in token of this, I shall kiss your hands.

"Your very humble servant, etc., etc."[1]

On learning that Mlle. de Trémoille had arrived at Taillebourg, Condé quitted his camp at Brouage and proceeded thither. He took with him the greater part of the Huguenot cavalry, and we may imagine with what a thrill of pleasure the romantic Charlotte must have beheld this valiant prince coming to woo her accompanied by so splendid an array of mail-clad horsemen. Nor was she less pleased when, at the gateway of the château, her suitor dismissed his imposing escort, and, to show his confidence, entered with three or four of his officers only.

All smiles and blushes the young châtelaine came forward to greet him, and, though Condé was usually very reserved with women, Mademoiselle was so pretty and so sympathetic that soon he found himself discoursing of his wars and his wanderings as though he had known her for years. Before the evening was over, Charlotte had decided that the hero of her dreams had indeed materialized; while the prince was completely charmed. "The two betrothed," writes a contemporary biographer of the latter, "promised henceforth to live and die together, provided that they obtained the consent of Madame de la Trémoille, of which Mademoiselle her daughter was sufficiently assured;"[2] and Condé might have said with Othello:

> " She loved me for the dangers I had passed,
> And I lov'd her that she did pity them."

Mlle. de la Trémoille gave that very night a proof of her devotion to her future husband. As the garrison of Taillebourg contained several men who, she had reason to suspect, were by no means well-disposed towards the Huguenot leader, "she

[1] Published by Édouard Barthélemy, " la Princesse de Condé : Charlotte Catherine de la Trémoille."

[2] "Véritable discours de la naissance et de la vie de Monseigneur le prince de Condé jusqu'à présent, à lui desdié par le sieur de Fiefbrun," publié par Eugène Halphen (Paris, 1861).

did not take any repose all night, but watched with extreme care over his safety until the morning, placing the sentinels herself and making hourly inquiries of the rounds if they had discovered anything which might trouble the repose of our amorous prince." [1]

Early on the morrow, Condé left Taillebourg, but, before his departure, he gave Mlle. de la Trémoille, "two lines in his own handwriting and signed by him, containing the assurance of his good faith touching their future marriage." Then, "after a thousand reiterated promises that death alone should be the separation of their union," he took leave of his betrothed and returned to Brouage.

The siege of this town was progressing rapidly; Condé's forces closely invested it on the land side, while the little Huguenot fleet blockaded the port; a portion of the outworks had already been captured, and its fall seemed assured, when the prince thoughtlessly engaged in a most disastrous enterprise.

It happened that a Huguenot captain named Rochemorte, attached to a small force which Condé had sent across the Loire to make an incursion into Anjou and Normandy, had succeeded, with a mere handful of men, in taking by surprise the citadel of Angers. The town, however, remained in the hands of the Catholics; the daring Rochemorte and his little band were being closely besieged, and, unless reinforcements speedily arrived, he would be obliged to capitulate. This news caused great excitement in the Protestant camp, and the prince, instead of contenting himself by the despatch of a force sufficient to enable Rochemorte to hold the captured citadel, was persuaded by his flatterers to go in person and attempt the capture of the town. So brilliant a success, they assured him, would entirely eclipse the military reputation of the King of Navarre, change the whole course of events, and strike such consternation into the enemy that very soon he might be able to carry the war to the very gates of Paris.

It was a most rash undertaking, for not only was Angers a

[1] Fiefbrun.

strongly-fortified town, but the neighbourhood was the point of concentration for the, Catholic armies destined to operate in the South, and was swarming with the enemy. However, his jealousy of his cousin, and his anxiety to distinguish himself in the eyes of his lady-love, rendered him deaf to the voice of reason ; and, after wasting a good deal of precious time in preparations for his expedition, he set off for Angers, at the head of some 2000 horse, three-fourths of whom were mounted arquebusiers.

On the way, he had an interview with the Duchesse de Thouars, who was journeying to Taillebourg to join her daughter. Henri III., it appears, had lately brought pressure to bear upon the duchess to persuade her to break off the negotiations for the marriage, and, as the latter was beginning to feel seriously uneasy as to the future of her prospective son-in-law, she received him very coldly and endeavoured to evade giving the consent which he demanded. Perceiving how the land lay, Condé refrained from pressing the matter ; and, after overwhelming her with protestations of friendship, took his departure, and despatched in all haste a courier to Taillebourg, with the following message, written on a leaf of his tablets :

" I have found Madame, your mother, whether from fear or otherwise, very much opposed to my happiness. I hope to conquer her severity by my perseverance and my conduct, swearing that you alone possess my heart, and that neither her prejudice nor any accident shall be able to prevent me from remaining until death your unchanging *serviteur*." [1]

On 21 October, the prince arrived beneath the walls of Angers. He came too late, for, two days before, Rochemorte had been killed, and the citadel had capitulated. His wisest course would have been to retreat at once, for, although he had received reinforcements after crossing the Loire, his army did not exceed 3000 men, and hostile columns were already gathering in his rear. However, he determined to endeavour

---

[1] Édouard de Barthélemy, "la Princesse de Condé : Charlotte Catherine de la Trémoille, d'après les lettres inédites conservées dans les archives de Thouars " (Paris, 1872).

to carry the town by storm, and made two assaults, both of which were repulsed with considerable loss. Then, very reluctantly, he gave the order to retire; but there was some delay in carrying it out, and scarcely had his vanguard crossed the Loire, than the enemy's cavalry appeared on both banks of the river. For a moment, he thought of endeavouring to make his way along the right bank of the Loire to the Huguenot stronghold of Sancerre, but, learning that the Catholics were in force in that direction, he abandoned it, and decided that the only course to adopt was for his followers to disperse and endeavour to creep through the meshes of the net which was closing round them. He himself, with a few officers, turned northwards, and succeeded in reaching Saint-Malo, where he embarked for Guernsey.

In that little island the unfortunate prince remained for more than two months. He was almost in despair, for he well knew that his folly, which had deprived the Huguenot forces of the West of their chief, many of their principal officers, and the greater part of their cavalry, must have ruined their operations in that part of the country, and compelled them to remain wholly on the defensive. Moreover, he saw no immediate prospect of being able to return to France, for, though he had applied for assistance to Elizabeth, that princess was unwilling at this juncture to offend the French Court, and he got nothing from her but expressions of sympathy. One day, however, in January, 1586, he perceived two ships-of-war flying the Rochellois ensign, approaching the island. They cast anchor; an officer landed, handed the delighted prince a letter from Mlle. de la Trémoille, and informed him that they had been sent to convey him to La Rochelle.

But let us see how Mlle. de la Trémoille had been faring during her lover's enforced absence from France.

CHAPTER IX

AFTER the disastrous expedition to Angers and the flight of Condé, the Duchesse de Thouars resolved to side definitely with the Catholic party, and to do everything in her power to prevent the marriage of which she had at first so warmly approved. She had now joined Charlotte at Taillebourg, "where mother and daughter did not get on too well together," [1] for, as is generally the case with young ladies of a romantic turn of mind, obstacles only served to fire Charlotte's imagination, and the more opposed did the duchess become to the marriage, the more firmly did the girl resolve to remain true to her lover.

At length, matters reached a climax. At the outbreak of hostilities, the young Duc de Thouars, who, as we have mentioned, had joined Condé's army, had installed a Huguenot garrison in the château. This garrison the duchess resolved to get rid of, and to replace it by a Catholic one ; and, one fine

---

[1] De Thou.

day, four companies of soldiers marched into the town, under the command of a certain M. de Beaumont, who was entrusted with a letter for the Duchesse de Thouars from the Maréchal de Matignon, general-in-chief of the royal forces in the West, in which he called upon her, in the King's name, to surrender the château, promising to restore it at the conclusion of the war. The duchess was joyfully preparing to obey, when her daughter intervened and informed her, very respectfully, but very firmly, that she should refuse to consent to the surrender, and that "she intended to keep inviolable the pledge which she had given Mgr. le Prince de Condé to preserve the château for him until her death."[1]

Madame de Thouars expostulated, coaxed, threatened ; all to no purpose. Charlotte was immovable as the rock upon which the château stood, and eventually the mortified lady ordered her coach and set out for Thouars, abandoning her rebellious daughter to the dangers of a siege.

The Château of Taillebourg was an old fortress of the thirteenth century,[2] situated on a steep rock, which rendered it perfectly safe from attack on three sides. On the one on which it was accessible, Charlotte ordered two culverins to be placed, so as completely to command the approach, perceiving which, Beaumont, who does not appear to have had any artillery with him, prudently refrained from any attempt to take the château by storm, and contented himself by very closely investing it. Aware that it was not provisioned for a siege, he felt confident that want of provisions must soon oblige the garrison to capitulate.

The days went slowly by. Every morning Beaumont formally summoned the defenders to surrender, only to receive a scornful defiance. But, in the meantime, famine was beginning to stare them in the face, and Charlotte recognized

---

[1] Fiefbrun.

[2] It had had an eventful history during the Hundred Years' War, when it was more than once taken and re-taken. In 1562, a daring Huguenot adventurer named Romegoux escaladed it, by means of poniards fixed in the interstices of the walls, and for some years used it as a base for his operations against the Catholics of the surrounding country.

that, unless help arrived, it would be impossible to hold out much longer. Just, however, when her situation seemed almost desperate, she learned that a body of Huguenot cavalry under the Sieur de la Boullaye, which had succeeded in escaping from the Angers fiasco, was in the neighbourhood ; and she at once determined to make an attempt to communicate with it. This, at first sight, seemed a hopeless undertaking, for the place, as we have said, had been very closely invested ; but she perceived that at the rear of the château, where the rock was a sheer precipice, Beaumont had placed only a very few men, deeming it impossible for any one to descend on that side. Accordingly, when darkness fell, she caused one of her servants to be lowered by a rope down the face of the cliff ; and the man, unperceived by the enemy, succeeded in making his way to La Boullaye's camp.

The besiegers, to guard against any attempt to relieve the château, had taken the precaution to fortify a large house which commanded the entrance to the town of Taillebourg. But, as soon as morning dawned, Charlotte "said good-day to the enemy with her culverins," and, turning them upon this house, kept up so persistent and well-directed a fire, that it was soon almost in ruins ; and when the Huguenots arrived, they had no difficulty in making their way into the town.

Fighting continued all day, with no decisive result ; but, during the night, the Catholics, who had lost some sixty men and whose commander had been taken prisoner, evacuated the town and retreated behind the Charente. La Boullaye did not pursue them ; but, after placing a strong garrison in the château, escorted its brave defender to La Rochelle, where she promptly caused two ships to be fitted out, at her own expense, and despatched to Guernsey, to convey her lover and his fellow-exiles back to France.

Within an hour or two of the arrival of Charlotte's ships, Condé was on his way to La Rochelle, where he landed a few days later. " I was there," writes Fiefbrun, " and had the honour of accompanying this princess (Mlle. de la Trémoille) to the port, where she received his Excellency with so many expressions of joy, that never was seen anything |in the world to surpass in mutual affection their caresses and welcomes, followed by public rejoicings on the part of the nobility and the people which it would be impossible to describe." [1]

The prince and his lady-love looked forward with impatience to their marriage, to which, however, the Duchesse de Thouars continued to show herself extremely hostile. At length, however, she was persuaded to give a grudging consent, though she absolutely refused to grace the ceremony with her presence. It took place very quietly at the Château of Taillebourg, on 16 March, 1586. A little while before, Charlotte had become a Protestant, her example being followed by her brother, the Duc de Thouars.

Almost immediately after his marriage, Condé took the field again. He was burning to distinguish himself and efface the memory of the disaster of the previous year, which had furnished the King of Navarre and his little Court of Nérac with material for many biting jests at his expense.[2]   Glory, however, continued to evade his pursuit, and his solitary success was gained in a cavalry skirmish before Saintes, which, however, cost him so dear that he is said to have been "more afflicted by his losses than elated by his victory." [3]

In August, an armistice was concluded, and the remainder of the year was spent in negotiations, which led to nothing. They enabled Condé, however, to spend a few weeks with his bride at Saint-Jean-d'Angely, where, as most of the prince's property had been sequestrated by the Crown, while it was not until nearly two years after the marriage that the Duchesse de Thouars condescended to pay her daughter's dowry, they were obliged to content themselves with a very modest establishment. Indeed, to judge from the following letter from the princess to Longuespée, her agent at Taillebourg, there must have been times when they found themselves greatly embarrassed for even comparatively small sums of money :

[1] " Veritable discours de la naissance et de la vie de Mgr. le prince de Condé."

[2] So incensed was the poor prince at these pleasantries that when his cousin summoned him to attend a Protestant conference at Bergerac, he declined to obey.

[3] De Thou.

"Longuespée, my knowledge of the good-will which you have long shown in our service has caused me to write you, to beg you to do me the favour of handing to the bearer of this the sum of one hundred écus, on account of larger sums which are due to her for bread that she has supplied while my husband and I have been here. And, if just now you have not the sum mentioned, I beg you to make arrangements to obtain it, so that I may satisfy her, assuring you that the favour which you will be doing me will be very agreeable to me, and hoping to remember it on the first occasion which presents itself as willingly as I shall remain your good mistress,

"X. DE LA TREMOILLE"

"At Saint-Jean-d'Angely, this 21 September 1586.

"I beg you again not to refuse me."[1]

On 30 April, 1587, the Princesse de Condé gave birth to "a daughter worthy of such a mother," who received the name of Éléonore, in memory of the prince's mother, and became in 1606 the wife of Philip William of Nassau, Prince of Orange.

Early in the new year hostilities were resumed, and Condé gained several successes in Poitou and Saintonge. In October, the King of Navarre and Condé marched from La Rochelle to the Loire to meet the latter's younger brothers, the Marquis de Conti and the Comte de Soissons, who, although Catholics, had been persuaded to cast in their lot with their relatives. Then they turned southwards, with the intention of concentrating all their troops in Gascony, and afterwards marching towards Berry, to effect their junction with a German force which was advancing to their assistance.[2] They were closely followed by a royal army under the Duc de Joyeuse, while another Catholic force under Matignon advanced against them from Guienne. To prevent the junction of Joyeuse and Matignon, the King of Navarre decided to give battle to the former in the plain before

---

[1] Édouard de Barthélemy, "La Princesse de Condé: Charlotte Catherine de La Trémoille.

[2] The Marquis de Conti had gone to Strasbourg to take the nominal command of the Germans.

K

Coutras, on the borders of Saintonge and Périgord. The Catholics had a considerable advantage in point of numbers; but Henri's army was almost entirely composed of veterans, and he was confident of success. As his officers were hastening to their posts, he stopped his cousins and exclaimed: "Gentlemen, I have only one thing to say to you: remember that you are of the House of Bourbon. *Vive Dieu!* I will show you that I am its head!" "And we will show you that we are good cadets," replied Condé.

Henri's confidence was justified; in less than an hour the Catholic army was completely routed, Joyeuse killed, and all the artillery, standards and baggage taken. It was the first victory in the open field which the Protestants had gained in twenty-five years of civil war, and stamped the King of Navarre as a bold and successful general.

Condé greatly distinguished himself, and, though his armour was hacked almost to pieces, he escaped unwounded from the battle itself. But in the pursuit he was not so fortunate. One of the bravest captains of the royal army, d'Espinay Saint-Luc, who had gallantly defended Brouage against the Huguenots in the preceding year, finding that his horse was too exhausted to carry him out of the field, resolved to do something to distinguish himself ere he surrendered. Having descried Condé almost isolated in the middle of the plain, he laid his lance in rest and charged him so furiously that both horse and man went down. Saint-Luc immediately dismounted, extricated the prince from his fallen steed, and tendered him his gauntlet, saying: "Monseigneur, Saint-Luc surrenders to you; do not refuse him."

Although the lance had not penetrated the prince's armour, which happened to be intact at the spot where he had been struck, he was badly bruised and shaken and scarcely able to stand. However, he embraced and pardoned the prisoner who had adopted this highly disagreeable mode of surrender, and was then carried to the King of Navarre's quarters.

The victory of Coutras although so complete, had no important results. D'Aubigné accuses the King of Navarre of having sacrificed his duty to love—to his eagerness to lay at the feet of his mistress, the Comtesse de Gramont (*la belle* Corisande), the standards which he had captured. But his inaction was more probably due to the fact that it was impossible for him to keep his army together, so eager were the soldiers to return to their homes with their booty. Anyway, he made no attempt to join the Germans, who were defeated by the Duc de Guise at Vimory, near Orléans, and again at Anneau, and driven across the frontier, with terrible loss.

Condé, who had in vain endeavoured to persuade his cousin to continue the operations, decided to lead the contingents of Poitou and Saintonge against Saumur, but so many of his men deserted that he was compelled to abandon this enterprise. He was, besides, far too unwell for further service, for, since his encounter with Saint-Luc, he had been suffering from severe pains in the side ; and on reaching Saintes, these were complicated by an attack of fever. The princess rejoined him there,[1] and early in January, 1588 he was sufficiently recovered to return to Saint-Jean-d'Angely. Shortly afterwards, the pains in the side returned ; but, passionately devoted as he was to all martial exercises, he no sooner felt better than he was in the saddle again ; and on Thursday, 3 March, spent some hours in tilting at the ring, on which occasion he rode a restive horse, which reared repeatedly.[2]

About an hour after supper that evening, the prince was seized with violent pains in the stomach, followed by repeated vomiting. He was attended by his chief surgeon, Nicolas Poget, and a physician named Bonaventure de Médicis, "who aided the movements of nature. The malady notwithstanding continued all night . . . and so great was his difficulty in breathing that he was unable to stay in his bed, and was compelled to sit in a chair.

"Whereupon, on the morrow, Maitres Louis Bontemps and Jean Pallet, also doctors of medicine, were called into

---

[1] The Duc d'Aumale (" Histoire des Princes de Condé ") says that the princess remained at Saint-Jean-d'Angely, but this is incorrect.

[2] Duc d'Aumale, " Histoire des Princes de Condé."

consultation; and they all of them succoured his Excellency with all diligence and fidelity, by all the means that they judged suitable, according to the symptoms of the malady. But on the Saturday, the fifth day of the month, and the second of the malady, at three o'clock in the afternoon, all things took a turn for the worse, and an entire suffocation of all the faculties supervened, in which he rendered his soul to God half an hour afterwards." [1]

"I was one of those," writes Fiefbrun, "who were chosen to report this piteous calamity to Madame his wife, whom I found descending the steps of her hôtel to come and visit him in his little lodging, where she expected to find him alive, since she had as yet no idea that he was so near his last day. As soon as she caught sight of me, she suspected her misfortune, and pressing me to tell her in a few words, she fell down in a swoon, and was carried immediately to her bed, where she broke forth into the most terrible lamentations, accompanied by so many sobs and sighs that they could not be imagined save by those who saw and heard them. They were so violent that I am often astonished that they did not occasion a miscarriage." [2]

In view of what we are about to relate, Fiefbrun's account of the 'manner in which the Princesse de Condé received the news of her husband's death is of extreme importance.

The rapidity of the malady, and the fact that decomposition set in within two hours after death, "gave cause to the doctors and surgeons to suspect that there had been some extraordinary and violent cause." By order of the prince's council, two other surgeons were called in, and an autopsy performed. This served to confirm their suspicions. "We have found," runs their report, "all the stomach, particularly towards the right part, black, burned, gangreened, and ulcerated, which, in our opinion, can only have been caused by a quantity of burning, ulcerating, and caustic poison, which poison has left evident traces of its passage

---

[1] "Rapport des médecins et chirurgiens sur la mort de Monseigneur le Prince de Condé," published by Édouard Barthélemy, "La Princesse de Condé: Charlotte Catherine de la Trémoille."

[2] She was three months pregnant.

in the esophagus. The liver, in the part adjoining the aforesaid channel, was altered and burned, and all the rest of the organ livid, as were also the lungs. There was not a single part of his Excellency's body which was not very sound and very healthy, if the violent poison had not destroyed and corrupted the parts mentioned." [1]

Meanwhile, orders had been given that all the late prince's servants were to be placed under arrest, and a courier had been despatched to the King of Navarre, who was at Nérac. Under date 10 March, 1588, we find Henri writing to the Comtesse de Gramont as follows:

"To finish describing myself, there has happened to me one of the greatest calamities that I could possibly fear, which is the sudden death of *Monsieur le Prince.* I mourn for him as he ought to have been to me, not as he was. I am assured of being the only target at which the perfidies of the Mass are aimed. They have poisoned him, the traitors!

"On Thursday, this poor prince, after tilting at the ring, supped, feeling well. At midnight, he was seized with a very violent vomiting, which lasted till morning. All Friday he kept his bed. In the evening, he supped, and having slept well, he rose on Saturday morning, dined at table, and then played at chess. He rose from his chair, and walked up and down his chamber, chatting with one and the other. All at once, he said : 'Give me my chair ; I feel a great weakness.' Scarcely was he seated when he lost the power of speech, and immediately expired. The effects of poison at once became apparent.

"It is incredible the consternation which this has caused in that part of the country. I am starting at daybreak to travel thither with all speed. I see myself on the way to encounter much danger. Pray to God for me earnestly. If I escape it, it must be because it is He who had protected me. Up to the grave, to which I am perhaps nearer than I think, I shall remain your faithful slave. Good-night, my soul ; I kiss your hands a thousand times." [2]

[1] " Rapport des médecins et chirurgiens sur la mort de Monseigneur le Prince de Condé."
[2] "Lettres missives de Henri IV."

Next morning, the King of Navarre set out for Saint-Jean-d'Angely, " to console my cousin, *Madame la Princesse*, and to prevent our enemies from profiting by our losses and misfortunes and by my absence." [1]   On the second day of his journey, however, he was met by a courier, with intelligence which convinced him that the bereaved princess was an object of something very different from sympathy.

"There arrived yesterday," he writes to his Corisande, "the one at midday, the other in the evening, two couriers.   The first reported that Belcastel, the page of *Madame la Princesse*,[2] and her first *valet de chambre*[3] had fled, immediately after seeing their master dead.   They found two horses worth two hundred écus at an inn in the faubourg, where they had been kept for a fortnight, and each had a wallet full of money.   On being questioned, the innkeeper stated that it was a person named Brilland who had given him the horses, and that he came every day to tell him to treat them well ; that if he gave four measures of oats to the other horses, he was to give them eight, and that he would pay double.   This Brilland is a man whom *Madame la Princesse* had placed in her Household and given the charge of everything.   He was immediately arrested.   He confesses to have given one thousand écus to the page and to have purchased the horses, by his mistress's order, to go to Italy.

"The second courier confirms all this, and says further that Brilland was compelled to write a letter to the *valet de chambre*, who was known to be at Poitiers, in which he requested him to come two hundred paces from the gate, as he wished to speak to him.[4]   Immediately, the ambuscade which was there seized him, and he was brought to Saint-Jean.   He has not yet been interrogated, but he said to those who were bringing him : ' Ah ! what a wicked woman Madame [the Princesse de Condé] is ! Let them arrest her treasurer ; I will tell everything frankly.' This was done.   That is all that is known up to the present.

---

[1] The King of Navarre to M. de Scorbiac, 11 March, 1588.

[2] He was a lad of about sixteen, a Périgourdin.

[3] His name was Antoine Corbais, and he was a native of La Fère.

[4] They could not, of course, arrest the man within the town, since it was in the hands of the Catholics.

CHARLOTTE CATHERINE DE LA TRÉMOILLE, PRINCESSE DE CONDÉ.

Remember what I have told you at other times. I am seldom deceived in my judgments. A bad woman is a dangerous animal (*une dangereuse beste*). All these poisoners are Papists. It was from them that the lady received her instructions. I have discovered an assassin for myself. God will protect me, and I will tell you more about it soon. . . My soul, I am very well in body, but very afflicted in mind. Love me, and let me see that you do ; that will be a great consolation for me."[1]

The King of Navarre did not carry out his original intention of proceeding straight to Saint-Jean-d'Angely, for, on reaching Pons, he turned aside to La Rochelle, and it was not until the evening of 29 March that he reached the scene of the tragedy. The probable reason for this delay was his wish to avoid committing himself until further light had been thrown upon the affair.

The princess, although, of course, under close supervision, was still nominally at liberty, for Fiefbrun, to whom, in his capacity of bailiff of Saint-Jean-d'Angely, Henri had entrusted the conduct of the inquiry, was a devoted servant of the Condés and was naturally very reluctant to take any definite steps against her. But, on his arrival, he found public opinion in the town so hostile to the lady that he felt obliged to order her arrest.

Personal considerations would appear to have been no stranger to this decision, and to the vigour with which he subsequently pushed on proceedings against the princess. The very strained relations which had existed for some time past between him and the late prince were common knowledge, and his enemies had not hesitated to circulate the report that he was privy to the death of his cousin. Théodore de Bèze had just written, warning him of this atrocious calumny, and urging him to take immediate steps to refute it :

" On this point I am constrained to add, knowing what might be the consequence of sinister counsels and your own clemency and good-nature, that your enemies have even dared, with that imprudence and wickedness which is the result of despair,

---

[1] " Lettres missives de Henri IV."

to spread the report that this detestable crime was instigated by you. You neither can nor ought to hesitate about this action, without making an irreparable breach in your reputation ; but, on the contrary, you ought to pursue the matter to judgment and execution, so as to stop the mouths of these detestable calumniators in the sight of God and man." [1]

After ordering the arrest of the Princesse de Condé, Henri despatched one of his gentlemen, the Sieur de Veau Limery, to the Court, with a letter for "the Queen, mother of the King, my lord," in which he informed her that the page Belcastel, "the principal instrument of the crime," had taken refuge in Poitiers, and begged her to give orders that search should be made for him, and that, when apprehended, he should be conducted to Saint-Jean-d'Angely, to be confronted with his accomplices. Instructions to that effect were sent to Poitiers ; but nothing was ever heard of the fugitive page, who seemed to have vanished off the face of the earth.

The position of the Princesse de Condé was a terrible one. It was not only at Saint-Jean-d'Angely that public opinion had pronounced against her. The more zealous Huguenots, furious at the supposed crime which had deprived them of the prince who had shared all their passions and prejudices, were loud in their demands that she should be brought to justice ; while the Catholics were very hostile to the princess, on account of her abjuration and her conduct in recent events, in which she had rendered such good service to the Protestant cause. To her relatives she looked in vain for help or sympathy. The Duchesse de Thouars, who, since the affair of Taillebourg, had been on the worst possible terms with her daughter, never seems to have even thought of coming to Saint-Jean-d'Angely to inquire if she were innocent or guilty ; and her absence still further prejudiced the princess's case in the eyes of the public. The young Duc de Thouars, who, one would naturally suppose, would have been eager to champion his sister, does not appear to have moved in the matter at all. As for her husband's relatives, the Prince de Conti and the Comte de Soissons seem to have at once made up their

<hr />

[1] Published by the Duc d'Aumale, " Histoire des Princes de Condé."

minds that she was guilty and did all in their power to hasten the prosecution; while the attitude of the Dowager-Princesse de Condé may be gauged from the following remarkable letter:

"Great as was the pleasure it gave me to address you as *Madame la Princesse*, I shall have reason to regret this name so long as you are not justified of the atrocious accusation which will cause you to lose honour and life together, if your innocence is not proved. That is what I desire intensely, since I am unable to believe that the heart of a woman so well-born and so well brought up could cherish such wickedness against the prince who had done you so much honour in wooing and espousing you. This loss is so great for all the family that the peculiar honour which I received from his father invites me to deplore it for the rest of my life. I have been among the first to demand justice of our King (Henri III.), who is neither able nor willing to refuse it. Their Majesties have declined to receive your letters, and the cardinals[1] to reply to them. I have also spoken of your story to the Queen, mother of the King, who replied that she is so much the friend of honour and virtue, and is so overwhelmed with horror at the deed of which you are accused, that she does not intend to intervene. . . . It is, therefore, your duty to endeavour to secure the arrest of your page, to whom, it is said, you caused a great deal of money to be given by your treasurer, and to whom one of your *valets de chambre* has confessed to have given the poison. This evidence makes matters very serious for you.

"It is further said that you love your page so passionately that he used to occupy your husband's place, with so many other dreadful things that the Court is horrified; and there is no conversation now except at the expense of your reputation, which, I think, is very unfortunate for you.

"Those who have counselled you (if such is the case) have done you more harm than if they had given you the same poison. Who would ever wish to see you, holding you to be without honour and without heart? Believe that God, who

---

[1] Presumably, the Cardinals de Bourbon and de Guise.

threatens poisoners with having no share in the Kingdom of Heaven, will permit the truth to be known and justice to be executed. I have very humbly entreated the King, on your behalf, that the page should be arrested. His Majesty desires it and has written about it; but it is not believed that you are anxious for it. I pray God that the contrary may be the case; but, however that may be, you are at present the fable and the malediction of France, and, as I believe, of all the world, even to the barbarians, if they hear of it. But can it really be possible that you have deprived of life a prince who has so much honoured and loved you? If it is, you have no worse enemy than yourself, and have consented to the damnation of your soul. Time, which is the father of truth, will speedily enlighten us on the matter of your conduct, which, I trust, is altogether contrary to the belief which everywhere prevails.

"When I knew that you were living as an honourable princess, and were respecting such a husband, a member of so great a family, I desired to do you service, and I esteemed myself happy. But now that I see you thus accused, if your justification does not appease this widespread rumour of so iniquitous a deed, I have received too much honour from the late Monseigneur my husband to be willing that any one should surpass me in the desire to be the most cruel enemy that you have ever had, although I shall nevertheless weep for your disgrace. . . . And if you have been instigated to this crime, as is reported, hasten to denounce those who have given you this pernicious counsel, for the sake of your life and honour; and I shall implore God to punish the guilty and protect the innocent.

"From Paris this IX. April 1588.

"She who was formerly your mother-in-law to do you service.

"FRANÇOISE D'ORLÉANS"[1]

---

[1] "Bibliothèque Nationale," Brienne Collection, published by Eugène Halphen in his introduction to Fiefbrun.

CHAPTER X

The King of Navarre appoints a special commission for the trial of Brilland—Brilland is put to the question—His confessions under torture implicate the Princesse de Condé, but on the following day he disavows them —He is found guilty and condemned to be dismembered by horses—The princess denies the competency of the court and appeals to the Parlement of Paris—But the King of Navarre and the commissioners ignore the decrees of that body—The commission directs that the princess shall be brought to trial—She gives birth to a son—The prosecution is dropped, but the princess remains in captivity—The Président de Thou interests himself in her case— Means by which he obtains from Henri IV. the recognition of her son's rights, and, with them, the acknowledgment of the princess's innocence.

AFTER ordering the arrest of the Princesse de Condé, the King of Navarre appointed a special commission, composed of twelve judges, for the trial of Brilland ; while, as the accused had protested against his examination being conducted by Fiefbrun, who appears to have been a personal enemy, Henri replaced him by Valette, Grand Provost of Navarre, the more willingly since he was aware that Fiefbrun was a devoted partisan of the princess.

The commissioners decided that Brilland should be put to the question. " On entering the torture-chamber, he protested, in the first place, that everything that he might say would be owing to the violence of the pain, and that he knew nothing about the poison, and that he was innocent. Nevertheless, when the torture was applied, he accused Madame in this sense, that she and he had plotted the poisoning of the late prince from the time that he [Condé] was aware of her behaviour, and that, on leaving this town, his Excellency had recommended him to keep watch over her actions, and to take care of her, declaring that, after she was brought to bed, he should chastise her for her misconduct ; and that when he

[Brilland] informed her of this, the said project was resolved upon . . . ; that the said poison had been sent to the . . . ; that it had come from M. d'Épernon. He further said that La Doussinière, *maître d'hôtel* of his aforesaid lord, had administered the aforesaid poison in a chicken stuffed with eggs." [1]

After this so-called confession had been extracted from him, the wretched man was released from the rack and taken back to prison. There, on the following day, he was visited by the commissioners, who ordered his confession to be read over to him. "He disavowed it ; protested that what he had said was false ; declared that what he had done was to escape the violence of the pain : exonerated those whom he had accused ; and maintained his innocence and that he was ignorant of the poison. At the same time, he confirmed the truth of all the aforesaid confessions that he had made and signed in the course of the trial, with the exception of that made under torture . . . and declared that he believed *Madame la Princesse* and those whom he had accused to be innocent, and that he knew nothing about the poison."

Brilland was found guilty and condemned to the most barbarous of all forms of punishment—to be dismembered by horses. Against this sentence he appealed.

In the meanwhile, the Princesse de Condé had been formally charged with complicity in the murder of her husband and summoned before the commission. She refused to appear, denying the competency of the tribunal and claiming the privileges of the peerage. The judges overruled the princess's objections, whereupon she petitioned Henri III. that her case should be tried by the Grande Chambre of the Parlement of Paris. His Majesty having returned a favourable answer, she appealed to the Parlement, and obtained from that body a degree calling the affair before it, prohibiting "all judges and others whom it may concern from taking any further proceedings," and ordering that all the documents

---

[1] Memoir published by Édouard de Barthélemy, " la Princesse de Condé : Charlotte Catherine de la Trémoille."

relating to the case should be immediately forwarded to the registrar of the court, on the ground that the wives of the Princes of the Blood were no more able than their husbands to be tried save by the Parlement of Paris. At the same time, it appointed two celebrated advocates, François de Montholon and Simon Marion, to act as counsel for the princess.

The commissioners at Saint-Jean-d'Angely appear to have paid no attention to these injunctions. The princess again appealed to the Parlement, which issued a second decree, confirming the first and ordering the commissioners to appear themselves before it, to answer for their disobedience. The King of Navarre, who had no intention of surrendering the conduct of an affair of such great consequence to himself to the royal judges, from whom he had everything to fear, replied by issuing a counter-decree, which rejected the pretensions of the princess, maintained the competency of the tribunal he had appointed, and ordered the commissioners to prosecute the affair, "in conformity with the procedure which they had followed hitherto."

In consequence, the sentence passed upon Brilland was confirmed, and on 11 July, 1588, the condemned man suffered his terrible fate. "He gave on this occasion," writes de Thou, "several proofs of madness, although he confessed that he was guilty of several other crimes, and that he recognized the justice of the sentence that the commissioners chosen to try him had pronounced. He began, however, to blaspheme in a scandalous fashion, so that those who assisted at the execution had great difficulty in making him return to his right senses, which caused people to think that his mind was not very sound, and that, in consequence, much reliance ought not to be placed on his evidence."

On the same day, the fugitive page, Belcastel, was executed in effigy. As for Corbais, the *valet de chambre*, who had fled with the page and had been trapped so neatly outside the gates of Poitiers, we are not told what was decided upon in regard to him. He is not mentioned again in the proceedings.

After the execution of Brilland, the proceedings against

the Princesse de Condé were continued.   The Prince de Condé
and the Comte de Soissons demanded to be received as parties
to the prosecution, and their request was granted by the
commissioners. The princess once more appealed to the
Parlement of Paris, which issued a third decree, forbidding
Conti and Soissons to pursue the affair except before the
Parlement, and ordering the arrest of the commissioners and
the seizure and sequestration of their property.

This decree, like the two which had preceded it, was treated
with contempt, since the Parlement was, of course, powerless
to enforce it, and on 19 July the commissioners directed that
the princess should be brought to trial, but that, on account
of her pregnancy, the trial should not begin until forty days
after her confinement. In the meanwhile, she was very
strictly guarded in the house of the Sieur de Saint-Mesme,
governor of Saint-Jean-d'Angely, in which she had been shut
up ever since her arrest, and only permitted to see a very few
persons. "During the six months that she was enceinte,"
writes Fiefbrun, "she was retained in her lodging, subjected
to a thousand slanders, and interrogated frequently by the
chosen and incompetent judges, not as a great princess, but
as a simple demoiselle, without any regard to her rank or
her privileges. I leave all those who have heard it spoken
about to imagine how many anguishes, how much despair,
assailed her soul during that long time, in which she was
not permitted to speak or to confer with any one save two or
three of her intimates, without any other counsel or assistance."

On 1 September, 1588, six months after the death of her
husband, the captive princess gave birth to a son, Henri de
Bourbon, second of that name, and third Prince de Condé.
Fiefbrun gravely assures us that, at the moment of the boy's
birth, "an extraordinary light was observed in the heavens, and
that, on the day of his baptism, the sky being serene and cloud-
less, a clap of thunder was heard, which several persons who
understood meteors regarded as of good augury."

Less importance, however, was attached to these happy
prognostications than to a circumstance which appeared to

remove the suspicion on which the charge against the princess
had been principally based, namely, that she was with child by
the page Belcastel, and had poisoned her husband to escape his
just vengeance. This was the striking resemblance which the
infant prince bore to the late Prince de Condé, which was
admitted even by some who had until then been inclined to
believe in the guilt of the princess. "To-day, at noon precisely,"
wrote the governor of Saint-Jean-d'Angely to the Duc de
Thouars, "*Madame la Princesse*, your sister, has been delivered
of the most beautiful prince imaginable, and with more
resemblance (so far as one can judge at his age) to the late
Monseigneur, his father, than one can describe. For which I
praise God, as do an infinite number of honourable people, your
servants."

And Gilbert, the mayor of the town, wrote that "he had
seen to-day the dead father born again in a child so like him in
every respect that there was not a man living but was of
opinion that never had son so closely resembled his father."

Desmoustiers, the pastor of the Protestant Church of Saint-
Jean-d'Angely, and Delacroix, the late prince's chaplain, bore
similar testimony, the former declaring that the boy resembled
his father "*en tout et partout*"; while the latter concluded his
letter by observing: "Thus does Our Lord (just Judge) cause
the truth concerning the poisoning to be known."[1]

Whether it was that the birth of a son had given the Princesse
de Condé a certain prestige with the Protestants, disposed to
see in this child a hope for the future, or that the want of proofs
rendered the prosecution difficult to continue, or that the King
of Navarre's attention was occupied by weightier matters, the
investigation was not resumed, and the members of the
commission which had been appointed to conduct it dispersed.
The princess, nevertheless, remained in captivity, although she
now enjoyed a certain amount of liberty, since she went twice a
week to see her little son, who had been put out to nurse at
Mazeroy, near Saint-Jean-d'Angely; and a path across the

---

[1] Édouard de Barthélemy, "Charlotte Catherine de la Trémoille, Princesse de
Condé."

fields between Beaufief and the road leading to that town, which she generally followed, bears to this day the name of " *le chemin de la princesse.*" [1] She was unable to obtain either the trial before the Parlement of Paris which she had repeatedly demanded or her liberty, and she appealed in vain to her relatives, to the neighbouring nobility, and to every person of importance whom chance happened to bring to Saint-Jean-d'Angely, to use their influence on her behalf. But neither her relatives nor the different nobles to whom she addressed herself seemed disposed to take any active steps in her favour, and it was left to a magistrate, the Président de Thou, to be the first to interest himself in the forsaken woman.

In the summer of 1589, de Thou, charged with a mission from Henri IV., passed through Saint-Jean-d'Angely, and the princess, since she was unable either to receive or to visit him herself, had the happy idea of sending to him her daughter Éléonore and the little Henri, with a request that he would accord them his protection. The kind heart of the worthy president was touched, and he promised to do everything in his power on behalf of the princess and her children. Several years passed, however, before circumstances permitted him to render any material assistance to his illustrious clients.

Henri IV., as the King of Navarre had now become, did not appear to cast any doubt upon the legitimacy of the little prince, since he consented to stand godfather to him, and conferred upon him indirectly the government of Guienne, which he himself had held before his accession to the throne. But this informal acknowledgment carried little weight, and, so long as the Princesse de Condé was not exonerated from the terrible charge which was still hanging over her, the boy's position remained doubtful and precarious. Moreover, when, after the conversion of Henri IV. and the submission of Paris, tranquillity was to some degree restored, and the new King's authority better established, the late prince's brothers wished to recommence the proceedings against their sister-in-law, and urged his Majesty to declare her child incapable of succeeding

[1] E. Halphen, " Introduction to Fiefbrun."

efforts of de Thou on behalf of the princess and her son, but at length he succeeded in outmanœuvring them.

In January, 1595, the King signed a new decree extending the provisions of an article of the Edict of Peace of 1577, which admitted Protestants to public office. The Parlement, however, refused to register it, except on the condition that no member of the Reformed Faith should be eligible for the post of governor or lieutenant-general of a province, and persisted in its refusal, notwithstanding all the efforts of the King to induce it to give way. The attitude of the Parlement placed Henri IV. in a very embarrassing position, and de Thou, adroitly seizing his opportunity, offered to secure the passing of the Edict, provided that the King would guarantee that the young Prince de Condé, the heir-presumptive to the throne, should be brought up in the Catholic Faith. His Majesty, at first received this proposition very ungraciously, but, seeing no other way out of the *impasse*, he eventually accepted it, and directed the attorney-general to announce to the Parlement that the Prince de Condé "would forthwith be taken out of the hands of persons of the Protestant religion to be brought up in that of Rome."

This announcement not only secured the registration of the Edict, but brought about the liberation of the Princesse de Condé, since to recognize the rights of the son was to acknowledge the innocence of the mother; and now that the favour of the King appeared to be gained, the prisoner of Saint-Jean-d'Angely had no lack of supporters. A few weeks later (June, 1595), Henri, Duc de Montmorency,[1] after having taken at Dijon his oath as Constable of France, presented to Henri IV. a petition signed by Diane de France,[2] widow of François,

---

[1] Until the death of his eldest brother François, Maréchal Duc de Montmorency, in 1577, Henri de Montmorency had borne the title of Baron de Damville, which was now assumed by the third of the Montmorency brothers, until then known as the Seigneur de Méru.

[2] Natural daughter of Henri II. by Filippa le Duc, a Piedmontese girl of humble origin, and not of Diane de Poitiers, as several historians have wrongly stated. She married, first, Orazio Farnese, Duke of Castro, and, *en secondes noces*, François de Montmorency, elder brother of the Constable.

Maréchal de Montmorency, Charles de Valois, Comte d'Auvergne,[1] the Duc de Thouars, the Duc de Bouillon, the Baron de Montmorency-Damville, and other relatives of the princess, praying him to direct that the accusations brought against her should be adjudicated upon. The King, by letters-patent, ordered the affair to be submitted to the Parlement of Paris, and that the minutes of the proceedings at Saint-Jean-d'Angely should be sent to the registrar of that body. At the same time, he ordered the princess to be set at liberty, on condition that the signatories to the petition should make themselves responsible for her appearance when called upon.

In November, 1595, the princess and her son quitted Saint-Jean-d'Angely, in charge of Jean de Vivonne, Marquis de Pisani, whom the King had appointed the boy's *gouverneur.* In the first days of December, they arrived at the Château of Saint-Germain, which had been provisionally assigned the little prince as a residence, and where, by Henri IV.'s desire, the Parlement of France came to salute him as first Prince of the Blood and heir-presumptive to the throne.

In the following May, the trial of the princess—if such a name could be applied to an affair, the issue of which was a foregone conclusion—came on for hearing. The Prince de Conti and the Comte de Soissons had protested against everything that might be decided as illegal, on the ground that the judgment of the case belonged to the King alone, "holding his court garnished with peers, legitimately assembled." The Parlement summoned the two princes to appear before it, and show cause why their sister-in-law should not be pronounced innocent of the death of her husband. They refused, where-upon the court declared all the proceedings in Saintonge null and void and of no effect, "as contrary to the authority of the King, and to the decrees of his Court of Parlement, and useful in no way whatsoever to the furtherance of justice." Finally, on 24 July, it issued a decree declaring the princess "pure and

---

[1] Afterwards Duc d'Angoulême. He was a natural son of Charles IX. by Marie Touché, and had married Charlotte de Montmorency, daughter of the Connétable Henri de Montmorency.

de la Trémoille, Princesse de Condé.

But, as an eighteenth-century historian very rightly points out, a case gained before the Parlement was not necessarily a victory at the tribunal of public opinion ; while over and over again that body had quashed the decrees of the lesser courts only to have its own verdict reversed by the judgment of history. The proceedings at Saint-Jean-d'Angely were declared null and of no effect, but the affair was not sent back for trial to the place where the supposed crime had been committed, nor submitted to a new examination. Thus, the Princesse de Condé, though pronounced innocent by the Law, was not exonerated by a large section of the public ; nor has time altogether effaced the suspicions which remained in so many minds.[1]

Since all the documents connected with the investigation at Saint-Jean-d'Angely were, by order of the Parlement, solemnly burned by the registrar of the Court, in the presence of the First President, Achille de Harlay, and the *rapporteur*, Édouard Molé, until some fresh evidence shall be forthcoming, historians must renounce the hope of discovering the truth of this *cause célèbre*, and content themselves with more or less hazardous conjectures.

That the prince died from the effects of poison was undoubtedly the firm belief of practically all his contemporaries. One writer of the time alone, so far as we are aware, Joseph Texeira,[2] takes a different view. In 1598, Texeira published an historical treatise, in Latin, dealing with the principal events of Henri IV.'s reign,[3] in the course of which he denied that the Prince de Condé had been poisoned, and attributed his death to the injuries he had received at Coutras,

---

[1] Désormeaux.

[2] He was a Portuguese Dominican monk, who settled in France, and became Almoner to Henri IV. and confessor to the Dowager-Princesse de Condé.

[3] "Rerum ab Henrici Borbonis Franciae protoprincipis majoribus gestarum Epitome."

from which, as we have mentioned, he had suffered a great deal of pain.   Texeira pretends that the doctors who performed the autopsy were divided as to the cause of death, and that the opinion of those who held that it was due to natural causes was adopted, after a solemn discussion, by the Faculty of Montpellier.   But Désormeaux, so devoted to the Condé family, confesses that, despite his active researches, he was unable to find the proof of the two facts advanced by Texeira in the documents of the time, whether published or in manuscript, and if, after this avowal, he inclines to the same opinion, it is because he cannot bring himself to believe that Texeira, Almoner to the King and Councillor of State, was capable of a lie.[1]

But, admitting that the unfortunate prince was poisoned, what evidence is there to connect his wife with the crime? Nothing whatever save the confessions of Brilland, made under torture, and which he subsequently denied, and the rumour of her undue intimacy with the page Belcastel, about which, singularly enough, nothing seems to have been heard until after her husband's death.   On the other hand, there are the strongest possible reasons for believing her to be entirely innocent.   She was, undoubtedly, deeply in love with her husband at the time of her marriage, and had given him, as we have seen, signal proofs of her devotion; and it is, indeed, difficult to believe that in less than two years her affection could have been transformed into a murderous hatred. Moreover, she had apparently nothing to gain and much to lose by his death, for in the line of succession he stood next to the King of Navarre, a childless man, whose life was spent in the midst of perils.   In conniving at the murder of the Prince de Condé, quite apart from the danger of detection and punishment, she would have deprived herself of the prospect of becoming Queen of France.

[1] " Recueil de l'Academie des inscriptions et belles-lettres." Halphen.

CHAPTER XI

Education of Henri II. de Bourbon, Prince de Condé—Appearance and character of the young prince—He is offered and accepts the hand of Charlotte de Montmorency, unaware that Henry IV. is desperately enamoured of the lady—Conversation of the King with Bassompierre—Marriage of Condé and Mlle. de Montmorency—Infatuation of the King for the young princess—Condé refuses to accept the odious rôle assigned him, and "plays the devil"—Violent scenes between him and the King—He removes with his wife to Picardy—Amorous escapade of Henri IV.—Condé, summoned to Court for the accouchement of the Queen, leaves the princess behind him—Indignation of Henri IV.—Condé flies with his wife to Flanders—Fury of the King, who sends troops in pursuit of the fugitives—Refusal of the Archdukes to deliver them up—Condé goes to Cologne, while the princess proceeds to Brussels.

HENRI IV. charged himself with all the expenses of the little Prince de Condé's education ; the Cardinal de Gondi, Bishop of Paris, was entrusted with the task of instructing him in the Catholic faith, and on 24 January, 1596, the boy attended Mass for the first time.

To assist the *gouverneur*, the Marquis de Pisani, in his important duties, the King decided to appoint a *sous-gouverneur*, and selected for that post Nicolas d'Aumale, Sieur d'Harcourt. D'Harcourt was a Protestant, and his appointment was probably due to Henri IV.'s desire to conciliate the Huguenots and to prove to them that, though the heir presumptive to the throne was to be brought up as a Catholic, there was no intention of separating him entirely from those of his father's faith. For preceptor, the prince was given Nicolas Lefebvre, Counsellor to the Departments of Waters and Forests, who was a devout, though a by no means intolerant, Catholic, and one of the most learned men of his time.

The education of the boy would have progressed smoothly

149

enough, but for the interference of the Dowager-Princesse de Condé, who aspired to direct everything herself, and continually countermanded the orders of Pisani, who was obliged to appeal to Henri IV. to uphold his authority. He complained that the princess refused to admit that anything was right that came from the King ; and there can be no doubt that the lady, who was aware that none but political motives had induced Henri IV. to put an end to her imprisonment, was but little disposed to respect his Majesty's wishes.

Not content with quarrelling with Pisani, the princess endeavoured to create dissension between him and d'Harcourt, by insinuating to the latter that he was distrusted by his superior, on account of his being a Huguenot. Then she tried to persuade the King to allow Texeira to be associated with d'Harcourt and Lefebvre in the education of her son—a proposal which was greatly resented by the *sous-gouverneur* and the preceptor.

The disputes to which his mother's meddlesome activity gave rise were very unfortunate for the young prince. And Pisani declared that it was "pitiable to see him thus guided, served, and treated," and expressed his fear "lest he should be found wanting, and that those who had been charged with his education should be blamed and despised for it." [1]

In October, 1559, Pisani died suddenly, at the Abbey of Saint-Maur-des-Fossés,[2] to which he had removed with his charge to escape a terrible epidemic—probably typhus—which was then ravaging Paris. The choice of his successor was not an easy one, for now that Queen Marguerite had given her consent to the dissolution of her union with the King, and negotiations had been set on foot for Henri's marriage with Marie de' Medici, the post was diminishing in importance. General astonishment, however, was expressed when it was known that the King had conferred it upon the Comte de Belin.

---

[1] Letter of Pisani to Villeroy, 5 March, 1598, cited by the Duc d'Aumale.

[2] The Abbey of Saint-Maur-des-Fossés, situated a little beyond the Bois de Vincennes, had been secularized in 1533, and afterwards sold to Catherine de' Médici, from whose executors the Dowager-Princesse de Condé had recently purchased it. It afterwards became one of the favourite country-seats of the Condés.

Duc de Mayenne, and had been one of the first of that party to attach himself to the cause of Henri IV. He had since testified great devotion to the monarch, but he was but little esteemed by the public, and had lost any military prestige he ever possessed by the promptitude with which he had capitulated at Arques, in 1596. Some privileged courtiers ventured to remonstrate with his Majesty on this appointment, to whom he drily replied: "When I wanted to make a King of my nephew, I gave him Pisani; when I wanted to make a subject of him, I gave him Belin."

The new *gouverneur* showed himself infinitely more complaisant towards the Princesse de Condé than had his predecessor; indeed, Tallemant des Réaux declares that they "made *belles galanteries* together," though no attention need be paid to the unsupported statement of this incorrigible scandalmonger. He was also far more indulgent with his pupil than Pisani had ever been—a change which is generally believed to have had a very injurious effect upon the character of the young prince, who was one of those lads who require a strong hand over them. Thanks, however, to the perseverance of Lefebvre, his studies were not permitted to suffer, and he received an education both sound and varied. He became a tolerable Latin scholar, spoke Italian fluently, understood Spanish, wrote his own language correctly—a rare accomplishment in those days—and had some knowledge of theology and mathematics. In appearance, he was rather below the middle height, with a slight, well-knit figure, and "the strongly marked features which generally distinguished the Bourbons."[1] He was passionately devoted to the chase and an excellent horseman; nor does he seem to have lacked the courage of his race, since in February, 1607, when the prince was in his nineteenth year, Henri IV. was obliged to exercise his authority to prevent a duel to which he had challenged the Duc de Nevers.

With the exception of this incident, his early youth appears to have been very uneventful, for, since France was now at

[1] Cardinal Bentiviglio, "Relazioni."

peace, no opportunity occurred for his initiation into the art of war. The King kept him constantly about his person, less through any affection for his kinsman than from a desire to protect him against the influence of ambitious and scheming persons who might seek to use him for the furtherance of their own ends. But the young prince did not possess the qualities which would have fitted him to shine in the gay and licentious society of the time, being shy and awkward, particularly in the presence of ladies, while his revenues were not at all commensurate with his rank; and after the birth of sons to Henri IV. had deprived him of all hope of the throne, he seems to have occupied a very inconspicuous position at Court.

Condé's comparative lack of fortune made a wealthy marriage a necessity, and when, at the beginning of the year 1609, the King announced his intention of bestowing upon him the hand of Charlotte de Montmorency, daughter of the Connétable Henri de Montmorency,[1] and one of the richest heiresses in France, he accepted the offer with a gratitude which was not diminished by the fact that Mlle. de Montmorency united to the advantages of wealth remarkable personal attractions.

There was, indeed, no more lovely girl at Court than the daughter of the Constable. Cardinal Bentiviglio, the Papal Nuncio at Brussels, who saw her towards the close of the same year, has left us the following description of her:

"She was then sixteen years old, and her loveliness was adjudged by all men to accord with the fame thereof. She was very fair; her eyes and all her features full of charm; an ingenuous grace in all her gestures and in her manner of speaking. Her beauty owed its power to itself alone, since she did not bring to its aid any of the artifices of which women are wont to make use."[2]

It is certain, however, that Condé would have received the proposition in a very different spirit if he had been aware of the reasons which had prompted the King to make it; for it was

---

[1] By his second wife, Louise de Budos, a woman of middling birth, but of such extraordinary beauty that some persons attributed it to supernatural agency.

[2] "Relazioni."

his Majesty had in mind.

One day in January, 1609, it happened that Henri IV. was passing through the great gallery of the Louvre, when he came upon a bevy of young ladies of the Court practising for a ballet, nymphs of Diana, armed for the chase. Among them was Mlle. de Montmorency, whose charms, enhanced by the classical costume she was wearing, made so profound an impression upon the susceptible monarch that he was quite unable to take his eyes off her.

Shortly after this encounter, his Majesty was laid up with an attack of gout. Several of the ladies of the Court came to visit him, and among those who were most assiduous in their attentions was the Duchesse d'Angoulême, who was invariably accompanied by Mlle. de Montmorency, her niece. Henri IV. was fifty-five, and his hair and beard, whitened by a life of peril and hardship, made him look considerably older. But his heart was still young, and he was as amorous as he had been at twenty. From the first, he took the keenest pleasure in Mlle. de Montmorency's society ; soon he was hopelessly in love, although for some time he appears to have deluded himself with the belief that his interest in the damsel was of a paternal nature only.

The fair Charlotte was already bethrothed, with the King's approval, to François de Bassompierre, a handsome young noble of Lorraine, high in favour with his Majesty, and one of the most redoubtable lady-killers of the Court. Henri, however, having himself become a candidate for the lady's affections, had no mind to endure a rival so formidable as the fascinating Bassompierre, and, accordingly, decided that the projected marriage must be broken off.

One night, when Bassompierre was on duty in the King's chamber, endeavouring to soothe his master's pain by reading to him M. d'Urfé's sentimental romance "l'Astrée," then at the height of its vogue, Henri informed him, after some preamble, that he intended to marry him to Mlle. d'Aumale, and to revive the duchy of that name in his favour. " You wish then, Sire, to give me two wives!" exclaimed the astonished courtier. "Baron," rejoined the King, "I wish to speak to you as a friend. I am not only in love, but distracted about Mlle. de Montmorency. If you marry her and she loves you, I shall hate you. If she loves me, you will hate me. It were better that the marriage were broken off, lest it should mar the good understanding between us, and destroy the affection I entertain for you. I have decided to marry her to my nephew, the Prince de Condé, and to keep her near the person of my wife. She will be the solace and support of the old age upon which I am about to enter. I shall give her to my nephew, who is only twenty, and prefers hunting a thousand times to ladies' society ; and I desire no other favour from her than her affection, without pretending to anything further."

Bassompierre, who was above all things a courtier, seeing that the King was determined, and that, unless he submitted with a good grace, he would lose both his bride and the royal favour, protested his willingness to obey, adding the hope that "this new affection would bring his Majesty as much joy as it would occasion him pain, but for his consideration for his Majesty."[1] His chagrin was, nevertheless, intense, and when, next morning, the young lady having been acquainted with the change that had been made in the disposition of her hand, greeted her too facile lover with an expressive shrug of her pretty shoulders and a glance of the most withering disdain, his grief and mortification were such that he fled precipitately to his lodging, where, he assures us, he spent three days without food or sleep.

The betrothal of Condé and Charlotte de Montmorency took place shortly afterwards (2 March, 1609), in the great gallery of the Louvre. The Constable gave his prospective son-in-law 100,000 écus ; while the King granted him an increase of his pension and a present of 150,000 livres. The bride received 18,000 livres from his Majesty, for the purchase of jewellery, as well as a magnificent trousseau. Owing to the necessity of obtaining the Papal dispensation for the union

---

[1] Maréchal de Bassompierre, " Mémoires."

of cousins,[1] the marriage-ceremony was postponed until 16 May, when it was celebrated at Chantilly, "very inexpensively, but very gaily."

This gaiety was not of long duration. Scarcely had the young couple rejoined the Court, which was then at Fontainebleau, than the King began to lay the closest siege to the princess's heart and strove by every means in his power to gain her affection. The girl, flattered by the homage of her Sovereign, of which she perhaps did not divine the end, was far from discouraging his attentions, and, if we are to believe Tallemant des Réaux, appeared one evening on the balcony of her apartments in a *peignoir*, with her hair falling over her shoulders, in order to please the King, who was transported with admiration. "*Dieu!*" cried she, "how foolish he is!" And she laughed heartily.

Her husband, however, did not laugh. The affair had become a public scandal. Even in the streets, people laughed and jested about the infatuation of the King, and "talked with the utmost freedom of his Majesty and of the corruption and debaucheries of his Court."[2] If Condé had little love for his wife, he was exceedingly jealous of his honour, and, to Henri's intense chagrin, absolutely declined to accept the odious rôle he had intended for him, and began, in his Majesty's phrase, "to play the devil."[3]

In vain, the King endeavoured to reassure him as to the innocence of his intentions; in vain, the Constable, at his Majesty's request, made the strongest representations to his son-in-law. Condé was deaf to all appeals, and, towards the middle of June, carried off his wife to Valery, in the hope that, during his absence, the King's passion might cool or be diverted to some fresh object.

Henri IV. was in despair. In obedience to his orders, the

---

[1] The Dowager-Princesse de Condé was, through her mother, a niece of the Constable.

[2] L'Estoile.

[3] "Mon ami—*M. le Prince* (Condé) est icy qui faict le diable; vous seriez en colère et auriez honte des choses qu'il dit de moi; enfin, la patience m'échappera et je me resous de bien parler à lui" (Henri IV. to Sully, 9 June, 1609).

poet Malherbe consented "to degrade his muse to the office of pander,"[1] and composed stanzas wherein the King, under the name of Alcandre, cries :

> Il faut que je cesse de vivre
> Si je veux cesser de souffrir ;

and the princess, under the name of Orante, replies :

> La cœur outrée du même ennui,
> Jurait que s'il mourait pour elle,
> Elle mourait aussi pour lui.[2]

Condé and his wife remained at Valery until the first week in July, when they were compelled to return to Court, in order to attend the marriage of César de Vendôme, Henri IV.'s eldest son by Gabrielle d'Estrées, and Mlle. de Mercœur. The King's passion became more violent than ever, and his conduct would have been ludicrous to the last degree had it been less culpable. Not only did he continue to commission Malherbe to bombard the princess with elegies and sonnets, but "one saw him alter in less than no time his hair, his beard, and his countenance." He who had hitherto been distinguished from the nobles of his Court by the simplicity and even negligence of his attire, might now be seen dressing and adorning himself with as much care as the youngest and most dandified of his courtiers, and, on one occasion, he appeared at a tilting-match wearing " a scented ruff, a doublet with sleeves of Chinese satin, and the colours of the Princesse de Condé, who called him ' her knight.' "[3] "The King is well and grows younger every day," wrote Malherbe to his friend Peiresc.

The unfortunate husband began to " play the devil " again, and, though Henri, in the hope of bending him to his will, had the meanness to give orders to Sully that the instalment of his pension due at Midsummer should not be paid him, and to threaten him with even more severe measures unless he mended his ways, his complaints grew louder than ever. Violent scenes took place between him and the King, in one of which Condé

[1] André Chénier, "les Poésies de Malherbe."
[2] Henrard, "Henri IV. et la Princesse de Condé."
[3] Tallemant des Réaux, " Historiettes."

allowed the word " tyranny " to escape him, and his Majesty, losing all control of himself, replied that the only occasion on which he had merited such a reproach was when he had recognized the prince for what he was not—that is to say, a legitimate son.

Finally, Condé took his wife back to Valery, and, though Henri employed every means in his power to induce him to return, it was to no purpose. "Beaumont," writes the King to the Constable, on 23 September, "returned yesterday, and says that he found our friend (Condé) more unmanageable than ever. He leaves Valery this morning for Muret." [1]

Muret was a château belonging to Condé in Picardy, not far from the Flemish frontier, and the prince's pretext for removing thither was the excellent hunting which the neighbourhood afforded. Early in November, he and his wife went to join a hunting-party at the Abbey of Verteuil, and, while they were there, M. de Traigny, governor of Amiens, invited the Princesse de Condé and the dowager-princess, who was with her, to dine at his country-house, situated some three leagues from the abbey. We will allow Lenet, the faithful servant of the Condés, who had the story from the princess's own lips, to relate what followed:

"It would seem very much as though this party had been concerted with the King, but he was, at any rate, informed of it by the Sieur de Traigny, who always abetted him in his pleasures, so that the princesses, while on their way thither, saw a carriage pass with the King's liveries and a great number of hounds. The princess-mother, who was passionately attached to her son, and watched the actions of the young princess very narrowly, feared that, under the pretext of some hunting excursion, the King had prepared for them a rendezvous. She summoned the huntsmen, whom she saw at a distance ; but one of them, advancing before the others, came to the door of the coach to answer the princess's questions, and disarmed her fears, by telling her that a captain of the hunt, who was in the neighbourhood to celebrate the feast of St. Hubert, had placed

[1] Cited by the Duc d'Aumale, "Histoire des Princes de Condé."

the relays where she saw them, because he was hunting a stag
with some of his friends. Whilst the princess-dowager was
speaking to the huntsman, the young princess, who was at the
coach-door, glanced at the others, who stood some little distance
off, and perceived that one of them was the King, who, the
better to disguise himself under the livery he wore, had put a
large black patch over his left eye and held two greyhounds in a
leash. · The princess told us that she had never been more
astonished in her life, and that she did not dare to mention
what she had seen to her mother-in-law, from fear lest she should
inform her husband. At the same time, she confessed to us
that this gallantry had not displeased her, and, continuing her
story, she told us that, having arrived at Traigny and entered
the salon, she remarked upon the extreme beauty of the view,
whereupon Madame de Traigny said to her that, if she cared to
put her head out of a window which she would show her, she
would see one still more agreeable. Advancing to it, she
perceived that the King was placed at the window of a pavilion
opposite, he having preceded her after having had the pleasure
of seeing her on the road, and that he held all the time one
hand to his lips, as though to send her a kiss, and the other to
his heart, to show her that he had been wounded.

"The surprise of this *rencontre* did not allow the princess
time to reflect what she should do, and she retired abruptly
from the window, exclaiming, ' *Ciel!* what is this? Madame,
the King is here!' On which the princess-dowager, greatly
incensed, divided her words between giving directions for the
horses to be immediately harnessed to her coach and loading
Traigny and his wife with reproaches. Even the King, who
hastened to the spot on hearing the commotion, did not escape
her anger. The enamoured prince employed all the entreaties
which his passion could dictate, and all the promises possible,
to induce her to remain, but to no purpose; for the princesses
re-entered their coach and returned forthwith to Verteuil, where
that same night the princess-mother broke the promise which
the King had extracted from her, and related the whole story
to her son."

. A few days later, Condé received a letter from the King, written in a strain half-coaxing and half-menacing, summoning him to Court, to be present at the approaching accouchement of the Queen. Etiquette required that the first Prince of the Blood should be in attendance on these auspicious occasions, and it was impossible for him to refuse. But he came alone. Henri was furious, and his anger and disappointment rendered him so insupportable to all about him, that Marie de' Medici herself begged Condé to send for his wife, promising to keep the strictest watch over her. Such was the King's wrath that he apparently could not trust himself to interview his cousin personally, but sent for the prince's secretary Virey,[1] and told him that, if Condé desired a divorce from his wife, he would not oppose it, and would even undertake to obtain the parents' consent. The prince, it should be explained, had no such wish, but, a few months before, after a stormy interview with the King, he had chanced to observe to the Duc de Villeroy, whom he had met on leaving the royal presence, and who had inquired the cause of his agitation, that, rather than consent to his own dishonour, or expose himself any longer to his Majesty's anger, he would get himself " dismarried " ; and these hasty words, which had been duly reported to the King, had been wrested into a request for a divorce.[2]

Virey withdrew, and the next day returned and handed the King a very skilfully-worded memorial from Condé, which had been drafted for him by the Président de Thou, wherein he begged his Majesty to appoint such persons as he might think fit to assist him with their counsel in this delicate affair; adding that, until the matter was decided, he did not doubt that the King would think it necessary that the princess should remain at Muret.

[1] Claude Enoch Virey (1566–1636). He was a Doctor of Laws, had fought as a Catholic volunteer in Henri IV.'s army at the battles of Arques and Ivry and at the sieges of Paris and Rouen, and was a poet of some distinction. The Président de Harlay, whose life he had saved on the Day of the Barricades, procured him a post on the educational staff of the young Condé, and he was subsequently appointed his private secretary.

[2] Duc d'Aumale, "Histoire des Princes de Condé."

This answer completely disconcerted the amorous monarch's plans, and made him more angry than ever. Ignoring the memorial, he turned furiously upon Virey, to whose influence he attributed the firm tone which Condé maintained, reproached him bitterly with the counsels he had given the prince, threatened him with his severe displeasure, and, finally, dismissed him, bidding him tell his master that, if he declined to yield to his will or attempted the slightest violence against the princess, he would give him cause to rue it. He¦ added that, had he been still only King of Navarre, he would at once have challenged the prince to a duel.

After receiving the King's message, Condé decided to feign submission, and accordingly begged his Majesty's leave to return to Muret to fetch his wife. His request, as we may suppose, was readily granted, and on 25 November, the day on which the ill-fated Henriette-Marie was born, he set out for Picardy.

On the evening of the 29th, while Henri was at the card-table, word was brought him that a messenger had arrived from Picardy with intelligence that *Monsieur le Prince* had early that morning left Muret, in a coach with his wife, accompanied by his chamberlain, the Baron de Rochefort, Virey, and two of the princess's ladies. Condé had given out that they were bound on a hunting-expedition; but the messenger—an archer of the Guard named Laperrière—had learned from his father, who was in the prince's service, that the party had taken the road to Flanders.

The consternation of the King knew no bounds. The moment he learned the news, he at once summoned his most trusted counsellors, who found him pacing up and down the room, with downcast eyes and hands clasped behind his back. As each arrived, he informed him of what had occurred and demanded his advice, refusing to give him even a moment for reflection. The prudent Sully advised his master to let the matter rest, pointing out that, in that case, the fugitive prince, being unable to draw his pension, would soon be reduced to sue for terms; whereas, if Henri showed anxiety to get him back, the enemies of France would be only too ready to assist him, in order to spite the King.

The infatuated monarch, however, was in no mood to follow such counsel, and that very night, without pausing to reflect on the probable effect of such a step, wrote to the governors of Marle and Guise, directing them to send the whole strength of their garrisons to capture Condé, "wherever he might be;" and despatched La Chaussée, an officer of the Guards, with orders to pursue the prince even over the frontier, "and if he should discover him in any town beyond his dominions to address himself to the governor and magistrates of that city, and to inform them that his Majesty had given him authority to require and entreat them to have the prince and his suite arrested and well guarded, assuring them that, in acting thus, they would be doing great service to the Archdukes."[1]

La Chaussée came up with the fugitives at Landrecies, the first Spanish fortress in Flanders, which they had reached in the early morning of the 30th. Since leaving Muret, they had only rested for a few minutes at a village inn; the almost impassable state of the roads had compelled them to abandon their coach before crossing the Somme, and the unfortunate princess had passed fifteen hours on the crupper of Rochefort's saddle, under a continuous downpour of rain.

La Chaussée produced the royal warrant for the arrest of Condé, but the authorities of Landrecies refused to allow it to be executed until they had referred the matter to the Archdukes. Rochefort, at the prince's request, was permitted to proceed to Brussels to beg the Archdukes to grant his master a safe-conduct through their dominions, in order that he might visit his sister, the Princess of Orange,[2] at Breda. An envoy from

---

[1] In May, 1598, Philip II. had ceded the Netherlands, the Franche-Comté, and the Charolais to his daughter Isabelle. The Archduke Albert, brother of the Emperor Rudolph, at that time governor of the Netherlands, renounced Holy Orders in order to marry the princess; and the pair had since exercised a sort of vice-regal authority, with very extensive powers. Their contemporaries always called them "the Archdukes."

[2] Éléonore de Bourbon had married Philip William, of Nassau, Prince of Orange, eldest son of William the Silent, in 1606.

M

Henri IV. arrived almost simultaneously to denounce the prince as a traitor and an enemy to the public peace, and to request their Highnesses to permit his arrest, or, at least, not to grant him an asylum in Flanders.

The Archdukes found themselves in a very embarrassing position, and took refuge in a compromise. They declined to allow the rights of nations to be violated by the arrest of Condé, and granted his wife permission to continue her journey, but gave orders that the prince should quit the Netherlands within three days.

Rochefort returned to Landrecies with this answer on the night of 2–3 December, and, without waiting for the day, Condé quitted the town and set out for Cologne, a city whose ancient liberties protected him from any attempt at molestation by his enraged Sovereign. On the following morning, the princess, under the charge of the faithful Virey, started for Brussels, where she arrived the same night, and was lodged at the Hôtel de Nassau, the residence of the Prince of Orange.

The Prince and Princess of Orange were at Breda, and their palace was only occupied by a few servants. Virey was very uneasy at the situation in which he found himself, since *Madame la Princesse* had for the moment no protector at hand but himself, and he feared lest Praslain, the envoy whom Henri IV. had despatched to Brussels, should take advantage of his helplessness and carry her off. Such, indeed, was Praslain's intention, but, before resorting to this extreme step, he wished to endeavour to obtain the consent of the Prince of Orange, for which purpose he set off for Breda. There he was received by the princess, who told him what she thought of his proposal in such very forcible language, that he was glad to beat a retreat. He hastened back to Brussels, but, on arriving there, found a guard, which Virey had contrived to obtain, posted before the Hôtel de Nassau, and was obliged to abandon all idea of a *coup de main*.

CHAPTER XII

Condé summoned by the Archdukes to Brussels—He places himself under the protection of Philip III. of Spain—Mission of the Marquis de Cœuvres to Brussels—His attempted abduction of the Princesse de Condé—Condé declared guilty of high treason—He leaves Brussels for Milan—Henri IV. and his Ministers threaten the Archdukes with war if the princess is not given up—Despatches of the Spanish Ambassador to his Court—Condé at Milan—Assassination of Henri IV.—Embarrassing position of Condé in regard to Spain—He returns to Brussels, but declines to see his wife—His return to France—He contemplates the dissolution of his marriage, but ultimately consents to a formal reconciliation with the princess—His turbulent conduct during the regency of Marie de' Medici—His arrest and imprisonment—The princess magnanimously shares her husband's captivity—Dangerous illness of the prince—Birth of Anne Geneviève de Bourbon—Release of the Condés.

TOWARDS the end of December, the Archdukes summoned Condé to Brussels, under the pretext that an interview with the French representative might induce him to return to France. But the real reason was that it had been suggested to them by Spinola[1] that, if the prince could be persuaded to place himself under the protection of Spain, he might be utilized as a very valuable instrument against France.

On his arrival in Brussels, Condé expressed himself willing to return, if guaranteed a place of surety in his government of Guienne; but Henri IV. refused even to consider such a proposal, and insisted on an immediate and unconditional return, promising him only a free pardon. At the instance of Spinola, who had rapidly acquired considerable influence over him, Condé thereupon decided to appeal to the King of

---

[1] Spinola, who had come to the Netherlands in 1602, at the head of a force maintained, like the old *condottieri*, at his own expense, had, after the reduction of Ostend, been given the command of all the Spanish and Italian troops in Flanders.

Spain for protection. The Council of State at Madrid was unanimously of opinion that the request should be acceded to ; and Philip III. accordingly charged his ambassador at the French Court, Don Inigo de Cardenas, to inform Henri IV. that he had taken the Prince de Condé under his protection, "with the object of acting as a mediator in the matter and contributing everything in his power towards the repose and happiness of the Very Christian King." The remainder of the despatch, however, leaves no doubt that his Catholic Majesty was animated by very different sentiments towards Henri IV. from those which Don Inigo was instructed to express.[1] At the same time, Philip wrote to Condé to assure him of his sympathy, and despatched one of his Council, the Count Anôvar, to Brussels, with instructions to watch over the interests of the prince, who, on his side, engaged to make no terms with Henri IV. without the consent of Spain.

Meanwhile, the Connétable de Montmorency, either because he really believed the reports which were being industriously circulated by French agents in Brussels that Condé was ill-treating his wife, or, more probably, out of dishonourable servility to the King, had intervened in the affair, and despatched to Flanders one of his relatives, Louis de Montmorency-Boutteville, father of the unfortunate gentleman whose execution for duelling caused such a painful sensation seventeen years later. Boutteville was the bearer of a letter to the Archdukes, in which the Constable complained bitterly of the alleged sufferings of his daughter, and besought their Highnesses to restore his beloved child to him. His request was refused, and the reports as to Condé's ill-treatment of his wife would appear to have been altogether devoid of foundation. Nevertheless, the young princess, who had little love for her husband and naturally resented the strict surveillance to which she was subjected, was becoming more and more dissatisfied with her life at Brussels. If she had done nothing to encourage the advances of Henri IV., she had certainly not been insensible to the homage of so

---

[1] Simancas Collection, cited by the Duc d'Aumale, " Histoire des Princes de Condé."

HENRY II DE BOURBON, PRINCE DE CONDÉ.

great a monarch, and many years later was wont to recall it with pride and emotion. Moreover, intrigues of all kinds were at work to further the King's odious designs. The wife of the French Ambassador at Brussels, Brulart de Berny, visited *Madame la Princesse* constantly and enlarged on the glories of which she was deprived by her husband's jealousy ; two of her waiting-women had been bribed and added their persuasions to those of the Ambassadress ; while Girard, a secretary of the Constable, was continually travelling to and fro between Paris, Chantilly, and Brussels, bearing letters and instructions.

Towards the end of January, Henry IV. despatched an envoy extraordinary to Brussels, in the person of Annibal d'Estrées, Marquis de Cœuvres, brother of the beautiful and ill-fated Gabrielle. Cœuvres very speedily perceived that there was small likelihood of being able to persuade the Archdukes to surrender the princess to her relatives, or rather to the King, and, on 9 February, wrote to his Majesty to obtain his consent to a plan which he had formed for the abduction of the young lady. Henri immediately sent the required authorization, but, unfortunately for the success of the enterprise, the mere prospect of once more beholding the object of his passion transported him to such a degree that he was quite unable to conceal his joyous anticipations, either from his *entourage* or even from his long-suffering consort. The jealous Queen took advantage of this indiscretion to acquaint the Nuncio Ubaldini, a devoted friend of the Medici family, with what was in the wind ; the Nuncio, in his turn, communicated the news to the Spanish Ambassador, who lost no time in sending a courier to Brussels to put Spinola on his guard.

Spinola, fearing lest Condé, if informed of the proposed abduction of his wife, might create a scandal, contented himself with arousing his suspicions sufficiently to induce him to beg the Archdukes to receive the princess into their own palace. To this their Highnesses readily consented, and 14 February was fixed for the departure of *Madame la Princesse* and her attend-ants from the Hôtel de Nassau.

Cœuvres was naturally much disconcerted on learning of

this change of residence, and recognizing that, were the lady once within the walls of the archducal palace, any such measures as he was contemplating would be foredoomed to failure, determined to make his attempt on the night of the 13th.

His plan was a bold one. The Princesse de Condé's apartments abutted on the garden of the Hôtel de Nassau, which was separated from the ramparts only by a narrow street. Under cover of the confusion and bustle which the preparations for her removal on the morrow would be sure to entail, she was to descend, or be carried into the garden, pass through it, and gain the street. A breach sufficient to admit of her egress was to be made in the ramparts, and on the far side of the moat, which was empty at this time, a body of horse, under the command of Longueval de Manicamp, governor of La Fère, would be waiting to escort her to the frontier, while another troop would cover their flight. Some difference of opinion seems to exist as to whether the lady herself was privy to this scheme ; but the fact that one of her waiting-women had carried that afternoon to the French Embassy a quantity of her mistress's clothes would certainly seem to point to her complicity.

It was only a few hours before the moment fixed for the execution of Cœuvres's design that Spinola learned of his intention, through the treachery of a French adventurer in the marquis's pay. This time he felt obliged to inform Condé, who hastened to the Archdukes to demand a guard, after which, beside himself with anger and excitement, he hurried hither and thither, calling upon every one he met to assist him to protect his wife. Soon the Hôtel de Nassau was surrounded by soldiers, reinforced by five hundred armed citizens, whom the Prince of Orange had procured from the Burgomaster, while cavalry, preceded by torch-bearers, patrolled the neighbouring streets. These warlike preparations brought almost the whole city to the spot, and "bred one of the greatest tumults ever known in Brussels ; and it was commonly reported and believed that the King of France was himself in person at the gates to carry away the princess by force." [1]

---

[1] Cardinal Bentivoglio, "Relazioni."

The same day, about three o'clock in the afternoon, Henri IV. had quitted Paris, "very jovial and much bedecked, contrary to his usual custom," accompanied by four coaches, "to go to meet his nymph,"[1] and proceeded to Saint-Germain-en-Laye. But the nymph did not arrive, and, in her stead, came a mud-bespattered courier with the news of the failure of the attempt. The discomfited monarch returned to Paris in a very ill-humour, and wrote a most unkind letter to Cœuvres, whom he stigmatized as "a blockhead and a fool."

That enterprising nobleman had, it would appear, very narrowly escaped capture, having actually entered the Hôtel de Nassau before he learned that he had been betrayed. However, being possessed of a large fund of assurance, he resolved to brave the matter out, and early next morning presented himself at the palace of the Archdukes, to complain of the insult put upon the King, his master, by the precautionary measures adopted the previous evening, and of the caluminous reports that were being circulated concerning himself. The Archduke Albert replied that he himself had given no credit to these reports, but that, as the Prince de Condé had insisted on the necessity for a guard, he had felt obliged to accede to his request.

On leaving the palace, Cœuvres, accompanied by the French Ambassador, Brulart de Berny, the Sieur de Préaulx, counsellor to the Parlement of Paris, and Manicamp, governor of La Fère, proceeded to the Hôtel de Nassau, where, with much solemnity, he handed Condé a formal indictment declaring him guilty of high treason, unless he forthwith made his submission to the King. To this indictment the prince at once drew up a reply, wherein he affirmed that "he had left France to save his life and his honour ; that he was prepared to return if any offer should be made him which would enable him to reside there in security ; that he would live and die faithful to the King ; but that, when the King should stray from the ways of justice and

---

[1] Letter of Jehan Simon, secretary to the Flemish Ambassador in Paris, to Pretorius, Secretary of State at Brussels, cited by Henrard, "Henri IV. et la Princesse de Condé."

should proceed against him by the ways of violence, he held all such acts as should be done against him null and invalid."[1]

After this, Condé, fearing or feigning to fear, that it was now no longer safe for him to remain in the Netherlands, determined, on the advice of Spinola and the Spanish Ambassador at Brussels, to seek an asylum at Milan. Accordingly, having exacted a solemn promise from the Archdukes that his wife should not quit their palace without his consent, on 21 February, he left Brussels secretly, in disguise, accompanied by Rochefort, Virey, and one of Spinola's officers named Fritima, who was to act as guide and interpreter. The season was an unusually severe one, and the travellers suffered many hardships, but on the last day in March they reached Milan in safety

The Spaniards attached great importance to the possession of Condé's person, for, as first Prince of the Blood and next in succession to the King's children, he might prove of the highest value to them in exciting troubles in France, should Henri IV. persist in his hostile projects against Spain, while, in the event of negotiations, his extradition might be dearly sold. In accordance with instructions from Madrid, the prince was received by the Spanish governor, Fuentes, with every possible honour, lodged in the ducal palace, and a numerous household appointed to wait upon him.

Henri IV. and his Ministers, finding persuasion of no avail with the Archdukes, had recourse to threats, and represented to them that, unless the fair Charlotte were surrendered, war would follow. "The repose of Europe rests in your master's hands," said the Président Jeannin to Pecquius, the Ambassador of the Archdukes in Paris; "peace and war depend on whether the princess is or is not given up." And the King himself reminded the Ambassador that Troy fell because Priam would not surrender Helen.

The gravity of these speeches was enhanced by the warlike preparations which were in progress all over France for the execution of the "Great Enterprise": the scheme of liberating

[1] Duc d'Aumale, "Histoire des Princes de Condé." Cardinal Bentivoglio, "Relazioni."

Europe from the domination of the House of Austria and giving France her rightful place in the world, which Henri IV. had cherished ever since his accession to the throne. It was, however, believed by many that these formidable preparations had no other object than the forcible recovery of the Princesse de Condé, and Malherbe wrote—

> " Deux beaux yeux sont l'empire
> Pour qui je soupire."

Such, undoubtedly, was the opinion of the Spanish Ambassador. "The King is so blinded and infatuated by his passion," he writes to Philip III., "that I know not what to say to your Majesty concerning it, and, if I find many reasons for holding peace to be secure, in regarding affairs from a political standpoint, I find many more for holding war to be certain on the ground of love." He goes on to say that he is informed that the King's infatuation has reached such a point that he is ready to sacrifice everything to it. His health is much affected by it ; he has lost his sleep, and some persons believe that he is losing his reason. And he adds that he is in daily expectation of seeing Henri IV. marching on Brussels at the head of a large force of cavalry.

A fortnight later, the Ambassador writes again—

"Within the last three days, the King has endeavoured to persuade the Queen to request her Highness the Infanta to send the princess (de Condé) for her coronation. The Queen, through the King's confessor (Père Cotton), has begged to be excused, observing that it did not seem to her to be becoming to appear as a third party and risk the indignity of a refusal from the Infanta. The King fell into a violent rage, and declared that the Queen should not be crowned, and that he would have nothing done to displease him. The Queen wept and was much distressed, both at this and at the ardour with which the King is pursuing one of her ladies."

Henri himself pretended to be entirely engrossed by his passion. "I am so worn out by these pangs," he wrote to Préaulx, "that I am nothing but skin and bone. Everything disgusts me. I avoid company, and if, to observe the usages of society, I allow myself to be drawn into some assemblies, my wretchedness is completed."

Fortunately for the fame of Henri IV., greatly as his mind was disturbed and his judgment distracted by this miserable infatuation, it is now generally admitted that the affair had little influence on the course of events. The war upon which he was about to enter was the outcome of twelve long years of persevering negotiations and carefully-prepared alliances, and if he had never set eyes upon the Princesse de Condé, the final result would have been the same. "The King and his Ministers," remarks Henri's latest English biographer, Mr. P. F. Willert, "used the large forces assembled for quite a different purpose as a bugbear to frighten the Archdukes. But, when they refused to purchase security by a compliance inconsistent with their honour, it was not on Brussels that the French armies prepared to march. On the contrary, four days before his death (10 May, 1610), the King in the most friendly terms asked the Archduke Albert's permission to lead his army across his territory to the assistance of his German allies : a permission granted by the Archduke, notwithstanding the opposition of Spinola and of the Spanish party in his Council." [1]

Nevertheless, almost up to the very last, there were many who still believed that, if the Princesse de Condé were given up, war might be averted. Among these was Henri IV.'s Jesuit confessor, Père Cotton, who, in an interview with Pecquius, informed him that, at the previous Easter, "the King was so sincerely desirous of securing his salvation that he had readily forgotten his affection for the princess ; but that all his passion had been rekindled by the perusal of the letters which she addressed to him." [2]

[1] "Henry of Navarre and the Huguenots in France."
[2] Pecquius to the Archduke Albert, 28 April, 1610. It appears to have been on this occasion that Père Cotton begged the Flemish Ambassador to intimate to the Archdukes that, though the solemn promise which they had given Condé might prevent them from surrendering his wife, they might, without any undue strain to their consciences, connive at her escape, since it was undoubtedly their duty to do everything in their power to avert so terrible a calamity as war. But this insidious suggestion their Highnesses very honourably declined to entertain.

Although she was treated with extreme kindness by the Infanta, the young princess had grown heartily weary of the dull little Court of Brussels, and not only stimulated the passion of her royal adorer by the tenderness of her replies to his letters, but complained bitterly of the restraints to which she was subjected, and which, she declared, would have a most serious effect upon her health, unless his Majesty procured her speedy liberation.

Meanwhile, Condé, at Milan, was becoming as bored with the imperturbable gravity and solemn pomp which surrounded him as was his young wife at Brussels, and, in order to find some distraction from the monotony of his existence, had been driven to the study of the antiquities of the neighbourhood and to beginning a translation of Tacitus, under the guidance of his learned secretary, Virey. Fearing that the prince might be persuaded to cast in his lot definitely with the Spaniards, the French Government despatched agents to represent to him that it would be more consonant with his dignity as a Prince of the Blood were he to remove to Rome and place himself under the protection of the common father of the faithful, rather than under that of the common enemy of his race and country. Condé seemed disposed to adopt this suggestion, but the arguments of Fuentes, and the news of the invasion of Lombardy by the Duke of Savoy and Lesdiguières, caused him to abandon all idea of leaving Milan, and to place himself entirely under the guidance of Spain.

Had Henri IV. lived, two things are tolerably certain to have happened : the first, that the Archdukes would sooner or later have been compelled to surrender the princess ; the second, that Condé would have been found in arms against his country. But, on 14 May, 1610, the knife of Ravaillac settled the question both of love and war, and Henri de Bourbon, with all his greatness and his littleness, his splendid schemes and his shameful passions, was but lifeless clay.

A letter from the governor of Alessandria informed Condé of the tragedy. He received the news with somewhat mixed feelings, in which, however, to his honour be it said, regret

seems to have predominated. His position was a very embarrassing one, as it was difficult for him to cast off the ties
which bound him to Spain. Virey, in the account in Latin
verse which he wrote of his master's adventures, part of which
he subsequently translated into French, under the title of
"l'Enlèvement innocent, ou la retraite clandestine de Monseigneur le Prince (de Condé) avec Madame la Princesse,"
affirms that Fuentes came to the prince to congratulate him as
the "legal heir" of the murdered monarch ; and there can be no
doubt that the Ministers of Philip III. approached the Pope, with
the view of ascertaining whether he would be prepared to annul
the marriage of Henry IV. and Marie de' Medici, in which event
it was their intention to put Condé forward as a candidate for
the throne. As they received no encouragement from Paul V.,
they were forced to abandon the idea, but they still cherished
the hope that the prince would, on his return to France, dispute
the Queen-Mother's title to the regency, and, consequently, no
objection was raised to his departure from Milan.

Condé left Milan on 9 June, and deeming it unsafe to cross
France in the then unsettled state of the kingdom, and while
still under the ban of high treason, proceeded to Brussels, where
he arrived nine days later. In spite of the remonstrances of the
Spanish members of the Archdukes' Council, he lost no time
in despatching the faithful Virey to Paris, with letters for
Louis XIII. and the Queen-Mother, wherein he protested his
devotion to the new King. His overtures were very graciously
received, and Virey returned to Brussels with an assurance that
a cordial welcome awaited his master. The secretary brought
also a letter from the Dowager-Princesse de Condé, in which she
endeavoured to incite her son against his wife, informing him
that up to the last moment she had continued to encourage the
late King's passion, and begging him to refuse to see her and to
leave her with the Archdukes. Condé did not see his way to
comply with the latter injunction, and accordingly consented to
the Constable "sending for his daughter ;" but he firmly refused
to meet her. "*Monsieur le Prince* has been some days in
Brussels," writes Malherbe to his friend Peiresc, under date

24 June, 1610. "The Infant (the Archduke) told him that he had a request to make to him. The latter, who did not doubt that it was that he should consent to see his wife, replied that he besought him very humbly not to lay any command upon him in which he should be reduced to the extremity of disobeying him. Thus matters remain in this affair. It is believed that he will take her back, but that he wishes to be requested to do so by the Constable and her relatives. All the letters which the King had exhibited, in which he was addressed (by the Princess) as '*mon tout*' and '*mon chevalier*' are disavowed."

On 8 July, Condé set out for France, and on the afternoon of the 16th he entered Paris by the Porte Saint-Martin, escorted by the Grand Equerry (the Duc de Bellegarde), the Ducs d'Épernon and de Sully, and a number of the nobility, who, by their Majesties' orders, had met him at Bourget. As he rode through the streets to the Louvre, he was obviously preoccupied and ill at ease, "now playing with the collar of his shirt, now biting his gloves, anon fingering his beard and chin ; and one saw clearly that he heard little of what was said to him, and that his thoughts were elsewhere."[1]

The cordiality of his reception by the young King and the Regent somewhat reassured him, and it was with a more confident air that he left the palace and rode to the Hôtel de Lyon, near the Porte de Bussy, where he was visited by the Comte de Soissons and other nobles. At nine o'clock that evening, he returned to the Louvre, and assisted at the *coucher* of the King, "*lequel il desguiletta, tira ses chausses, et ne partit qu'il ne l'eut mis au lit,*" thus demonstrating publicly that he repudiated the ambitious views which some attributed to him, and had no other desire than to be the first of his Majesty's subjects.

For some little time, Condé persisted in his refusal to be reconciled to his wife. He was much incensed, not only against the lady herself, but also against her father, on account of the request he had addressed to the Archdukes, and the accusation of cruelty to the princess which he had not hesitated to bring

[1] "L'Estoile."

against his son-in-law, though the Constable pleaded, in extenuation of his conduct, that he had acted under constraint, and that his letters to the Archdukes had been drafted by the Président Jeannin, by order of the King. Urged on by the princess-dowager and his sister, the Princess of Orange, Condé actually appears to have contemplated taking steps towards getting his marriage annulled, in the hope that, if this could be effected, the Regent might offer him one of her daughters, or, failing a royal princess, he might espouse the wealthy widow of the Duc de Montpensier. Finally, however, recognizing the difficulties of the undertaking and the danger of incurring the enmity of so numerous and powerful a family as the Mont-morencies, he yielded to the solicitations of the Constable and the Duchesse d'Angoulême, and, at the beginning of August 1610, he and his wife were formally reconciled at Chantilly.

We shall not attempt here more than a very brief account of the career of Condé during the troublous minority of Louis XIII. For a moment it seemed as though the prince were well disposed towards the new government, and Marie de' Medici certainly did everything in her power to confirm him in his pacific intentions. She purchased, for 400,000 écus, the Hôtel de Gondi, in the Faubourg Saint-Germain, the finest residence in Paris after the Louvre, and presented it to him ; she confirmed him in all his offices and appointments, increased his pension to 200,000 écus, and gave him a large sum to pay his debts. But Condé was ambitious and meddlesome ; he could not forget that he had once been heir to the throne, and that ill-fortune had in all probability alone deprived him of the regency.[1] Scarcely had he returned, than he became the principal factor in fomenting opposition to the Government, with the design of diminishing the Queen-Mother's authority to the advantage of the great nobles of the realm, and for a time found the *métier*

---

[1] The regency in France belonged, in theory, to the first Prince of the Blood. As, however, Catherine de' Medici had created a precedent in the Queen-Mother's favour, and, as Henri IV. had as good as named her Regent, Marie de' Medici had seized the office immediately on the late King's death. But for the circumstance that Condé was in exile at the time, it is open to question whether she would have been permitted to do this.

of rebel a highly profitable one. At the peace of Sainte-Ménéhould (May, 1614), he received Amboise as a place of surety, and the sum of 450,000 livres in cash ; and at the Peace of Loudon (February, 1616), so enormously had the wages of rebellion risen in the interval, the government of Berry and 1,500,000 livres were required to purchase his neutrality. But, at length, he went too far, and a rumour having spread that his principal adherents, the Ducs de Bouillon, de Longueville, de Mayenne and de Vendôme, were about to make an attempt to place him on the throne, on 1 September, 1616—which, by a singular coincidence, happened to be his birthday,—the Regent, on the advice of Richelieu and Sully, caused him to be arrested at the Louvre, whither he had come to attend a meeting of the Council.

For three weeks Condé remained a close prisoner in an upper apartment of the palace, none of his Household being permitted to have access to him, with the exception of his apothecary, " whose attentions were necessary after two months of a somewhat dissolute life." But in the night of 24-25 September, he was transferred to the Bastille, where he was treated as a State criminal, and subjected to a most rigorous confinement in a gloomy chamber, the windows of which were so closely grated that scarcely a ray of light was permitted to enter.

Ever since their formal reconciliation six years before, the relations between Condé and his wife had been very cool ; indeed, it would appear that the tie which bound them had become merely a nominal one. Nevertheless, on learning of the arrest of her husband, the princess, who was at Valery, showed real magnanimity. Without a moment's delay, she set out for Paris, sent the prince messages assuring him of her sympathy and devotion, and begged the Regent to allow her to share his captivity. Her request, however, was refused, and she received orders to leave Paris at once and return to Valery.

After the assassination of Concini and the departure of the Queen-Mother for Blois, Condé's principal adherents were restored to favour, but he himself still remained in the Bastille.

However, Louis XIII.'s favourite, the Duc de Luynes, sent his uncle, the Comte de Modène, to visit the prince and report upon his state of health. Condé begged him to convey to the King his hope that, if reasons of State required that he should remain a prisoner, his Majesty would at least consent to ameliorate his captivity, and, particularly, to permit his wife to join him. *Madame la Princesse*, it should be mentioned, had recently obtained permission to leave Valery, and had taken up her residence at Saint-Maur.

The immediate result of this interview was to procure the captive a little more air and light; but the unfortunate man's health had been so much affected by the rigour of his confinement that, when the windows of his room were opened he fainted away. Some days later, the favour which he had so earnestly requested, was also granted. We read in a journal of the time:

"26 May, 1617. The Princesse de Condé went to salute the King, and to entreat him to permit her to share her husband's captivity. The King accorded her permission, and to take with her one demoiselle. Upon which, her little dwarf, having begged him to consent to his not abandoning his mistress, his Majesty permitted him also to accompany her. The same afternoon, *Madame la Princesse* entered the Bastille, where she was received by *Monsieur le Prince* with every demonstration of affection, nor did he leave her in repose until she had said that she forgave him."[1]

The prince and princess remained in the Bastille until 15 September, when they were transferred to the Château of Vincennes. Here Condé was allowed a good deal more liberty than had been permitted him in the Bastille, and took exercise daily "on the top of a thick wall, which was in the form of a gallery." In the last days of December, *Madame la Princesse* gave birth to a still-born son, "and was more than forty-eight

---

[1] "Journal historique et anecdote de la Cour et de Paris," MSS. of Conrart, cited by Victor Cousin, "la Jeunesse de Madame de Longueville." The chronicler speaks frequently of the prince's ill-treatment of his wife, for which he appears to think there was no justification.

5 September, 1618, the princess gave birth to twin sons, neither of whom survived, and, in the following March, Condé fell dangerously ill, and for some days his life was despaired of. The physicians who attended him attributed his illness to the state of profound melancholy into which his captivity and the death of his children had thrown him, and, when this was known, the prince became the object of universal sympathy, and Louis XIII. was strongly urged to consent to his release. His Majesty promised to set the prisoner at liberty, "so soon as he had placed his (Condé's) affairs in order," but several months passed, and Condé still remained at Vincennes, though granted every indulgence consistent with a due regard to his security. However, at the end of August, another domestic event, which, happily, had a different termination from the others, came to relieve the monotony of his captivity, *Madame la Princesse* giving birth to a daughter, Anne Geneviève de Bourbon, the future Duchesse de Longueville, the heroine of the Fronde.

The birth of this little girl was the turning-point of her parents' fortunes, for on 20 October Condé was at length set at liberty, and five weeks later the Parlement of Paris solemnly registered "the declaration of innocence of *Monsieur le Prince*,[2] who was restored to all his honours and offices."

His three years' captivity, which cannot be said to have been altogether undeserved, had worked a great change in the

---

[1] "Journal historique et anecdote de la Cour et de Paris."

[2] In the preamble of this document, Louis XIII. strove to throw the responsibility for his cousin's long detention upon Marie de' Medici and her adherents, although the real cause seems to have been the fears of Luynes lest Condé should attempt to dispute his ascendency over the young King. "Being informed," said his Majesty, "of the reasons by which his detention has been excused, I have found that there was no cause save the machinations and evil designs of his enemies."

N

character of Condé. Like so many others, he had learned wisdom from adversity. Until then he had struggled against the royal authority with almost as much zeal as his father and grandfather, though, since the death of Henri IV., without their justification. But the lesson he had received had been a severe one, and henceforth the King had no more loyal servant, his Ministers no stauncher supporter, than the first Prince of the Blood. His enemies have accused him, and with only too much reason, of servility towards those in power and of an excessive regard for his own interests ; but, on the whole, the line of conduct he pursued seems to have been patriotic as well as prudent.

Two years after Condé's release from Vincennes, on 8 September, 1621, his wife bore him a son, Louis, Duc d'Enghien, who was to confer so much lustre on the name of Condé ; and in 1629 a second son was born to them, Armand, Prince de Conti.

CHAPTER XIII

Birth of Louis de Bourbon, Duc d'Enghien (the Great Condé)—His early years at the Château of Montrond—His education—His personal appearance and character—Wealth of the Condés—Life at Chantilly—Isabelle de Boutteville and Marthe du Vigean—Tender attachment of the Duc d'Enghien and Mlle. du Vigean—Subserviency of the Prince de Condé towards Richelieu—He solicits for Enghien the hand of the Cardinal's niece, Claire-Clémence de Maillé-Brézé—The young prince protests against the sacrifice demanded of him, but eventually consents—He is presented to Mlle. de Maillé-Brézé—First campaign of the Great Condé—He denies the rumour that he has "no taste for his *fiancée*"—Fête at the Palais-Cardinal : a ludicrous incident—Marriage of the Duc d'Enghien.

VOLTAIRE has observed that the sole claim of the third Prince de Condé to remembrance is that he begat one of France's most famous generals. To be just, he should have added that the claim is a twofold one, inasmuch as not only was he the father of the Great Condé, but gave him one of the most thorough military educations that prince ever received, and but for which, though his fiery valour would doubtless have gained him some distinction in the field, it is scarcely probable that he would ever have earned the title of " *le Grand.*"

The birth of this shoot of the royal race was an event of importance, for, after five years, the union of Louis XIII. with Anne of Austria still remained without result, and the Duc d'Orléans, the King's younger brother, did not seem inclined to take a wife ; but, at the moment when it occurred, the attention of the Parisians was occupied by the arrival of a Carmelite monk, Père Dominique de Jésus-Maria, to whom miraculous powers were ascribed, and it passed almost unnoticed.

Condé was in his government of Berry when the news that he had a son reached him, and, as soon as she was able to travel,

Madame la Princesse set out for Bourges, to take the boy to his father. The latter had already made up his mind as to the way in which his heir was to be brought up. As the little prince was fragile and sickly, and he dreaded for him the air of Paris, the cares of an over-indulgent mother, and the influence of the fashionable ladies by whom the princess was always surrounded, he had decided to break with tradition and to establish him at the Château of Montrond, a fortified castle belonging to him, situated at the confluence of the Marmande and the Cher, overlooking the little town of Saint-Amand, where he would be placed under the care of some intelligent women of the middle class, who could be trusted to carry out his instructions with unquestioning obedience.

Such an arrangement was naturally but little to the taste of *Madame la Princesse*, who was indignant at being thus separated from her son, but it was amply justified by the results. In the pure country air the boy's health steadily improved, while his intelligence was quickly perceived to be far in advance of his age. No sooner did he begin to speak than he displayed a remarkable strength of will, which resisted, as far as a child can resist, the orders of his nurses ; and they found it no easy task to persuade him to rise, take his meals, or go to bed at the hours which they considered good for him. He feared no one but his father, and, when the latter was not at hand to correct him, it was difficult to restrain him in anything.

On 2 May, 1626, the little prince, who assumed from that day the title of Duc d'Enghien,[1] was taken to Bourges to be baptized, the ceremony being performed, in solemn state, by the archbishop of the diocese, Roland Hébert. But, save on this occasion, he was never permitted to leave Montrond, where he led a healthy out-door life, the lessons he received being frequently imparted under the guise of games, so as to tax the mind as little as possible, while leaving the most pleasant impression. He made astonishing progress, particularly in Latin, and quickly began to evince the keenest interest in

[1] Enghien is the modern spelling; in the seventeenth century it was written Anguien.

military matters, the result of conversations with a distinguished engineer named Sarrasin, who was then engaged in repairing the defences of Montrond, and who superintended the boy's amusements. "When, towards the end of the year 1629," writes the Duc d'Aumale, "the Prince de Condé, returning from Languedoc, stopped at his Berry fortress, his suite beheld with some surprise a young captain of seven, who ranged in order of battle, in the trenches of the château, the children of the neighbouring town of Saint-Amand, evoked the heroes of ancient Rome, and harangued them in Latin."

At the close of the following year, Condé removed his son from Montrond to Bourges, to continue his studies at the Jesuit College of Sainte-Marie, one of the most celebrated of the schools which the Fathers had established in France. Wishing to avoid the complications which might arise from the presence near his son of a man of quality, he selected as his *gouverneur*, a simple gentleman of Dauphiné, La Buffetière by name, "a good man, faithful, and well-intentioned, who knew how to follow to the letter *Monsieur le Prince's* instructions for the conduct of his son." [1] Associated with him, as tutor to the prince, was a learned Jesuit, Père Pelletier; while a doctor named Montreuil watched over his health, which was still such as to occasion his father some anxiety.

For six years the Duc d'Enghien attended the Jesuit College at Bourges. The only distinction which was made between him and the other pupils was a little gilded balustrade which encircled his chair, and, by *Monsieur le Prince's* orders, his schoolfellows were strictly forbidden to give way to him, either in class or at play. Condé himself, who, as governor of Berry, resided part of each year at Bourges, watched over and directed the education of his son, examined his compositions and the notes which he took at lectures, and made him dance and play tennis before him. When absent at the Court or with the Army, he corresponded regularly with the boy, and, the better to judge of his progress, he directed him, after he was eight years old, always to write to him in Latin. *Gouverneur*,

[1] Lenet, "Mémoires."

tutor, and doctor were kept busy replying to the letters full of questions, instructions, and recommendations with which the anxious father bombarded them ; whilst the rector of the Jesuit College was perpetually being enjoined "to pay attention to the studies and conduct of my son."

The pains bestowed upon the Duc d'Enghien's education were well repaid ; his progress delighted his instructors, and must have satisfied even *Monsieur le Prince.* At twelve years of age, when he finished his course of rhetoric, such was his proficiency in Latin that he wrote and spoke it, we are told, as though it were his mother-tongue. The next two years were devoted to the study of philosophy and the sciences, which latter term included logic, ethics, mathematics, and physics, after which Condé, notwithstanding that his son had already received an education far in advance of that which was then considered sufficient for the son of a *grand seigneur,* arranged that he should go through a course of law under the direction of Merille, Professor of Jurisprudence in the University of Bourges.

The vacations were passed at Montrond, to which the young prince was permitted to invite some of his schoolfellows. But his tutors and certain masters came also, and his studies were by no means suspended, though physical training—lessons in dancing, fencing, and riding—received the larger share of attention.

At the end of the year 1635, Condé judged that the time had come for his son to lay aside the scholar's gown, and accordingly the Duc d'Enghien bade farewell to the Jesuits of Bourges and set out for Paris, where he was presented to Louis XIII. After a short visit to his mother at Saint-Maur, he set out for Dijon to join his father, who had lately added the government of Burgundy to that of Berry, and remained there until the beginning of the following year. He then returned to Paris and entered the famous "Académie royale pour la jeune noblesse," established some years previously by a retired officer of the army, named Benjamin, and recently transformed into a kind of military school under the protection

LOUIS I DE BOURBON, PRINCE DE CONDÉ, (THE GREAT CONDÉ)
FROM AN ENGRAVING BY JACQUES LUBIN

of Louis XIII. and Richelieu. Here he was taught everything which concerned the profession of arms: geography, mathematics, fortification, drawing, fencing, horsemanship, being treated, by his father's wishes, in every respect as the other young noblemen, several of whom became his close friends, and in after years shared his labours and his fame.

After twelve months of earnest work, varied by short visits to Saint-Maur, and a few appearances at the Court and in Society, the duke quitted Benjamin's academy, and in the spring of 1638, the Prince de Condé having been called to the command of the army in Guienne, Louis XIII. entrusted him with the government of Burgundy during his father's absence.

It was a very striking-looking, as well as a very learned, young man who, one fine April morning, took his seat in the Parlement of Dijon, "with every honour and testimony of affection possible." "His eyes," writes a contemporary, "were blue and full of vivacity, his nose was aquiline, his mouth very disagreeable, from being very large, and his teeth too prominent. But in his countenance generally there was something great and haughty, somewhat resembling an eagle. He was not very tall, but his figure was admirably well-proportioned. He danced well, had a pleasant expression, a noble air, and a very fine head." [1]

Unhappily for the Duc d'Enghien and for France, his father and his teachers, while sparing no pains to develop his talents and to strengthen his body, had not succeeded in correcting certain grave defects of character, which, as he grew older, were to become more pronounced and to end by tarnishing his fame. The lad was fearlessly brave, open-handed, quick-witted, and full of energy and determination. But he was haughty and overbearing, thoroughly selfish, and supremely indifferent to the sufferings or susceptibilities of others, when he had ends of his own to serve.

When the Prince de Condé had married Charlotte de Montmorency, he was, for his rank, a poor man; but during the last few years the family had become one of the wealthiest in

---

[1] Madame de Motteville, "Mémoires."

France. The prince himself held the rich governments of Berry and Burgundy, and several other offices, and had received, at different times, immense sums from the Crown ; while, after the execution of the unfortunate Henri II., Duc de Montmorency, for high treason, in 1632, the princess and her two elder sisters, the Duchesses d'Angoulême and de Ventadour, had divided between them the vast fortune of the Montmorencies.[1] To *Madame la Princesse* fell the largest share of the landed property, including the estates of Écouen, Mello, Châteauroux, Méru, and La Versine ; while, some time afterwards, Chantilly and Dammartin were also bestowed upon her, though she appears to have been granted merely the enjoyment of them for life ; and it was not until the autumn of 1643 that they became the absolute property of the Condés, in recognition of the military services of the Duc d'Enghien.

Although the Princesse de Condé paid occasional visits to her country seats of Mello, Méru, and La Versine, the greater part of the summer was always passed by her at Chantilly, whither she came with a little party composed of the most intimate friends of her children, and a sprinkling of wits and men of letters. *Monsieur le Prince*, who did not care for country pleasures, usually remained in Paris, and, in his absence, etiquette was laid aside, and the guests permitted to amuse themselves as they pleased. Lenet, in his "Mémoires," has left us an interesting account of how the company at Chantilly passed their time :

"The excursions were the most agreeable possible to imagine. The evenings were not less amusing. After the

---

[1] By a will made shortly before his death, the Duc de Montmorency, who left no children, had designated as heir to the greater part of his immense estates the little François de Montmorency-Boutteville, afterwards the celebrated Maréchal de Luxembourg, the posthumous son of the Comte de Montmorency-Boutteville, executed for duelling in 1627. But the duke's condemnation rendered this document of no effect, and the whole of his property reverted to the Crown. Louis XIII., however, contented himself with retaining possession of Chantilly and Dammartin, for the sake of the hunting, without, however, uniting them to his demesne, and caused the rest of the property to be divided between the Princesse de Condé and her two sisters, Richelieu, we may presume, not being minded to set up another great feudal noble in the place of the deceased duke.

usual prayers had been read in the chapel, which were attended by every one, all the ladies retired to the apartments of the princess, where they played at various games and sang. There were often fine voices and very agreeable conversations, stories of Court intrigue and gallantry, which made life pass as pleasantly as possible. . . . Rhymes and riddles were composed, which occupied the time in spare hours. Some were to be seen walking on the edge of the ponds, and some in the alleys of the park or gardens, on the terrace or on the lawn, alone or in parties, according to the state of mind in which they were ; while others sang airs, or recited verses, or read romances on a balcony, or as they walked or reposed on the grass. Never was there seen so beautiful a place in such a beautiful season." [1]

Lenet wrote of the spring of 1650, when the Princes (Condé, Conti and Longueville) were in prison, and Madame de Longueville an exile, and when, as he admits, the amusements of the young people were often disturbed by bad news. But before the Fronde, which divided all French society, Chantilly was an even more delightful resort. The young Duc d'Enghien came there, bringing with him many of the young nobles who had been his friends at Benjamin's Academy, and who were to fight by his side on many a fiercely-contested field ; the two sons of the Maréchal Duc de Châtillon, Maurice, Comte de Coligny, and Gaspard, Marquis d'Andelot ; Guy de Laval, son of the Marquis de Sablé ; Léon d'Angennes, Marquis de Pisani ; Louis and Charles Amédée de Savoie, who successively bore the title óf Duc de Nemours; La Moussaye, the hero of the battle of La Marfée; the two du Vigeans, Nangis, Tavannes, and others, amongst whom grew up a little humpbacked boy, who was one day to be known to fame as the Maréchal de Luxembourg.

And there also was Enghien's lovely sister, Anne Geneviève de Bourbon, who, in 1642, was to marry the Duc de Longueville, and with her a bevy of young beauties, light-hearted, laughter-loving damsels, bandying jests with the wits, rallying the more

[1] Lenet, " Mémoires."

serious, and exercising, under the indulgent eyes of *Madame la Princesse*, their precocious coquetry upon the Duc d'Enghien and his comrades. Among them may be mentioned Marie Antoinette de Brienne, daughter of the Minister of that name, afterwards the Marquise de Gamaches; the two sisters of the future Maréchal de Luxembourg, Marie Louise and Isabelle de Boutteville; the celebrated Julie d'Angennes, afterwards Duchesse de Montausier; and Anne and Marthe du Vigean, the former of whom married the Marquis de Pons, and *en secondes noces* the young Duc de Richelieu, the Cardinal's heir.

Of these nymphs, two—Isabelle de Boutteville and Marthe du Vigean—were destined to figure very prominently in the life of the Great Condé. They presented a singular contrast. Isabelle de Boutteville, who, under the name of the Duchesse de Châtillon, was to achieve celebrity as the most finished coquette of her time, was an imperious young beauty, who already appreciated to the full the power of her own attractions. Insatiable for admiration, she disdained no conquests, encouraging and rebuffing by turns the troop of adorers who gathered about her, and rehearsing thus early with the Duc d'Enghien and the younger of the two boys who were to bear the title of Duc de Nemours the part she was one day to play with them on another stage. None of the young beauties of Chantilly, with the exception of Mlle. de Bourbon, inspired the poets who foregathered there to celebrate their charms and deplore their coldness more often than she. Among a multitude of verses of more or less merit, composed in her honour, may be mentioned those of the poet Charpy, wherein he draws an ingenious comparison between the destruction wrought by the sword of his father, the notorious duellist, and the havoc created by the *beaux yeux* of Isabelle :

> " Quand je vois de rapport de votre père à vous,
> Divinité mortelle, adorable Sylvie !
> Il tenait dans ses mains et la mort et la vie :
> Vos yeux se sont acquis les mêmes sur nous."

Marthe du Vigean was a very different kind of girl. Modest

and gentle, she hardly seemed to be aware of the admiration
which she aroused :

> " Sans savoir ce que c'est qu'amour
>   Ses beaux yeux le mettent au jour,
>   Et partout elle le fait naître
>   Sans le connoître,"

wrote Voiture. Unfortunately, no portrait of her, either painted
or engraved, has been preserved, nor have we any detailed
description of her among the writings of her contemporaries
which can supply its place. But her beauty would appear to
have been of a peculiarly appealing type, the reflection of a
character gentle, pure and unselfish.

In love, it is said, people are most frequently attracted by
those who least resemble them. However that may be, the
haughty, vain, egotistical young Duc d'Enghien, for a moment
subjugated by the more dazzling charms of Isabelle de Boutteville, to whose yoke he will return in years to come, speedily
transferred his affections to this gentle, retiring maiden, for whom
he conceived the one great and pure passion of his stormy life.
The girl reciprocated his affections, and loved him with an
intensity of devotion which never wavered for a moment to her
life's end. To her, this young prince, with his eagle glance and
his fiery courage, was a veritable hero of romance, a seventeenth-
century Bayard, " *sans peur et sans reproche.*"

Although not in the first rank of the French nobility, the
Du Vigeans were high in favour at Court, and Madame du
Vigean was one of *Madame la Princesse's* most intimate friends.
She was very rich and gave magnificent fêtes at her country-
seat of La Barre, and Marthe was a considerable heiress. In
ordinary circumstances, therefore, the Duc d'Enghien might
not have despaired of obtaining his father's and the King's—
that is to say, Richelieu's—consent to the match, for the princes
of the House of Bourbon had often sought their wives among
the daughters of noble and wealthy French families. But,
unhappily for the lovers, *Monsieur le Prince* had other views for
his son, and had long since selected a wife for him.

Among the courtiers who so eagerly sought the favour of

Richelieu no one was more obsequious than the Prince de Condé, who had not only willingly consented, contrary to all ancient usage, that the Princes of the Blood should yield precedence to cardinals, but had even, it is asserted, carried his servility to such a point as to raise the tapestry and hold it when the all-powerful Minister passed through a door. Omnipotent though Richelieu was, he could hardly have flattered himself with the hope of an alliance with the Princes of the Blood ; and it must therefore have been with feelings of astonishment and contempt mingling with gratification that " he beheld M. de Condé ask of him almost on his knees the hand of his niece, and plead for this object as eagerly as though he had in view for his son the sovereignty of the world." [1]

The niece in question was Claire-Clémence de Maillé-Brézé, daughter of the Maréchal Duc de Brézé, who had married " solely for her beauty," as he was never tired of reminding the Cardinal, Richelieu's pretty but eccentric sister, Nicole du Plessis. Born on 28 February, 1628, Claire-Clémence's infancy was passed with her parents at the Château of Milly, in Anjou. But when the unfortunate Nicole's eccentricity turned to madness,[2] and the marshal began to console himself openly with the widow of one of his *valets de chambre*, the Cardinal decided that it was time to remove his niece ; and, in 1633, took advantage of an epidemic which was then ravaging Anjou to send her to the Château des Caves, near Nogent-sur-Seine, to the Bouthilliers, whose fortune he had made, and who were entirely devoted to him.

It is probable that Richelieu would not have shown himself so solicitous for the welfare of the little girl had he not already foreseen that she would become an instrument of his policy. In point of fact, most flattering proposals for her hand had already been made him. The first was from the Duc de la Trémoille, on behalf of his eldest son, afterwards the Prince de

---

[1] Mlle. de Montpensier, " Mémoires."

[2] According to Tallemant des Réaux, at one time, the poor woman imagined that she was made of glass, and never sat down except with infinite precautions ; at another, she thought that her hands and feet had turned to ice, and was continually warming them, even in the hottest weather.

Duc d'Enghien, then twelve years of age.

So anxious was *Monsieur le Prince* to be reconciled with the Minister whom he had failed to conquer, and to convert his former adversary into a complaisant ally—or rather a beneficent patron, that he had already taken the precaution to assure himself of the consent of Louis XIII. The Cardinal, on his side, who saw in this union the most dazzling proof of his influence and of the triumph of his policy, received his Highness's overtures very graciously, and, early in 1633, gave him the promise he desired.

The joy of *Monsieur le Prince* was such that Richelieu had all the difficulty in the world to prevent him from confirming the rumours of the Court and publicly announcing his good fortune ; but the Cardinal insisted that it should remain a secret between them until the bride-elect had reached a marriageable age, and, very reluctantly, the other consented. As for the Maréchal de Brézé, Richelieu did not even think it worth while to mention the arrangement to him, deeming that the right of disposing of his niece's hand belonged to himself alone.

Thus matters remained until the end of the year 1640, when Condé, having gone through the form of obtaining the consent of the Maréchal de Brézé, acquainted his son with the honour in store for him. The Duc d'Enghien, as might be supposed, protested strongly against the sacrifice that was demanded of him, but *Monsieur le Prince*, always terribly in earnest when it was a question of pleasing those in power, was inexorable ; and eventually the duke gave a reluctant consent, somewhat consoled by the reflection that, as the Cardinal's nephew by marriage, advancement in his profession must be both sure and speedy.

Under date 11 February, 1640, we find Condé writing to Richelieu from Dijon :

"My son, who burns with the same desire as myself to be allied to you, will write to you on the instant, and will set out

with me to-morrow for Paris, to offer his services to his mistress.
I have spoken to him about it, and have received from him not
only the proofs of the obedience that he owes me, but also
those of very great joy on this subject." [1]

The Duchesse d'Aiguillon, the Cardinal's beloved niece,
conducted Mlle. de Brézé to Paris, where the Duc d'Enghien
and his father arrived shortly afterwards. The young duke
was "presented to his mistress," as was said then, and authorized to visit and to write to her, while awaiting their marriage,
which, much to the disappointment of *Monsieur le Prince*,
Richelieu had decided to postpone until the following year, on
account of the extreme youthfulness of the bride-elect.

The Prince de Condé overwhelmed Claire-Clémence with
attentions and declared that he was all impatience to call her
his daughter-in-law. On presenting her *fiancé* to her, he assured
her "it would never be possible for her to espouse a person
who would show her more respect or more affection ; " and when
Enghien was about to take the armchair that was offered him,
he stopped him, saying sharply : "That is not the place for a
serviteur ; go and sit down on a little *placet* with your mistress." [2]

Nothing less than the paternal exhortations were required
to persuade the young duke to pay his court to his betrothed,
and, in point of fact, he limited his visits to those which the
exigencies of etiquette required. Claire-Clémence was "far
from plain ; she had beautiful eyes, a fine complexion, and a
pretty figure." [3] But she was barely twelve years old, and
very small even for her years, and, besides, so childish in her
ways that *la Grande Mademoiselle* declares that two years after
her marriage she still amused herself with dolls. Very young
men are more often attracted by ripe than by immature charms,
and it was therefore scarcely to be expected that Enghien should
have shown any inclination for the society of his betrothed—
even if his affections had not been already engaged elsewhere.

[1] Duc d'Aumale, "Histoire des Princes de Condé."
[2] Letter of Henri Arnauld to Barillon, April 11, 1640, cited by Homberg and
Jousselin, "la Femme du Grand Condé."
[3] Mademoiselle de Montpensier, "Mémoires."

Little time, however, was given the young people for becoming better acquainted with one another, as other matters than courtship and marriage were demanding Enghien's attention. Since 1635 war had been declared against Spain, and France had come openly into that field in which her secret influence had long been exercised. The clash of arms which resounded throughout Europe had strongly affected the young prince, and he had long sighed for an opportunity of displaying his courage. So early as 1636 he had written to his father: "I read with pleasure the heroic actions of our kings in history. . . . I feel a holy ambition to imitate them and follow in their track, when my age and capabilities shall have made me what you wish."[1] Condé, however, thinking that his son's strength was not yet equal to the hardships of active service, had hitherto refused to gratify his ambition; but, in the spring of 1640, he at length gave his consent, and, at the end of April, the lad set out for Picardy to make his first campaign with the army operating against the Spaniards on the North-Eastern frontier. He was greatly disappointed that he was not to receive his baptism of fire under the eyes of his father, who commanded the French forces in Roussillon. But Richelieu had chosen the Army of Picardy, because its commander, the Maréchal de la Meilleraie, was the sworn enemy of *Monsieur le Prince*, and might, consequently, be trusted neither to allow the young soldier to shirk his duties nor to exaggerate his services To mitigate his disappointment, the Cardinal overwhelmed his future nephew with compliments, and presented him with two splendid chargers.

This first campaign of the Great Condé was short and easy, terminating on 9 August with the taking of Arras. The young soldier earned golden opinions from all his superiors by the promptitude and intelligence with which he executed everything entrusted to him, and gave abundant proofs of the courage for which he was soon to become so celebrated in a cavalry skirmish before the beleaguered town.

The campaign over, the duke, by his father's instructions,

[1] Earl Stanhope, "Life of Louis, Prince de Condé, surnamed the Great."

returned to Dijon without passing through Paris, to the great chagrin of his sister and her friends, who were naturally anxious to celebrate his exploits. But *Monsieur le Prince*, like a prudent father, had decided that, until his son was safely married, it would be as well for him to shun the society of those dangerously fascinating damsels, and of one of them in particular. The Cardinal, unaware that Enghien had been merely following the paternal orders, saw in this avoidance of Paris a confirmation of the persistent rumour that was going about the Court that the young prince "had no taste for his *fiancée*." In high indignation, he despatched Chavigny to Dijon, to invite him to explain his conduct and to say candidly whether or no he desired the alliance which his father had solicited for him. There can be very little doubt what answer Enghien would have returned had circumstances permitted him to express his real sentiments; but, with the fear of both the Cardinal and *Monsieur le Prince* before his eyes, he indignantly denied the truth of the report that was in circulation, and begged Chavigny to assure his Eminence that his heart was entirely set upon the marriage.

"I feel myself obliged to inform you," he writes to his father, "that M. de Chavigny came yesterday to see me and told me that he had something of importance to say to me. It is that a gentleman had told him that a rumour ran that I had no inclination for Mlle. de Brézé; that I regarded this marriage with aversion, and that people remarked that my countenance was very melancholy, and, finally, that he begged me to be on my guard. I replied that the person who had told him this was a wicked man, as were those who circulated these false reports; that I looked upon this marriage as a great honour and favour; that it was the thing in the world that you and I desired the most, and that all those who spread these reports were his enemies and mine, and that, far from being melancholy, I had never been so gay."[1]

Notwithstanding these indignant protestations, the Cardinal, who, while naturally very anxious for a marriage which would

---

[1] "Archives de Chantilly," cited by the Duc d'Aumale.

connect him with the Royal House itself and serve to consolidate his power, was anxious also to assure the happiness of his niece, was still somewhat uneasy. In consequence, he showed himself a trifle cold when the marriage was mentioned, to the profound alarm of *Monsieur le Prince*, who redoubled his attentions both to his Eminence and his niece, and was as impatient for the conclusion of the affair "as if his son were about to espouse the queen of all the world."

The marriage was finally fixed for 11 February, 1641. Early in January, the Duc d'Enghien arrived in Paris with his father, who accompanied him everywhere he went, apparently from fear lest he should fail to manifest sufficient enthusiasm for the fate in store for him. Mlle. de Brézé had already arrived and was lodged at the Hôtel d'Aiguillon, in charge of Madame Bouthillier; and, on 14 January, Richelieu gave a magnificent fête in honour of the young couple at the Palais-Cardinal. The principal attraction of this entertainment was the representation of "Mirame," a "*tragi-comédie*" which his Eminence had written in collaboration with Desmarets. Richelieu had spared no expense to give his work—which was probably neither better nor worse than the mediocre pieces of the time—a setting in every way worthy of it. The theatre, constructed expressly for it, had cost 200,000 écus; the scenery had been brought from Italy, and the costumes had been designed by the Cardinal himself. All the effective passages in the play were rapturously applauded by the spectators, which is scarcely surprising, since the celebrated author, carried away by admiration for his own genius, invariably gave them the signal; and if the fall of the curtain did not leave his Eminence under the pleasing illusion that he was not only a great statesman, but a great poet as well, it was certainly not the fault of his guests.

The play was followed by a grand ball, in which the little Mlle. de Brézé appeared in a marvellous toilette and decorated with a part of the Queen's jewels, which her Majesty had lent her for the occasion. *Monsieur le Prince*, who, with some of his intimates, watched the scene from the gallery, pretended to be in

o

raptures of admiration, and every time that his future daughter-in-law danced, kept repeating : " Ah ! how pretty she is ! Ah ! how pretty she is !" It is to be hoped that the report of these praises served to console their object for a trifling but ludicrous mishap of which she was the victim, and which must have occasioned her profound mortification.

She had come to the fête furnished with a pair of enormously high-heeled shoes, which she had been made to don in order to increase her stature, which, as we have said, was very short, even for her years. It was only with the greatest difficulty that she was able to preserve her equilibrium, and, while dancing a *courante*, she slipped and fell sprawling on the floor. *La Grande Mademoiselle*, who recounts this misadventure, declares that " no considerations of respect could hinder all the company from giving vent to their merriment, not even excepting the Duc d'Enghien." [1]

On 7 February, the marriage-contract was signed in the King's cabinet at the Louvre, as was the custom when Princes of the Blood were wed. The Prince and Princesse de Condé promised the young couple settlements to the value of 80,000 livres a year and an annual pension of 40,000 livres. His Eminence gave his niece the seigneuries of Ansac, Moy, Cambronne, and Plessis-Billebault, together with the sum of 300,000 livres, but under the express condition that she should renounce all claim to the rest of his property in the event of his death.

" It was impossible," observe Claire-Clémence's biographers, MM. Homberg and Jousselin, " to manifest more clearly, in the eyes of all, that the niece of Richelieu had been sought by the House of Condé, less for wealth, which was by no means out of the ordinary, than for the advantages of a connexion with him whom the courtiers called " the All-powerful." [2]

The stipulation regarding Richelieu's property greatly disgusted *Monsieur le Prince*, who was as greedy as he was ambitious ; and, though he had not ventured to contest the matter with the Cardinal, he made, together with his son, a formal

[1] Mademoiselle de Montpensier, "Mémoires."
[2] "La Femme du Grand Condé."

protest, in the presence of a notary, against the renunciation exacted by his Eminence.

After the signing of the contract, Richelieu gave a magnificent ballet at the Palais-Cardinal, entitled " La Prosperité des armes de France." This ballet, we are told, delighted every one save the King, who appeared to be displeased at the sight of the Duc d'Enghien descending from heaven, surrounded by dazzling sunbeams, to make his entry.

On 11 February, the marriage was celebrated in the chapel of Palais-Cardinal, by the Archbishop of Paris. After the ceremony, the bridal pair and their relatives were entertained to a sumptuous banquet, and in the evening a play, followed by a supper, was given by Richelieu at the Palais-Cardinal. " Never had his Eminence been seen in a better temper,"[1] writes a witness of the marriage fêtes, on which the Cardinal is said to have expended upwards of a million livres. Supper over, the company adjourned to the Hôtel de Condé, to put the bridal pair to bed, according to custom.

[1] Letter of Henri Arnauld to the President Barillon, cited by MM. Homberg and Jousselin, "la Femme du Grand Condé."

CHAPTER XIV

Serious illness of the Duc d'Enghien—Tyranny exercised over him by Richelieu—An amusing anecdote—Death of the Cardinal—His will—Lawsuit between the Prince de Condé and the Duchesse d'Aiguillon—Enghien contemplates the dissolution of his marriage, neglects his wife, and devotes himself to Marthe du Vigean—He receives the command of the Army of Flanders, gains the brilliant victory of Rocroi, and takes Thionville—The Duchesse d'Enghien gives birth to a son—Indifference of the duke—He returns to Paris and endeavours to procure the dissolution of his marriage—But this project is frustrated by the interference of the Prince de Condé—Enghien is wounded at the battle of Nördlingen, and has a dangerous attack of fever—To the astonishment of his friends, he suddenly breaks off his tender relations with Mlle. du Vigean—Despair of the lady, who, in spite of the opposition of her family, enters the Carmelites of the Faubourg Saint-Jacques.

A FEW days after his marriage, the Duc d'Enghien fell dangerously ill, an event which was attributed by the Court to his despair at having been forced into an alliance so distasteful to him. Certainly, he behaved like a man who had little desire to live, and it was only with great difficulty that he could be persuaded to see the doctors whom *Monsieur le Prince* called in. At one time, his condition was so serious that hope was almost abandoned, but these apprehensions were fortunately unfounded, and in six weeks he was convalescent. His spirits, however, did not return with his strength, and he remained for some time in a state of profound melancholy, refusing to go into Society, or to receive his friends, and spending "the entire day and a part of the night" reading romances. At length, he succeeded in shaking off his lethargy, and on 13 May celebrated his return to health by giving a grand fête at Charonne to his sister and her fair friends, including, needless to say, Mlle. du Vigean.

The Cardinal, already irritated by the coldness with which Enghien had from the first treated his child-wife, in spite of the affection which she lavished upon him, was much displeased on learning of this entertainment, for, in his opinion, no society was more calculated to wean his nephew from the domestic hearth than that of these charming young ladies. He had another, and more serious cause for resentment against the young prince, in the fate which had befallen one Maigrin, a creature of his own, whom Condé, at his suggestion, had appointed comptroller of his son's Household. Incensed by the surveillance which he suspected Maigrin of exercising over his actions, Enghien had inveighed against him in such violent terms before some of his confidential servants, that two of them, with the idea of pleasing their master, picked a quarrel with the unfortunate comptroller, and wounded him so severely that he died a few hours later.

The Cardinal, furious at the death of his *protégé*, wrote a very angry letter to the Prince de Condé, complaining bitterly of "the disorders and the want of dignity in M. d'Enghien's Household," and demanding that "his conduct should be aided and guided by a single mind." The obsequious prince hastened to reply : " He is *your creature:* do with him what you will." And the luckless Enghien found that he had escaped from the paternal control only to fall under the tyranny of Richelieu, who reorganized his Household, which he filled with persons devoted to his own interests, fixed the number of days which he was to spend in any one place, and regulated everything which concerned him down to the smallest details. No wonder that the young duke was glad when the time arrived for him to rejoin the army of Picardy, with which he took part in the sieges of Aire, La Bassée, and Bapaume !

Although Enghien's manner towards his wife continued very cold, in other respects his conduct, during the remainder of the Cardinal's life, gave his Eminence little cause for complaint. On one occasion only does he appear to have offended the great man, when, thanks to the diplomacy of *Monsieur le Prince*, he was enabled to make atonement. This was in the autumn of

1642, when, on his return from the campaign of Roussillon, he was so ill-advised as to pass by Lyons without visiting the Cardinal Alphonse de Richelieu, Archbishop of Lyons, and brother of the Minister. At the first interview which he had with the latter on his arrival in Paris, the Cardinal inquired after the health of his brother, and it became necessary to acknowledge that he had not been visited. The Cardinal made no remark, but, when the prince had departed, he gave full vent to his feelings, and vowed that he would make him regret the slight he had offered him. The Prince de Condé, informed of what had occurred, was terribly alarmed, and hastened to intercede for his son with the angry Minister, promising that he should make the fullest atonement; and when Enghien joined him at Dijon, he ordered him to return immediately to Lyons, and repair his fault. And so the delinquent found himself obliged to make a long journey in very bad weather, not to Lyons, but to Orange, whither the Cardinal Alphonse had gone, on purpose, it was said, to give the prince the trouble of going further in search of him.

A few weeks later (4 December, 1642), Richelieu succumbed to the one enemy whom he was unable to subjugate, in full possession of all the power and splendour for which he had laboured so unceasingly. Save to his family and his immediate followers, his death brought little regret, for all classes had felt his iron hand; and Enghien, who, since his marriage, had been subjected to such galling restraints, must have felt very much like a boy emancipated from the control of some stern and unbending preceptor. Now, at last, he was free to order his life as he pleased, to follow his taste for pleasure, and to indulge his passion for Mlle. du Vigean.

When the will which the Cardinal had executed some months before at Narbonne was opened, it was found that the Duchesse d'Enghien's brother, Armand de Maille-Brézé, had been left the duchies of Fronsac and Caumont, but that the duchess's hopes—or rather the Condés'—were extinguished by the following clause:

" I make no mention in this will of my niece, the Duchesse

Tres-haulte & Tres puissante princesse CLAIRE-
Clemence de Maillé femme de Monseigneur Louis de
Bourbon Prince De Condé &c Danguien
par son tres humble serviteur Moncornet

CLAIRE CLÉMENCE DE MAILLÉ-BRÉZÉ, PRINCESSE DE CONDÉ

d'Enghien, inasmuch as, by her marriage-contract, she has renounced her claim to my property, in consideration of the dowry I have bestowed upon her, and with which I desire her to be content."

Great was the indignation of the haughty and greedy family into which poor little Claire-Clémence had entered on discovering that the Cardinal had strictly adhered to the conditions which he had imposed at the time of her marriage; and the Prince de Condé lost no time in embarking on a lawsuit against the Duchesse d'Aiguillon, in whose presence the will had been drawn up, and who had benefited largely under it, while her nephew, Armand de Vignerot, was the principal legatee. He pretended that the will had been dictated by the duchess and executed by the Cardinal under the influence of an incestuous passion, and ought, therefore, to be declared void; and counsel on both sides fairly surpassed themselves in the violence of their harangues. A first decision of the Court condemned the Duchesse d'Aiguillon to restore 400,000 livres; but there were so many points to be debated, and the gentlemen of the long robe found the business so very profitable, that it was not until the case had dragged its weary length along for more than thirty years, and *Monsieur le Prince* had been more than a quarter of a century in his grave, that the parties, weary of the interminable litigation, arrived at a settlement (May, 1674).

The Duc d'Enghien, if he eventually showed himself willing enough to profit by it, did not at first take any part in this scandalous lawsuit, and it was his father who directed all the proceedings. His abstention was probably due to the fact that now that the "All-powerful" was no more, he was seriously contemplating an attempt to get his marriage dissolved, on the ground that his consent had been obtained by force while he was still only a boy, after which he intended to marry Marthe du Vigean, and, in view of this, he felt that it would be as well for him not to appear in the case. While awaiting a favourable opportunity for getting rid of the matrimonial fetters, he neglected his poor little wife entirely, notwithstanding that she was now enceinte, and paid such assiduous attentions to the

lady of his heart that they were soon the talk of the Court.
Learning that the Maréchal de Guiche was about to demand
Mlle. du Vigean's hand for his son, the Marquis de Saint-
Mesgrin, great-nephew of Henri III.'s *mignon*, he hastened to
put a stop to this project, and showed himself so violently
jealous of all the damsel's admirers that they scarcely dared to
approach her.

As for the duchess, she attempted no remonstrance, but went
into retreat at the Carmelite convent in the Faubourg Saint-
Jacques, where she remained until the departure of her husband
for the wars.

Enghien had just received the command of the Army of
Flanders, which had been promised him by Richelieu, in
recognition of his fidelity to the Cardinal during the conspiracy
of Cinq-Mars and of the submission to which ambition had
lately prompted him. The Spaniards were laying siege to
Rocroi, a town at the head of the Forest of Ardennes, poorly
fortified and garrisoned, and of considerable strategic importance, since its fall would leave France open to invasion.
Contrary to the advice of the Maréchal de l'Hôpital, who had
been sent to restrain the fiery ardour of the youthful commander,
and counselled him to be content with throwing reinforcements
into the beleaguered town, he determined to give them battle
without delay. The armies met in the plain before Rocroi in
the early morning of 19 May, the same day and almost at the
same hour as Louis XIII., who had died on the 16th, was laid to
rest at Saint-Denis, and, mainly owing to a brilliant cavalry
charge delivered by Enghien at a critical moment, the French
gained a complete victory. The loss of the Spaniards was very
great, while the whole of their baggage and artillery fell into
the hands of the victors.

The news of the victory of Rocroi was received with frantic
delight in Paris. On all sides nothing was heard but praises
of the Duc d'Enghien: of his bravery, his military genius, his
humanity towards the wounded, both victors and vanquished,
and his magnanimity in demanding for his lieutenants all the
rewards of victory, since he himself desired nothing but the

glory. In a single day, he had become a popular hero. The enthusiasm abated only to burst forth again three months later, when intelligence arrived that Thionville had surrendered to the young general, and that the entrance to Germany, by way of the Moselle, lay open to the French.

A few days before Thionville fell, on the evening of 30 July, the little Duchesse d'Enghien gave birth to a very fine boy. "The size of this child is a marvel, in view of the smallness of the mother," writes Perrault to Girard, secretary to the Duc d'Enghien, "and the doctors who have assisted her wonder at it, and are not less astonished at the facility of the accouchement, which has been such that one would suppose that this little one has never done anything else." [1]

Monsieur le Prince at once sent off one of his gentlemen, named La Roussière, to announce the glad tidings to the duke; but Enghien showed no eagerness to express his paternal joy, and, instead of sending the messenger back, kept him to assist at the reduction of Thionville. Nor was it until after the town had capitulated, and Condé had despatched another messenger, informing him that the boy "resembled him and was the most beautiful in the world," that he finally condescended to write a few lines to the young mother.

About the middle of November, the duke returned to Paris to receive the felicitations of his family and friends, and to resume his "chaste amours" with Mlle. du Vigean. His eulogistic historian Désormeaux declares that, on arriving at the Hôtel de Condé and perceiving his son, "his tender and magnanimous soul enjoyed a pleasure more dear and more pure than that of victory"; while the *Gazette* asserts that "to express the pleasure which his [Enghien's] presence had occasioned the Prince de Condé and all his family would be as difficult as to represent the joy which the duke experienced at the sight of the son born to him in the midst of so many laurels and popular acclamations."

It is, however, unnecessary to see in such testimony anything except the blind respect of a *protégé* of the Condés and

[1] Letter of 30 July, 1643, published by the Duc d'Aumale.

the optimism of the editor of an official publication. For the family correspondence proves that, at this time, Enghien certainly gave no indication of the intense affection which he was to bestow upon his son in later years, 'and he took advantage of the fact that the Court was still in mourning for the late king to have him baptized without the customary rejoicings. The child, to whom Mazarin and *Madame la Princesse* stood sponsors, received the name of Henri Jules and took the title of Duc d'Albret.

If the poor Duchesse d'Enghien had anticipated that the birth of her son would prove a link between herself and her husband, she was doomed to disappointment, for she found herself more neglected than ever. Soon after her confinement, she had fallen so seriously ill that the duke had been able for a moment to count upon her death and to look forward to a honeymoon with Mlle. du Vigean ; and it is to be feared that he received the news of her convalescence with very mixed feelings. Disappointed in the hope of receiving any assistance from Nature, he appealed to his mother to use her influence with the Regent to obtain the dissolution of his marriage, and found in her a willing ally.

Madame la Princesse, although she had never forgiven Richelieu the execution of her brother, Henri de Montmorency, whom all her prayers and tears had not sufficed to save, had raised no objection to her son's marriage with his niece, and had, so long as the Cardinal lived, shown the girl every considera-tion. But, since the death of Richelieu, she seemed to have transferred to her innocent daughter-in-law the hatred she had vowed against the Minister, and sought to atone for the hypocritical attitude she had been forced to assume by treating her with the coldest disdain. The prospect of humiliating the family of the man whom she had regarded as her brother's murderer naturally appealed to her, and she lost no time in approaching Anne of Austria on the subject.

The prestige of Enghien was just then so great that it was difficult for the Regent and Mazarin to refuse him anything, and, though Anne expressed her disapproval of the project in unmistakable terms, and Mazarin was anxious to protect the niece of his benefactor, it is quite probable that they would eventually have yielded to pressure, and that the young duchess would have been repudiated by her unscrupulous husband, if the Prince de Condé had not intervened in her favour.

To his honour, be it said, *Monsieur le Prince* had never wavered in his loyalty to the compact which he had made with Richelieu over the Cardinal's niece. If it were not in his nature to show the girl much affection, he understood, at least, how to constitute himself her protector, and had not ceased to employ every means to bring back his son to a wife who was so worthy of his affection. Informed by his daughter, the Duchesse de Longueville—who, though she had hitherto been the sympathetic confidante of her brother and Mlle. du Vigean, had declined to be a party to so discreditable an intrigue—of the projects which were being discussed in his family, he showed the utmost indignation. Sending for Enghien and Mlle. du Vigean, " he said a thousand cruel things to both lover and mistress," after which he advised the duke to return to his military duties as speedily as possible. The latter obeyed, and, shortly afterwards, bade a touching farewell to his lady-love[1] and set out for the army.

In August 1544, Enghien added to the laurels he had gained at Rocroi in three days' sanguinary fighting before Freiburg, and a year later gained the victory of Nördlingen over the Imperialists. In the latter engagement he was wounded, and an attack of fever which supervened nearly cost him his life. In the autumn he returned to Paris, in a very weak state of health, when, as a general rule, man is particularly susceptible to feminine blandishments. The astonishment of his friends and the despair of poor Mlle. du Vigean may, therefore, be imagined, when it was perceived that he seemed to regard the girl whom he had once so passionately loved with as much indifference " as if he had never heard her voice."

To what are we to attribute so sudden a revulsion of feeling ?

---

[1] According to some chroniclers, such was his emotion at parting from his inamorata, that he fell down in a swoon at her feet.

The ingenuous Désormeaux ascribes it to the fact that "his love had vanished with the prodigious quantity of blood that had been taken from him"; others to the effect of the paternal remonstrances. But the most probable reason is that, with increasing years and experience of life, common-sense had at last asserted itself, and that, in despair either of obtaining the dissolution of his marriage or of overcoming the virtuous scruples of his inamorata, he had decided no longer to abandon himself to a passion which could have no other result than that of troubling his peace of mind.

It is possible, however, that he may have been prompted by a more worthy motive. Finding that his equivocal attentions had somewhat compromised the lady, while, on the other hand, her devotion to himself had caused her to reject the honourable advances of more than one highly eligible suitor, he may at length have awakened to a sense of the selfishness of his conduct and have determined to yield his place to some one with a better right.

If such were the reason of his withdrawal, the sacrifice was a vain one. Marthe du Vigean, though she permitted no complaint to escape her, remained inconsolable. She turned a deaf ear to Saint-Mesgrin and other suitors, who crowded round her as soon as the brusque retreat of Enghien was known, and resolved to become the bride of the Church. Lest, however, the resolution which she meditated should be deemed by the world the "outcome of grief or of mortification," she took no immediate steps to carry it out, and for some time continued to receive the visits of her friends, even of those who had been the witnesses of her passion. But, at length, in the summer of 1547, ignoring the counsels and entreaties of her relatives, she quitted her father's house and took refuge with the Carmelites of the Rue Saint-Jacques, whither the poor little Duchesse d'Enghien had been accustomed to repair, on account of her, to appease her jealousy and find resignation. Anne du Vigean, the future Duchesse de Richelieu, in a letter to her brother, the Marquis de Fors, gives an interesting picture of her sister's last days in the world :

"   . We went to Rueil, where we spoke every day of the affair [Marthe du Vigean's resolution to become a nun], and where many tears were shed ; and the conclusion arrived at was that, at any rate, nothing should be done for six months, my mother hoping, in asking this delay of her, that she might be able to induce her to alter her mind.   Finally, we returned here, because I was very ill ; I had fever so badly that I did not move from my bed.   One fine day, she said to me : 'Sister, I shall not give them all the time I promised, for I shall go before another week has passed ! '   I begged her to give me time to write to my mother, in order that she might come and speak to her, since I was not strong enough to retain or to counsel her. I wrote, accordingly, ill though I was.   In the meanwhile, I had sent to the Hôtel de Longueville to learn your news [the news from the army], because I had been told that a courier had arrived, and Madame de Longueville wrote to me to send for it ; and at the end of her letter she asked my sister to go and see her.   She went out, therefore, to go thither, and when she had gone half the distance, told her people that she must turn aside to the 'Grandes Carmélites,'[1] but that she had only a word to say to them.   She made them turn her carriage and went thither, where she is still and does not intend to come out. My mother arrived an hour later. . . .   My father wished to kill every one, all the Missionaries and Carmelites in the world, but he is beginning to be somewhat appeased.   I go to see her every day ; she is merry and resolute, and watches me weeping without shedding a tear."[2]

Marthe du Vigean seems to have been very happy in her new life, and declared that she would not change her condition to be empress of the whole world.[3]   She made profession in 1649, and took the name of Sœur Marthe de Jésus.   She held the

---

[1] There were two convents of Carmelite nuns in Paris at this period, one in the Faubourg Saint-Jacques, the other in the Rue Chapon.   The first, which was the parent-house of the order in France, was known as the "Grandes Carmélites."

[2] Published by MM. Homberg et Jousselin, "la Femme du Grand Condé."

[3] Letter of Mère Agnes de Jésus, Prioress of the Carmelites of the Faubourg Saint-Jacques, to Mlle. d'Épernon, cited by Victor Cousin, "la Jeunesse de Madame de Longueville."

office of sub-prioress from 1659–1662, and died three years later, at the age of forty-four.

The peace of the cloister had descended upon her, but the memory of her grace and beauty lingered long in the world she had quitted:

> "Lorsque Vigean quitta la Cour,
> Les Jeux, les Grâces, les Amours
> Entrèrent dans le monastère.
>   Laire la laire, lon lère
>   Laire la laire, lon la.
>
> Les Jeux pleurèrent ce jour-la ;
> Ce jour-là la beauté se voilà
> Et fit vœu d'être solitaire
> .   .   .   .   .   .[1]"

The man whom she had loved with such devotion did not seek to see her again, but always preserved for her "a recollection full of respect."[2]

---

[1] Voiture.   [2] Lenet, "Mémoires."

CHAPTER XV

Notwithstanding his rupture with Mlle. du Vigean, the Duc d'Enghien continues to treat his wife with coldness—The heart of the prince is fiercely disputed by the ladies of the Court—Dissipated life of Enghien : paternal remonstrances—*Liaison* between the duke and Ninon de l'Enclos—Death of Henri II. de Bourbon, Prince de Condé—Failure of the new Prince de Condé before Lerida—His brilliant victory at Lens—Beginning of the Fronde—Condé remains faithful to the Court, and takes command of the royal troops—The Duchesse de Châtillon becomes his mistress—Peace of Rueil—The arrogance and ambition of Condé causes the Court and the Frondeurs to join forces against him—The arrest of the Princes—The Princesse de Condé at Bordeaux—Death of the dowager-princess—Equivocal conduct of Madame de Châtillon—Episode of an unaddressed letter—Exile of Mazarin and release of the Princes—Continued indifference of Condé towards his wife, notwithstanding her courageous efforts on his behalf—Negotiations between him and the Regent—His rupture with the Frondeurs, who draw towards the Court—Condé retires to Saint-Maur—Alliance between the Court and the Frondeurs—Proceedings against Condé—The prince retires to Montrond and "draws the sword."

THE brusque and unexpected rupture of the Duc d'Enghien with Marthe du Vigean for a moment encouraged the hope of a better understanding between the prince and the legitimate object of his affections. Although she could not, of course, compare in outward attractions with Mlle. du Vigean, the little duchess, now in her eighteenth year, had improved greatly in appearance since her marriage, and, if not regularly pretty, she was, with her open countenance, her fine dark eyes, her beautiful complexion, and her trim figure, a decidedly pleasing personality. Moreover, she was highly intelligent, conversing well and agreeably on a number of subjects, and showing a good sense and a keenness of observation beyond her years, possessed a singularly sweet disposition, and was, notwithstanding the indifference with which her husband had treated her, sincerely attached to him.

Unhappily, this hope proved illusive, for Enghien did not depart from that studiously courteous but cold and distant attitude which he had adopted towards his wife from the first day of his marriage. The poor little duchess was bitterly disappointed, but she had schooled herself to suffer in silence, and courageously refused to allow the world to perceive how keenly she felt her husband's neglect. Fresh trials, however, awaited her. Hitherto, she had, at least, had the consolation of believing that Enghien was still faithful to his marriage-vows, in deed, if not in thought, for the virtue of Mlle. du Vigean had proved a more impregnable fortress than Thionville, and his passion for her seems to have preserved him from the wiles of more facile beauties. But now even this was to be denied her. The moment it became known that Enghien had broken definitely with Mlle. du Vigean, the heart over which the latter had so long reigned supreme was fiercely disputed by the ladies of the Court, and the young hero became the object of the most singular advances. The majestic Duchesse de Montbazon,[1] the fire of whose splendid eyes "penetrated even the most insensible hearts,"[2] charged their common friend, the Duc de Rohan, to acquaint the prince with the sentiments which she entertained for him. Mlle. de Neuillant, afterwards Duchesse de Navailles, one of the Queen-Mother's *filles d'honneur*, made similar overtures, with more diplomacy, but with equal ardour, and left no means untried to engage the affections of his Highness. But neither of these ladies appear to have made much impression upon their quarry, and it was a colleague of Mlle. de Neuillant, the charming Louise de Prie, Mlle. de Toussy, who came nearest to success. For some little time Enghien paid her the most assiduous attentions, and negotiations of a very equivocal nature were carried on between the prince and the damsel's relatives, through the medium of the Chevalier de la Rivière. But, either because Mlle. de Toussy's

---

[1] Marie de Bretagne, daughter of the Comte de Vertus, and wife of Hercule de Rohan, Duc de Montbazon.

[2] Madame de Motteville, "Mémoires."

family was inclined to be too exorbitant in its demands upon Enghien's generosity, or, more probably, because she herself was only willing to be a mistress in the poetic acceptation of the term, the ducal ardour soon cooled, and the young lady consoled herself for her admirer's defection by marrying the Duc de la Mothe-Houdancourt.

But, if no woman were permitted to succeed to the place which Marthe du Vigean had occupied in Enghien's affections, the ardent nature which he had inherited together with the courage of his ancestors soon found satisfaction in amours of a less sentimental character, and his life became so dissipated that, during the summer of 1646, the Prince de Condé felt obliged to remonstrate with him in the strongest terms. "My son," he writes, "God bless you. Cure yourself, or, it is better to poniard yourself than lead the life that you are doing. . . . I pray God to console me. I write to you in despair, and am, Monsieur, your good father and friend. . . . "[1]

The Duc d'Enghien did not poniard himself, but neither did he amend his ways to any appreciable extent. His conquests in the *pays de tendre* far outnumbered those beyond the Rhine, but the very ease with which they were achieved deprived them of all value in his eyes and speedily quenched the flame of passion : indeed, the only woman to whose charms he seems to have been really sensible was the celebrated Ninon de l'Enclos, to whom his attention seems first to have been drawn by the enthusiastic praises of their common friend Saint-Évremond. For a year or two the prince was a frequent visitor at Ninon's hôtel in the Rue des Tournelles, and the lady, whose vanity was flattered by the admiration of the hero of the hour, was very kind to him indeed. But it was not in Ninon's nature to be faithful to any one for long—" I shall love you for three months," she once wrote to a new admirer, "and three months is an eternity ! "— and, besides, the victor of Rocroi made war a great deal better than he made love, and preferred to receive homage rather than to offer it. So gradually her affection cooled, and when the

[1] Letter of 18 August, 1646, Archives de Chantilly, cited by MM. Homberg and Jousselin, " la Femme du Grand Condé."

prince, on his return from the campaign of 1648, reproached her for having encouraged the intrigue between his sister Madame Longueville and La Rochefoucauld, and for permitting the lovers to meet at her house, she dismissed him and consoled herself with the Marquis de Villarceaux, who had long sued for her favours.

At the beginning of December, the Prince de Condé, who had been in failing health for the last eighteen months, was taken seriously ill, and at midnight on the 26th he died, in his fifty-seventh year. He made, we are assured, a very Christian end, in the presence of his wife and his two sons—Madame de Longueville had followed her husband to the Congress of Münster—and "parted from *Madame la Princesse* as though he had loved her all his life." [1] In his will, he left large sums to the poor, "deeming it incumbent upon him to restore the profits of the benefices that he had wrongly enjoyed," and even the humblest of his servants was not forgotten. His body was interred in the parish church of Valery ; his heart he bequeathed to the Jesuits of the Rue Saint-Antoine, an example which was followed by his descendants.

Morose and bigoted, self-seeking and avaricious, the third Prince de Condé is far from an attractive personality. Nevertheless, his death was a sensible loss both to his family and to France. Selfish and turbulent though his conduct had been during the regency of Marie de' Medici, when once he had decided that his own interests would be better served by loyalty than by opposition to the Crown, he certainly spared no effort to deserve the important offices and immense pensions which were the reward of his fidelity ; and the steady support he gave to Anne of Austria and Mazarin since the beginning of the new reign had been of the highest value to the Government. "As sparing of the King's money as his own," writes the Duc d'Aumale, "his ideas on financial matters were sound ; he desired that the public debts should be regularly discharged, and opposed extravagance and the constant augmentation of expenses, as well as increased taxation. He inspired confidence

[1] Madame de Motteville, "Mémoires."

NINON DE L'ENCLOS

in serious men of affairs, who never wished to conclude a treaty when he did not assist at the Council. The quack financiers, the d'Émeris and the rest, feared him and rejoiced at his death. They played a fine game after he was gone." [1]

His authority over his family was absolute. His children, if they did not love him, both feared and respected him, and to the last Enghien, so impatient of all control, showed towards his father the greatest deference. Had Henri de Bourbon lived a few years longer, his sound common-sense would certainly have saved them from the disasters they brought upon themselves and France ; and the Fronde might have been, after all, merely " a blaze of straw."

Charlotte de Montmorency had the enjoyment for her life of the whole of her deceased husband's property, subject only to an annual charge of 80,000 livres in favour of her elder son, and 10,000 in favour of the younger. This arrangement was no doubt a just one, seeing that the large fortune which his wife brought him had been the basis of Henri de Bourbon's great wealth. But it, nevertheless, weighed very hardly on his suc- cessor, who had received comparatively little with Mlle. de Brézé, and, being as liberal as his father was the reverse, soon found himself seriously embarrassed to maintain his position as first Prince of the Blood, notwithstanding the revenues he derived from his offices and governments.

In the spring of 1647, the new Prince de Condé was despatched to Catalonia to endeavour to retrieve the reverses sustained in that province, which had of late years earned an unenviable notoriety as the grave of French military reputations. He determined to lay siege to the fortress of Lerida, and, on 18 May, the trenches were opened gaily to the sound of violins. It was a fashion of the time, which made of a war a fête ; but it was the hitherto invincible general who had, on this occasion, to pay the expenses of the music ; for Lerida was resolutely defended, while the supplies and siege-artillery promised him by the Government did not arrive, and, after severe losses, he

[1] " Histoire des Princes de Condé."

decided to raise the siege. Condé deserved credit for having placed the safety of his army before his pride; but it was his first reverse, and, though he was aware that he had done everything possible to ensure success, his mortification was none the less keen.

The memory of the Catalonian fiasco was brilliantly effaced in the following year, when, in command of the Army of Flanders, he gained, with comparatively trifling loss, the splendid victory of Lens, over an enemy much superior in numbers, whom, by a feigned retreat, he had succeeded in drawing from an almost unassailable position into a battle on level ground (20 August). This success hastened the conclusion of peace with the Emperor, and, on 24 October, 1648, the Treaty of Westphalia terminated thirty years of war and twelve years of negotiations, and extended the frontiers of France to the coveted line of the Rhine.

Left with Spain alone to face, there seemed every reason to hope that a great future awaited France, and that, as the result of two or three successful campaigns, she would be enabled to secure the same advantages in the North-East and South-West as she had already secured in the East. That this hope was only very partially realized, and that not until after more than ten years of further warfare, was due to that miserable internecine strife which, under the name of the Fronde, checked the victorious career of Condé at the age of twenty-seven, plunged France into a welter of anarchy, and sapped the very vitals of the nation.

This sanguinary and farcical struggle began with a contest between the Court and the Parlement of Paris, which, encouraged by the weakness of the Government and backed by popular feeling, was neglecting its judicial duties to encroach upon the political rights of the Crown and to claim an authority which even the States-General had never possessed. The " Importants " —the aristocratic cabal, headed by the two great turbulent Houses of Vendôme and Guise, which from the beginning of the regency had bitterly opposed the ascendency of Mazarin—and a number of discontented and ambitious princes, prelates, nobles and great ladies: Paul de Gondi, afterwards the Cardinal de Retz, La Rochefoucauld, the Duc and Duchesse de Longueville, the Prince de Conti, Turenne, and the Duc and Duchesse de Bouillon, threw in their lot with the popular cause.

Although Condé detested Mazarin and sympathized to a large extent with the opposition to the Minister, and though Madame de Longueville, who exercised great influence over both her brothers, made every effort to win him over to her cause, the sentiment of duty, which was not yet obscured, kept him faithful to the Court, and to the solicitations of the rebels he replied simply: "My name is Louis de Bourbon, and I do not wish to weaken the Crown." An admirable maxim, which, however, he was very soon to abandon.

In the early morning of 6 January, the Court quitted Paris for Saint-Germain, a picturesque exodus of which the pen of *la Grande Mademoiselle* has traced an inimitable picture, and the rebellious capital was forthwith invested by the royal troops, under the command of Condé. The forces at the prince's disposal were, however, insufficient to invest the city completely, and, though some roads were effectually closed, others remained open. Occasional skirmishes took place, but the only serious fighting occurred at Charenton on 8 February. In this affair, the Duc de Châtillon, husband of the beautiful Isabelle de Montmorency-Boutteville, was mortally wounded and expired the following day at Vincennes, whither he had been carried. With his death, the male line of the illustrious Admiral became extinct.

The widowed duchess received the sad news with comparative indifference, but, according to Madame de Motteville, "counterfeited grief, after the manner of ladies who love themselves too well to care for any one else." She had not, indeed, waited for the death of her husband to establish tender relations with the fascinating Duc de Nemours, and was already aspiring to resume over the heart of Condé the empire which she had for a brief while exercised in former years.[1] Hitherto, the prince would

---

[1] It must be admitted that she had some excuse for her conduct, as the deceased duke had been far from a faithful husband, and had gone into his last fight with a garter of his lady-love, Mlle. de Guerchy, bound round his arm.

appear to have given the lady but scant encouragement, for, though very far from indifferent to her charms, Châtillon was one of his closest friends, and the idea of engaging in a *liaison* with his wife was repugnant to his sense of honour. But, with the death of the duke, his scruples vanished, and not long afterwards Isabelle became his mistress, without, however, renouncing the Duc de Nemours, her relations with whom she was, of course, very careful to conceal from her titular lover.

On 12 March, 1649, the Peace of Rueil put an end to the war, though it was not until 18 August that the Court returned to Paris, after an absence of seven and a half months.

To the Parliamentary Fronde succeeded, at a short interval, the Fronde of the Princes, more difficult to characterize, since it was composed of little save disappointed ambitions and interested calculations, but also more difficult to conquer. The good understanding between *Monsieur le Prince* and Mazarin had been merely of a temporary nature, called into being by the danger to which the royal authority had found itself exposed, and it did not long survive the restoration of order. Condé's natural pride and arrogance had been enormously increased by the events of the last few months, and he believed his support absolutely indispensable to the Government. The Regent and her Minister were willing to go to great lengths to secure a continuance of it, but no ordinary concessions were likely to satisfy a man who regarded himself as the saviour of the Crown, and believed that he held its fate in the hollow of his hand, and whose jealous and suspicious mind, skilfully played upon by his sister, seemed to see in every action of Mazarin a carefully calculated move to strengthen the Cardinal's position or to diminish his own prestige. His increasing pretensions rendered him more of a rebel than the Frondeurs themselves ; his arrogance disgusted every one. He exacted from Mazarin a written agreement whereby he undertook not to make any appointment of importance in Church or State unless he had first been consulted, or to arrange any marriage for his nephews and nieces without his consent.

" In his ordinary life he had such mocking airs that no one was able to endure him. However high their rank, people were obliged to wait an interminable time in *Monsieur le Prince's* ante-chamber. In the visits which were paid him he manifested so disdainful an ennui, that he showed plainly that they were wearying him."[1]   Finally, having exasperated the Regent and Mazarin beyond endurance, while, at the same time, he had contrived to alienate the Frondeurs, who had been eager for his alliance, the latter and the Court joined forces against him, and, on 18 January, 1650, he, with his brother, the Prince de Conti, and the Duc de Longueville, were arrested at the Palais-Royal, whither they had come to attend a meeting of the Council, and conducted to the Château of Vincennes. Madame de Longueville, whose arrest had also been determined upon, succeeded in making her escape to her husband's government of Normandy.

Anne of Austria and Mazarin appear to have been in some doubt whether to arrest the two Princesses de Condé, with the little Duc d'Enghien, then between six and seven years old.[2] " But considering," says Lenet, " that the dowager was a princess of a timid and indolent disposition, and that the young princess was without friends, without money, and without experience, and not very well satisfied with the conduct of the prince, her husband, they had decided merely to order them to retire to Chantilly."

In sparing the young princess, they committed a grave error, for Claire-Clémence concealed beneath her gentle and retiring nature great courage and energy of character, which only awaited the occasion to manifest themselves. While all her *entourage* were bewailing the misfortune which had befallen them, she thought only of effecting her husband's liberation. The Duc de la Rochefoucauld had formed a plan of resistance in the South, always ready to rise in insurrection on the smallest provocation, and had united his fortunes to those of his powerful neighbour, the Duc de Bouillon. The two dukes

[1] Duchesse de Nemours, "Mémoires."
[2] On his father becoming Prince de Condé, the little Duc d'Albret had assumed the title of Duc d'Enghien.

determined to link to the cause of the imprisoned princes that of the citizens of Bordeaux, who had been for months past in a state of semi-revolt against the tyranny of their detested governor, the Duc d'Épernon ; and La Rochefoucauld despatched his confidant, Gourville, to Chantilly, to inform the Princesse de Condé of their intentions. The courageous princess at once determined to join them, and, with the aid of Lenet, on the night of 11–12 April, 1650, she and the little Duc d'Enghien escaped from Chantilly and made their way to Montrond, and thence to Bouillon's château of Turenne, in the Limousin.

The gentry of the South flocked to offer their services to the princess, who soon found herself at the head of a considerable force ; and at the end of May she appeared before Bordeaux. The Parlement and the municipal authorities hesitated to receive her, in the face of the formal prohibition of the King ; but the populace, incited by the agents of Bouillon and La Rochefoucauld, took the matter out of their hands, flung open the gates and welcomed her with frantic enthusiasm. The following day, leading her son by the hand, she presented herself at the Palais de Justice, to implore the protection of the Parlement. "Act as a father to me, Messieurs, since the Cardinal Mazarin has taken my own father from me," cried the little duke, falling upon his knees ; and the magistrates, partly out of compassion for this touching spectacle, and partly out of fear of the mob which was clamouring at the doors, voted that "the dame Princesse de Condé and the seigneur Duc d'Enghien might reside in that town in safety under the protection of the laws."

Next day, notwithstanding the protests of the Parlement, Bouillon and La Rochefoucauld entered the city, borne, so to speak, on the shoulders of the mob. Soon appeared a Spanish envoy, with promises of prompt and powerful assistance from Philip IV. ; and Bordeaux and the greater part of Guienne were in open rebellion.

The revolt in Guienne quickly assumed such alarming proportions that Mazarin decided that the presence of the King and the Regent in that province was indispensable, and having left the Maréchal du Plessis-Praslin to hold in check the insurrection in the North, on 4 July, the Court quitted Paris to join the royal army of the South, commanded by the Maréchal de la Meilleraie. La Meilleraie soon succeeded in confining the revolt within the walls of Bordeaux, but all attempts to induce the city to open its gates proved unavailing, and on 5 September the siege was begun.

While the novelty of the affair lasted, the Bordelais displayed the most desperate resolution. Encouraged by the example of the Princesse de Condé, even the wives of the wealthiest citizens took part in the defence of the town, and carried baskets of earth decorated with bows of ribbon to the trenches. The little Duc d'Enghien rode to the ramparts and cried to his attendants to give him a sword, "that he might go and kill Mazarin." Bouillon and La Rochefoucauld directed the defence-works, and, as if the siege had been a pleasure-party, "regaled the ladies with fruit and sweetmeats and the workmen with wine." Every evening there was dancing under the ramparts, and the Princesse de Condé held a court in a brilliantly-illuminated gallery. The festivities, indeed, were continuous, notwithstanding that skirmishes, often very sanguinary, took place almost daily.

However, the assistance promised by Spain did not arrive ; the better-class citizens soon grew tired of a struggle into which they had been forced against their better judgment ; while the bellicose ardour of the populace was cooled by the scarcity of provisions. Moreover, the season of the vintage was approaching, and to lose the chief crop of the year would be nothing short of disaster. Perceiving how matters were tending, the Princesse de Condé resolved to anticipate the surrender which she felt was imminent, and, on 11 September, proceeded to the Hôtel de Ville, where the city fathers were assembled in conclave, and informed them that, "since she sought only their satisfaction and tranquillity, she would do nothing to hinder the peace which they might be able to conclude with the Cardinal."

The authorities took her at her word ; and, on 1 October,

articles of peace were signed between the Regent and the insur-
gents, whereby a full and complete amnesty was granted the
Bordelais, on condition that the King and his troops were
admitted to the town; while the Princesse de Condé, Bouillon,
and La Rochefoucauld were permitted to retire to their estates
in the full enjoyment of all their dignities, on the promise
that they would lay down their arms and "continue henceforth in fidelity and obedience." It was also agreed that the
Duc d'Épernon should be temporarily suspended from his
duties as governor of the province. The treaty contained no
mention of the Princes, although the revolt had been made
in their name and for their deliverance.

On 3 October, the Princesse de Condé and her son sailed
from Bordeaux, "amid a rain of flowers," and proceeded to
Bourg-sur-Mer, where the Court had taken up its residence.
Claire-Clémence went to salute Anne of Austria, and, throwing
herself at the Queen's feet, demanded pardon for her husband.
Her Majesty received her very kindly and made her sit by
her side, but her answer to the princess's petition was not
very encouraging. "I am well pleased, my cousin," said she,
"that you acknowledge your fault; you have taken a bad
way to obtain what you ask for; now that you intend to take
a different one, I will see when and how I can give you the
satisfaction you desire."

While Condé's neglected wife was promoting insurrections
and confronting the perils and hardships of war in her
husband's interests, his mistress was very differently employed.
The Dowager-Princesse de Condé, although she was still
only in her fifty-fourth year and had hitherto enjoyed excellent
health, had not been able to survive the misfortunes of her
House. As sensible to the present disgrace of the children
whom she so fondly loved as she had been to their former
triumphs, she¹ had grieved over it to such a degree that she
fell seriously ill, and died on 2 December, 1650, at Châtillon-
sur-Loing, the residence of the Duchesse de Châtillon, to which
she had obtained permission to retire.

During her last days, the old princess had fallen very much

under the influence of Madame de Châtillon, who, as avaricious as she was unprincipled, had determined to obtain a share of her property. In this she was but too successful "The Duchesse de Châtillon, who was the most astute woman in the world," observes Lenet, "had so well understood how to employ her adroit and subtle mind and her agreeable and insinuating manners as to make herself so completely mistress of the princess-dowager, that she saw only with her eyes and spoke only with her mouth."

It was with the idea of separating the old princess from all the friends and servants who might endeavour to frustrate her designs that the duchess had persuaded her to take up her residence at Châtillon-sur-Loing, where she was careful not to permit any one to approach her, except Madame de Bourgneuf, the *gouvernante* of Madame de Longueville's children, and *Madame la Princesse's* confessor, a worldly and intriguing abbé named Cambriac, both of whom she had succeeded in gaining over to her cause. The outcome of these manœuvres was that the dowager bequeathed to Madame de Châtillon nearly the whole of her jewellery—in itself a respectable fortune—and the revenues for life of several of her estates, including that of Merlou, near Pontoise.

The young Princesse de Condé was at the Château of Montrond, whither she had proceeded on leaving Guienne, when she learned of the death of her mother-in-law. Well aware of the rapacity of the fair Isabelle, she at once despatched Lenet to Châtillon to watch over her husband's interests ; and this intervention obliged the impatient legatee to make a journey to Montrond to ask the princess's permission to take possession of the jewellery bequeathed to her. The interview between the two ladies was rendered the more piquant by an incident which afforded Claire-Clémence an opportunity for enjoying a malicious triumph over the too-coquettish mistress of her husband.

Before the arrival of Madame de Châtillon at Montrond, a courier arrived from Paris, bearing a packet without any super-scription, which was brought to the Princesse de Condé and opened by her. It contained a tender letter for the duchess from her *amant de cœur*, the Duc de Nemours, in which he assured her that, since her departure from Paris, he was changed to the point of being no longer recognizable, and was gradually pining away. To these lamentations the lovelorn nobleman joined some very practical counsels, advising his inamorata to take possession of the estate of Merlou—which, as we have mentioned, the late princess had left her for life—before Condé was set at liberty. Claire-Clémence had the satisfaction of handing this missive to her rival, when the latter arrived at Montrond a day or two afterwards. But Madame de Châtillon, so far from exhibiting the confusion which she had anticipated, declared, with superb audacity, that the letter was a forgery, since M. de Nemours was nothing but a mere acquaintance. Notwithstanding these denials, the story of the letter had a great success, and circulated through all the *ruelles*, where Madame de Châtillon was unmercifully bantered about it. However, she could well afford to disregard these railleries, since Condé, too much enamoured not to forgive the equivocal part she had played towards the dowager-princess, showed no intention of disputing the will, and sent instructions to his wife to authorize her to take possession of Merlou.

Notwithstanding the suppression of the revolt in Guienne and the crushing defeat inflicted on the rebels and Spaniards by Du Plessis-Praslin at Rethel (9 December, 1650), the party of the Princes gained adherents every day, while the unpopularity of Mazarin steadily increased. The Old Fronde, which he had alienated by his refusal to accede to their exhorbitant demands, made common cause with the friends of Condé, and persuaded the fickle Gaston d'Orléans, the King's uncle, to side with them. Encouraged by them, the Parlement loudly demanded the liberation of the Princes and the dismissal of the Cardinal, and the Regent in vain endeavoured to defend her Minister. By the middle of February, 1561, Mazarin was on his way into exile, and Condé was a free man once more.

As soon as she was informed of the approaching liberation of her husband, the princess had made preparations to set out for Paris and bid him welcome at the Hôtel de Condé, but she was suddenly taken ill and obliged to remain at Montrond. Such, however, was her impatience to rejoin him that, while still barely convalescent, she insisted on starting on her journey, travelling the first part of the way in a litter. After having given her husband so many proofs of love and devotion, after having supported with so much courage so many trials and dangers for his sake, it was but natural that she should have expected some return on his part; and, for the moment, it indeed seemed as though Condé was by no means insensible to the noble conduct of the princess. He came to meet her as far as Sainte-Geneviève-des-Bois, near Montchéry, assured her that henceforth he should devote himself entirely to her, and desired that she should make a sort of triumphal entry into Paris in his own carriage, and sitting by his side. But, though he was probably sincere enough at the time, the supreme selfishness of his character rendered him incapable of any lasting gratitude, and very soon the astute Madame de Châtillon had resumed her former empire over him, and the poor princess found herself almost as neglected as ever.

Unlike his father, Condé did not learn wisdom from adversity. The turbulence of the third Prince de Condé had, as we have seen, been effectually cooled by the three years' imprisonment he had suffered in the early part of the previous reign; but Louis de Bourbon was entirely destitute of the prudence which had tempered his father's greed and ambition. His year of confinement seemed only to have accentuated that impatience of all control, that haughtiness of manner, and that contemptuous disregard for the feelings and opinions of others which he had always shown. Restored to liberty, in circumstances which seemed to promise him an almost undisputed ascendency, he returned to Paris more than ever determined to carry matters with a high hand. But, to exercise the power which he desired, the maintenance of the alliance between the Old Fronde and the party of the Princes, which had opened his prison doors and procured the exile of Mazarin, was essential, and Condé, though possessed of the highest military gifts, had none of the qualities necessary for successful political leadership.

Anne of Austria, on the advice of her exiled Minister, with whom she was in constant communication, sought to break up the combination between the two Frondes by a *rapprochement* with Condé, and secret negotiations were accordingly opened with the prince. The latter, who cared nothing for his new allies, professed himself ready to give or rather to sell his support to the Court, and even to consent to the return of Mazarin ; but the price he demanded would have rendered him the virtual sovereign of the South of France. Acting always on Mazarin's instructions, Anne encouraged the belief that these preposterous terms would eventually be accorded, until Condé had completely alienated the Old Fronde, by breaking off the marriage arranged between his brother Conti and Mlle. de Chevreuse, which had been one of the conditions of their alliance. The Old Fronde, indignant at the prince's bad faith, drew towards the Court, and, on the night of 5-6 July, 1651, Condé, in the belief that his liberty, if not his life, was threatened, fled to Saunt-Maur. *Madame la Princesse* and her son, Conti, Madame de Longueville, and a number of his partisans followed him, and he had soon "a Court which was not less imposing than that of the King."

His more prudent supporters urged him to be reconciled to the Regent, who had sent to assure him that his retreat had been due to an entire misapprehension. But Madame de Longueville and others were in favour of an open rupture with the Court, and the prince's impetuosity of character and ambitious views inclined him to the same course. However, he was not yet prepared for an armed struggle against the royal authority, and, having despatched his wife and son and Madame de Longueville to Montrond, he returned to Paris and entered into negotiations with the Queen. But his demands were so outrageous and his conduct so insolent that the exasperated Queen decided to transform without delay the understanding which she had had for some weeks past with the Frondeurs into a definite alliance, and towards the middle of August articles of agreement between the two parties were drawn up and signed.

Being now assured of the co-operation of the Frondeurs,

Anne felt strong enough for an open struggle with Condé, and, having engaged Retz to maintain her cause in the Parlement, she, on 17 August, launched against the Prince a declaration, in which she charged him with ingratitude, contempt for the royal authority, criminal alliances with the enemies of the realm, and a desire to subvert the State. These charges led to violent scenes at the Palais de Justice, in one of which Retz narrowly escaped being assassinated by some of Condé's friends. They were not, however, pressed; indeed, on 5 September, the Queen, on the mediation of Gaston d'Orléans, sent to the Parlement a letter formally exonerating the prince. But, under the pretext of giving more solemnity to the decree, she requested that it should not be promulgated until after the majority of Louis XIV., which he would attain on the following day, on completing his thirteenth year, the age fixed by the laws of France for the majority of her kings.

Condé excused himself, by letter, from assisting at the proclamation of his Sovereign's majority, on the ground that his enemies had rendered him so odious in his Majesty's eyes that he could not be present without danger; and while the King, in the midst of a magnificent *cortège*, was wending his way through the cheering crowds to the Palais de Justice, the first Prince of the Blood, whose place should have been by his side, was hastening to his brother-in-law's château of Trie in Normandy, with the object of persuading the Duc de Longueville to join him in resistance to the royal authority. He came, however, on a bootless errand, for Longueville, unlike his consort, had had enough of civil war, and declared that he was not in a position to render him any effective support.

From Trie, Condé proceeded to Chantilly, whence he sent an envoy to Louis XIV., offering to return to the capital, if the changes in the Ministry which he understood that it was his Majesty's intention to make were deferred for three days. But the young King haughtily refused even to consider this proposition. The prince thereupon summoned a meeting of his partisans at Chantilly; but, now that he had actually come to the very verge of the abyss, he found many reasons to deter him from taking the final step : his reluctance to plunge his country into the miseries of another civil strife ; the many defections in his party, for to make war on the King of France was a very different matter from resisting the will of a Spanish regent and an Italian minister ; the danger of placing any reliance on the promises of help he had received from Spain ; and, finally, the knowledge that war would mean an indefinite separation from Madame de Châtillon, of whom he was more than ever enamoured, and who, having been gained by the Court, had been using all her influence to bring her lover to a more pacific frame of mind.

At length, fearing that, if he remained longer at Chantilly, he might be arrested, he decided to withdraw to his government of Berry, and on 13 September arrived at Montrond. Here, two days later, a final conference was held, and the bellicose Madame de Longueville succeeded in triumphing over her brother's last scruples. It was then that Condé uttered the prediction so often quoted, and which was to prove so true : "You compel me to draw the sword. Well, let it be so. Remember that I shall be the last to replace it in its scabbard."

CHAPTER XVI

Condé proceeds to Bordeaux, where he is rejoined by his relatives—He opens the campaign with success, but is soon obliged to remain on the defensive—Return of Mazarin—Condé on the Loire—Battle of Bléneau—He leaves his army and proceeds to Paris—His futile negotiations—Battle of the Faubourg Saint-Antoine—Massacre of the Hôtel de Ville—The Fronde grows daily more discredited—Condé quits Paris and joins the Spaniards on the Flemish frontier—The Fronde at Bordeaux—Sanguinary affrays between the *Ormée* and the *Chapeau Rouge*—Courage and presence of mind displayed by the Princesse de Condé and Madame de Longueville in separating the combatants—Surrender of Bordeaux—The princess sails for Flanders to rejoin her husband—Her reception at Valenciennes—She is cruelly neglected by Condé—She removes from Valenciennes to Malines—Her miserable existence—Condé applies to the Spanish Court for financial assistance—Brilliant military qualities displayed by him in the service of his country's enemies—The princess gives birth to a daughter—Peace of the Pyrenees—Return of Condé and his wife to France.

THE fatal resolution once taken, Condé acted with his customary vigour and decision. He despatched Lenet to Madrid to conclude a treaty with Spain; wrote to his staunch adherent, the Comte de Marsin, who commanded in Catalonia, begging him to join him in Guienne with all the troops he could induce to follow him, and directed his brother and sister and the Duc de Nemours to proceed to Bourges and endeavour to incite that town and the whole of Berry to revolt. Then, accompanied by La Rochefoucauld, he set out for Bordeaux, which he had resolved to make his headquarters.

Condé was received at Bordeaux with transports of joy, and the town and the greater part of the province at once rose in revolt. But Madame de Longueville and Conti failed entirely in the task entrusted to them, and, on the approach of the royal army, were obliged to retire to Montrond, where *Madame la*

Princesse and her son had remained, and subsequently to Bordeaux. A much more severe blow to the prince's cause was the defection of Turenne, upon whose support he had confidently counted, but who, together with his brother, the Duc de Bouillon, had decided to throw in his lot with the Court. Nevertheless, he resolved to take the offensive, and for a while carried all before him in the South-West. But his forces were much inferior in number to the Royalists, and by the end of the year he was obliged to fall back to the Garonne.

The sudden reappearance of Mazarin upon the scene in the following January reanimated the hopes of the prince, and appeared to give new strength to his party. The Parlement, which, on 4 December, had issued a decree proclaiming *Monsieur le Prince* and his principal adherents "attainted and convicted of high treason and *lèse-majesté*," now voted that this sentence should be suspended and renewed its old decrees against the Cardinal. Gaston d'Orléans, with whom the prince had been for some time past negotiating, believing that he had been the dupe of the Queen, concluded an alliance with him, and, shortly afterwards, most of the Frondeurs also declared for Condé.

Towards the end of March, Condé, having entrusted the government of Guienne to his brother, Conti, assisted by a council composed of *Madame la Princesse*, Madame de Longueville, Lenet, Marsin, and the Président Viole, set out to take command of the Frondeurs on the Loire. After an adventurous journey, in which he only escaped capture by a miracle, he reached the army in safety, and falling upon the division of the royal forces commanded by Hocquincourt, completely routed it. But his attack on Turenne's position failed, and, shortly afterwards, he quitted his army and set out for Paris, with the object of inducing the capital to espouse his cause. Here, he found his beloved Madame de Châtillon, and, largely through her influence, "allowed himself to be drawn into an abyss of negotiations of which one never saw the bottom."[1] These negotiations led to no result, and, in the absence of their chief, the Frondeur army suffered a severe reverse at Étampes, where it was suddenly

[1] La Rochefoucauld, "Mémoires."

attacked by Turenne. Nor did he secure the adhesion of the capital, for, though the populace espoused his cause, the better-class citizens stood aloof.

At length, at the end of June, Condé, comprehending the fatal error he had committed in leaving the field to engage in futile intrigues, and of having preferred the counsels of an avaricious mistress [1] to those of his best friends, left Paris to resume the command of his weakened and disheartened forces. It was too late. Forced back upon Paris by superior numbers, he was obliged to fight the bloody combat of the Faubourg Saint-Antoine, which would probably have ended in the total destruction of the rebel army, had not *la Grande Mademoiselle*, by dint of tears and supplications, wrested an order from her irresolute father to open the gates to the hard-pressed Frondeurs and for the cannon of the Bastille to cover their retreat (2 July).

Two days later, a ferocious mob, among which are said to have been many of Condé's soldiers, disguised as artisans, attacked the Hôtel de Ville, where some three hundred delegates from the clergy, magistracy, and the various parishes were assembled in conclave, murdered several of them, and set the building on fire. This atrocious act, worthy of the worst days of the League, had the effect of terrifying the city into submission to Condé, but, at the same time, proved the death-blow of the Fronde, since all save the refuse of the people were filled with horror and loathing for a party which sought to compass its ends by such means. Every day saw the prince's followers falling away from him and the desire for peace growing stronger; and the skilful effacement of Mazarin, who, on 19 August, left Pontoise and retired into a second and voluntary exile at Bouillon, and afterwards at Sedan, removed the only pretext for continuing the war. Condé attempted to negotiate, but was informed that no proposal from him would be considered until he had laid down his arms, disbanded his troops, and renounced his alliance with Spain ; and, at length,

---

[1] In his negotiations with the Court, Madame de Châtillon had persuaded Condé to stipulate that her services in the cause of peace and concord should be recognized by a *gratification* of 100,000 écus.

on 13 October, disdaining to accept the general amnesty which had been proclaimed, but finding his position in the capital no longer tenable, he left Paris with the few troops which still remained faithful to him and joined the Spaniards on the Flemish frontier. A week later, Louis XIV. and Anne of Austria made their entry into the city amid general rejoicings, and in the following February Mazarin returned in triumph, to remain until the hour of his death the absolute ruler of France.

The Fronde of Bordeaux survived the Fronde in Paris by nearly ten months. Its chief feature was the bitter struggle between the advanced and moderate parties among the citizens. The former, recruited from the lower middle-class and the populace, desired to carry on the war *à outrance*, and was quite ready for an alliance with Spain, England, or half Europe for that matter. Its most violent spirits held republican views, which had been fostered by recent events in England, and, imitating the League or anticipating the Jacobins, formed themselves into a regular society, called, from its favourite place of assembly—a little terrace bordered by elms in the environs of the town—the *Ormée*, and persecuted with the utmost virulence all whom they suspected of hostility to the popular cause. The latter, which comprised the great majority of the better-class citizens, though hostile in general to the Court and Mazarin, were desirous of keeping the insurrectionary movement within bounds, and looked with marked disapproval on Condé's negotiations with Spain. To resist the tyranny of the *Ormée*, they organized themselves into a kind of aristocratic league, which was called, from the fashionable quarter of the town, the *Chapeau Rouge*. Sanguinary encounters between the two factions were of frequent occurrence, and, but for the courage and presence of mind of the Princesse de Condé and Madame de Longueville, who, at great personal risk, repeatedly intervened to separate the infuriated combatants, Bordeaux would have become a shambles.

On one occasion, we read that *Madame la Princesse*, "*fort allumée de colère*," vowed that the next time there was a breach of the peace, she would, notwithstanding that she was with child,[1] place herself at the head of those who obeyed her, and cause the offenders to be cut to pieces.[2]   Scarcely, however, had she and Madame de Longueville withdrawn, than the *Ormistes*, undismayed by this terrible threat, stormed the Hôtel de Ville and held it throughout the night.   In the morning, flushed with success, they marched in great force upon the Quartier du Chapeau Rouge, and attacked the house of a certain M. Pichon, a president of the Parlement, who appears to have been the object of their peculiar animosity.   Unhappily for them, M. Pichon had received warning of their intentions, and had taken the precaution to convert his residence into a kind of fortress, from which a withering fire of musketry was opened on the besiegers.   Exasperated by their losses, the *Ormistes* proceeded to storm and set fire to the neighbouring houses ; reinforcements came up rapidly on both sides, and it seemed as though the whole town would be delivered up to fire and blood. So fierce was the fighting that it appeared hopeless for the princesses to intervene ; but, at length, they bethought themselves of a happy expedient.   Hastening to the curé of the Church of Saint-Messan, they ordered him to accompany them to the scene of the fray, bearing the Holy Sacrament, preceded by the cross and candles.   The *cortège* advanced into the very midst of the combatants, who desisted, vanquished by the courage and presence of mind of these young women.

On 23 July, 1653, Bordeaux surrendered on honourable terms, the troops which Marsin had brought from Catalonia being permitted to join Condé, and a full pardon being granted to the inhabitants, with the exception of the leaders of the *Ormée*, one of whom was executed.

The most generous offers were made by Mazarin to *Madame la Princesse*, on condition that she should remain in France and separate her interests from those of her husband.   But, ever constant to her duty, Claire-Clémence declined them, and

---

[1] In the night of 19–20 September, 1652, the Princesse de Condé gave birth to a son.   The little prince, who was baptized Louis de Bordeaux and received the title of Duc de Bourbon, only lived a few weeks.

[2] Lenet, "Mémoires."

announced her intention of rejoining Condé. On 3 August, accompanied by the Duc d'Enghien and the faithful Lenet, she sailed for Flanders on board a Spanish ship-of-war. Her health had been so much affected by the trials and anxieties of the last few months that her physicians assured her that she would not survive the voyage ; but, happily, these gloomy prognostications were not realized, and on 26 August she landed safely at Dunkerque. Thence she journeyed slowly, by way of Nieuport, Bruges, Ghent, and Oudenarde, to Valenciennes, where, by her husband's orders, she took up her residence.

By order of the Viceroy of the Netherlands, she was received everywhere with royal honours and the most splendid hospitality. At Valenciennes, the governor, the municipal authorities, and all the nobility of the surrounding country, came to pay her homage, and to compliment her on her heroic Odyssey from Bordeaux. The Viceroy did everything in his power to amuse her, and sent from Brussels a company of actors, who gave before the illustrious exile a series of performances, in a theatre constructed specially for the occasion.

The consideration and sympathy with which strangers were so eager to surround the princess presented a striking contrast to the coldness and indifference of her husband. After all that she had done and suffered for his sake, she might well have expected to receive from him some proof of affection, or at least, of respect. But for eight months after her arrival he never once condescended to visit her, and, to add to the mortification which she must have felt, he deprived her of her son, who had never yet left her, whom he sent to the Jesuit College at Namur. At last, at the end of June, 1654, he sent orders to her to meet him at Mons. They passed one night together at an inn in the town, and on the morrow separated again, the husband proceeding to Brussels and the army, the wife returning to Valenciennes.

At the beginning of September, the approach of the French obliged *Madame la Princesse* to quit Valenciennes and seek another asylum. She chose Malines, where she installed herself at the Hôtel Hoogstratin. In spite of the fine promises which had been made by the Viceroy, she did not receive any assistance from the Government and soon found herself in terrible straits. The meagre sums sent her at rare intervals by Condé, who was himself in scarcely better case, were quite insufficient to defray the expenses of her Household, and she was obliged to dismiss the greater number of her attendants and to dispose successively of the few jewels she had kept, less for their value than for the associations connected with them, of her horses and carriages, and, finally, of part of her wardrobe. Sometimes she and her servants were even in need of food, for her *maître d'hôtel* had the greatest difficulty in obtaining credit from the humble tradesmen of the town.

The princess continued this wretched existence for several years. She rarely saw her son, but received occasional visits from her husband, an honour for which she seems to have been indebted to the fact that Condé was no longer able to spend his leisure at Brussels, where he was in debt to every one. "I am in such disrepute with the tradesmen," he writes, under date 28 October, 1655, to the Comte de Fiesque, his envoy at Madrid, "that they look upon me as a bankrupt. I borrow in every direction, and I pay no one back." And, a month later: "I doubt if I shall dare to return to Brussels, on account of the multitude of creditors of all kinds whom I have there. My wife and my son are accustoming themselves to live on air."

When, on 2 January, 1656, Condé arrived at Malines, he found his unfortunate wife without a fire in her room, and learned that the exasperated landlady of the inn had just caused the princess's *maître d'hôtel* to be thrown into prison. Moved with pity, despite his egoism, by the wretched condition to which his conduct had reduced this courageous and devoted woman, he humbled his pride sufficiently to write to Don Luis de Haro, Prime Minister of Spain, to demand assistance. "Finally, Monsieur," he writes, "I beg your Excellency to consider that without prompt pecuniary assistance it will be impossible for me to continue my services to the King with honour and usefulness. . . . I beg you to inform me what his Catholic Majesty wishes me to become ; for, so long as I have

no money, as my troops are without recruits and without
remounts, as my general-officers are without a sol, as my for
tresses are dismantled, as all my friends are in poverty, as I
myself, my wife, and my son are in a continual beggary, I
cannot be capable of rendering service to his Majesty in such a
condition." [1]

Condé certainly had every claim upon the gratitude of the
Spanish Court, for in the service of the enemies of his country
he displayed the most rare qualities. As a general, he compelled the admiration of all by his courage, energy, and fore-
sight. His masterly retreat on Mons, after the raising of the
siege of Arras, whereby he saved the routed Spaniards from
complete destruction, must rank as one of his finest feats of
arms, and scarcely less brilliant were his relief of Cambrai and
the manner in which he forced Turenne's lines before Valenciennes. Badly seconded by the Spanish Government, who
furnished him neither with subsidies nor capable generals, he
was obliged to give his personal attention to everything. He
superintended the recruiting of his armies, their provisioning,
their encampments, descended even to the most trifling details,
and led the life of the soldier, sharing his privations that he
might communicate to him his energy.

As the result of the visit paid by Condé to Malines at the
beginning of 1656, in the following spring *Madame la Princesse*
found herself again in an interesting condition. The approach
of this event added to the poor woman's anxieties, for she
could not but feel many misgivings as to the fate reserved for a
child to be born in exile, the offspring of a rebel prince, who had
been deprived, by a decree of the Parlement, even of the name
of Bourbon. She was, besides, much disquieted by the prospect
of the privations which it might be required to face at Malines,
in that inn where she was reduced to live so miserably. She
accordingly took counsel with the faithful Lenet, and, on his
advice, decided to petition Louis XIV. and Mazarin for permission to return to France, and, at the same time, to appeal to
the Parlement of Paris and her relatives to make intercession

---

[1] Archives de Chantilly, cited by the Duc d'Aumale.

on her behalf. But the touching letters which she addressed to the King and the Minister were without result ; she was merely informed that circumstances did not lend themselves to her return to France, and her only resource was to have a protest drawn up by Flemish lawyers, "in order that her accouchement out of France might not be laid to her charge, nor prejudice the child which would be born of her pregnancy."

In November, 1656, the Princesse de Condé gave birth, contrary to all her hopes, to a daughter, who was baptized Louise. While this little girl was still only a few months old, Jeanne Baptiste de Bourbon, Abbess of Fontevrault, wrote to Condé, offering her the succession to her abbey. The prince thanked the abbess for her good intentions, but suggested that it would be preferable to wait for better times, and that it was, besides, rather early to make his daughter a nun. The little princess did not assume the cross and mitre, since she died before she was three years old.

The campaign of 1657, which opened with Condé's brilliant relief of Cambrai, closed with the loss of Mardyke and other places, for the incurable indolence of the Spanish generals hampered the prince at every turn. England had now formed an alliance with France, and, in the following year, the Spaniards, having, against the advice of Condé, marched against the allies, who were besieging Dunkerque, sustained a crushing defeat in the battle of the Dunes. This disaster, followed by the capitulation of Dunkerque and the invasion of Flanders by Turenne, decided Philip IV. to make peace ; and, on 24 November, 1657, the Treaty of the Pyrenees brought the long war to a close.

It closed also the exile and disgrace of Condé, who, thanks to the firmness of Spain, was not only permitted to return to France, but re-established in possession of all his property, honours and dignities, with the exception of the governments of Guienne and Berry, and the charge of Grand Master of the King's Household, which he was to surrender to the Duc d'Enghien, retaining, however, the reversion of the post. In return for Philip IV.'s cession of Jülich to the Duke of Neuburg and of the fortress of Avesnes to France, Louis XIV. conferred upon Condé the government of Burgundy and Bresse, of the château of Dijon, and of Saint-Jean-de-Losne; and, as compensation for the duchy of Albret, which he had given to the Duc de Bouillon, he invested him with that of the Bourbonnais. This last arrangement restored to this branch of the Royal House of France the title of Duc de Bourbon, by which three of the later Princes de Condé preferred to be known.

In return, nothing was demanded of the rebellious prince, except that he should disband his forces within two months, and declare his intention "to make reparation for the past by an entire obedience to all the commands of his Sovereign" in a letter which he was to write to his Majesty. Early in December, this missive reached Toulouse, where the Court then was, and, on the 29th of the same month, Condé, accompanied by the Duc d'Enghien, quitted Brussels and set out for France. *Madame la Princesse* followed, after a short interval, with the little Mlle. de Bourbon. She, at least, was able to return to her native land without bitterness and without remorse, since she had only acted in accordance with what she believed to be her duty to her husband.

CHAPTER XVII

ON 4 January, 1660, Condé arrived at Coulommiers, whither the Duc and Duchesse de Longueville had come to welcome him. After remaining there a week, the princess and her little daughter, who had joined her the day after her arrival, set out for Trie ; the Duc d'Enghien was sent to Augerville, to the house of the Président Perrault, a partisan of *Monsieur le Prince*, who had himself recently returned from exile ; while Condé, accompanied by his brother-in-law, continued his journey to Aix, in Provence, where the Court then was, to salute the King. At Lambesc, they were met by the Prince de Conti, who, after the surrender of Bordeaux, had made his peace with the Court and espoused one of Mazarin's nieces, the beautiful and virtuous Anne Marie Martinozzi. Conti must have felt a little uneasy as to the reception he was likely to meet with from the brother whose cause he had abandoned. However, Condé greeted him affectionately, and, though the intimacy which had once existed between them was never renewed, they remained on friendly terms.

On 27 January, *Monsieur le Prince* reached Aix and went at once to visit Mazarin, to whom, since the Peace of the Pyrenees, he had written several "rather civil" letters. The interview between the two old enemies, though necessarily somewhat constrained, passed off satisfactorily enough. Condé recognized that the Cardinal was now far too firmly seated in the saddle ever to be dislodged, while Mazarin felt that he could afford to be magnanimous. At its conclusion the prince was "introduced into the Queen's chamber, where he presented his respects to their Majesties."[1] The memoirs of the time,—even those of *la Grande Mademoiselle*, who does not conceal her chagrin at not having been able to learn anything—are silent regarding this interview, which lasted more than an hour. No one seems to know what passed, but all are agreed that, when it was over, the Prince de Condé appeared to be as much at his ease at Court as if he had never left it.

The following evening the prince supped with Mazarin, who entertained him magnificently, and who, a few days later, in writing to Lenet, spoke in the warmest terms of their "friendship and cordial relations."

But, if the past were forgiven, it could not be forgotten, at least until time had enabled the prince to show that he was sincere in his professions of fidelity to his Sovereign. Condé, recognizing this, did not prolong his stay at the Court, and on 4 February he set out for Paris, where he was soon rejoined by his wife. In the capital he met with a most cordial reception ; the Parlement and the other Courts presented him with an address of welcome ; all Paris hastened to follow their example ; and the Hôtel de Condé, so long deserted, was for some weeks the centre of animation.

It was in this splendid residence which she had not entered since the death of her mother-in-law, ten years before, that a fresh and final disillusion awaited the long-suffering wife of the Great Condé. On her return from exile, Claire-Clémence might well have believed that a new life was about to begin for

---

[1] "Gazette de France," January, 1660.

her—a life in which she would be restored both to her place in Society and in her husband's house, and receive abundant compensation for all the hardships and humiliations which she had experienced. Under what immense obligations had she not placed her husband! Twice within two years she had brilliantly played the rôle of a party leader. At the peril of her life she had traversed the seas to bring him his son and to take her place by his side, and for long years had uncomplainingly endured all the bitterness of poverty and exile. Was it conceivable that a man could fail to be touched by so much courage, so much devotion? Was it conceivable that, now that it was in his power to show his appreciation of all that she had suffered for his sake, he should not hasten to take advantage of the opportunity?

And the changes which had taken place since their departure from France seemed to favour a better understanding between husband and wife. To "*le temps de la bonne régence*," [1] that era of facile and romantic gallantry, had succeeded one of regularity, order, and outward decorum, revealing a profound change in taste and morals. Of the salons which had been so much frequented before the Fronde, some were already nothing but a memory; others retained the merest shade of their former reputation. Condé's old *entourage* no longer existed; the band of pretty women whom his sister had gathered round her, and among whom he had moved as a kind of demi-god, was dispersed. Madame de Longueville herself had turned *dévote*, and divided her time between her husband and children and her religious duties. Madame de Châtillon had found a second husband in the Duke of Mecklenburg, and, though she was still residing in France, she seemed more anxious to secure his intervention in her lawsuits and her conjugal difficulties than to pick up the thread of their interrupted intrigue.

Besides, Condé himself was no longer the dashing cavalier

[1] "J'ai vu le temps de la bonne régence,
  Temps où régnait une heureuse abondance,
  Temps où la ville aussi bien que la cour
  Ne respirait que les jeux et l'amour."
  Saint-Évremond, "Stances à Ninon."

of former times. Never very robust, his health had been severely tried by the fatigues of so many years of active service; and already he was beginning to suffer from those attacks of gout which were to be the torment of his old age. Now, on the threshold of his fortieth year, weary and disillusioned, it seemed but natural that he should seek solace for his hardships and his thwarted ambition in the society of his wife and children.

Condé had too much family pride to neglect his duties towards his son, but, notwithstanding all the claims which she had upon his consideration, his behaviour towards his wife showed no improvement. It was, indeed, more cold and distant than ever. In the winter, which he generally passed in Paris, he and the princess each had their apartments under the same roof; they were seen together at State ceremonies; on great occasions, it was the latter who did the honours of the Hôtel de Condé. But in the summer, Claire-Clémence never appeared at Chantilly, where *Monsieur le Prince* was accustomed to gather round him all the celebrities of the time, save on the rare occasions when her presence was formally requested; soon she ceased to come there at all. Apart from attendance at official ceremonies and occasional visits to Saint-Maur, accompanied by a few persons of her suite, she seldom left the Hôtel de Condé, and led almost as retired a life as she had formerly passed among the Carmelites of the Faubourg Saint-Jacques. For the last and cruel disillusion which she had experienced had deprived her of all desire to mingle with the gay world around her. Too proud and too generous to complain, she gave as an explanation of her retirement the cares which her delicate health imposed, and the dignity of her behaviour gained for her the admiration and sympathy of all who penetrated the secret of this princely *ménage*.

But Condé's neglect was not the only trial which the poor princess had to endure. In the early years of her married life, she had been able to find some consolation for her husband's indifference in the affection of her son, the Duc d'Enghien, whom she had kept constantly with her and to whom she was passionately devoted. But the boy, as we have mentioned, had

ANNE OF BAVARIA, DUCHESSE D'ENGHIEN

been separated from his mother soon after their arrival in Flanders, and sent to the Jesuit College at Antwerp, since which time she had only seen him at long intervals. *Monsieur le Prince*, on the other hand, had superintended his son's education, and, as the lad grew older, he spent more and more of his time with his father, for whom he soon conceived the warmest admiration and affection ; while Condé, on his side, was tenderly attached to his son. Unhappily, these pleasant relations were established at the cost of the princess ; for the little consideration which his father, who could do no wrong in his eyes, showed for his mother was naturally not without its effect upon Enghien, and gradually the affection which as a boy he had entertained for the latter was replaced by the most complete indifference.

Almost as soon as he re-entered France, Condé began to occupy himself with matrimonial projects on behalf of his son. If we are to believe *la Grand Mademoiselle*, overtures were made to her, and the Duc d'Enghien was "ardently desirous for this marriage, and very assiduous in his attentions to her." The princess, however, excused herself, "on the ground of the great disparity of age between herself and the duke," though she informs us, in her "Mémoires," that it was her suitor's "want of merit," and his "base mind," to which she objected.

No difficulty would, however, have presented itself had Condé been willing for his son to marry *Mademoiselle's* half-sister, Mlle. d'Alençon. *Madame la Princesse* was very anxious for this alliance, as were several of the prince's counsellors ; but Condé had other views for his heir, and had determined to marry him to Anne of Bavaria, second daughter of Edward of Bavaria, Prince Palatine, and of Anne de Gonzague, sister of the Queen of Poland.[1]

His reason for preferring an alliance with a foreign princess of the second rank and of little fortune to one which would have strengthened the position of the Condés, by uniting them

---

[1] Louise Marie de Gonzague. She had married in 1645 Ladislas IV. King of Poland, and, after his death, she became wife of his brother, John Casimir.

to the younger branch of the Royal Family with its great possessions, was the belief that his son's marriage with a niece of the King and Queen of Poland would be of material assistance to him in the realization of an ambition which he had for some time cherished.

This ambition was nothing less than Enghien's succession to the elective crown of Poland, which the reigning sovereign, the childless John Casimir, was prepared to abdicate so soon as a candidate likely to be aceeptable to the great majority of his subjects could be found. This idea seems to have originated with the Queen of Poland, one of Condé's most intimate friends, who was using all her influence to secure the support of her husband and the Polish nobles, who in that State were masters of the throne, for the Duc d'Enghien.

Louis XIV. was not ill-disposed towards the Polish project, and, on 10 December, 1663, the marriage of the Duc d'Enghien and Anne of Bavaria was celebrated in the King's chapel at the Louvre. A clause in the marriage contract stated that the King and Queen of Poland adopted the bride "as their only daughter." Meanwhile, however, it was becoming apparent that Condé himself was likely to be far more acceptable to the Poles than his son, and the French Court seemed to approve of this solution. At the beginning of 1665, John Casimir decided to abdicate, and Condé was preparing to start for Warsaw with Enghien—whether it was his intention to get himself or his son elected is a moot point—when Louis XIV., fearing to offend the Duke of Neuburg, a rival competitor, whose possessions of Berg and Jülich commanded the passages of the Rhine and covered the Spanish Netherlands on the North-East, ordered him to renounce his candidature. "My cousin," said he, "think no more of the Crown of Poland ; the interest of my State is concerned in it." Condé reluctantly obeyed, and when, in June 1669, John Casimir, who had been persuaded by the prince's friends in Poland to retain the crown until then, in the hope that circumstances might permit him to renew his candidature, Michael Wisnowiecki was elected.

Condé received some compensation for the mortification

Chantilly. Without allowing himself to be discouraged, Condé secretly applied himself to drawing up a plan for the conquest of Franche-Comté. This plan he submitted to Louvois, the Minister for War, who persuaded the King to approve it, and to entrust its execution to the prince himself. On 4 February, 1668, Condé crossed the frontier, and so skilfully had his measures been taken and so rapid were his movements, that in little more than a fortnight the whole province was at his feet. Louis XIV. immediately gave to the prince the government of the conquered territory ; but the Triple Alliance between England, Sweden and Holland was already forming, and the King was soon obliged to consent to peace, retaining his conquests in the Netherlands, but restoring Franche-Comté to Spain.

The Princesse de Condé had figured at the marriage of her son and at the subsequent festivities, but, after the young couple had established themselves at Chantilly, where a portion of the château had been placed at their disposal, she gradually disappeared from the Court and Society, and was never seen except at great official functions, where her rank necessitated her presence. Often she was ill and invisible for months at a time, and Condé and Enghien appeared very embarrassed when people inquired after the princess's health, and hastened to change the subject. A few notes preserved in the archives of Chantilly serve to explain what seems to have remained an enigma, even to the best-informed of contemporary chroniclers. In the autumn of 1664, we find Condé writing to his secretary Caillet as follows :

"Make yourself acquainted with everything that my wife does at Saint-Maur ; inform me of everything that she does or says, and whether she still persists in her transports (*emportements*). M. Perrault writes me that she spoke to him with

R

moderation. I am a little dubious about that, for I hear from others that she is anything but moderate. . . . Endeavour, at any rate, to discover what has become of Duval, and if my wife has not seen him at Saint-Maur. . . . I will inform you of what will have to be done in this matter. Show my letter to the Abbé Roquette and to Père Bergier (the two spiritual directors of the family)." [1]

From these letters, it is very evident that *Madame la Princesse's* mind was affected, a fact which is not surprising, when we consider that her mother, Nicole du Plessis, had always been eccentric, and, in her later years, quite insane; that her father had been noted for his morose disposition and violent temper, and that she herself had passed through so many agitations, hardships, and deceptions. It is, indeed, sad to reflect that the reason of this truly noble woman, who in war and exile had shown such admirable courage and fortitude, should have given way at the very moment when she should have been enjoying the repose and happiness which she had so well earned. For this calamity the neglect and indifference of her ungrateful husband and her unnatural son were undoubtedly largely responsible.

Abandoned by those who should have lavished upon her the most tender care, the unhappy Claire-Clémence became the prey of greedy and unscrupulous attendants. The man Duval mentioned by Condé in one of his letters to Caillet was a footman of the princess, a person of some education and "*de bonne conversation*," to whom the lonely woman had attached herself. She gave him expensive presents and promised him a pension ; and Condé, warned of the influence which he was beginning to exercise over his wife, insisted on her dismissing him from her service.

The dismissal of the only person who appeared to feel for her any sympathy aggravated for a time the malady of Claire-Clémence, and was no doubt the cause of the "*emportements*" of which her husband speaks. But they do not appear to have lasted long, and by Holy Week 1655, she was sufficiently

[1] Letters of 28 September, 7 and 8 October, published by the Duc d'Aumale.

when the Queen, in accordance with ancient custom, served at table twelve poor women, whose feet she washed. The Princesse de Condé, aided by Mlle. d'Alençon and the Princess of Baden, carried the dishes to her Majesty.

During the next six years, Claire-Clémence continued to lead the same secluded life, emerging now and again from her retirement to assist at some Court ceremony, such as the baptism of the Dauphin at Saint-Germain-en-Laye, on which occasion she was one of the princesses to whom fell the duty of dressing the infant prince. After this brilliant ceremony, however, the appearances of the princess in public became so rare that people appear to have almost forgotten her existence, when, at the beginning of 1671, a mysterious affair, which was to complete the ruin of her life, came to make her, for a moment, the talk of both Court and town.

About two o'clock in the afternoon of 13 January, Claire-Clémence, having just dined, was alone in her apartments at the Hôtel de Condé, when the door opened, and her former favourite, the dismissed footman, Duval, entered the room unannounced. The ease with which he had succeeded in making his way to the princess's apartments is explained by the fact that at this hour of the day all the servants were at dinner, and that there was no one at hand to inquire his business. Duval had come to demand money—the arrears of the pension which the princess had promised him, but which, owing to the unsatisfactory state of her finances, had only been paid very irregularly. On being told that it was impossible to comply with his request at once, he became very insolent and spoke in so loud a tone that a young musketeer, the Comte Jean Louis de Bussy-Rabutin, formerly page to the Princesse de Condé, who had just entered the ante-chamber, opened the door to see what was the matter. Rabutin, after asking the impudent rascal how he dared to address her Highness in such a manner, ordered him to leave the house immediately ; Duval angrily refused, and both drew their swords and rushed upon each other. The princess endeavoured to separate them, and received a wound "above the right breast," [1] which, though not dangerous, bled profusely. She fell to the ground in a swoon ; the servants, attracted by the noise, came rushing in, and the combatants, profiting by the confusion, succeeded in effecting their escape, though not before they had both been recognized.

Such was the version which spread in Paris and was generally accepted, until the singular attitude of Condé piqued the curiosity of the public and invested the affair with an atmosphere of mystery and scandal. The prince, who had long sought an occasion for disembarrassing himself of a wife whom he had never loved, and who was no longer able to be of use to him, did not hesitate a moment to place the very worst construction upon what had occurred. Although suffering cruelly from the gout, he at once ordered his coach and set out for Paris, and, refusing even to see his wife, demanded of the King the punishment of a crime of *lèse-majesté* and a *lettre de cachet* against the princess. Louis XIV., who had been himself so far from conceiving any suspicions that he had already paid a personal visit to the injured lady, refused at first to accede to the latter request, and Condé returned to Chantilly in a very bad temper.

However, he was not the kind of person to be easily discouraged, and on 15 January, in the presence of the captain of his guards and the curé of Chantilly, he drew up and signed a document authorizing the Princesse de Condé to make a donation of her property to her son, the Duc d'Enghien. At the same time, he caused a deed to be prepared which stated that the princess, "on account of the tenderness and affection which she had always had for the person of the very high, very excellent and puissant prince Monseigneur Henri Jules de Bourbon, Duc d'Enghien, her son, Prince of the Blood, peer and Grand Master of France, etc., etc., and to recognize the great respect and obedience which he had always had for her, made a donation to him of all her movable property, furniture, titles, actions, immovables, pretensions, in whatsoever place they might be situated, reserving, nevertheless, the enjoyment

[1] "Gazette de France," 17 January, 1671.

by usufruct of all her said goods, during her lifetime, to dispose of them as might seem good to her."[1]

The same day, the Duc d'Enghien, accompanied by two notaries, proceeded to the Hôtel de Condé, informed his mother of the wishes of *Monsieur le Prince*, and presented the deed for her signature. The unfortunate princess signed without demur this kind of anticipated will, in which it seemed that her husband desired to cut her off from the world of the living. She was no doubt under the impression that her compliance might suffice to appease the conjugal wrath, and did not appear to understand that it was tantamount to a confession that she was no longer responsible for her actions.

As the Duc d'Aumale observes, this deed had not the character of a spoliation, since the usufruct was respected and the free disposition of the princess's jewels and plate assured. Yet, when viewed in the light of what followed, it had an odious appearance, and nothing in this sad affair has more disposed public opinion against Condé and his son.

Meanwhile, an active search had been made for the culprits. Duval was discovered at the house of a canon of the Sainte-Chapelle, whom he had persuaded to give him shelter, and conducted, with his hands tied behind his back, to the prison of the Faubourg Saint-Germain. Rabutin was more fortunate. After lying hidden for a week at the Hôtel des Mousquetaires, he succeeded in effecting his escape to Germany, where he married a lady of royal blood, the Princess Dorothea of Holstein, and rose to high rank in the Imperial service.

As the crime with which Duval was charged was that of having attempted the life of a Princess of the Blood, he was tried by the Grande Chambre and the Tournelle, sitting together. The evidence of Claire-Clémence, taken on commission on 17 January, proved most unfortunate for her, since, from a generous but mistaken desire to shield two men who had been in her service—Rabutin had not yet succeeded in effecting his escape from Paris, and the police were hunting for him high

---

[1] By a separate deed, the princess was permitted to dispose as she wished of her jewels and plate.

and low—she professed entire ignorance of the cause of the affray. Duval, she declared, had come to ask for money, of which he explained that he was in great need, and she had promised to give it to him in two or three days. (It will be observed that she said nothing about the loud and insolent tone in which he had demanded it, and which had been the cause of Rabutin's appearance upon the scene.) *After he had left her,* she had heard a commotion in the ante-chamber adjoining her salon, and, going out to see what was the matter, had received a wound in the breast, from which she immediately lost consciousness, without having recognized the persons who were fighting.

Duval was three times interrogated. On the first two occasions he stoutly denied that he was in any way culpable, but on the third he confessed, and admitted that it was he who had wounded the princess. In view of the latter's reticence, however, the Court regarded these admissions with considerable suspicion, and, being of opinion that the charge was not fully proved, instead of condemning him to death, merely sentenced him to the galleys.

The result of the proceedings against Duval, joined to the singular attitude of *Monsieur le Prince,* gave to the affair, in the opinion of a considerable section of the public, a new complexion ; and it was now freely asserted that the two men who had drawn upon each other in the princess's presence had been rivals in her affections. Such was the view taken by Madame de Sévigné, who, in a letter to her cousin Bussy,[1] thus expresses herself:

"I have just been told of an extraordinary adventure which occurred at the Hôtel de Condé, and which deserves to be related to you. Here it is : *Madame la Princesse* having conceived an affection for one of her footmen named Duval, the latter was foolish enough to suffer impatiently the good-will which she likewise testified for the young Rabutin, who had

---

[1] Roger de Rabutin, Comte de Bussy (1618–1693), the celebrated letter-writer and author of the scandalous " Histoire amoureuse des Gaules," which procured him a year in the Bastille and a sixteen years' exile from the Court.

been her page. One day, when they both happened to be in her chamber, Duval having said something that was wanting in respect to the princess, Rabutin drew his sword to chastise him. Duval drew his also, and the princess, throwing herself between them to separate them, was wounded in the breast. Duval has been arrested, and Rabutin has taken to flight. However honourable the subject of the quarrel may be, I like not the name of a footman coupled with that of Rabutin." [1]

To which her scandal-loving correspondent replies:

"Our cousin's adventure is neither beautiful nor ugly; the mistress does him honour, and the rival shame."

At the same time, most of her contemporaries refused to believe that the sweet and unfortunate Claire-Clémence had been seriously culpable, and, though several of Condé's biographers, to efface a stain on the escutcheon of their hero, have not hesitated to reproduce this calumny, others, such as Louis Joseph de Bourbon and Earl Stanhope, are of a different opinion, and blame severely the conduct of the prince. [2] "How is it possible," asks the latter, "to think that the suspicion of the prince was well founded? How can we believe that a princess married nearly thirty years, and, up to this time, entirely free from the slightest imputation—always held sacred by calumny, which spares so few, ever irreproachable in the midst of a most corrupt Court—could have waited till the age when passions have subsided to indulge them? How reconcile such irregularities with that exalted piety which she had practised from her youth upwards? How can we, without any proof, admit such accusations against the woman who had always devoted herself so courageously and constantly to the service of a husband who slighted her? Against the heroine of Montrond and Bordeaux; against Clémence de Maillé? And again, what accusations? Not only of an illicit attachment, but the shameless sharing of her favours between two of her own domestics!" [3]

[1] Letter of 23 January, 1671.

[2] The best informed of all, the Duc d'Aumale, adopts a neutral attitude, being of opinion that there is not sufficient evidence to condemn either Condé or his wife.

[3] "Life of Louis, Prince of Condé, surnamed the Great." It should be

Condé, who had never scrupled to jeer at the conjugal misfortunes of others, now, in his turn, became an object of ridicule. Chansons and epigrams at his expense began to circulate in Paris, and served to exasperate him still further against his wife. In the first days of February, he again demanded of the King a *lettre de cachet*, and this time Louis XIV. did not refuse, and signed an order which exiled the princess to the Château of Châteauroux, in Berry. No time was lost in executing it, and as soon as the doctors pronounced her able to stand the fatigue of the journey, she left Paris.

On the day of her departure, she sent for the curé of Saint-Sulpice, with whom she had a long conversation. " Monsieur," said she, as she bade him farewell, "this is the last time that you will speak to me, since I shall never return from the place to which the King is sending me. But the confession which I now make to you will proclaim my innocence for ever." Her parting from her son was heartrending, and, after embracing him again and again, she swooned away in his arms. As soon as she recovered, the carriage started for Châteauroux.

The château which Condé had selected as his wife's prison, and where she was destined to remain for the rest of her days, stands upon a hill on the left bank of the Indre, and commands a magnificent view of the surrounding country. It was built by Raoul *le Large*, seigneur de Déols, about the middle of the tenth century,[1] an age when security was naturally the primary consideration, and, though its sombre appearance had been a good deal modified from time to time, it was still far from a cheerful habitation.

The princess was followed thither by her whole Household : *dame d'honneur, chevalier d'honneur*, equerry, almoner, physician, apothecary, comptroller, waiting-women, chef, scullions, coachmen and footmen ; and an allowance of 50,000 livres a year was made her for the maintenance of this establishment. She was

mentioned that the distinguished historian declines to believe that the princess had as yet exhibited any signs of insanity, but in this he is quite mistaken.

[1] The seigneurie of Châteauroux was in 1497 erected into a county in favour of André de Chauvigny. In 1613 it was acquired by Henri II., Prince de Condé, who, three years later, obtained letters-patent evicting it into a duchy-peerage.

permitted to walk in the grounds of the château, and even to take carriage exercise in the vicinity, but always very carefully watched and guarded ; while no stranger was under any pretext allowed to approach her. Apart from these restrictions, she was treated, at any rate at first, with all the consideration and respect due to her exalted rank, and her captivity was not of the harsh and brutal character with which some writers have invested it.

Nevertheless, the isolation to which she was subjected, the deadly monotony of her existence in this gloomy fortress, soon began to have its effect upon her already tottering reason. Her disorder took the form of terror. From incessant brooding over her wrongs, the husband who had repaid her unselfish devotion with such harshness and ingratitude became, in moments of hallucination, a monster who, not content with burying her alive, was resolved to rid himself of her altogether, and frequently she refused to touch dishes that were offered her, from fear lest they should contain poison.

In 1675, in consequence of some rumours which had reached her that her sister-in-law was being ill-treated by those to whose care she had been entrusted, Madame de Longueville, more compassionate than the rest of her family, requested Père Tixier, a Benedictine monk in whom she had every confidence, to proceed to Châteauroux and ascertain if there were any justification for these reports. The monk, however, before undertaking this mission, considered it advisable to inquire if it would be agreeable to *Monsieur le Prince*, who was likewise a valued patron of his. Condé raised no objection. "You will go to Châteauroux," said he, "since my sister wishes it, and will see whether *Madame la Princesse* has everything she requires ; for, such as she is, she is my wife, and I do not wish her to want for anything. But do not speak of me to her at all, you understand."

On his arrival at Châteauroux, Père Tixier was presented to the princess, who was about to sit down to dinner. "Father," said she, "you belong to *Monsieur le Prince*, who sends you to see me." "No, Madame," replied the good man, "I am a monk, and the monks belong to God." "Oh!" rejoined the princess, "I understand;" and she declared her conviction that Condé had sent him to confess her, because he intended to have her made away with. Tixier endeavoured to reassure her, and the officer whom Condé had placed in charge of his wife, and "who I saw clearly," says the monk, "treated her very roughly," exclaimed: "*Morbleu!* Madame, at your usual fables again! Will you never be sensible?"

Dinner was served, and, after the soup, a dish of cod was brought in. The princess partook of it with relish, and asked for a second helping. The dish, however, had just been removed, and, when it was brought back, she declined to touch it, saying that it had been to the kitchen and that there had been suffi- cient time to mix with it some fatal ingredient. The officer remonstrated. "But," said he, "does not everything that is served you, Madame, come from the kitchen?" Nevertheless, the unfortunate woman refused to listen to reason.

The princess, having at length been persuaded by Père Tixier that he had merely come, at Madame de Longueville's request, to inquire as to her welfare, begged him to convey her most grateful thanks to her sister-in-law. For her husband, she had no message and spoke of him with aversion. "*Monsieur le Prince*," said she, "greatly despised me, but I greatly despised him also."[1]

[1] "Père Tixier," by MM. Lemoine and Lichtenberger, "Revue de Paris," 15 November, 1903.

CHAPTER XVIII

Termination of Condé's military career—His retirement at Chantilly—
His improvements of the château and estate—His son, the Duc d'Enghien
(*Monsieur le Duc*)—Portrait of this prince by Saint-Simon—His tyrannical
treatment of his wife—His singular habits—Malicious practical joke which
he perpetrates on the Duc de Luxembourg—His amours with the Duchesse
de Nevers, the Marquise de Richelieu, and the Comtesse de Marans—His
natural daughter by Madame de Marans legitimated and married to the
Marquis de Lassay—His lack of military capacity—His children—The
education of his only son, the Duc de Bourbon, superintended by Condé—
Marriage of the young prince to Mlle. de Nantes, elder daughter of Louis XIV.
and Madame de Montespan—The wedding-night—Conversion of Condé
—His last illness—His death—His funeral oration by Bossuet—The
Princesse de Condé remains in captivity—Her death.

MONSIEUR LE PRINCE probably troubled himself
very little about his unhappy wife's feelings towards
him. Having brought his military career to a
triumphant close by restoring the fortunes of France in
Alsace and driving the Imperialists across the Rhine, he had
retired definitely to Chantilly, to spend the remaining years
of his life in as much peace as his implacable enemy, gout,
would permit.

In this delightful spot, his leisure was cheered by the society
of all the celebrities of his time. There were to be met warriors,
statesmen and ambassadors, divines and philosophers, poets,
painters, scientists and wits. No general set out to join his army
without coming to take leave of the great captain and discuss
with him his plan of campaign ; no distinguished foreigner
visited Paris without paying homage at Chantilly ; no author of
repute published a book without sending a copy to the prince
who was "thought the best judge in France both of wit and
learning."[1]

[1] Bishop Burnet, "History of his own Time."

And so he grew old, honoured and adulated by all :

> "Tranquille et glorieux
> Il vit à Chantilly comme on vit dans les cieux." [1]

Condé had a natural taste for gardening—even during his imprisonment at Vincennes he had amused himself by cultivating carnations—and his greatest pleasure in his declining years was to embellish the retreat which he had chosen for himself.   In 1662, he had begun the enlargement of the park, and, under the direction of the celebrated gardener Le Nôtre, parterres were traced around the château, long alleys, bordered by trim hedges, stretching away into the forest began to make their appearance, and trees, shrubs, and rare plants were gathered from all quarters. But want of money imposed prudence, and it was not until some years later, when *Monsieur le Prince's* finances were once more in a satisfactory condition, that the work took a wide scope. Then it was that Gitard constructed the grand staircase ; that Mansart built the Orangerie, and commenced the Ménagerie ; that the aqueduct which brought to Chantilly the water of the fountain of the Hôtel-Dieu-des-Marais was made ; that the parterres were completed and new avenues pierced in all directions ; that the fountains which " were silent neither day nor night" [2] were erected, and that Chantilly began to assume the appearance which it was to retain until the Revolution.

Condé, however, had another and more important occupation in his retirement than the embellishment of Chantilly.

One of the greatest disappointments of the prince's life was his only son, the Duc d'Enghien, to whom, as we have mentioned, he was most tenderly attached.   As a child, *Monsieur le Duc*—to give him his official designation—had been charming, but this early promise had unhappily not been fulfilled, either in appearance or in character ; while, though he undoubtedly possessed great abilities, he was quite incapable of employing them to any useful purpose.   Saint-Simon has drawn of him one of his most arresting portraits :

"He was a little man, very thin and slenderly made, whose

[1] Saint-Évremond. "Stances irrégulières."
[2] Bossuet, " Oraison funèbre du Grand Condé."

HENRI JULES DE BOURBON, DUC D'ENGHIEN (AFTERWARDS
PRINCE DE CONDÉ.)

countenance, though somewhat mean, was still imposing from the fire and intelligence of his eyes ; while his nature was a compound as rare as could be met with. No man was ever endowed with a keener or more varied intelligence, which extended even to the arts and mechanics, and was joined to an exquisite taste. No man had a more frank or more natural courage, or a greater desire to shine ; and, when he wished to please, he did so with so much tact, grace, and charm that it seemed spontaneous. Neither was any man more accomplished in invention and execution, in the pleasures of life, in the magnificence of fêtes, by which he often astonished and delighted in every conceivable way. But, then, no man had ever before so many useless talents, so much futile genius, or so lively and active an imagination, solely employed to be his own curse and the scourge of others. Abjectly and basely servile, even to lackeys, he scrupled not to use the lowest and paltriest means to gain his ends. Unnatural son (to his mother), cruel father, terrible husband, detestable master, pernicious neighbour ; without friendship, without friends—incapable of having any—jealous, suspicious, ever restless, full of artifices to discover everything and to scrutinize all (in which he was unceasingly occupied, aided by an extreme vivacity and a surprising penetration) ; choleric and headstrong to excess, even over trifles, never in accord with himself and keeping all about him in a tremble, he caused the unhappiness of every one who had any connection with him. To conclude, impetuosity and avarice were his masters, which monopolized him always. With all this, he was a difficult man to resist, when he brought into play the pleasing qualities he possessed."

To his unfortunate wife, Anne of Bavaria, he was a veritable tyrant. She was ugly, virtuous, and stupid, a little deformed, and not very clean in her person ; but this did not hinder him from being furiously jealous till the end of his life. Nor were her piety, the unwearying attentions she lavished upon him, her gentleness, and her novice-like submission able to protect her from frequent insults, and even from blows and kicks. The poor woman was hardly allowed to call her soul her own. " She was not mistress even of the most trifling things; she did not dare to propose or to ask anything.   He would make her start on a journey the moment the fancy took him, and often, as soon as she was seated in the carriage, he would make her descend again, or return from the end of the street, and recommence the journey after dinner or the next day.   Once this kind of thing lasted for fifteen days running, before a journey to Fontainebleau. At other times, he would summon her from church, and make her leave High Mass, and sometimes would even send for her when she was on the point of receiving the Communion; and she would be obliged to return on the instant and defer her Communion until another occasion.   This he did, not because he wanted her, but merely to gratify his whim."

He was always uncertain in his movements, and had four dinners prepared for him every day: one in Paris, a second at Écouen, a third at Chantilly, and a fourth wherever the Court might be at the moment.   But the expense of this arrangement was not so great as might be supposed, for the *menu* consisted merely of soup and half a chicken roasted upon a *croûton* of bread, the other half serving for the following day.   He rarely invited any one to dine with him, but, when he did, no one could be more courteous or more attentive to his guests.

He delighted in practical jokes, generally of an extremely malicious kind, of which the following will serve as an example:

The Duc de Luxembourg,[1] son of the celebrated marshal, had a young and pretty wife,[2] who suffered, like a good many other ladies about the Court, from excessive sensibility, a fact which was "known to everybody in France except her husband."   On the occasion of a visit of the Court to Marly, both M. de Luxembourg and his consort were invited to take part in a masquerade.   *Monsieur le Duc* undertook to provide the former with what he declared to be a highly original costume, and, since he enjoyed the reputation of being a great authority on such matters, his offer was gladly accepted.

---

[1] Charles François Frédéric de Montmorency-Boutteville.
[2] Marie de Clérambault.

DIANE GABRIELLE DE THIANGES DUCHESSE DE NEVERS

Thereupon the malicious prince proceeded to array his unconscious victim in various fantastic garments, which he crowned with a gigantic pair of antlers, which almost touched the candelabra. Thus attired, he was conducted into the ballroom, where, by a sudden shifting of his mask, his identity was quickly revealed. When the company perceived who it was who was thus parading the emblem of a deceived husband, a great shout of laughter rang through the room, which redoubled when the luckless Luxembourg, mistaking the hilarity which his appearance aroused for a tribute to the originality of his costume, bowed repeatedly.

In his youth, *Monsieur le Duc*, like most of his family, was very much addicted to gallantry. When his affections were engaged, nothing cost too much, and "he made some amends for a shape which resembled a gnome rather than a man."[1] "He was grace, magnificence, gallantry personified—a Jupiter transformed into a shower of gold. Now, he disguised himself as a lackey; another time, as a female vendor of articles for the toilette; anon, in some other fashion. He was the most ingenious man in the world."[2]

Among the great ladies who smiled upon him was the lovely and fascinating Gabrielle de Thianges, who became, in 1670, the wife of the Duc de Nevers, the brother of the famous Mancini sisters.[3] "Few women," says Saint-Simon, "have surpassed her in beauty. Hers was of every kind, with a singularity which charmed." And he declares that when she died, at the age of sixty, she was "still perfectly beautiful."

If we are to believe Madame de Caylus, the duchess, after the fall of her aunt, Madame de Montespan, had, at that lady's suggestion, made an attempt to capture the affections of the King, "in order to keep the royal favour in the family," and that it was only upon the failure of this intrigue that she resolved to content herself with *Monsieur le Duc*. But, whatever may have been the lady's feelings towards

---

[1] Madame de Caylus.   [2] Saint-Simon.

[3] Philippi Mancini. Mazarin had bequeathed to him the duchy-peerage of Nivernois and Donzois, which he had purchased from the Duke of Mantua, in 1659.

him, *Monsieur le Duc* was desperately enamoured of her, and the fertility of resource which he displayed and the sums he appears to have expended in order to enjoy her society were really astonishing.

Voltaire asserts, in a note to the first edition of the *Souvenirs* of Madame de Caylus, that, for the purpose of entering secretly into the apartment of the duchess, he had bought the two houses on either side of the Hôtel de Nevers. Saint-Simon goes much further and says that, to conceal their rendezvous, "he rented all the houses on one side of a street near Saint-Sulpice, furnished them, and pierced the connecting walls." If we are to believe this anecdote, the Maréchal de Richelieu must have been but a feeble plagiarist when, many years later, he adopted a similar means of entrance into the Palais-Royal and the Hôtel de la Popelinière.[1] But since Saint-Sulpice, though close to the Hôtel de Condé, was a long way from the Hôtel de Nevers, we must confess that we do not quite see how such operations were to bring *Monsieur le Duc* to the side of his beloved. Perhaps, however, Saint-Simon intends us to understand that, in order not to excite the least suspicion, the prince was in the habit of entering a house at one end of the street, and the lady one at the other extremity, and of meeting in the middle. Any way, it seems rather a tall story, even for Saint-Simon.

Despite so many precautions, the Duc de Nevers scented treason, and resolved to escape it by the procedure which he usually adopted in such circumstances, namely, by carrying his wife off to Rome.[2] "M. de Nevers," writes Madame de Caylus, "was in the habit of setting off for Rome in the same way as any one else would go out to supper; and Madame de Nevers had been known to enter her carriage in the persuasion that she was only going for a drive, and then to hear her husband say to the coachman: "To Rome." In time,

---

[1] See the author's "The Fascinating Duc de Richelieu" (London, Methuen; New York, Scribner, 1910).

[2] The Duc de Nevers had inherited under his uncle's will the Palazzo Mazarini, at the foot of the Quirinal, and frequently spent the winter there.

however, the lady began to know her husband better and to be more on her guard against him, and happening to discover his intention of taking her upon another of these sudden journeys, she promptly warned her lover and begged him to devise some means of averting, or, at any rate, of postponing, their threatened separation.

Now, the Duc de Nevers, like all the Mancini, had a very pretty turn for verse-making, of which he was inordinately vain, and nothing delighted him more than to hear his poetical effusions recited before an appreciative audience.   Aware of this little weakness, *Monsieur le Duc* resolved to lay a trap for him, into which he felt convinced he could not fail to fall. But let us listen to Madame de Caylus ·

"*Monsieur le Prince*,[1] equally fertile of invention as reckless of expense whenever his tastes or passions were concerned, judged, from the knowledge he possessed of the character of M. de Nevers, that he might easily divert him from his intended expedition, by affording him an opportunity of employing his talent and exercising his passion for making verses.   He proposed, therefore, to give a fête to *Monseigneur*[2] at Chantilly. The invitation was given and accepted, when he hastened to M. de Nevers, informed him of the entertainment, and, pretending that he was in a great difficulty about the choice of a poet to write the words of the *divertissement*, begged him, as a favour, to find him one.   Upon which M. de Nevers offered himself, just as *Monsieur le Duc* had foreseen.   To conclude, the fête took place—it cost more than one hundred thousand crowns —and Madame de Nevers did not go to Rome."

Thus Madame de Caylus.   But Saint-Simon gives another version of this story, according to which the laugh, at the last, was on the side of M. de Nevers:

"The Duc de Nevers, all jealous, all Italian, all full of intelligence that he was, had never conceived the least suspicion of this fête, although he was not ignorant of the love of

---

[1] This episode occurred in 1688, nearly two years after the death of the Great Condé, when *Monsieur le Duc* had become *Monsieur le Prince*.

[2] The Grand Dauphin, only son of Louis XIV.

Monsieur le Prince for his wife. However, five days before it took place, he ascertained the reason why it was being given. He said not a word about it, but started for Rome the very next day with his wife, and remained there for a long time ; and, in his turn, scoffed at *Monsieur le Prince*."

Another *grande dame* whom the duke honoured by his attentions was the Marquise de Richelieu,[1] a lady whom Saint-Simon mentions, "because she is not worth the trouble of being silent about." According to the same chronicler, he fell madly in love with this siren, and "spent millions upon her, and to keep himself informed of her movements." One fine day, he discovered, to his profound indignation, that he had a successful rival in the person of the Comte de Roucy. He reproached the marchioness bitterly with her treachery, and, though she assured him that she had been cruelly maligned, he had her so closely watched that very soon the charge was brought home to her beyond any possibility of denial. In vain, did the culprit entreat his forgiveness ; in vain, did she swear by all that she held sacred that Roucy's love was as nothing to her in comparison with his, and that she would never see him again. The infuriated prince refused to be placated and turned to leave her. Then the fear of losing so prodigal a lover "suggested to the marchioness an excellent expedient for setting his mind at rest." She proposed to give Roucy a rendezvous at her house, and that some of *Monsieur le Duc's* people should lie in wait ; and, when the count appeared, make away with him. But, instead of the success she appears to have expected from this very Italian proposal,[2] the prince was so horrified that he immediately sent to warn Roucy, and never saw Madame de Richelieu again.

A third inamorata of *Monsieur le Duc*, of whom we should have perhaps spoken before, since she was one of the loves of his youth, whereas his *liaisons* with the Duchesse de Nevers

---

[1] Marie Charlotte de la Meilleraye-Mazarin. She was a daughter of Armand de la Porte-Meilleraye-Mazarin, Duc de Mazarin, and the beautiful Hortense Mancini, Mazarin's favourite niece. On his marriage, the former added the cardinal's name to his patronymic, and was created Duc de Mazarin.

[2] Madame de Richelieu was, of course, an Italian on her mother's side.

and the Marquise de Richelieu belong to his riper years, was
the widowed Comtesse de Marans, often mentioned in the
letters of Madame de Sévigné, who speaks of her with unusual
bitterness, owing, it is believed, to some disparaging remark
which she had once let fall concerning the writer's beloved
daughter, Madame de Grignan. The countess was an extremely
pretty woman, but the most inconsequent and extravagant
creature in the world. According to Madame de Sévigné, she
had been heard to declare that she would rather die than
surrender herself to a man whom she loved ; but, if a man loved
her and she did not find him altogether odious, she would be
willing to yield. Whether or no she loved *Monsieur le Duc*,
she surrendered herself to him, and, in 1668, presented him
with a daughter. The girl was at first known as Mlle. de
Guenani, which is the anagram of her father's duchy of Anguien
(the old orthography of Enghien). But, in 1692, she was
legitimated, and took the name of Julie de Condé, Mlle. de
Châteaubriant. Brought up at first at Maubuisson, she was
later sent to the Abbaye-aux-Bois, from which retreat, however,
she occasionally emerged to pay visits to her relatives at
Chantilly or Saint-Maur. At this time, there seems to have
been some idea of her taking the veil, but she was so pretty,
intelligent, and amusing, that it was eventually decided that
she should remain in the world, and, in 1696, she married the
Marquis de Lassay, a middle-aged widower, celebrated for his
amorous adventures, who had been for some time past
desperately in love with her. The bride received a dowry of
100,000 livres, as well as 20,000 livres for the expenses of her
trousseau; while Lassay was appointed the King's lieutenant
in the Bresse. It is to be feared, however, that the amorous
marquis had reason to regret his bargain, for, if gossip does not
lie, before she had been married a week, the lady had provided
herself with a lover.

Many and grave as were the faults of *Monsieur le Duc*, it is
probable that Condé would have suffered them with comparative
equanimity if his son had inherited in any degree his own
genius for war. But, singularly enough, with all the intelligence

and quickness of perception which he displayed in other directions, Enghien never showed the smallest aptitude for his
father's profession. "So great a warrior as *Monsieur le Prince*,"
writes Saint-Simon, "was never able to make his son understand the first principles of the art of war. He made this
teaching for a long time the principal object of his care and
study. His son tried to do the same, but was never able to
acquire the slightest aptitude for any portion of the art,
although his father concealed nothing from him, and was
constantly explaining all that relates to it at the head of his
army. He always took him with him, and endeavoured to give
him a command near himself, of course, in order to counsel
him. This plan of instruction succeeded no better than the
others. Finally, he despaired of his son, gifted though he was
with such great talents, and ceased his endeavours, with what
grief may be imagined.

In fairness to *Monsieur le Duc*, however, it should be
mentioned that, if he had inherited none of his father's military
genius, he had at least inherited his valour, and, on more than
one occasion, he displayed conspicuous courage. Thus, at the
sanguinary battle of Seneffe (11 August, 1774), when Condé's
horse had been killed under him, and the prince had been
thrown with great violence to the ground, Enghien threw
himself before him, and was himself wounded in assisting him
to rise.

Of nine children whom Anne of Bavaria had borne the Duc
d'Enghien, four daughters and a son had survived.[1] The boy,

---

[1] 1. Marie Thérèse de Bourbon, born 1 February, 1666 ; married in 1688 Louis
François, Prince de Conti ; died in 1732.

2. Louis de Bourbon, born 11 October, 1668; became Louis III., Prince de
Condé in 1709 ; died the following year.

3. Anne Marie Victoire de Bourbon, Mlle. de Condé, born 11 August, 1675 ;
died unmarried 23 October, 1700.

4. Anne Louise Bénédicte de Bourbon, Mlle. de Charolais, born 8 November,
1676 ; married in 1692 the Duc de Maine, son of Louis XIV. and Madame de
Montespan.

5. Marie Anne de Bourbon, called Mlle. de Montmorency, and later Mlle.
d'Enghien, born 24 February, 1678 ; married in 1710 the Duc de Vendome ; died in
1718.

Louis, Duc de Bourbon, was in his eighth year when Condé retired definitely to Chantilly, and *Monsieur le Prince*, in the hope of developing in the son the qualities which he had not found in the father, and of perhaps living to see him rise up and continue the glorious traditions of the family, desired to direct his education himself. *Monsieur le Duc*, whose time was fully occupied by his duties at the Court, and who still retained his former habits of submission to his father's will, consented ; and Condé decided to have his grandson educated on the same system which had proved so successful in his own case. Established : at the Petit-Luxembourg, with his *gouverneur* Deschamps,[1] his tutors the Jesuit Fathers Alleaume et du Rosel, and one of *Monsieur le Prince's* equerries, Le Bouchet, who directed his physical exercises, the young duke attended the courses of the Collège de Clermont, passing his vacations at Chantilly, whither his tutors always accompanied him.

All the masters and professors under whom the boy studied were vigorously seconded by Condé, who maintained with them an almost daily correspondence, while he was continually exhorting his grandson to apply himself to his studies. The Duc de Bourbon, however, though he was not without ability, was incurably indolent, and, despite all the efforts of his teachers and the reprimands of *Monsieur le Prince*, his progress both at the Collège de Clermont and at Louis-le-Grand, to which he was transferred when he was fourteen, was most disappointing. It was evident that Condé had not taken into sufficient consideration the great difference in temperament between himself and his grandson, and that a system which had produced such splendid results in his own case was quite unsuited to this idle, pleasure-loving lad.

The duke was accordingly removed from college, and, on the advice of Bossuet, Condé decided to keep him under his own eye at Chantilly, and to entrust the rest of his education to La Bruyère and the distinguished mathematician Sauveur. This plan worked excellently for some months, and *Monsieur le Prince* was full of hope ; but, unfortunately, the Duc d'Enghien,

---

[1] Jean Auguste Deschamps, Sieur de Cotecoste.

to whom the possession of the royal favour was of infinitely more importance than anything else in the world, considered that the time had now arrived to bring his son to the notice of the King and initiate him into his duties as a courtier, and desired that he should pay occasional visits to Versailles. These visits, which, on some pretext or other, were frequently prolonged far beyond the limit which Condé had fixed, naturally did not make for the young gentleman's progress in his studies, for, though his tutors always accompanied him, he soon became so absorbed in the pleasures of the Court that they thought themselves fortunate if they could obtain from him an occasional hour of distracted attention. La Bruyère was in despair and appealed to *Monsieur le Prince*, who remonstrated vigorously with Enghien. "Your son," he writes, "will become a very good huntsman, but ignorant of everything that he ought to know. It is for you to remedy it, and to think of his life, his health, and his good education. I beg you to consider it, and not to wait to remedy it until it is too late."

Condé and Enghien were, however, at cross-purposes ; the one wished to form a man, a prince, a captain ; the other thought only of making his son an accomplished courtier. That the hope of the Condés should be an invariable guest at Marly was in the latter's eyes a more desirable thing than that he should command armies ; that he should secure the reversion of the governments and offices which had been bestowed upon his father was of more importance than that he should inherit his grandsire's fame.

It must be admitted that Enghien was indefatigable in his endeavours to further what he conceived to be the interests of his son. "With the prudence and calculation of an officer experienced in sieges, he pursued his plan, seeking to take possession of all the avenues which could conduct him to the heart of the King ; hunting and shooting-parties, masquerades, ballets, fêtes at Marly, served him as approach-works ; a direct attack that he was preparing could not fail to assure for his son the royal favour."[1]

[1] Duc d'Aumale, "Histoire des Princes de Condé."

made public.

This was not the first alliance between the fruit of *le Grand Monarques* amours and the Princes of the Blood. In January, 1684, Condé's nephew and ward the young Prince de Conti[1] had espoused Louise de la Vallière's daughter, Mlle. de Blois, on which occasion, we learn from Madame de Sévigné that *Monsieur le Prince*, who had always clung to the bygone fashion of moustaches and a chin-tuft, astonished the Court by appearing clean-shaven, with his hair curled and powdered, and a *justaucorps* adorned with diamond buttons.[2] But, although Condé approved of the marriage arranged for his grandson, he was far from approving of the latter interrupting his studies to take upon himself conjugal responsibilities. However, such was the *Monsieur le Duc's* impatience to see the young prince become the son-in-law of the King that he ultimately withdrew his

---

[1] Louis Armand de Bourbon (1661–1685). He must not be confused with his younger, and far more celebrated brother, François Louis de Bourbon (1664–1709) who succeeded him in the title, up to which time he was known as the Prince de la Roche-sur-Yon.

[2] "I will tell you a great piece of news ; it is that *Monsieur le Prince* was shaved yesterday. This is no mere rumour or gossip; it is a fact ; all the Court witnessed it ; and Madame de Langeron, choosing the time when he had his paws folded like a lion, made him put on a *justaucorps* with diamond buttons. A *valet de chambre* also, taking advantage of his patience, curled his hair, powdered it, and at last reduced him into being only the best-looking man at Court, and with a head of hair that puts all wigs out of competition. This was the prodigy of the wedding." Letter of 17 January, 1680.

objections, and Louis XIV. having also proved complaisant, the marriage was celebrated, in the chapel at Versailles, on 24 July, 1685.

So far as people were able to judge from features which were hardly yet formed, the twelve-year-old bride gave promise of being very pretty ; and this promise was duly fulfilled. As much could not be said for the bridegroom. Both the Duc and Duchesse d'Enghien were short, though of no unusual diminutive-ness, but their son was almost a dwarf,[1] and a very ugly one to boot, with an abnormally large head, an unwholesome com-plexion, and a surly expression.

The union of these two marionettes, as the Marquis de Sourches calls them, was celebrated with extreme magnificence, and "the Great Condé and his son left nothing undone to testify their joy, just as they had left nothing undone to bring about the marriage."[2]   The King secured to the duke the reversion of all the offices held by his father and gave him a pension of 90,000 livres, and to his daughter one of 100,000 livres.

In the evening, the happy pair proceeded to the pretended consummation of their marriage, without which the ceremony through which they had just passed would not have been con-sidered binding. In the presence of the King and all their relatives, they entered a state bed, where they remained for half an hour, the Duchesse d'Enghien standing by the bridegroom's side, and Madame de Montespan by that of the bride. This solemn farce terminated, they separated, not to meet again for several months, except in the presence of witnesses ; and the Duc de Bourbon went back to his interrupted studies, which *Monsieur le Prince* had insisted on his continuing.

The year which saw the marriage of the Duc de Bourbon marks a very important event in the life of his grandfather. The religious instruction of Condé had been as thorough as the other branches of his education, and, in early youth, he appears to have been as orthodox a Catholic as any one could desire,

---

[1] The Great Condé, who was tall, used to say, laughing, that, if his race thus continued to dwindle, it would at last come to nothing.

[2] "Souvenirs et Correspondance de Madame de Caylus."

LOUIS III, DUC DE BOURBON, PRINCE DE CONDÉ (CALLED
MONSIEUR LE DUC)

life of war and pleasures soon brought indifference, and the society of fashionable freethinkers, like Saint-Évremond and the celebrated Princess Palatine, combined with the difficulty he experienced in reconciling the doctrines of the philosophers whose works he was fond of studying with the theological teaching of the time, raised doubts in his mind which eventually led to a very pronounced form of unbelief. At the same time, he declared himself to be always open to conviction of his errors, and one of his favourite occupations in his later years was to engage in theological discussions with Bossuet, the Oratorian Malbranche, and other eminent divines.

The death of his beloved sister, Madame de Longueville, who, in April, 1679, crowned twenty-seven years of penitence and good works by a truly Christian death, at which Condé was himself present, made a profound impression upon him, and he was even more impressed by that of his old friend, the Princess Palatine, who, after declaring that the greatest of all miracles would be her conversion to Christianity, had for the last twelve years been leading a life of almost equal devotion. From that time, the discussions between Condé and Bossuet became more frequent, and little by little the prince began to surmount the obstacles which barred his return to the fold.

It was, however, a Jesuit, Père des Champs, formerly a fellow-pupil of Condé at Bourges, who was to finish the work which the great bishop had begun. At the beginning of Holy Week, 1685, the prince summoned him to Chantilly; for several days they remained closeted together, after which Condé descended to the chapel and received the Sacrament, in the presence of all his Household. Some weeks later, he communicated publicly at the Church of Saint-Sulpice, in which parish the Hôtel de Condé was situated.

For some time past Condé's health had been such as to occasion grave anxiety; his attacks of gout were becoming more frequent and more severe, and he was often so feeble that he was unable to walk without assistance. When, at the end of May, 1686, although in great pain, he insisted on coming to

Versailles to attend a Chapter of the Ordre du Saint-Esprit, at
which the *cordon bleu* was to be bestowed on the Duc de Bourbon
and the Prince de Conti, the fatigue which the journey and the
ceremony entailed exhausted him to such a degree that, according to Sourches, those present " expected every moment to see
him die."

Towards the middle of the following November, news reached
Chantilly that the little Duchesse de Bourbon had been taken
seriously ill with small-pox at Fontainebleau, where the Court
was then in residence. Notwithstanding that he was again
suffering from the gout, *Monsieur le Prince* at once ordered his
coach and set off for Fontainebleau. On the road he met the
Duc de Bourbon and his eldest sister, Mlle. de Condé, whom the
King had sent to Paris, so that they should not be exposed to
the contagion. Alarmed at their grandfather's appearance, they
endeavoured to persuade him to turn back, but he insisted on
continuing the journey. Arrived at Fontainebleau, he shut
himself up with the Duchesse de Bourbon and " rendered her
all the cares not only of a tender father, but of a zealous
guardian." [1] The girl, however, grew worse, and Louis XIV.,
on learning of his daughter's danger, wished to come and see
her. " *Monsieur le Prince*," writes Madame de Caylus, " placed
himself at the door to prevent him entering, and there ensued a
great struggle between parental love and the zeal of a courtier,
very glorious for *Madame la Duchesse*." The writer adds that
the King, being the stronger, went in, notwithstanding Condé's
resistance, but, according to other chroniclers, his Majesty was
so touched by his cousin's zeal for his safety that he ended by
allowing him to have his way.

Soon after this incident, the Duchesse de Bourbon's illness
took a turn for the better, and at the end of a fortnight she was
pronounced convalescent. Condé's presence was no longer
necessary ; but the change in his manner of life, the sleepless
nights, the fatigue and the anxiety he had endured, had been
too much for an old man whose constitution was already so
shattered, and it was evident that his days were numbered.

[1] " Souvenirs et Correspondance de Madame de Caylus."

He had expressed a wish to die at Chantilly, and it was hoped that it might be possible to gratify it. But, on the morning of 10 December, he became much weaker, and was warned that it was time to think of the Sacraments. He desired that Père des Champs should be summoned from Paris, and, turning to Gourville, observed : " Ah well ! my friend, I believe my journey will be a longer one than we thought. But I wish to write to the King." And, after a vain attempt to write himself, he dictated to his confessor, Père Bergier, a letter to Louis XIV., to implore his pardon for the Prince de Conti, who had been for some time in disgrace and seemed likely to remain there.

In the middle of the night, feeling worse, he made his confession and received absolution from Père Bergier, Père des Champs not having yet arrived, and at daybreak the curé of Fontainebleau brought him the Viaticum. Shortly afterwards, *Monsieur le Duc* arrived with the news that the King had, on his own initiative, pardoned the Prince de Conti, for the letter which *Monsieur le Prince* had dictated the previous day had not yet been despatched. This intelligence was a great relief to Condé, who caused a few lines to be added to the letter, thanking his Majesty for his kindness and assuring him that he should now die content.

Conti and Père des Champs arrived a little later, and, with the Duc and Duchesse d'Enghien, remained with him to the end, which came very peacefully between seven and eight o'clock in the evening. " No one," wrote the British Ambassador, the Earl of Arran, to his Government, " ever died with less concern, and he preserved his senses to the last minute."

After lying for some days in the mortuary chapel at Fontainebleau, which had been transformed into a *chapelle ardente*, the body of Condé was conveyed to Valery and interred in the family vault. His heart was deposited in the Jesuit church in the Rue Saint-Antoine. " In carrying to the same place the heart of my uncle, the Comte de Clermont," writes his great-grandson, " I had an opportunity of seeing all the hearts of our ancestors, which were deposited there, enclosed in silver-gilt cases ; and I remarked (as did also those who accompanied me) that the heart of the Great Condé was nearly double the size of all the others." [1]

On 10 March, 1687, a solemn service was held at Notre-Dame. The funeral oration, pronounced by Bossuet, is generally considered the masterpiece of that famous preacher, and is the greatest of all the tributes rendered to the memory of Condé.

" At that moment " (during his last hours), exclaimed the orator, " he (Condé) extended his consideration to the most humble of his servants. With a liberality worthy of his birth and of their services, he left them overwhelmed with gifts, but still more honoured by the proofs of his remembrance." But for the woman who had so gloriously borne his name, who had so uncomplainingly shared his misfortunes, Condé, on his deathbed, had not a word of tenderness, of gratitude, or of pardon. Nay, if we are to believe *la Grande Mademoiselle*, on the morrow of his master's death, Gourville carried to Louis XIV. a letter written some time before, to be given him after that event, in which Condé entreated the King never to allow the princess to leave her prison at Châteauroux.[2]

However that may be, Claire-Clémence never quitted that gloomy fortress, either living or dead ; for, when she died, after surviving her husband more than seven years (18 April, 1694), she was interred in the Church of Saint-Martin, which lay within the precincts of the château. " No member of her illustrious family appears to have attended her obsequies, and doubtless the twelve poor people whom she had had the charity to maintain out of her meagre allowance, with some Capuchins from the neighbouring convent, were the only persons who came to pray over the grave of her who, for her misfortune, had become " the very high, very excellent and puissant Princesse de Condé." [3]

---

[1] Louis Joseph de Bourbon, Prince de Condé, " Histoire de la Maison de Bourbon."

[2] Mademoiselle de Montpensier, " Mémoires."

[3] MM. Homberg & Jousselin, " la Femme du Grand Condé." During the Revolution, some ruffians forced open the chapel in which was the tomb of the unfortunate princess, carried off the leaden coffin and scattered its contents.

CHAPTER XIX

THE son and grandson of the Great Condé have left but few traces in history, and the little which is recorded of them does not, as a rule, redound to their credit.

Succeeding to the offices as well as to the titles of his father, Henri-Jules de Bourbon was appointed colonel of the infantry Regiment of Condé and *mestre de camp* of the cavalry corps of the same name, and took part in several campaigns, being present at the capture of Mons in 1691, and of Namur in the following year. During the latter part of the campaign of 1692, he was nominally second in command of the Army of Flanders, but no opportunity for distinction seems to have come his way, and soon afterwards ill-health obliged him to retire from active service. Henceforth, he divided his time between the Court, Paris, and Chantilly, though, as he grew older, the Court appears to have lost the attraction it had once had for him, and, when there, he remained most of the day in his apartments, only emerging to attend the King at his *lever* and *coucher*, or to visit the Ministers, whom, when he happened to want anything from them, it was his habit to importune to the verge of distraction.

Chantilly was "his delight." When he walked in the gardens, he was followed by four secretaries, to whom he dictated any ideas which occurred to him for the improvement of the château or the estate. He spent immense sums upon them, and with the happiest results, for he possessed the most exquisite taste. It was he who finished the parish church, erected upon land which had been given by his father to the inhabitants of the town, completed the Ménagerie, and built the gallery in the *Petit Château*, the *Galerie des Batailles*. In the pictures representing the history of the Great Condé which by his orders were painted for it, he was very reluctant to omit the actions which Condé had performed when in command of the armies of Spain. At the same time, he felt that he could not venture to expose to the eyes of Frenchmen the exploits which had been directed against themselves. The painter professed himself unable to suggest any means of reconciling his patron's wishes with his scruples, but, at length, the prince bethought himself of a most ingenious way out of the difficulty. He caused a picture to be painted in which the Muse of History was represented tearing with indignation, and flinging far away from her, the pages of a book which she held in her hands. On these pages were inscribed: "The Relief of Cambrai"; "The Relief of Valenciennes"; "The Retreat from before Arras"; while in the centre of the picture stood the Great Condé, endeavouring to impose silence on Fame, who, with trumpet in hand, was proclaiming his exploits against France.[1]

The prince could well afford to indulge his taste for the embellishment of Chantilly, since he had inherited the business acumen of his grandfather and amassed a great fortune, though, according to Saint-Simon, he was "a beggar in comparison with those who came after him." He does not appear to have been over scrupulous in his methods of acquiring wealth, and made a practice of lending large sums to the members of the Parlement

---

[1] Désormeaux, " Histoire de la Maison de Bourbon " ; Stanhope, " Life of Louis, Prince de Condé, surnamed the Great."

of Paris, in order to ensure their support in the lawsuits in which he was perpetually engaged, in view of which it is not surprising to learn that it was very rarely that a verdict was given against him.

With his son, who, on the death of the Great Condé, had retained the title of Duc de Bourbon, instead of assuming that of Enghien, which both his grandfather and father had borne, but was now officially styled *Monsieur le Duc*, he appears to have been on anything but cordial terms, though the harshness with which he sometimes treated him was tempered by a wholesome fear of the King, whose son-in-law he was. It must be admitted, however, that the Duc de Bourbon was scarcely the kind of son to inspire affection, even in a parent with an infinitely greater capacity for it than *Monsieur le Prince* possessed. Not only was he almost repulsive in appearance, but he was cursed with so violent a temper that it was positively dangerous to contradict him. One evening, when entertaining some friends at Saint-Maur, he had an argument with the Comte de Fiesque over some historical incident. When the count refused to admit that he was wrong, *Monsieur le Duc* sprang to his feet in a violent rage, and, snatching up a plate, hurled it at his guest's head, and then turned him out of the house, although, having been invited to stay the night, he had sent away his coach. The unfortunate Fiesque was obliged to make his way to the house of the curé of the parish and beg a bed from him.

He was, moreover, exceedingly vindictive, and any one whom he even suspected of doing him an ill turn speedily had cause to rue it. Thus, on one occasion, having reason to believe that a certain escapade of his in Paris, which had earned him a severe reprimand from his royal father-in-law, had been brought to the King's notice by the Marquis de Termes, one of his Majesty's *premiers valets de chambre*, he despatched several of his servants, armed with stout canes, to lie in wait for the supposed informer. They ambushed him successfully and administered so unmerciful a castigation that he was obliged to keep his bed for several days.

Saint-Simon accuses him of a love of brutal practical jokes, and asserts that the death of the Latin poet Santeuil, at Dijon, in 1694, was due to his having given him a glass of champagne into which he had emptied the contents of his snuff-box. But we can find no confirmation of this story, and probably there is no more truth in it than in a good many other of Saint-Simon's anecdotes.

Notwithstanding the indolence which in his youth had been the despair of his tutors, the pains bestowed upon his education had been by no means wasted, and even his enemy Saint-Simon is fain to admit that he was a well-read and intelligent man. In war his abilities were infinitely superior to those of his father, and had he enjoyed, like him, the advantage of the Great Condé's training, it is quite probable that he would have made a name for himself, that is to say, if Louis XIV., who had little liking for his son-in-law, could ever have been persuaded to entrust him with an independent command. Between 1688 and the Peace of Ryswick he served in several campaigns, and proved himself a very capable officer, as well as displaying brilliant courage, notably at the siege of Namur and in the battles of Steenkirke and Neerwinden. In the campaigns of the War of the Spanish Succession he took no part, and it would seem that, in spite of his military talents, or perhaps because of them, Louis XIV. did not desire to employ him.

With his wife *Monsieur le Duc* lived on good terms, though, in common with most aristocratic husbands of the time, he unfortunately found it impossible to concentrate his affections upon their lawful object. Of his mistresses the most noted was the beautiful Madame de Mussy. She was a little woman, but exquisitely shaped, "with a dazzling complexion and ravishing arms and bosom." The wife of a counsellor to the Parlement of Dijon, "who was too much in love with the wine of Beaune to guard a treasure so difficult to defend," *Monsieur le Duc* had met her when he was presiding over the Estates of Burgundy in place of his father, and, profiting by her husband's addiction to the bottle, had paid her a court which was soon crowned with success. When, at length, the bibulous counsellor learned what

had been going on under his very nose, he was furious, and
" carried his resentment even so far as to give his wife several
blows." His violence furnished the lady with a pretext for
leaving him which she was not slow to seize, and, while M. de
Mussy was petitioning the Parlement of Dijon for a decree
empowering him to have her shut up in a convent, she effected
her escape, followed her lover to Paris, and threw herself upon
his protection. This the prince readily promised, and, shortly
afterwards, Madame de Mussy found herself the occupant of
a luxuriously-furnished house in the precincts of the Temple,
where she was soon surrounded by a little Court, which was
composed not only of the Marquis de la Fare, the Abbé
Chaulieu, the Comte de Fiesque and other friends of *Monsieur
le Duc*, but also of several ladies of the Court, such as the
Duchesse de Bouillon and the Marquise de Bellefonds, who
were not too particular what company they kept, so long as it
was sufficiently amusing.

La petite Mussy, if she had been prudent, might have con-
tinned to live a life of luxury and pleasure for many years, for
the passion which she had inspired in the heart of *Monsieur le
Duc* was no ephemeral one. But, unfortunately for her, she
happened to meet, one night at the Opera, that notorious lady-
killer, the Comte d'Albert, who, after being banished from
France, on account of his intrigue with Madame de Luxembourg, had recently been expelled from Brussels, for making
himself too agreeable to the Mlle. Maupin—the heroine of
Théophile Gauthier's romance—then mistress of the Elector of
Bavaria.

The count, having no other amorous engagement on hand just
then, decided to make a conquest of Madame de Mussy. The
task was, of course, easy enough for a gentleman who, we are
assured, had only to show himself to ensure an immediate
capitulation, and soon Madame de Mussy had become as indifferent to her titular lover as she had formerly been to her
husband. *Monsieur le Duc*, "finding that she no longer
responded to his caresses with her accustomed ardour," had her
watched, and ere long discovered the truth. His wrath was

terrible, though, happily, he contented himself by venting it upon the furniture, mirrors, and porcelain of his perfidious mistress, among which he raged with such fury that in a few moments the apartment was strewn with the wreckage of what had represented a comfortable little fortune.

Madame de Mussy, whom love for her fascinating count had inspired with a courage of which she might not have otherwise been capable, boldly faced the storm, and informed the infuriated prince that "she was not his wife, that he had nothing wherewith to reproach her, and that she was in love with the Comte d'Albert, who was far more amiable than his Highness, as he might judge for himself by taking the trouble to look in a mirror."

Monsieur le Duc, beside himself with passion, swore that he would hand her over to her husband, who would take good care to have her shut up in a convent for the rest of her days, and took his departure, vowing vengeance.

Knowing enough of the vindictive character of the prince to be aware that this threat was no idle one, Madame de Mussy recognized that she ought not to lose a moment in placing herself beyond his reach. The Comte d'Albert, now reinstated in the good graces of the Elector of Bavaria, had recently set out for Madrid, where he had been appointed that prince's envoy, and she at once resolved to follow him thither. That same night, accompanied by her confidential *femme de chambre* and subsequent historian, Mlle. Valdory, she left Paris, disguised in masculine attire, and, after many adventures, for the War of the Succession was then raging in Spain, reached Madrid in safety. She had expected to find there the Comte d'Albert and consolation for her hardships and misfortunes in his arms; but not only was she deceived in this hope, but she learned that her lover was false to her, and that he had recently consented, doubtless for a substantial consideration, to make an honest woman of Mlle. de Montigny, a cast-off mistress of the Elector of Bavaria. Worn out by the fatigues and privations she had suffered during her journey from Paris, devoured by jealousy, and tortured by remorse, the unhappy

Madame de Mussy fell into a decline and died six months later.[1]

As for *Monsieur le Duc*, he consoled himself for his mistress's perfidy by a *liaison* with Madame de Rupelmonde—the wife of a Flemish gentleman in the Spanish service—whom Saint-Simon describes as " brown as a cow and possessed of unparalleled impudence." To this lady succeeded a certain Madame Locmaria, who was soon replaced, in her turn, by the pretty daughter of an upholsterer in the Rue des Fossés-Monsieur-le-Prince.[2]

Madame la Duchesse, however, had certainly no right to take exception to her husband's little affairs, for, though Madame de Caylus assures us that she " lived with him like an angel," it would seem that her marriage vows sat very lightly upon her. This daughter of Madame de Montespan was an exceedingly pretty, accomplished, and charming young woman ; but, if she had inherited her mother's beauty, intelligence, and fascination, she had also her full share of that too celebrated lady's less agreeable qualities, being selfish, extravagant, and deceitful, while her mordant wit made her universally dreaded. " Her wit shines in her eyes," writes *Madame ;* " but there is some malignity in them also. I always say that she reminds me of a pretty cat which, while you play with it, lets you feel its claws." " Although she was slightly deformed," says Saint-Simon, " her face was formed by the most tender loves and her nature made to dally with them. . . . She possessed the art of placing every one at their ease ; there was nothing about her which did not tend naturally to please, with a grace unparalleled, even in her slightest actions. She made captive even those who had the most cause to fear her, and those who had the best of reasons to hate her required often to recall the fact to resist her charms . . . Sportive, gay, and merry, she passed her youth in frivolity and in pleasures of all kinds,[3] and, whenever the opportunity presented itself, they extended even to debauchery. With

---

[1] " Histoire de Madame de Muci," par Mlle. B—— (Valdory), Amsterdam, 1731; "le Nouveau Siècle de Louis XIV. " ; Desnoiresterres, " les Cours galantes."

[2] " Mémoires du Comte de Maurepas."

[3] Her chief pleasure appears to have been gambling, which is scarcely surprising, when we consider that she was the daughter of a woman who had been accustomed

these qualities, she possessed much intelligence and much capacity for intrigue and affairs, with a suppleness which cost her nothing. She was scornful, mocking, bitterly sarcastic, incapable of friendship and very capable of hatred ; mischievous, haughty, implacable, prolific in base artifices and in the most cruel *chansons*, with which she gaily assailed persons whom she pretended to love and who passed their lives with her.[1] She was the siren of the poets ; she had all their charms and all their perils."

The charms of the young princess naturally drew around her many adorers ; but, though she had neither affection nor esteem for her husband, and was far from insensible to the homage which was paid her, her conduct would not appear to have merited any very severe censure until some years after her marriage, when a *soupirant* presented himself whom it would have been difficult for any woman to resist. This was Louis François de Bourbon, Prince de Conti, the young man for whose pardon, it will be remembered, the Great Condé had petitioned Louis XIV. on his death-bed. This pardon had unfortunately been a merely formal one, for the prince had far too much of his famous uncle's temperament, that is to say, the temperament of the Condé of the Regency and the Fronde, ever to secure the favour of *le Grand Monarque*, who always regarded with suspicion those who showed any independence of character, particularly if they happened to belong to the Royal House. In consequence, though he possessed a natural instinct for war, combined with the most superb courage, and appeared destined for a brilliant military career, nothing would induce the King

to win and lose several hundred thousand francs at a single sitting, and had on one memorable occasion lost over two million. In May, 1700, Dangeau informs us that *Madame la Duchesse* wrote to Madame de Maintenon to tell her that she had lost " from 10,000 to 12,000 pistoles [from 100,000 to 120,000 livres], which it was impossible for her to pay just then." Madame de Maintenon showed the letter to the King and begged him to come to his daughter's assistance. His Majesty consented, and, after requesting that a detailed statement of the whole of the lady's liabilities should be drawn up and submitted to him, paid them in full, without saying a word to her husband, which was distinctly kind of him.

[1] In the *chansons* attributed to her, some of which are undeniably clever, she exercised her satirical wit at the expense of the Duc and Duchesse de Bourgogne, Madame de Maintenon, her husband, and even her royal father.

LOUISE FRANÇOISE, DUCHESSE DE BOURBON (CALLED MADAME
LA DUCHESSE)

to allow him to hold high command, and he had the mortification of seeing himself passed over in favour of generals who were manifestly his inferiors.

Conti was a tall and rather awkward-looking man, with irregular but pleasing features, and the most charming manners which made him a universal favourite. He was married to Marie Thérèse de Bourbon, the eldest daughter of *Monsieur le Prince*, who adored him and of whom he appears to have been fond ; but this did not prevent him from falling in love with *Madame la Duchesse*, who returned his passion with equal fervour. *Monsieur le Duc* was furious, but he did not dare to quarrel openly with his brother-in-law, and, besides, thanks to the complaisance of the Dauphin, who was much attached both to his half-sister and to Conti, and gave the lovers many opportunities of meeting at his country-house at Meudon, " the affair was conducted with such admirable discretion that they never gave any one any hold over them." [1]

It has sometimes been asserted that the prince's infatuation for *Madame la Duchesse* lost him the throne of Poland, to which, through the skilful intrigues of the Abbé de Polignac, the French envoy at Warsaw, he had been elected, by a majority in the Diet, on the death of John Sobieski, in 1697. But, although it is true that he was exceedingly loth to leave France and his mistress, and employed every possible pretext to delay his departure for Poland, it is very doubtful whether, without far stronger support than Louis XIV. was prepared to give him, an earlier arrival upon the scene would have enabled him to triumph over so formidable a competitor as Augustus of Saxony.

At the beginning of 1709, Louis XIV.'s dislike of Conti at length yielded to the danger of the country, and the prince was informed that he had been selected to command the Army of the North in the approaching campaign. This tardy recognition of his undoubted merits came, however, too late. For some time past he had been in very bad health, and on 21 February he died, at the early age of forty-five.

[1] Saint-Simon.

His death, which was regarded as a public calamity, so great had been his popularity and so high the opinion formed of his military talents, was a terrible blow to *Madame la Duchesse.* "He was the only one to whom she had been faithful," writes Saint-Simon ; "she was the only one to whom he had not been fickle ; his greatness would have done homage to her, and she would have shone with his lustre." "She had need of all the command which she had naturally over herself," observes Madame de Caylus, "to conceal her grief from *Monsieur le Duc.* She succeeded, the more easily, I believe, because he was so relieved at no longer having such a rival that he cared neither to investigate the past nor the depths of the heart."

The untimely death of the Prince de Conti was followed, at an interval of a few weeks, by that of *Monsieur le Prince*, who had long been in failing health.

During the latter years of his life the eccentricity for which he had always been noted had become more and more pronounced, until at last, if Saint-Simon is to be believed, it was hardly distinguishable from madness. Calling one morning on the Maréchale de Noailles, at the moment when her bed was being made, and there only remained the counterpane to be put on, he paused for a moment at the door, and then, crying out in a transport of delight : "*Oh ! le beau lit, le beau lit, qu'il est appétisant !*" he took a flying leap on to the bed and rolled over several times. Then he got down and made his excuses to the astonished old lady, saying that her bed looked so clean and so beautifully made that he had been unable to resist the temptation to roll in it.

It was whispered that there were times when he imagined himself a dog or some other animal, and Saint-Simon declares that "people very worthy of belief had assured him that they had seen the prince at the King's *coucher* suddenly throw his head into the air several times running and open his mouth quite wide, like a dog while barking, yet without making a noise."

He also began attending in a ridiculously minute manner to

accordingly brought in, who pretended to be dead, but ate nevertheless. This trick succeeded, and for the remaining weeks of his life the prince consented to take food, but only in the presence of the doctors and his fellow-corpses.

As *Monsieur le Prince* grew worse, his wife summoned up sufficient courage to beg him to think of his conscience and to see a confessor. He angrily refused, and persisted in his refusal, notwithstanding her tears and supplications. As a matter of fact, he had been seeing Père de la Tour of the Oratory for some months past, though in the strictest secrecy. He had at first demanded that the reverend father should come to him by night, and in disguise. Père de la Tour replied that he would be quite willing to visit *Monsieur le Prince* under cover of darkness, but that the respect he owed to the cloth would not permit him to masquerade in the attire of a layman. After some hesitation, the penitent consented to waive this condition ; but he caused the most elaborate precautions to be taken to prevent his visitor being recognized. He was admitted, at dead of night, by a little back door, where a confidential servant of the prince, with a lantern in one hand and a bunch of keys in the other, was waiting to receive him, and conducted to the sick-room along dark passages and through many doors, which were unlocked and locked again after him as he passed. Having at length reached his destination, he confessed *Monsieur le Prince*, and was then conducted out of the house by the same way and in the same manner as he had entered it. Similar precautions were observed on each of his subsequent visits.

Henri Jules de Bourbon, fifth Prince de Condé, died on

1 April, 1709, at the age of sixty-six. His last instructions to his son were to carry out all the improvements which he had projected at Chantilly, and to take care that none of the honours due to his rank were omitted at his funeral.

And so he passed away, "regretted by no one, neither by servants nor friends, neither by child nor wife. Indeed, *Madame la Princesse* was so ashamed of her tears that she made excuses for them." [1]

The Duc de Bourbon, for he preferred to retain his old title, instead of assuming that which his grandfather had rendered so illustrious—an example which was followed by his son, and, a century later, by the last head of his House—did not live to carry out his father's projects at Chantilly, since he survived him less than a year. He had been suffering for some time from continual pains in the head, "which tempered the joy he felt at being delivered from his troublesome father and brother-in-law." [2] His mother, much alarmed, had besought him to think of his soul, and this he had promised to do, as soon as the Carnival and its pleasures were over and the fashionable season for penitence had arrived. On the evening of Shrove Monday (3 March, 1710), as he was driving home over the Pont-Royal from the Hôtel de Coislin, he was seized with a fit and carried in an unconscious condition to the Hôtel de Condé. Priests and doctors were speedily in attendance, but he never recovered consciousness, and died about four o'clock in the morning.

"*Madame la Duchesse*," writes Madame de Caylus, "appeared infinitely afflicted by his death, and I believe she was sincere." But the chronicler is careful to explain that this affliction was not caused by any love for the departed prince, but "because, since the death of the Prince de Conti, her mind and heart were occupied by nothing but ambition, [3] and *Monsieur le Duc* possessed all the qualities necessary to make her conceive great hopes in that direction."

[1] Saint-Simon.   [2] Ibid.

[3] But, if we are to believe Saint-Simon, her heart was partially occupied by the Comte de Léon, a son of the amorous Lassay by his first marriage, who, "although he had the face of a monkey, was perfectly well-made."

CHAPTER XX

Louis Henri de Bourbon-Condé—He assumes the title of Duc de Bourbon, instead of that of Prince de Condé, and is known as *Monsieur le Duc*—His personal appearance—He loses an eye by a shooting-accident—His military career—He becomes President of the Council of Regency on the death of Louis XIV.—His protection of John Law—His wealth—His character—His marriage with Marie Anne de Bourbon-Conti—Singular intrigue which precedes it—His indifference to his wife—His amours—The financier Berthelot de Pléneuf—Gallantries of Madame de Pléneuf—Saint-Simon's portrait of her—Her daughter, Agnès de Pléneuf—Singular beauty and intelligence of this young girl—Violent jealousy which her mother conceives for her—Marriage of Agnès to the Marquis de Prie, who is soon afterwards appointed Ambassador at Turin—Her life at Turin—Disgrace and bankruptcy of Berthelot de Pléneuf—Financial straits of the de Pries—Madame de Prie comes to Paris to intercede with the Government on her husband's behalf—Calumnies concerning her spread by her mother and her partisans—Her elations with the Regent.

BY his marriage with Mlle. de Nantes, Louis III., Duc de Bourbon, had had nine children—three sons and six daughters—all of whom survived him.[1] The eldest son, Louis Henri, hitherto known as the Duc d'Enghien, was, at the time of his father's death, in his eighteenth year. Like the latter, he preferred the title of Duc de Bourbon to that of Prince de Condé, and, like him, was henceforth styled *Monsieur le Duc*. In contrast to his father, who had been very

---

[1] Here is the list:

1. Marie Gabrielle Éléonore (1690-1760), Abbess of Saint-Antoine-lez-Paris.
2. Louis Henri, Duc de Bourbon, Prince de Condé (1692-1740).
3. Louise Elisabeth, Mlle. de Bourbon (1693-1775).
4. Louise Anne, Mlle. de Charolais (1697-1741).
5. Marie Anne, Mlle. de Clermont (1697-1741).
6. Charles, Comte de Charolais (1700-1760).
7. Henriette Louise Marie Françoise Gabrielle, Mlle. de Vermandois (born in 1703).
8. Elisabeth Alexandre, Mlle. de Sens (1705-1765).
9. Louis, Comte de Clermont (1709-1771).

short and rather thick-set, Louis Henri de Bourbon-Condé was tall
and thin, with a long face and prominent cheek-bones. At this
period, however, he was not considered an ill-looking young
man, but two years later [he had the misfortune to meet with an
accident which disfigured him.

In the winter of 1712—that fatal winter which witnessed the
successive deaths of the charming Duchesse de Bourgogne,
her husband, and their eldest son, the little Duc de Bretagne—
he took part in a battue at Marly with the Dauphin and that
prince's younger brother, the Duc de Berry. *Monsieur le Duc*
and the Duc de Berry were standing facing one another, on
opposite sides of a frozen pool. The latter fired at a bird, which
was flying very low, and missed it ; and part of the charge,
rebounding from the ice, struck *Monsieur le Duc* in the left eye,
the sight of which was destroyed.

The young prince succeeded to his father's post of Grand
Master of the King's Household, to his government of
Burgundy, and to the command of the cavalry and infantry
regiments of Condé. In 1711 he took part in the Flemish campaign under Villars, and in the assault on Hordain showed that
he had inherited the courage of his race. In the following year,
he was in nominal command of the cavalry of the Army of
Flanders, and assisted at the sieges of Douai, Le Quesnoy, and
Bouchain ; while in 1713 he followed Villars to the Rhine, was
present at the sieges of Landau and Freiburg, and was made
maréchal de camp.

In his will, Louis XIV. had named the Duc de Bourbon a
member of the Council of Regency, as soon as he should reach
the age of twenty-four ; but on the death of *le Grand Monarque,*
his wishes were immediately set aside, and the Regent, the
Duc d'Orleans, proceeded to appoint the Council himself, with
Monsieur le Duc as its president. Apart, however, from the
share he took in the campaign against the legitimated sons of
the late King, the Duc du Maine and the Comte de Toulouse,
with the object of reducing them to the rank of simple peers of
the realm, the prince appears to have occupied himself very
little with politics during the first years of the Regency, and

confined his activities to the financial speculations in which half Paris was then engaging. With so much ardour, indeed, did he espouse the cause of the Scotch adventurer Law that he was accused of being one of the authors of the "System" which involved the country in such disaster. Any way, he had the courage to defend the fallen idol to the very last, and when Law, his life being no longer safe in Paris, made his escape to Flanders, it was one of the Duc de Bourbon's carriages which conveyed him to the frontier.

Very wealthy before the "System," his great fortune was materially increased by successful speculation. In 1720 it was computed at not less than sixty million livres.

The character of the prince is very diversely estimated by his contemporaries. Some writers, such as Marais, Barbier, and Duclos, judge him severely, and describe him as hasty in temper, brusque in his manners, debauched, dishonourable, rapacious, and entirely destitute of political capacity. Others, like Saint-Simon and the Dowager-Duchess d'Orléans, recognize in him a certain merit. The former acknowledges that, with all his faults, he had "an indomitable obstinancy, an inflexible firmness ;" while the mother of the Regent, whose opinions at least possess the advantage of being consistently sincere, writes of him in 1719 :

"*Monsieur le Duc* has many good qualities and many friends. He is polished and knows how to behave well, but his attainments are not very extensive. Nor is he better informed, but there is a loftiness and a nobility in his character, and he knows how to uphold his rank."

Louis Henri de Bourbon-Condé, in fact, was neither the odious nor the incapable person whom certain historians have depicted. His courage was indisputable ; if he was rapacious, he was also generous and open-handed ; if he was a bad enemy, he was also a faithful friend ; he possessed cultured tastes, and beneath his love of pleasure and his apparent indifference to public affairs he concealed qualities which only required to be stimulated into activity to make of him, if not a statesman, at least a formidable party-leader.

In the summer of 1713, *Monsieur le Duc* was married to his cousin, Marie Anne de Bourbon-Conti, at the same time as his second sister, Mlle. de Bourbon, became the wife of the young Prince de Conti. This double marriage, which was regarded with more or less repugnance by all four of the parties concerned, affords a curious illustration of the despotism exercised by Louis XIV. over the members of the Royal House.

The death of *Monsieur le Prince*, in 1709, had been followed by a most acrimonious lawsuit over his will between the Condés and Contis, which, suspended for a while by the sudden demise of his successor, had been resumed with redoubled bitterness as soon as decency permitted. Nothing was further from the thoughts of the Contis than an alliance with their detested cousins, and, in point of fact, secret negotiations had been for some time in progress between them and the Orléans family for the marriage of the Prince de Conti to Mlle. de Chartres, second daughter of the future Regent.

Now, *Madame la Princesse*, a pious and gentle soul, had been terribly distressed by this family quarrel, and had made several futile efforts to induce the litigants to come to an arrangement. By some means, she got wind of the matrimonial negotiations just mentioned, which opened her eyes to a very natural means of accommodation which had not yet occurred to her, namely, a double marriage between her grandchildren. Aware that she herself would never be able to bring this about, she determined to appeal to Louis XIV., who had also endeavoured to reconcile the parties, and had been more than once on the point of employing his authority to put a stop to proceedings so prejudicial to the dignity of the Royal House, and who, she knew, would be the more ready to listen to her, since he could hardly fail to be extremely irritated to learn, from an outside source, of the projected marriage of the Prince de Conti and a daughter of the Duc d'Orléans.

She had not miscalculated. The King at once expressed his warm approval of her proposal, and lost no time in sending for *Madame la Duchesse*, whom he informed of his wishes. That lady began to remonstrate vigorously, but his Majesty "spoke to her, not as a father, but as a master who intends to be obeyed without hesitation," and she reluctantly yielded. Next came the turn of the Princesse de Conti, who offered the same stubborn resistance, and only capitulated when the King, losing all patience, informed her that, if she refused to give her consent, he would cause the double marriage to be celebrated without it. As for the parties most nearly concerned, his Majesty did not even trouble to go through the form of consulting them, and on 9 July the marriages were celebrated, in the chapel at Versailles, by the Cardinal de Rohan.

The new Duchesse de Bourbon, who was nearly five years older than her husband, was an extremely pretty young woman, and "possessed of much intelligence, amiability, and charm of manner." [1] Neither the attractions of her mind nor of her person, however, appear to have made any impression upon *Monsieur le Duc*, for which he was not perhaps wholly to blame, having regard to the peculiar circumstances in which the marriage had taken place, besides which it would seem that his wife made very little attempt to understand him. Any way, he never entertained for her the smallest affection, and the tie which bound them was never more than a nominal one.

Such being the relations between *Monsieur le Duc* and his consort, it was but natural that the former should have become the quarry of all the *dames galantes* of the time. Madame de Sabran, one time mistress of the Regent, Madame de Zurlauben, Madame de Polignac, Madame de Nesle, mother of the too-celebrated sisters who were to succeed one another in the affections of Louis XV., and other facile beauties seem to have dipped their pretty fingers freely into his coffers; but none of these *liaisons* was of long duration, and it was not until the prince was approaching his thirtieth year that he found a woman capable of fixing his affections.

In the closing years of the reign of Louis XIV. there lived in a magnificent hôtel at the corner of the Rues de Cléry and Poissonière a family of the name of Berthelot de Pléneuf. The

---

[1] Saint-Simon.

father of the family, Étienne Berthelot de Pléneuf, was a wealthy Government official and army-contractor, a younger son of François Berthelot, a person of comparatively humble origin, who had amassed an enormous fortune, partly by judicious land-speculation in Canada, where he owned "estates of the value of a province," which the King had transformed for him into the county of Saint-Laurent, and partly as a revenue-farmer and commissary. Old Berthelot had employed a considerable portion of his wealth in the purchase of lucrative Government posts and estates in France, which he distributed among his sons, to Étienne's share falling the office of Director General of the Powders and Saltpetres of France and the seigneurie of Pléneuf, which entitled him to style himself the seigneur de Pléneuf.

In 1696, Pléneuf, who was then about thirty-five, had married, *en secondes noces*, a Mlle. Agnès Riault d'Ouilly, a daughter of a rich bourgeois family, which, like his own, had been recently ennobled. The second Madame de Pléneuf, who, it may be mentioned, was nearly twenty years her husband's junior, had been one of the prettiest girls in Paris, and in due course she became one of its most beautiful aud fascinating women. "Tall, perfectly shaped, with an extremely agreeable countenance, intelligence, grace, tact, and *savoir-vivre*," [1] she triumphed like a queen, and as Pléneuf, proud of her success, denied her nothing, the salons in the Rue de Cléry soon became the rendezvous of all fashionable Paris.

If in beauty and intelligence Madame de Pléneuf left little to be desired, the same, unfortunately, could not be said for her reputation. The prolonged absences of her husband with the army provided her with abundant opportunities for receiving the homage of her numerous admirers, and she took advantage of them so freely that she earned for herself the name of the Messalina of her time. To no lady in Paris did gossip ascribe so many lovers, and, in most cases, it is to be feared, with only too much justification. There was a Lorraine prince, the Prince Charles d'Armagnac; the Cardinal de Rohan; the Ducs de

[1] Saint-Simon.

Duras and de la Vallière ; the versatile Marquis de Dangeau, author of the famous "Journal"; Canon Destouches, father of Néricault-Destouches, the diplomatist and playwright ; young La Baume, son of the Maréchal de Tallard; the Marquis de Cany, son of the War Minister Chamillard ; the dashing Comte de Gacé, who, in February, 1716, fought the famous midnight duel with the Duc de Richelieu in the middle of the Rue Saint-Thomas-du Louvre. And the list might be considerably extended.

But if Madame de Pléneuf were an immoral, she was also a very clever woman, and displayed really remarkable address in managing her crowd of *soupirants* and avoiding anything approaching a scandal. " Enamoured of herself to the last degree," writes Saint-Simon, " she desired that others should be so, but it was necessary to obtain permission. She knew how to pick and choose among her admirers, and so well did she understand how to establish her empire that complete happiness never exceeded, in appearance, the bounds of respect and propriety ; and there was not one of the chosen band who dared to show either jealousy or mortification. Each one hoped for his turn, and, while waiting, the choice more than suspected was respected by all in perfect silence, without the least altercation amongst them. It is astonishing how this conduct gained her friends of importance, who always remained attached to her, without there being any question of anything more than friendship, and whom she found, in case of need, the most eager to serve her in her affairs. She was at this time in the best and the most aristocratic society, as much as the wife of Pléneuf was able to be ; and there she has remained since, among all the vicissitudes which she has experienced."

Saint-Simon does not exaggerate. Madame de Pléneuf never encountered among her admirers any resistance to the regulations which she imposed upon them. All submitted to them with a good grace; all passed without protest from the rank of candidates for her favour to that of lover, and from that of lover to that of friend, and of friends, in some instances, ready to make considerable sacrifices for her sake.

Among several children, Madame de Pléneuf had a daughter,

born in 1698, some two years after the marriage of her parents, to whom she had given her own name of Agnès. Beautiful as was the mother, the daughter promised to be more beautiful still, and with her physical perfections she combined vivacity, intelligence, and the most charming manners. "A figure supple and above the middle height, the air of a nymph, a delicate face, pretty cheeks, a well-formed nose, blonde hair, eyes a trifle small, but bright and expressive; in a word, a physiognomy refined and distinguished, and a voice as charming as her face." Such is the description given of her, when she was fifteen, by the Président Hénault, and his praises are echoed by practically all contemporary writers. Saint-Simon declares that she was "beautiful, well-made, more charming by reason of those indescribable things which captivate, and with much intelligence carefully cultivated"; Marais admits that there was "much that was agreeable in her countenance, in her mind, and in all her manners"; d'Argenson proclaims her "*la fleur des pois*"; while in the eyes of Duclos, she "possessed more than beauty," and "everything about her was seductive."

Now, while Agnès remained a child, Madame de Pléneuf would appear to have been quite a devoted mother, and "it was the passion and occupation of her life to bring her up well." But, as the little girl advanced towards womanhood, and gained every day what she herself was losing in attractions, with the result that the homage of some of the gallants who frequented the Hôtel de Pléneuf began to be transferred from the mother to the daughter, the affection which she had once entertained for her gradually changed to dislike, and eventually to the bitterest jealousy and hatred. "In proportion as the daughter pleased by a hundred attractions," writes Saint-Simon, "she displeased her mother. Madame de Pléneuf could not endure the sight of homage addressed to others than herself at her own house. The advantages of youth irritated her. Her daughter, whom she was unable to prevent from perceiving it, suffered her dependence, endured her murmurs, supported the constraints imposed upon her, but she began to be annoyed by them. Pleasantries concerning the jealousy of her mother escaped her, which were reported to Madame de Pléneuf. The latter felt the ridicule of them. She flew into a passion. The girl retorted, and Pléneuf, more prudent than she was, dreading a scandal which might prejudice the establishment of his daughter in life, decided to provide her with a husband."

It was certainly high time to separate mother and daughter, for the enmity between them was increasing every day, and at the beginning of 1713 an incident occurred which brought matters to a crisis and made it impossible for them to remain any longer under the same roof.

Among the admirers of Madame de Pléneuf was a certain Comte d'Angennes. Young, handsome, and of charming manners, he had not been permitted to sigh in vain; indeed, the lady appears to have conceived for him a most violent passion. In a surprisingly short time, however, she perceived that the ardour of her new lover was beginning to cool, for, though frequenting the house as assiduously as ever, he no longer sought opportunities of being alone with his hostess. Madame de Pléneuf, her suspicions aroused, watched him closely, and more than once detected him talking in low tones to Agnès, with an expression on his face which there was no mistaking.

Thenceforth the jealous woman's hatred of her too attractive daughter knew no bounds. No longer did she trouble to dissimulate her feelings from her friends, but actually incited the most devoted of them to imitate the attitude she adopted towards the girl, with the result that poor Agnès's life became almost unendurable.

Unendurable, too, was the sight of her to her unnatural mother, and she importuned her husband until he consented that the girl should leave the house and be placed in a convent, while awaiting the appearance on the scene of an eligible suitor. Several gentlemen who answered more or less to this description speedily presented themselves, and, after some hesitation, M. de Pléneuf decided in favour of the Marquis de Prie.

The marquis was twenty-five years older than Agnès and,

U

though he was the possessor of large estates, they were either
so unproductive or so heavily mortgaged that they brought
him in next to nothing. But he was a member of a very
ancient House, connected with several of the most illustrious
families in France, was governor of Bourbon-Lancy, colonel
of the cavalry regiment which bore his name, held the rank
of brigadier-general in the Army, and, finally, was one of the
godfathers of the heir to the throne.

This last honour, which he owed to his good fortune in
happening to be with his aunt the Duchesse de Ventadour,
gouvernante to the Duc d'Anjou, in Louis XIV.'s cabinet, at
the moment when the infant prince was brought thither for
his Majesty's inspection, seems to have had great weight with
M. de Pléneuf, who was intoxicated with the idea of an alliance
with the godfather of his future King. As for the marquis,
it is probable that M. de Pléneuf's money-bags constituted
a far more potent attraction for him than the *beaux yeux* of
his lovely daughter. He was not only poor, but ambitious, and,
now that the approach of peace threatened to put an end to
his hopes of military distinction, he had decided to embark
upon a diplomatic career, and aspired to an embassy, for which,
of course, the possession of a long purse was an indispensable
qualification.

The preliminaries were soon concluded, and on 27 December,
1713, Agnès Berthelot de Pléneuf became the Marquise de Prie.
Taken to Versailles by the Duchesse de Ventadour, to be
presented to Louis XIV., she astonished all the Court by her
dazzling beauty and her precocious airs of a woman of the
world ; and even those who had been inclined to condemn M. de
Prie for having contracted a *mésalliance* were obliged to admit
that he had married a wife of whom any man might be proud.
Almost immediately after his marriage, the marquis was nominated Ambassador to the King of Sardinia, and set out for
Turin, whither, after a short interval, his wife followed him.

At Turin Madame de Prie remained five years. For the
first two or three, during which a little daughter was born to
her, everything went smoothly. Her husband was kind and

attentive, and, if she felt for him no affection and some contempt—for he was a pompous and self-opinionated person, with abilities as slender as his ambitions were lofty—she, at least, tolerated him ; while, as the Ambassadress of the greatest King in the world, and one of the most beautiful women in the Piedmontese capital, she was the object of universal homage, and no social gathering was deemed complete which she did not grace with her presence. But towards the end of 1716 an event occurred which was to effect a great change in the fortunes of the Pries.

For some time past a very ugly cloud had been slowly gathering over the head of M. de Pléneuf. At this period, and, indeed, until a very much later date, most gentlemen connected with the commissariat department of the Army were but indifferently honest ; but long impunity had rendered Pléneuf unusually audacious, and so outrageously did he rob the Army of Italy, of which he had acted as chief commissary, that in 1706 Louis XIV. ordered an inquiry to be instituted.

Matters would probably have gone hardly with Pléneuf, if he had not had the good fortune to possess powerful protectors. Thanks to their efforts, not only were the charges against him not pressed, but, a little while afterwards, he was actually appointed chief clerk at the War Office.

Nevertheless, his peculations, and those of his colleagues, were not forgotten, and in 1714 the Government decided upon a new revision of the accounts of the Army of Italy. This investigation, temporarily interrupted by the last illness and death of Louis XIV., was resumed some months later, when Philippe d'Orléans, eager to court popularity, determined to make the revenue-farmers and commissaries disgorge their ill-gotten gains ; and Pléneuf was the first to be summoned before the Court instituted for that purpose. This time, there was no one to intervene in his favour, and, warned that his arrest was imminent, he fled to Switzerland, and thence made his way to his daughter at Turin.

In saving his person, however, he had not succeeded in saving his property ; and his hôtel in Paris and his country-estates were sequestrated until such time as he should make restitution of the immense sums of which he had defrauded the State.

The disgrace and bankruptcy of Pléneuf was a terrible blow to the de Pries. They might have stomached the loss of the old gentleman's reputation, for the offence of which he had been guilty was of such common occurrence in those days as to be regarded with a very lenient eye, and, indeed, he appears to have received quite a warm welcome at the Court of Turin; but the loss of his money was another matter altogether.

With the laudable desire of upholding the honour of France, both the Ambassador and his wife had incurred heavy expenditure during their residence in Italy ; de Prie's small fortune was entirely exhausted, and very little was left of Agnès's dowry. It was to the purse of Pléneuf that they had been looking to replenish their empty coffers, and here he was quartered upon them, with a healthy appetite and extravagant tastes, but without a crown in his pocket. In short, the ambassadorial *ménage* found itself reduced to the direst extremities, and it was only by pawning his plate and borrowing money at usurious interest that the unfortunate representative of the might and majesty of France was able to continue at his post.

Towards the end of the year 1718, matters had reached such a pass that no hope of escaping from his difficulties remained to him save by the intervention of his Government. Again and again he had appealed to Torcy, the Minister for Foreign Affairs, for assistance ; but the answer was always the same : the Royal Treasury was empty ; it was impossible at present even to pay his Excellency's salary, much less to discharge his debts.

In despair, the Ambassador determined to send his wife to Paris to plead their cause with the Government, and at the beginning of December Madame de Prie set out for France.

The young woman who returned to Paris was a very different person from the girl who had quitted it five years before. Not only had she gained in outward attractions, but she had gained enormously in worldly knowledge. She had learned the ways of Courts, and had learned them at one where falsehood and dissimulation were considered the first essentials of every good politician. She had learned some of the subtleties of diplomacy, for the Marquis de Prie, who had been no match for Victor Amadeus and his Ministers, had been only too thankful to avail himself of the advice and assistance of his clever wife and father-in-law; indeed, for some months past it was they who had conducted the real work of the embassy. She had learned too to understand the power of her beauty, for, though there would appear to be no reason to believe that she had ever surrendered to love, she had certainly known how to inspire it, and a prince of the Royal House of Savoy—the Prince di Carignano—the Baron Ferron, Prime Minister of Victor Amadeus, the Chevalier de Lozilières, first secretary to the embassy, and the Marquis d'Alincourt, son of the Maréchal de Villeroy, who stayed for some time in Turin on his return from a campaign against the Turks, had been all devoted admirers. "But, above all," observes her admiring biographer, M. Thirion, "she had learned how to toil, to suffer, to defend herself against the ills of life, to struggle and to combat, in order to satisfy the exigencies of an uncertain hand-to-mouth existence, in such fashion that, beneath the frail envelope of this adorable young body, there beat an almost virile heart, there resided a soul matured before its time, disciplined and for ever superior to cowardly weaknesses." [1]

And it was a very different Paris to which she returned. The austere and bigoted *régime* of Louis XIV. and Madame de Maintenon, where even the most profligate and reckless had been constrained to some semblance of decorum, was no more, and the pent-up impatience of a corrupt society was finding relief in a veritable saturnalia of sensuality. Vice, which for so many years had scarcely dared to rear its head, now stalked abroad, naked and unashamed; virtue, and even ordinary decency, was mocked at and derided. The Regent himself set the tone in moral depravity, and his example was followed by the Princes and Princesses of the Blood, by the bulk of the nobility and by a considerable proportion of the wealthy middle-class.

[1] "Madame de Prie (1698–1727)," Paris, 1905.

"The disorderly and foolish life in Paris," writes the old Duchesse d'Orléans, "becomes every day more detestable and more horrible. Every time it thunders I tremble for this town."[1]

To send a beautiful and unprotected young woman into the midst of so licentious a Court was, to say the least of it, a very injudicious action on de Prie's part, and some contemporary writers are of opinion that it was his deliberate intention to launch her upon some gallant adventure. In this, as we shall presently see, they have probably done him an injustice; but, however that may be, nothing in the conduct of his wife during the first months after her arrival in Paris indicates that she had the least idea of speculating in her charms.

Since it was, of course, out of the question for her to demand the hospitality of her detestable mother, she installed herself with her little daughter in a small house close to the Convent of La Conception, belonging to one of her aunts, Madame de Séchelles, to whom she paid an annual rent of 500 livres, for the use of a portion of it. She lived very quietly, for she was almost entirely without resources, and seldom went into Society, though, in accordance with her husband's instructions, she solicited audiences of the Regent, the Abbé Dubois, Torcy, and, indeed, every one who might be able to be of assistance to the impecunious Ambassador.

The interviews which took place between her detested daughter and these distinguished persons did not escape Madame de Pléneuf, and, thanks to the malevolent activity of her and her friends, a rumour soon began to spread that the young Ambassadress, whose beauty never failed to cause a sensation wherever she appeared, was employing her charms to mend her broken fortunes. She was accused of prostituting herself to the Maréchal de la Feuillade, to d'Alincourt and to Torcy, and of having made an attempt to subjugate the heart of the Regent, who, it was added, had repulsed her, either because she had not pleased him, or because he regarded her as too dangerous a mistress.

[1] "Correspondance complète de Madame, duchesse d'Orléans," Letter of 27 Septembre, 1720.

There seems to have been no truth whatever in these allegations. La Feuillade was in very bad health; d'Alincourt on the eve of espousing a wealthy heiress, and Torcy approaching his sixtieth year. As for the Regent, well, the post of chief sultana to his Highness was not just then vacant, being occupied by Madame de Parabère; and Madame de Prie was certainly not the kind of woman either to risk the humiliation of a rebuff or to be content with a subordinate position. Moreover, no trustworthy contemporary chronicler has charged the lady with any such ambition as gossip ascribed to her.

If, however, the Regent did not fall in love with Madame de Prie, she seems to have made a very favourable impression upon him, and she was several times invited to assist at those too-celebrated *petits soupers* at which the ruler of France was accustomed to seek relaxation from the cares of State. However, such orgies were but little to her taste, and when she had at length succeeded in obtaining from him a promise that her husband's debts at Turin should be settled, or that he should be permitted to resign his post, she ceased to appear at the Palais-Royal.

Meanwhile, the favour with which Madame de Prie was regarded in high places had begun to alarm Madame de Pléneuf and her coterie. Since her daughter's return to Paris that amiable lady had not ceased to aim at her every kind of shaft that hatred and malice could forge and to incite her docile admirers to do the same. When, however, they saw her a welcome guest at the Palais-Royal, they began to ask themselves if they had not carried their hostility a little too far; and, though Madame de Pléneuf herself professed to be implacable, some of her friends began to make overtures to her daughter, with a view to bringing about a reconciliation. Nothing, however, came of these negotiations, for, before they had proceeded very far, an event occurred which was to fan the dying embers of the old feud into the flame of a new and interminable war.

CHAPTER XXI

Origin of the *liaison* between *Monsieur le Duc* and Madame de Prie considered—Extraordinary ascendency which the latter acquires over her lover—For a while, the favourite leads a life of pleasure, but is soon obliged to give her attention to politics—Exasperation of Madame de Pléneuf's coterie against her—Insecurity of *Monsieur le Duc's* position—The Orléans faction—Intrigues of the War Minister Le Blanc and the Belle-Isles—Hatred of Madame de Prie for Le Blanc—She resolves to crush the common enemies of herself and *Monsieur le Duc*—Her skilful conduct—Murder of Sandrier de Mitry, chief cashier of La Jonchère, treasurer of the Emergency War Fund—Sinister suspicions concerning La Jonchère and Le Blanc—Madame de Prie determines to get to the bottom of the mystery—Her alliance with the Pâris brothers against the War Minister—Dubois persuades the Regent to withdraw his protection from Le Blanc—Arrest of La Jonchère and examination of his accounts—Disgrace and exile of Le Blanc—The death of Dubois puts a stop to the proceedings—Death of Philippe d'Orléans—*Monsieur le Duc* becomes Prime Minister.

ONE night, in the autumn of 1719, so the story goes, the Duc de Bourbon attended a ball at the Opera, where his attention was attracted by two masked ladies, who remained inseparable throughout the evening. One of them in particular piqued his curiosity, as much as by her liveliness and wit, as by the perfection of her shape and the grace of her movements. He entreated her to unmask, but was met by a refusal, and she and her companion took their departure, laughing merrily at his mortification. At the next Opera-ball, the two ladies appeared in the same costume. *Monsieur le Duc*, who was again present, hastened to join them, but, though, on this occasion, he succeeded in ascertaining that the elder was a Madame Auxy, he was unable to discover the identity of the one who most interested him, for nothing could persuade her to unmask. On leaving him, however, she hinted that, if he cared to attend the next ball, he might find her less obdurate.

The prince was faithful to the rendezvous, but the fair *inconnue* seemed disinclined to fulfil her promise ; and it was only after many refusals and many protestations that she at length consented to remove her mask, and to reveal the adorable features of Madame de Prie, at sight of which *Monsieur le Duc* incontinently succumbed.

Such is the version of the affair which has found favour with the majority of historians. It is doubtful, however, if it is the correct one, and, any way, it is strangely inconsistent with the account given by Caylus—no friend, by the way, of Madame de Prie—of the repulsion with which the first solicitations of *Monsieur le Duc* inspired the object of his desires :

" However ambitious Madame de Prie may have been, when she saw herself on the point of surrendering to a man whose face was extremely repulsive, although he was rather well-made, she experienced a frightful repugnance, and was a hundred times ready to renounce her project."

A more plausible explanation of the origin of this passion, which, owing to its consequences, belongs to history, is that Madame de Prie's aunt, Madame de Séchelles, who was on friendly terms with Marie Anne de Bourbon-Conti, the first wife of *Monsieur le Duc*, and a frequent visitor at the Hôtel de Condé, brought her niece there ; that *Monsieur le Duc* saw her and fell desperately in love with her, and that certain partisans of the House of Condé, who were anxious to find some intelligent woman capable of guiding the prince amidst the bewildering chaos of passions and intrigues in which he found himself, and of awakening in him those ambitions which they themselves had vainly endeavoured to arouse, persuaded her, weary as she was of the trials and humiliations of poverty and eager once again to possess the good things of life, to become his mistress.

What, however, is incontestable, is the completeness of her triumph. From the first hour until the time, six years later, when circumstances over which neither of them had any control came to force them apart, she dominated *Monsieur le Duc* entirely, and he adored her with an intensity of devotion of which no one had believed him capable. The Sabrans, the Nesles, the Polignacs and the rest were as entirely forgotten as if they had never existed ; never was there so much as a whisper of a rival in his affections. He consecrated himself to her body and soul.

Nor is this a matter for surprise, since Madame de Prie was no ordinary mistress. Not only did she possess in a superlative degree all that could charm the senses, but she had intelligence, culture, and exquisite tact, and, she understood to perfection the art of pleasing. "She amused him, she distracted him, she showed a profound respect for his decisions, which flattered him in confirming him in the idea that he acted always on his own initiative. She never gave him advice except after being asked for it, and in subordinating it, in appearance, to the superior intelligence of her lover, although it was frequently her counsel which prevailed."[1] Thus, she insinuated herself into the mind and heart of the prince and "disposed of him as a slave."[2] Never did he dream of rebelling against his fetters, since he was barely conscious of them.

For a while, Madame de Prie gave herself up to the enjoyment of all the luxury and splendour with which her princely lover hastened to surround her with the zest which only a pretty young woman can feel who, after once being in a position to indulge all her caprices, has for several years been compelled to deny herself even the necessaries—or what the feminine mind considers the necessaries—of existence. She passed long delightful hours in the shops of fashionable *couturiers* and made extensive purchases, which, let us hope, *Monsieur le Duc* paid for in hard cash, and not in the notes of his *protégé* Law's unfortunate bank. She visited the *ateliers* of the artists, of whom she had in former days been a generous patron, and commissioned a portrait of herself from Van Loo, and another from Rosalba, whom she had patronised at Turin, and who had just completed a pastel of Madame de Parabère. Arrayed in ravishing toilettes and blazing with diamonds, she did the honours of the Hôtel de Condé, of Chantilly and of Saint-Maur, for, very opportunely for her, the unloved wife of

---

[1] H. Thirion, "Madame de Prie."
[2] Henri Martin, "Histoire de France jusqu'en 1789."

Monsieur le Duc had, after a long and painful illness, recently departed to another world, leaving the field quite free for the sultana. And she profoundly troubled the salons by launching an entirely novel method of arranging the hair, which became her *à merveille*, but caused serious inconvenience to some of the fashionable dames who felt constrained to adopt it.

But, after some weeks, she was obliged to give her mind to more serious matters. The " elevation " of a *petite bourgeoise*, daughter of a fraudulent financier and of a woman universally depised, to be the favourite of a prince who stood so near the throne and might even one day ascend it, had not taken place without exciting the most rancorous jealousy and hatred. *Chansons*, venomous satires, slanders, calumnies, rained upon her, until, if she had been a more sensitive woman, she might well have been driven to the verge of despair. She was charged with having led a life of debauchery from her earliest youth ; of having bewitched *Monsieur le Duc* by initiating him into vices imported by her from Italy and hitherto unknown in France ; of having ruined her husband by her scandalous extravagance ; of having treated an unselfish and devoted mother with the most outrageous cruelty and ingratitude. She learned that in Madame de Pléneuf's circle it was predicted that her triumph would be of very brief duration ; that they would soon succeed in disgusting *Monsieur le Duc* with his choice, and that when she had fallen from her high estate and had been abandoned by the prince, they would make her bitterly repent of her victory.

She learned, too, that the position of *Monsieur le Duc* was far from secure, and that he had many powerful enemies, who were continually intriguing against him and who would not scruple to employ every possible means to reduce him to political impotence. This, however, requires a word of explanation.

For some years past the bitterest antipathy had existed between the Houses of Orléans and Condé. This feud had its origin in the aversion which the two daughters of Louis XIV. and Madame de Montespan had always entertained for each other, and which, in their younger days, had so much disturbed the harmony of the royal circle that the King was at length obliged to threaten them with banishment from the Court if they could not live peaceably together. The hatred between the two sisters had been communicated to their sons, the Duc de Chartres and *Monsieur le Duc*, and intensified by the lawsuit over the will of the late *Monsieur le Prince* and by the prominence taken by *Monsieur le Duc* in the campaign against the legitimated princes, whose cause the Duchesse d'Orléans had espoused with the most passionate enthusiasm.

The Regent did not share the antipathy of his wife and son to the Condés; indeed, he regarded the proceedings of them and the faction which they had gathered about them with the gravest suspicion, which is hardly surprising, having regard to the ambitions with which they were generally credited. These included his own deposition and the substitution of the Duchesse d'Orléans as Regent, the banishment of *Monsieur le Duc* and the Condés, the re-establishment of the legitimated princes in their titles and dignities, the constitution of a new Ministry, and a *rapprochement* with Spain.

The party was numerically powerful, including as it did a number of the *protégés* of the House of Orléans, and many discontented and ambitious persons. It also comprised some very distinguished names: the Duc and Duchesse du Maine, the Comte de Toulouse, the Prince de Condé, the Rohans, the Duc de Montemart, and the Maréchaux de Villeroy, Berwick and Tallard. But its most active and formidable members were three men of middle-class origin: the Secretary of State for War, Le Blanc, the Comte, afterwards the Maréchal de Belle-Isle, and his younger brother, the Chevalier de Belle-Isle.

Claude Le Blanc was the son of Louis Le Blanc, who had been at one time intendant of Normandy; his mother was a sister of the Maréchal de Bezons. Born in 1669, he practised for some years at the Bar, but in 1704 was appointed intendant of Auvergne. He was an exceedingly able man, "full of intelligence, capacity and resource,"[1] and in the intendancy of Flanders, to which he was transferred towards the close of the

[1] Saint-Simon.

LOUIS HENRI, DUC DE BOURBON, PRINCE DE CONDÉ (CALLED
MONSIEUR LE DUC)

War of the Austrian Succession, he rendered such admirable service that Louis XIV. summoned him to Court in order that he might thank him personally.

On the old King's death, the functions of Secretary of State for War were suppressed and replaced by a council, of which Le Blanc was a member, but, after trying this experiment for two years, the Regent decided to revert to the old order of things, and the office was conferred upon the ex-intendant.

Although Le Blanc possessed few of the qualities of a Louvois, and during the war with Spain which followed the Cellamare conspiracy was guilty of more than one grave error, he was, on the whole, far from an incapable Minister, and the Army owed to him several useful reforms, while he always enjoyed great popularity with the troops. But, on the other hand, he was greedy, ambitious, unscrupulous, and an incorrigible intriguer, with whom no consideration of gratitude or honour would be permitted to weigh for a moment.

In the Comte de Belle-Isle, who, a quarter of a century later, during the War of the Austrian Succession, was to earn undying renown by his gallant defence of Prague and the masterly manner in which he subsequently conducted the retreat of the garrison to Eger, through the midst of an enemy's country and in the depth of winter, he possessed a most valuable ally.

Although Belle-Isle was the grandson of the Surintendant Fouquet, whose ill-gotten wealth had brought upon him so terrible a punishment, he had, nevertheless, entered the service of Louis XIV. and risen to the rank of brigadier-general. He accompanied Villars to the negotiations of Rastadt, and, after the conclusion of peace, was made governor of Huningue. Appointed *maréchal de camp* on the outbreak of the war between France and Spain, he contributed to the capture of Fontarabia and San Sebastian, and, without having done anything very notable, contrived, thanks to the adroit manner in which his friend Le Blanc represented his services, to acquire a considerable military reputation and with it a footing at the Court, of which he did not fail to profit. Ambitious, enterprising, and persuasive, he succeeded in insinuating himself into the favour of the Regent, and soon began to be regarded as a very important personage.

The third member of the triumvirate, the Chevalier de Belle-Isle, was a young man of twenty-seven, noted for his dashing valour in the field and his innumerable gallantries. His abilities were, however, considerable, and his ambition perhaps even more excessive than that of his elder brother, whose entire confidence he enjoyed.

Le Blanc and the Belle-Isles, while secretly the protagonists of the opposition party, remained, in appearance, devoted adherents of Philippe d'Orléans, and this made them doubly dangerous. Profiting by the confidence which the Regent reposed in them, they had lately attempted a master-stroke, by imputing to the Duc de Bourbon machinations of their own cabal which were on the point of being discovered. They accused him of conspiring to supplant the Regent, and so cleverly did they manufacture evidence in support of this charge that *Monsieur le Duc* had all the difficulty imaginable to prove his innocence. Eventually, the Duc d'Orléans accepted his indignant protestations, but from that moment the chief of the House of Condé began to be regarded by the public as a possible rival of his Royal Highness.

Now, by a singular coincidence, the same three men who had so nearly succeeded in bringing about the disgrace of *Monsieur le Duc* were the most devoted of all the friends of Madame de Pléneuf, and, in consequence, implacable enemies of Madame de Prie. Le Blanc had rendered himself particularly odious to the Duc de Bourbon's mistress. For some years past the Minister had been completely infatuated with Madame de Pléneuf and obedient to her slightest behest, and in the miserable days which had followed the discovery of Agnès's flirtation with M. d'Angennes he had ably seconded her mother in making the girl's life a burden to her. Moreover, whether justly or no, she strongly suspected him and the Belle-Isles of having been concerned in the tragic end of the unfortunate d'Angennes, who, shortly after the episode in question, had been found dead in the street, pierced by three sword-thrusts, in circumstances which pointed to his being the victim of some private vengeance.   Again, Le Blanc had, at his own special request, been appointed a member of the commission appointed to investigate the accounts of M. de Pléneuf and his fellow-commissaries ; and the animus he had displayed against the principal delinquent on this occasion—which, it was generally believed, had been prompted by the desire to please Madame de Pléneuf, who had been for some years past on very bad terms with her husband, and, at the same time, to obtain greater facilities for enjoying that lady's society—had largely contributed to his ruin.

And, finally, he had committed an action which would alone have sufficed to assure him the undying hatred of Madame de Prie.

We have mentioned that among the admirers of Madame de Prie at Turin was the Marquis d'Alincourt, son of the Maréchal de Villeroy.   Whether there had ever been anything serious between them is very doubtful, but, at any rate, the lady had been indiscreet enough to write d'Alincourt several letters which were capable of such an interpretation.   Now, Le Blanc, who was a friend of d'Alincourt, knew of the existence of these epistles, and, soon after Madame de Prie became the mistress of *Monsieur le Duc*, he contrived, by some means, to get possession of them, and handed them to Madame de Pléneuf, who carried them straight to her daughter's lover.   The precious pair doubtless hoped thereby to bring about a rupture between the prince and his inamorata, but they had sadly underrated the strength of the former's infatuation ; and the only result was to disgust him with persons who could make war with such weapons and to intensify the hatred with which Madame de Prie regarded her mother and the Minister for War.

As soon as Madame de Prie understood the precarious situation of *Monsieur le Duc*, and that her mother's friends, Le Blanc and the Belle-Isles, were his most redoubtable enemies, she recognized that her interests were one with those of her lover, and that, by placing him in a position in which he would be able to defy them, she would shelter herself from their blows.

From that moment, the line of action which it behoved her to follow was clear, and she determined to devote all her talents and all her energies to rallying the prince's partisans around him and thwarting the machinations of their common foes. Nor did she intend to rest from her labours until she had crushed them utterly, and raised *Monsieur le Duc* so high that they would be powerless to injure either him or herself.

But, to accomplish this, it was necessary to begin by freeing herself from certain embarrassments: by appeasing her husband's indignation and preventing a scandal, which might prejudice her in the eyes of those old-fashioned persons who consented to condone immorality only so long as the conventionalities were duly observed; by rehabilitating her father, whose delinquencies were a continual reproach to her; and by persuading the Condés, and, in particular, the Dowager-Duchesse de Bourbon to accept the situation and admit her to their intimacy,

All these matters were satisfactorily arranged. M. de Prie, who, at the beginning of 1720, had resigned his post at Turin, returned to Paris vowing vengeance against his erring wife, and, if gossip is to be believed, did actually go so far as to give her several blows with his cane. But he was a man of feeble character, and, besides, desperately in need of money; and soon, perceiving in which direction his interests lay, he calmed down, and eventually took himself off to Languedoc, with the title of lieutenant-general of that province, which *Monsieur le Duc* had been instrumental in obtaining for him.

Thanks to the same influence, the Government consented to throw a veil over the misdeeds of M. de Pléneuf, and to permit him to return to Paris, though it refused to restore him his property. His daughter, however, hastened to provide for his necessities, and soon afterwards secured for him the post of secretary to Sennecterre, who had been despatched to England to discuss with the British Government the question of the restoration of Gibraltar to Spain.

The question of her relations with the Condé family presented some difficulty. The Duc de Bourbon's two brothers,

Madame la Duchesse had very little affection for the latter, but she aspired to control all his actions, and she strongly resented the appearance upon the scene of a rival influence. For some time she made no secret of her dislike of Madame de Prie, and treated her with the coldest disdain ; and the favourite had need of all her suppleness to overcome her hostility. At length, however, the princess decided to accept the situation, and, though she continued to cherish for her son's mistress a strong aversion, their relations were, to all appearances, perfectly cordial.

Next, the astute young woman proceeded to ingratiate herself with the Regent, Cardinal Dubois, and other members of the Government.

By Philippe d'Orléans she was, as we have seen, already very favourably regarded, and very soon she was admitted to the circle of his intimate friends.

Profiting by the knowledge that Dubois, although he had little liking for *Monsieur le Duc*, cared still less for the adversaries of the Condés, she sought eagerly for opportunities of rendering herself useful to him, and succeeded so well that before long she was able to reckon with confidence upon the support of his Eminence, who was becoming more powerful every day.

Nor did she neglect persons who, although they did not occupy any important ministerial office, were, nevertheless, possessed of influence. Thus, she succeeded in detaching, temporarily at least, the Cardinal de Rohan from the opposing

x

faction—a distinct triumph, since the cardinal was generally believed to have been one of the lovers of Madame de Pléneuf—and in deciding the Maréchal de Villars, d'Alincourt, Livry, first *maître d'hôtel* to the King, her uncle by marriage; the Maréchal de Matignon, the Duc de Richelieu, of gallant memory, for whom, when *Monsieur le Duc* became Prime Minister, she obtained the Embassy of Vienna, and several other nobles who had been hesitating between the two parties, to throw in their lot with the Condés.

She supported Law, too; and that adventurous financier was not ungrateful, and repaid her protection by filling her purse so full that she became quite independent of her lover's bounty, and was able to maintain a whole company of spies, who brought her early information of the movements of the enemy.

And so, shrewd, vigilant, resolute, and courageous, she pursued the path she had marked out for herself, to all appearance satisfied to remain on the defensive, but, in reality, carefully noting the weak points in her adversaries' position, and watching for the occasion to deliver a crushing blow. Nor was the occasion long in presenting itself.

On 25 March, 1722, Sandrier de Mitry, receiver-general of the finances of French Flanders, and secretary and principal cashier to La Jonchère,[1] treasurer of the Emergency War Fund,[2] disappeared from his home, and nothing more was heard of him until the 18th of the following month, when his body, partially clothed and pierced by two wounds, was discovered in the Seine, near Marly.

---

[1] Gérard Michel, Seigneur de la Jonchère.

[2] The Emergency War Fund had been instituted by Louis XIV.'s celebrated War Minister, Louvois, who wished to have large sums of money always at hand for his great projects, without being obliged to take the Minister of Finance into his confidence, and was maintained, in time of war, by contributions levied on conquered territory, and, in time of peace, by a variety of means. The treasurers were not bound to render accounts annually, as in other Government offices, but were permitted to retain the money and employ it in their own affairs. This system had its advantages, but, on the other hand, it lent itself readily to malversation on the part of those who had the management of the Fund.

This mysterious crime created an immense sensation in Paris, and a strong suspicion prevailed that La Jonchère, who did not bear too high a character,[1] had been plundering the State ; that the unfortunate Sandrier had detected the defalcations, and that the treasurer had caused him to be made away with in order to close the matter.

But rumour, in certain quarters, went further than this, and accused the War Minister, Le Blanc, of being a party to the crime, or, at any rate, to what was believed to be the cause of it. For Le Blanc was not only La Jonchère's official chief, but his patron and friend, and it would have been almost impossible for the treasurer to have falsified his accounts without the Minister being aware of it.

The authorities, however, declined to see the least connexion between the murder of Sandrier and the position which he had occupied, and nearly a year passed without any steps being taken against La Jonchère. It is, indeed, highly improbable that they would ever have been stirred to action had not Madame de Prie taken upon herself to intervene.

No sooner did that energetic lady hear of the crime that had been committed and of the rumours that were in circulation concerning La Jonchère and Le Blanc, than she resolved to employ every means in her power to get to the bottom of the affair. Fortune favoured her quest, in bringing her allies, wealthy, enterprising, and capable, and as determined to compass the ruin of the Minister for War as she was herself.

Quite apart from the Condé faction, Le Blanc possessed many enemies. Of these the most powerful were the four brothers Pâris, the famous bankers, who, after the Mississippi crash, had been entrusted by the Regent with the task of restoring the public credit. In the days before they had attained their present eminence, the Pâris had been in business as army-contractors, and Le Blanc, at that time Intendant of Flanders, had caused the third brother, Pâris-Le Montagne, to

---

[1] In 1717, he had been summoned before the tribunal appointed to investigate the accounts of the commissaries and revenue-farmers, and ordered to make restitution to the amount of 600,000 livres to the State.

be arrested on a charge of rendering fraudulent accounts. More recently become Minister for War, he had accused the ablest of the four, Pâris-Duverney, of infringing the edicts forbidding the export of gold, and, though Duverney had succeeded in exculpating himself, both he and his brothers were provisionally banished from the realm. Hence, the bankers hated Le Blanc and had sworn to be avenged on him as soon as they were able.

The task of re-establishing the finances which had been entrusted to them, and which they conducted with undeniable skill, of course included an examination of the accounts of the public services. Scarcely had they begun to investigate those of the Ministry for War than they discovered such flagrant irregularities as to leave little room for doubt that a system of wholesale robbery prevailed. They immediately drew up a report to that effect and despatched it to the Regent, but, in their eagerness to bring their enemy to account, they had not waited to substantiate the charges they made ; and Philippe d'Orléans, with whom Le Blanc was just then in high favour, excused himself from moving in the matter, on the ground that the Minister for War had rendered undoubted service to the State, and was extremely popular with the Army, and that, in the present critical condition of affairs, it would be better to watch his future conduct than to criticize his past acts.

The bankers were greatly mortified by this repulse. Nevertheless, they were too embittered against Le Blanc, and too apprehensive of reprisals on his part, to abandon the struggle ; and they accordingly began to look about them for some powerful ally, whose assistance might enable them to resume it with some prospect of success.

Naturally, their thoughts turned in the direction of the Duc de Bourbon, but, since they had been the most strenuous opponents of his *protégé* Law, and they feared that the prince might harbour some resentment against them on that account, they hesitated to approach him. Great therefore was their satisfaction, when one day they received a letter from Madame de Prie proposing an alliance between them and the House of Condé against the common enemy.

the whole weight of the Condé influence, and encouraged in secret by Dubois, whose jealousy of Le Blanc Madame de Prie had artfully fanned, the Pâris brothers again advanced to the attack, and demanded that a commission should be appointed to investigate the accounts of the Ministry for War.

Their demand was conceded, the commissioners had been already nominated, and every one was expecting to hear that Le Blanc and La Jonchère had been summoned to appear before them, when the faction opposed to the Condés, with the Duc de Chartres, the Prince de Conti, and the legitimated princes at its head, started a violent agitation in favour of Le Blanc, and carried the war into the enemy's camp by accusing the Pâris brothers of having themselves despoiled the State. This furnished the Regent with a pretext for intervening between the accused and justice, and the meeting of the commission was postponed *sine die*.

Madame de Prie, however, did not despair. She had made sure of the support of Dubois, who in August, 1722, had been named *ministre principal*—the same title which had been given the Cardinal de Richelieu—and her several agents were everywhere at work. Daily the evidence against Le Blanc was accumulating in her hands; towards the end of the spring of 1723, it was so overwhelming that she felt that it would be impossible for the Regent to ignore it.

She had ascertained that, apart from their official relations, Le Blanc and La Jonchère were on terms of the closest intimacy; that the latter had a pretty and coquettish wife, whom he had complacently surrendered to his chief, being himself in love with the wife of the unfortunate Sandrier; that he lived in almost princely style, and had, moreover, advanced large sums of money to the Comte de Belle-Isle, to defray the cost of a magnificent hôtel which he was building on the banks of the Seine, opposite the Tuileries; that, on learning of the death of Sandrier, Le Blanc had shown so much emotion that every one present was astonished, and that a day or two later he fell ill and was obliged to take to his bed. And, finally, she discovered that it was practically certain that, in robbing the State, Le Blanc and La Jonchère had been acting with the connivance of the Palais-Royal, and that a considerable portion of the spoil had found its way into the Regent's coffers.

When she judged that the moment for action had arrived, Madame de Prie communicated with Dubois, who, armed with the reports she had sent him, went to the Regent, laid them before him, and told him very plainly that he could no longer support Le Blanc without being immediately compromised.

Philippe d'Orléans, after a perusal of the documents, was obliged to acknowledge that the Minister was right, and authorized him to take what steps he considered advisable in the matter. Dubois lost no time in setting the Law in motion ; the commission met at the house of the Maréchal de Villars, who had been appointed president ; and on 24 May La Jonchère was arrested as he was returning from Versailles, in virtue of a *lettre de cachet* signed by the Cardinal, and conducted to the Bastille, while the seals were placed on his hôtel in the Rue Saint-Honoré, and all his registers and papers seized by the police. At the Bastille, La Jonchère was subjected to two long interrogatories by Ravot d'Ombreval, a relative of Dubois, who acted as attorney-general to the commission. He appeared very agitated, contradicted himself several times, and ended by admitting that he had acted dishonestly, and that he was not the only one guilty, though he obstinately refused to give the names of his accomplices.

A few days later, two of La Jonchère's principal clerks were also arrested, and on 18 June the treasurer was conducted to his house to be present at the raising of the seals and the sorting of his papers. This operation lasted from eleven o'clock in the morning until nine in the evening, when he was escorted back to the Bastille, guarded by forty archers and followed by two carts filled with his registers and papers. The examination of these, which was carried out under the supervision of the Lieutenant of Police, d'Argenson, revealed immense defalcations, and, moreover, left no room for doubt as to the culpability of Le Blanc. It also showed that La Jonchère had received a commission, which was now established at the Arsenal, summoned the two Belle-Isles to appear before it, together with the Marquis de Conches and the Comte de Mayières, two lieutenant-generals attached to Le Blanc, and several other persons. The Belle-Isles adopted a haughty tone, and protested their innocence with such indignation that the commission were visibly impressed. However, the discovery of a note concealed behind the grate in La Jonchère's bedroom, in the Rue Saint-Honoré, in which the elder brother acknowledged the receipt of 1,800,000 livres from the treasurer, put a different complexion upon the matter.

The utmost consternation now reigned among the Orléans faction, and it seemed as though Madame de Prie had succeeded in reducing the enemies of herself and her lover to complete impotence, when the death of Dubois, which occurred on 10 August, 1723, intervened to save them, or, at any rate, to procure them a respite of some months.

With the disappearance from the political scene of the ambitious cardinal, whose will had so long dominated his own, Philippe d'Orléans resumed his liberty of action. On the very day on which Dubois died, he demanded and obtained from the King the post of Prime Minister, cleverly forestalling *Monsieur le Duc*, who, on the advice of his mistress, had decided to ask for it himself; and thus united in his own person the titles of heir-presumptive to the Crown and Prime Minister.

[1] The letter in which Breteuil received his nomination stated that Le Blanc had begged the King to permit him to retire. This was to soften his disgrace, which was none the less real.

The question as to which of the two parties the prince would incline greatly agitated the public mind, and it was the opinion of most that he would favour that of his wife and son. It is very probable that he would have done so, had *Monsieur le Duc* been so maladroit as to display any mortification at his having stolen a march upon him, in which case the work of so many months might have been undone in a few hours. But Madame de Prie was far too astute to permit her lover to commit a blunder of this kind ; and, prompted by her, the Duc de Bourbon hastened to repair to the Palais-Royal, to present his compliments to the new Prime Minister and to assure him of his devotion to his person.

Thanks to this prudent conduct, although they were not allowed to follow up their victory, they retained possession of the greater part of the field. Le Blanc remained in exile, and his successor, Breteuil, who, as we have mentioned, was devoted to their cause, was confirmed in his office : La Jonchère remained under lock and key ; while the Belle-Isles and their creatures, though they remained at liberty, were kept under observation. Finally—and this, we may be sure, was not the least satisfaction to Madame de Prie—her mother found herself neglected and reduced to poverty.

Such was the position of affairs when, on 2 December, 1723, the Duc d'Orleans was suddenly attacked by apoplexy at Versailles, and expired almost immediately, in the arms of his latest inamorata, Madame de Phalaris. Of all the princes, *Monsieur le Duc* happened to be the only one on the spot, and he did not fail to profit by his good fortune. Following the procedure adopted by the deceased prince on the day of Dubois's death, he hastened to the King, informed him of the loss which he had just sustained, and, almost in the same breath, demanded the vacant post of Prime Minister. His youthful Majesty, " without being moved by the news," conferred it upon him ; the prince, in accordance with custom, forthwith took the oath and received the patent ; and when, a few hours later, the Duc de Chartres, who had received the news of his father's death at the Opera in Paris, or, according to another account, in the boudoir of an Opera-girl whose society he affected, came galloping madly into Versailles, he found, to his profound disgust, the place to which he himself aspired already filled. *Monsieur le Duc* was the master of the realm, and Madame de Prie mistress of all that was his.

CHAPTER XXII

OUTSIDE the faction opposed to the Condés, the
elevation of *Monsieur le Duc* was not ill received.
With the bulk of the nation Philippe d'Orléans had
never been popular. The people had been unable to forget the
horrible suspicions concerning him which the successive deaths
of the Duc and Duchesse de Bourgogne, the little Duc de
Bretagne and the Duc de Berry had aroused, and many worthy
persons steadfastly refused to see in the really touching respect
and affection which he had always shown for the young King
anything but a cloak for the most sinister designs. The
middle-classes blamed him for the financial disasters which had
involved so many of them in ruin, and credited him, very
absurdly, with the intention of recalling Law. The clergy and
the devout had been alienated by his debauched life and his
contempt for religion. Thus, the very real service which he had

rendered France in maintaining peace, with the exception of a brief interval, for eight years, was forgotten, and the advent of his successor hailed with almost a sigh of relief.

It is true that there were not a few, such as the advocate Barbier, who regretted the change of rulers, and predicted that it was Madame de Prie who would govern the kingdom, and " lay her hands on as much money as she could " ;[1] but, on the whole, the possibility of a term of petticoat government does not appear to have aroused much uneasiness.

Monsieur le Duc, on his side, neglected nothing to make himself popular. Though his manners were usually somewhat brusque, he could be charming when he chose to take the trouble, and, during the first few weeks of his Ministry, he was so affable and so courteous, so considerate and so obliging, that he pleased everyone who approached him. The good impression thus created was strengthened by the diminution of several taxes which had weighed very hardly on the Parisians, and by the magnanimity he displayed towards those whose hostility to him was notorious ; and soon the gazettes were chanting in unison the praises of the new Prime Minister, and declaring that France was indeed fortunate to have so admirable a prince at the head of affairs.

But this popularity was only momentary, for the difficulties of the situation were immense, the task before him one of the most ungrateful that could well be imagined ; and it would have needed a far more experienced and subtle politician than *Monsieur le Duc* to have steered a safe course amid the shoals and quicksands that surrounded him. The Treasury was empty and the follies of the " System " still unpaid for ; commerce was almost annihilated ; the Church rent by the Jansenist schism ; the Court a battle-ground for contending factions, one of which regarded the new Prime Minister with the bitterest hostility. And, in place of the Regent and Dubois, three new powers had arisen ; two close at hand, the young King and his preceptor, Fleury, Bishop of Fréjus ; the other distant, Spain, represented by Philip V.

[1] " Journal de Barbier," December, 1723.

The young Louis XV., whose majority had been proclaimed six months before, on completing his thirteenth year, was a most perplexing factor in the situation. D'Argenson calls him "an impenetrable personage"; Luynes "an indefinable being"; in a word, he was a mystery to the whole Court. Ostensibly, he cared for nothing but the chase, gambling[1] and the pleasures of the table; but many were of opinion that this frivolity and indifference were but assumed; that very little that took place escaped him; and that the time was not far distant when he would begin to assert his authority in no uncertain manner. Morose, uncommunicative, egotistical, he repulsed all the efforts of the courtiers of both sexes to ingratiate themselves with him, and reserved his confidence, and the little affection of which he seemed capable, for one person—his preceptor, the Bishop of Fréjus.

The rise of André Hercule Fleury had been remarkable. Though without great talents or high connexions—he was the son of a collector of taxes at his native town of Lodève—he had understood so well the art of insinuating himself into the good graces of every one who was in a position to advance his fortunes, that obstacles disappeared before him as snow melts in the sun. "He was what one might call a true wheedler," writes Saint-Simon, who allows us to perceive in the portrait which he has drawn of him something of the jealousy which his extraordinary good fortune had inspired. He wheedled himself into the favour of the Cardinal de Bonzy, who brought him to Court and obtained for him the post of almoner to Queen Maria Theresa; he wheedled himself into that of his royal mistress, of the Duchesse de Bourgogne, of the Duc and Duchesse du Maine, and, finally, into that of Louis XIV., who a few months before his death nominated him preceptor to the Dauphin.

If he failed to cultivate the good qualities which Louis XV showed as a child, and cannot therefore escape some of the responsibility for the scandals and the disasters of that unfortunate reign, he succeeded little by little in gaining the entire

---

[1] Louis XV.'s love of play first revealed itself towards the end of 1722. In July, 1724, Marais writes that "the King is a terrible gambler."

ANDRÉ HERCULE, CARDINAL DE FLEURY

NTHE RIGAUD

confidence of his pupil. Jealous of his influence, Philippe d'Orléans endeavoured to separate him from the boy by the offer of the archbishopric of Rheims, the first episcopal dignity in the realm. But Fleury knew where his true interests lay, and declined it. Nothing, he declared, should distract him from the duty which he owed to his young Sovereign. When, in 1722, Louis XV.'s *gouverneur*, the Maréchal de Villeroy, was banished by the Regent from Court, Fleury, deeming that his honour obliged him to share the disgrace of his superior and protector, followed him into exile. But his departure occasioned the young King such distress that he lost no time in recalling him, by a letter in his own hand—an action upon which it is probable the astute old gentleman had confidently counted.

At the time of the death of Philippe d'Orléans, Fleury was in his seventy-first year, an age at which most men have renounced ambition and are thinking only of repose. The Bishop of Fréjus, however, felt that he had some years of activity yet before him, and he was resolved to climb to the very pinnacle of fortune. He might easily have persuaded Louis XV. to make him Prime Minister, but he counselled the young King to entrust the direction of affairs to the Duc de Bourbon ; perhaps, because he hoped to govern through him ; more probably, because he foresaw that *Monsieur le Duc's* Ministry must be of brief duration, and that his own elevation would be far better received after the prince had been allowed his chance.

Monsieur le Duc and Madame de Prie were not blind to the danger which threatened from this quarter. In his quality of priest, Fleury could not fail to disapprove of the relations existing between them, and that he had communicated his sentiments to his royal pupil was very evident from the coldness with which his Majesty treated the marchioness. Nor could it be said that the King regarded *Monsieur le Duc* with any marked degree of favour ; indeed, he appeared to avoid him, and not infrequently when the Prime Minister had requested an audience, he was informed that M. de Fréjus would receive any communication that he might wish to make.

Encouraged by this, the Orléans party began to make over-tures to Fleury with a view to an alliance. But the preceptor preferred to retain his liberty of action, and their advances met with no formal response. It was, however, impossible to say how long he would continue to remain neutral, and the possibility of so powerful a coalition being formed against them occasioned the Duc de Bourbon and his mistress profound uneasiness.

The third power was Philip V. of Spain.

After the conclusion of peace between France and Spain at the beginning of 1720, the Regent and Dubois, anxious to re-establish friendly relations between the two great branches of the House of Bourbon, proposed a triple matrimonial alliance, to which Philip V. and Isabella Farnese readily consented. In accordance with this arrangement, the Infanta Isabella Luisa, then in her fifth year, was sent to the Court of France, to be brought up until she had reached a marriageable age, when she was to become the wife of Louis XV. ; the fourth of the Regent's six daughters, Mlle. de Montpensier, was married to the Prince of the Asturias, heir to the Crown of Spain ; while the fifth of the Orléans princesses, Mlle. de Beaujolais, who was only six years old, was sent to Madrid, where it was proposed that, in due course, she should wed Don Carlos, the eldest son of Philip V. and his second wife, Isabella Farnese.

Connected thus closely with the Orléans, Philip V. had everything to lose by events which excluded his allies from power. In January, 1724, he had abdicated in favour of the Prince of the Asturias, though the new king's authority was merely nominal, and on the son's death, some months later, the father resumed the Crown. Some writers maintain that this abdica-tion was in fulfilment of a vow that he had made in 1720 ; others believe that it was intended to facilitate his designs on the French throne ; and this is far from improbable. For it is certain that Philip had not abandoned the hopes which he had cherished since the death of his grandfather, and which the feeble health of Louis XV., the well-known incapacity of the new Duc d'Orléans, and the false reports of his partisans concern-ing the popularity which he enjoyed in Paris, served to sustain.

only natural that *Monsieur le Duc* should have proceeded at first with caution and moderation, and have gone as far as he could reasonably be expected to go to disarm the malice of his foes. Such a course, indeed, was dictated by the most elementary prudence. It served, however, no useful purpose beyond proving to him the futility of attempting to conciliate those whom nothing but a virtual renunciation of his authority would be likely to satisfy. The Duc d'Orléans, it is true, declared himself, in his own name and that of his party, perfectly willing for an immediate reconciliation, and offered to marry Mlle de Sens, the youngest sister of his rival. But the conditions he desired to impose—the recall of Le Blanc and his restoration to the Ministry for War, and his own admission to every audience which *Monsieur le Duc* had with the King—were quite impossible for the other to accept.

However, the Prime Minster, on the advice of his mistress, begged to be excused from giving an immediate answer and demanded a few weeks for reflection. A brief truce followed, during which *Monsieur le Duc* still further strengthened his reputation for impartiality by including a number of combatants from the opposite camp in an important promotion to the Ordre du Saint-Esprit. The new *cordons bleus* also included the husband and personal friends of Madame de Prie, who, at the same time, obtained for herself a lodging in the Château of Versailles. This was a move of the first importance, since it enabled *Monsieur le Duc* to have close at hand in every emergency the woman who was not only his mistress, but his most trusted counsellor.

In these early days of the new *régime*, the favourite appeared to be taking little or no interest in politics and to be absorbed wholly in pleasure. Never had Chantilly received so many visitors ; while, when *Monsieur le Duc* was in Paris or at Versailles, the Hôtel de Condé or the Hôtel of the Grand Master was always the centre of animation. The latter hôtel, which the King had lately purchased from the Dowager-Princess de Conti and presented to the prince, was transformed by *Monsieur le Duc* and his mistress, whose good taste was indisputable, into the most charming residence imaginable. The two Coypels, Jean François de Troy, Louis de Boulogne, Lemoine, Verdier, Restout, Cazes—all the best painters and sculptors of the day—were employed in the decoration of its salons ; splendid tapestries, exquisite porcelain, costly *objets d'art* were to be seen on every side.

The favourite possessed a beautiful voice and a wonderful talent of interpretation. During her residence at Turin she had conceived a passion for the works of the Italian composers, up to this time very little known in France. With the aid of Crozat, a wealthy banker of the Rue des Petits-Champs, who shared her enthusiasm, she proceeded to organize a company of amateurs, who gave concerts at the houses of several persons of distinction. These artistic reunions soon became popular and undoubtedly contributed to form the taste of the nation.

But while Madame de Prie, all smiles and gaiety, seemed to have no thought beyond the enjoyment of life, she was in secret carefully maturing her plans. Since the hostile faction refused to be placated, save at a price which would entail the virtual sacrifice of all that the Condés had gained, she was determined to continue the struggle ; and she had persuaded *Monsieur le Duc* that the wiser course was not to wait to be attacked, but to take the offensive themselves.

Towards the middle of February, 1724, no small sensation was aroused by the news that Ravot d'Ombreval had been appointed Lieutenant of Police in place of d'Argenson, whom the Duc de Chartres had persuaded to resign his office, and that Pâris-Duverney had become Guardian of the Royal Treasure. These appointments were very significant, for d'Ombreval, besides being a devoted adherent of *Monsieur le Duc* and Madame de Prie, had acted as prosecuting counsel before the Commission, while Duverney and his brothers were the surprise was expressed at the announcement, a few days later, that the proceedings against La Jonchère were to be resumed forthwith.

The indignation and alarm of the Orléanists knew no bounds, for those already summoned before the Commission were not the only persons who had had interesting financial transactions with the treasurer of the Emergency War Fund, and, now that the Condés were in power, there was no saying how far the net might not be cast, added to which there was the murder of Sandrier, which would without doubt be closely investigated.

From several quarters warnings reached *Monsieur le Duc* and Madame de Prie that the lives of Duverney and d'Ombreval, if not their own, were in danger. They refused to attach any importance to them, for, though they were aware of the unscrupulous character of some of their adversaries, they could not bring themselves to believe that they would carry their enmity to such lengths. However, they had soon cause to alter their opinion.

One evening, at the end of February, 1724, a M. de la Guillonière, a cousin of the Pâris brothers, had just alighted from his coach at the door of Duverney's hôtel in the Rue Saint-Antoine, when he was set upon by masked men, who stabbed him in several places, and then took to flight, leaving him apparently dead upon the ground. Happily his wounds, though dangerous, were not mortal, and eventually he recovered.

Now, La Guillonière, both in build and gait, bore a strong resemblance to Duverney, and no reasonable doubt existed that the blows aimed at him had been intended for his cousin, for the would-be assassins had been observed loitering round the banker's hôtel for some time previously.

A warning which *Monsieur le Duc* received a day or two later made it equally clear that, Duverney disposed of, the scoundrels intended to turn their attentions to more exalted personages.

The Cardinal de Noailles, Archbishop of Paris, demanded

an audience of the Prime Minister on a matter of the most urgent importance, and, when admitted, told him, in great agitation, that he had just learned from one of his priests that, in a confession which had been made to him, the penitent had spoken of a plot to murder both *Monsieur le Duc* and Madame de Prie. The prelate had hesitated before violating the secret of the confessional, but reasons of State had prevailed.

Almost at the same time, a letter which the Chevalier de Belle-Isle had endeavoured to pass into the Bastille to La Jonchère was intercepted. This letter, among other pressing recommendations to the prisoner, contained that of maintaining silence in all circumstances in regard to his relations with Le Blanc, and promised that, if he did this, the friends of the latter would undertake to save him.

So astounded were *Monsieur le Duc* and the majority of his counsellors at such tactics on the part of their enemies that, for a moment, they were at a loss how to proceed. Madame de Prie, however, retained her presence of mind and insisted on prompt and energetic action, pointing out that it was now a case of war to the knife in the most literal sense of the expression, and that, if they did not hasten to crush their adversaries, they would certainly be crushed themselves.

It was ultimately decided to follow her counsels. The Chevalier de Belle-Isle was forthwith arrested and conveyed to the Château of Vincennes. On 5 March, Du Val, commandant of the mounted police, furnished with a *lettre de cachet*, proceeded to Doué, where he arrested the late Minister for War and conducted him to Paris and the Bastille. The same night, the police surrounded the hôtel of the Comte de Belle-Isle, with orders to apprehend both the count and his friend the Marquis de Conches, who was staying with him. They secured Belle-Isle and escorted him to the Bastille, whither his younger brother had been transferred a few hours previously ; but Conches disguised himself and succeeded in effecting his escape by a secret door. He did not, however, remain long at large, for he was captured the following day at a house in the Rue Tavannes, where he had taken refuge, and sent to join his friends in misfortune. Numerous other arrests followed, including that of Moreau de Séchelles, a high official at the Ministry of War and an intimate friend of Le Blanc. But what aroused the most sensation was the apprehension of a man named Lempereur and his two sons and of two brothers called Mestre, sons of a soldier in the Cent-Suisses.

This Lempereur, who lived in an isolated house near the wood of Rueil, had formerly been a gardener at the Château of La Jonchère, and he was suspected of having murdered Sandrier, with the assistance of his sons and the Mestres. He was also suspected of being concerned in another crime, which the police believed to be closely connected with the first. One evening in September, 1722—that is to say, about five months after the discovery of Sandrier's body—a carter in the employ of the tenant of La Malmaison, a farm upon the La Jonchère estate, afterwards celebrated as the residence of the Empress Josephine, had been murdered close to his master's door. As nothing upon him had been touched, and he was not known to have any private enemies, the inference was that he had been in possession of certain facts concerning the death of Sandrier which had made his removal necessary to the safety of the assassins.

It was the intention of the new Government to concentrate all their efforts to secure the total ruin of Le Blanc, the very life and soul of the hostile faction. He was to be brought to trial on two charges: the old one of embezzlement of public funds, the new one of homicide. The first would be easy to prove; in fact, his culpability, if not the exact extent of it, had been clearly revealed by the examination of La Jonchère's papers. The second presented much greater difficulties, but it was obvious that a conviction on the charge of embezzlement would greatly facilitate the task of the prosecution.

The Orléanists, on their side, made the most desperate efforts to intimidate their adversaries into abandoning their designs against the ex-Secretary of State. Insults and menaces rained upon *Monsieur le Duc*, upon Madame de Prie, upon the Pâris brothers, upon d'Ombreval, and upon all their most prominent supporters ; the most disgusting effusions concerning the Prime Minister and his favourite were scattered about in the gallery and salons of Versailles and even in the bedchamber of the young King ; the most biting *chansons* circulated in Paris ; almost every day came warnings that their lives were in danger ; and a relative and staunch adherent of Madame de Prie died suddenly, in circumstances which left little doubt that he had been poisoned.

The Government, however, refused to be diverted from its course. The proceedings against La Jonchère were continued, and on 15 April, 1724, the Commission *censured* him, declared him incapable of holding any office under the Crown, and condemned him to restore to the King 2,100,000 livres—a very small part of the amount of which the State had been defrauded.[1] The Comte de Belle-Isle was to be surety for 600,000 livres of this sum.

This mitigated condemnation was intended to convey the impression that La Jonchère had only been acting under the orders of the late Minister for War, and that the latter was the real culprit.

In the meanwhile, the Government had decided to endeavour to bring home to Le Blanc yet another mysterious crime. In the spring of 1718, a certain Gazan de la Combe, of whom very little is known, had been found dead, strangled by a cord attached to the foot of his bed, at the house of La Barre, lieutenant of the constabulary, in the Rue Notre-Dame de Bonne-Nouvelle. Le Blanc and other Ministers had, it appeared, been in the habit of consigning to the care of La Barre certain persons who had incurred their displeasure, and it was given out that the dead man had been confined there on account of intrigues on behalf of the Spanish Ambassador, the Duc and Duchesse du Maine, and their accomplices, and that, knowing that it was the intention of the Government to bring him to trial, he had, in his despair, committed suicide. Now, however, an officer in the Army came forward who informed the police that, at the time

---

[1] The total amount of the defalcations was estimated at 12,000,000 livres at the very least.

of the death of La Combe, he happened to be detained in the same house, by orders of Le Blanc ; that one morning, attracted by cries of terror from the wife of La Barre, he had hurried to La Combe's room, where he found him lying dead, but that, from the position of the body, he was of opinion that it was impossible for him to have taken his own life. He added that, while he was in the room, Le Blanc had entered, accompanied by La Barre ; that the Minister, on perceiving him, had appeared very agitated, and had demanded of La Barre why he had not set him at liberty two days before, in accordance with his instructions, and had then ordered him to leave the house. This evidence was subsequently confirmed by one of La Barre's servants.

In the opinion of the police, there was little doubt that the unfortunate La Combe had, like Sandrier, been in possession of certain facts concerning the Emergency War Fund which made his removal advisable ; and La Barre and his wife were promptly arrested and conducted to the Bastille.

Matters now began to look very black indeed for Le Blanc, and there were not a few who declared that he might consider himself very fortunate if he did not terminate his career on the gibbet. But, fortunately for the ex-Minister for War, he was, through his title of honorary *maître dès requêtes*, a member of the Parlement of Paris, and had therefore the right to demand to be judged by all the Chambers sitting together ; and just as he was about to be brought to trial, he presented to the Parlement a petition to that effect, which was immediately granted.

This move on the part of the accused was a serious check to *Monsieur le Duc* and Madame de Prie, who for a moment had imagined that they had their enemy in their power, and that they were on the point of dealing, through his condemnation, an overwhelming blow to the hostile faction. For the Parlement was not unnaturally inclined to indulgence when the misdeeds of one of its own members was in question, and Le Blanc had had the good fortune to ingratiate himself with it during the Regency. Moreover, the Orléans counted many friends among the magistracy, the Condés comparatively few.

However, as the trial was not to come on for several months, they hoped, in the interval, so to strengthen their position that, even if the issue were unfavourable to them, the consequences would be of comparatively small importance. Their great object was to ingratiate themselves with Louis XV. and to combat the increasing influence of Fleury over the young monarch's mind, in which they perceived an even greater danger than the enmity of the Orléans.

"The Prime Minister governs certainly," writes that shrewd observer, the Venetian Ambassador, Morosini, "and directs the affairs of the kingdom, as well as its foreign policy. The bishop appears to court effacement and to be reluctant to meddle with anything. But nothing is concluded without the King's consent, and the King decides nothing without the bishop's approval. A few days ago, for example, *Monsieur le Duc* presented himself to beg him to name an hour which would be convenient to him for work. The King was playing cards with the Duc de Noailles, and, not seeing the Bishop of Fréjus, gave orders that he should be summoned immediately. After which he continued to play until the arrival of the bishop, whom he then caused to enter into his cabinet with *Monsieur le Duc.* What passed on this occasion is constantly happening. . . . I hear that the Prime Minister has never had a conversation with the King alone, while the bishop speaks to him when and where he pleases.

" Moreover, it is continually being said in public that, if an ecclesiastic is to continue the traditions of the Dubois, the Mazarins, and the Richelieus, it will be without doubt the Bishop of Fréjus.

" *Monsieur le Duc* and his *entourage* perceive with mortification the continual encroachments of the bishop. They fear and detest him, but they dare not attack him openly, finding his position too strong."

However, if Fleury's position were too strong to be carried by a direct attack, it was not too strong to be undermined, and the idea occurred to Madame de Prie to draw the aged Maréchal de Villeroy, Louis XV.'s former *gouverneur*, from his retirement and oppose him to the Bishop of Fréjus. The marshal, it will be remembered, had been banished from Court by the Regent in 1722, since which time he had been vegetating in his government of Lyons. The young King had been attached to Villeroy and had shed bitter tears when he learned of his disgrace, and if, in the interval, his sentiments had not changed, the ex-*gouverneur* might easily become a formidable rival to the bishop.

Louis XV. seemed quite delighted at the prospect of seeing his old friend again, and the hopes of the conspirators ran high. But they were fated never to materialize, for, though his Majesty received the marshal graciously enough, he subsequently took so little notice of him, that the old man, deeply mortified, almost immediately quitted the Court and never appeared there again. Thus, the influence of Fleury remained as potent as ever, and, since he had not failed to penetrate this little manœuvre, the antipathy which he had always felt for *Monsieur le Duc* and the favourite was not lessened.

But Madame de Prie was a young woman of infinite resource and she had many cards in her hands. Every day *Monsieur le Duc* relied more on her counsels, not only because he had formed the highest opinion of her intelligence, but because, as he explained after his disgrace, he felt that she was devoted to his interests, "up to the annihilation of every other sentiment."

No longer did she make any pretence of being absorbed in pleasure, as in the first weeks of her lover's Ministry. She had become a politician of the most ardent kind, and the greater part of her time was passed in her cabinet, dictating to the two secretaries she employed for her immense correspondence, discussing with the Ministers, who, by their chief's desire, invariably consulted her, the most difficult questions, and making notes on the *placets* presented to *Monsieur le Duc*, every one of which was submitted to her. All who approached her were astonished at her industry, at the shrewdness of her judgment, and at her grasp of matters which are usually considered quite beyond the comprehension of a young woman. "She was," wrote the Abbé Legendre, "a heroine capable of regulating the affairs of a vast empire."

The immense patronage which *Monsieur le Duc* exercised in both his private and official capacities was almost entirely directed by her, and, though she was, of course, guided chiefly by party considerations, some of her selections showed sound judgment. Thus, her choice of the Duc de Richelieu, in 1725, for the Embassy at Vienna, though ridiculed at the time, was really a very happy one ; and this is admitted even by historians so little favourable to Madame de Prie as Lemontey.[1] Without allowing herself to be discouraged by the failure of the Villeroy affair, the marchioness promptly proceeded to make another and more important move.

The surest way to gain the good graces of the young King was to exploit his passion for the chase. Well, no one was better able to procure him this diversion than *Monsieur le Duc*. His forests of Chantilly and Halatte abounded in big game, already beginning to fail in those in the vicinity of Versailles, owing to their being too constantly hunted. The hunting establishment of the prince, moreover, enjoyed an almost European reputation, while he himself was a famous man when hounds were running.

At the suggestion of his mistress, *Monsieur le Duc* proposed to the King that he should honour him by hunting his forests and spend the months of July and August at Chantilly, by which means not only would they have every opportunity of gaining the young monarch's favour by gratifying his taste for sport and amusement, but he would be removed for a time from the influence of Fleury, and also from that of the Orléans' faction, which was continually bombarding him with petitions on behalf of Le Blanc and complaints as to the alleged ill-treatment to which the ex-Minister and his fellow-prisoners were being subjected in the Bastille.

Louis XV. received the proposal with delight, and on the last day of June he set out for Chantilly, accompanied by a splendid *entourage*, from which *Monsieur le Duc* and Madame de Prie had taken care that every one avowedly hostile to their cause should

---

[1] See his " Histoire de la Régence," and the author's " The Fascinating Duc de Richelieu " (London, Methuen : New York, Scribner, 1910).

be excluded, although they had decided to admit several of the more moderate partisans of the Orléans, whom they hoped to win over. The weather was magnificent, and Chantilly had never looked more beautiful. The King "indulged every day in the amusement of the chase, either of the stag or the boar, and appeared very satisfied with the cares which *Monsieur le Duc* took without ceasing to render his stay at this superb château agreeable." His Majesty dined daily with the princes and nobles whom he did the honour to select, and in the evening supped with *Madame la Duchesse*, Mlle. de Clermont, and a few ladies and nobles, whom he named in rotation, his table being served with extreme magnificence. After supper, the company adjourned to a gallery adjoining the King's apartments, where high play went on until a late hour, to the accompaniment of *Monsieur le Duc's* private band.

Thus the days went by, and his Majesty was so delighted with the splendid sport provided for him, and the unceasing efforts of *Monsieur le Duc* and Madame de Prie to keep him amused, that his former prejudice against them seemed to have disappeared entirely. He laughed and jested with his host, invited the marchioness to sup at his own table and to ride in his carriage to the chase, and, indeed, was so gracious to that lady that a rumour circulated in Paris that she and her fair friends had designs upon the virtue of the young monarch. In short, everything was proceeding as well as could possibly be desired, and the King had even decided to prolong his visit beyond the time he had originally fixed, when a most unexpected and un-fortunate event brought it to an abrupt conclusion, and with it all the calculations of Madame de Prie.

On the afternoon of 31 August, the young Duc de Melun, one of the few of his courtiers for whom Louis XV. had shown any partiality, was charged by a stag which he was pursuing, and so badly gored that he died in the early hours of the following morning. This tragedy produced so painful an impression upon the young King that it was only with great difficulty that he could be prevented from returning to Versailles that very evening, and, though he consented to postpone his departure until 3 September, he scarcely left his apartments and refused to share in any amusement.   He quitted the splendid residence of *Monsieur le Duc* with very different feelings from those which he had shown a few days previously, and there could be little doubt that the death of the Duc de Melun had effaced the good impression which the prince and his mistress had been at such infinite pains to create, and that it would be many a long day ere he consented to return to a spot which possessed such dolorous associations.

And so, like the recall of Villeroy, the Chantilly visit had failed to produce the desired effect, though through no fault of those who had planned it ; and at the beginning of 1725 the Condé party sustained another check.

On 7 January, the late Minister for War, Le Blanc, was arraigned before the assembled Chambers, charged with being an accomplice of the murders of Gazan de la Combe, Sandrier, and the carter of La Malmaison, and of the attempted assassination of La Guillonière.   The trial, into the details of which it is impossible to enter here, lasted a fortnight, but almost from the first day it was evident that the result was a foregone conclusion.   The entry of the Duc d'Orléans, the Prince de Conti and their suites into the Grande Chambre was greeted with loud murmurs of approbation ; that of the peers of the Condé party, the Ducs de la Feuillade, de Brancas, and de Richelieu, with derisive laughter.   The Bishops of Sarlat and Avranches, Le Blanc's brothers, the Maréchal de Bézons, his brother-in-law, the Chevalier Le Blanc, his son, and other relatives and intimate friends of the accused, sat together in a body and displayed so much emotion that many of the judges could hardly restrain their tears.   And the line taken by the defence—that Le Blanc was a victim of party rancour and that the charges against him had been manufactured by the Government—was admirably calculated to appeal to the prejudice of a magistracy which almost invarably found itself in opposition to the Ministry of the day.

The proceedings, contrary to custom, were conducted with closed doors, the public being rigorously excluded ; a great part

CLAUDE LE BLANC

of the evidence for the prosecution was ruled out, while every-thing that was likely to tell in favour of the accused was at once admitted. On the third day, the Ducs de la Feuillade, de Brancas, and de Richelieu withdrew, and were followed by all the coun-sellors of the Condé party ; but the Duc d'Orléans and the Prince de Conti continued to encourage the defence by their presence for some days longer. Finally, on 21 January, the Parlement, by the unanimous vote of sixty-nine judges, acquitted Le Blanc on all four changes—a verdict which was received with applause by the public, with whom, owing to various reasons, of which we shall speak hereafter, the Ministry of *Monsieur le Duc* was fast losing what popularity it had once possessed, and who, ignorant of the strength of the evidence against Le Blanc, saw in him only a victim of the hatred of the Pâris brothers and Madame de Prie. Notwithstanding what certain historians, who were unacquainted with the facts as they are known to-day, have asserted to the contrary, there can be very little doubt that the ex-Minister for War had benefited by one of those scandalous miscarriages of justice of which the records of the Parlement of Paris afford only too many examples. Before an impartial tribunal he would have been almost certainly found guilty on the charges relating to Gazan de la Combe and La Guillonière, and probably on the others also ; and, whatever may be thought of the motives of Madame de Prie, she had rendered a public service by her efforts to run to earth this highly-placed criminal.

Le Blanc, although, as a wag remarked, "after being very black, he had been made white (*blanc*) again," was not immedi-ately released, but remained in the Bastille until the following 12 May, when he was set at liberty and exiled to Lisieux. On the same day, the Comte de Belle-Isle was also liberated, and exiled to Carcassonne. Two months later, La Jonchère also found himself a free man.

The ex-Minister's accomplices were brought to trial before the Tournelle,[1] and were all acquitted, with the exception of La Jonchère's gardener Lempereur, who was found guilty of the La Malmaison murder and broken on the wheel. He paid for all.

[1] The Tournelle was the court of criminal jurisdiction of the Parlement.

CHAPTER XXIII

Monsieur le Duc and Madame de Prie determine to break off the marriage of Louis XV. and the Infanta, and to marry the young King to a princess capable of at once giving him an heir—Double interest of the favourite in the accomplishment of this design—Question of the remarriage of *Monsieur le Duc*—Madame de Prie, unable to oppose this, selects Marie Leczinska—Rupture of the Spanish marriage—Exasperation of the Court of Madrid—Difficulty of finding a suitable consort for Louis XV.—Madame de Prie accused of having barred the way of Mlle. de Vermandois to the crown matrimonial—The favourite advocates the claims of Marie Leczinska, who is eventually chosen—Triumph of Madame de Prie—Arrival of the new Queen —A model husband—Growing unpopularity of the Government and increasing influence of Fleury—An unsuccessful intrigue—Madame de Prie retires from Court, but *Monsieur le Duc* insists on her return— Disgrace of *Monsieur le Duc*—His mother and his mistress follow him to Chantilly—Madame de Prie is exiled to Normandy—A touching farewell—Chivalrous behaviour of the prince—Death of Madame de Prie—Remarriage of *Monsieur le Duc*— His death.

*M*ONSIEUR LE DUC and Madame de Prie did not allow themselves to be cast down by the reverse which they had sustained at the Palais de Justice, since for some months they had been meditating a most daring project, which, they believed, would render them absolute masters of the field.

We have mentioned that in 1721 the Infanta Luisa Isabella, then in her fifth year, had been sent to the French Court to be brought up there until she had reached a marriageable age, when she was to become the wife of Louis XV. Well, this arrangement had always been regarded with the strongest disfavour by *Monsieur le Duc* and his mistress. In the first place, years must elapse before the " Infanta-Queen," as the little princess was called, would be able to bear an heir to the throne, and should Louis XV. die without male issue, their enemy, the Duc de Chartres, would become King. In the second, should the of the Orléans.

During the visit of the King to Chantilly in the previous summer they had taken counsel with Pâris-Duverney and their principal advisers, and had decided that the Infanta must be sent back to Spain, even at the risk of an open breach with Philip V.; and Louis XV. married to some princess who could at once make him a father.

Madame de Prie had personally a double interest in the accomplishment of this design, for not only would it remove the greatest dangers which *Monsieur le Duc* had to fear and immensely strengthen his position, but the marriage of the King and the birth of a prince would serve to retard perhaps indefinitely the marriage of her lover. For while only two lives stood between *Monsieur le Duc* and the throne, it was obviously his duty to take a second wife, and *Madame la Duchesse* was continually urging him to do so. Such a prospect was naturally most distasteful to Madame de Prie, not because she had much reason to fear a rival in the prince's affections, but because she had become so attached to him that she could not bear the thought of surrendering him, even nominally, to another woman, Moreover, his remarriage must interfere to some extent with that free intercourse which had hitherto existed between them, and which, for political as well as sentimental reasons, might occasion serious inconvenience.

However, since she did not see her way to offer any opposition to the affair without the risk of an open quarrel with *Madame la Duchesse,* she decided to accept the inevitable, and to occupy herself in finding a wife for her lover who, while not possessing sufficient personal attractions to cause her any jealousy, would be sufficiently complaisant to reduce the incoveniences which she feared to a minimum.

She accordingly lent *Madame la Duchesse* her most devoted adherents, the same whom she was presently to employ on behalf of Louis XV.; and the Courts of Europe were ransacked to find a suitable partner for the chief of the Condés. The search proved to be a difficult one, for Madame de Prie's requirements naturally caused not a few otherwise eligible young ladies to be passed over by her agents ; but, at length, her old admirer Lozilières, formerly secretary to the Embassy at Turin, who journeyed under the name of the Chevalier de Méré and in the character of a wandering artist, reported the discovery of one whom he thought might answer her purpose.

The princess in question was Marie Leczinska, daughter of Stanislaus Leczinski, the dethroned and fugitive King of Poland, who was now vegetating sadly at Weissembourg, in Alsace. She was described as pleasing in appearance, though without any pretensions to beauty, very amiable, very kind-hearted, and entirely devoid of ambition ; in short, exactly the kind of young woman to make *Monsieur le Duc* a good wife, without threatening any danger to his mistress. The favourite's suggestion of an alliance between the Duc de Bourbon and the Polish princess was well received by *Madame la Duchesse*, for, though the young lady's father was at present in exile, it was far from improbable that a turn of fortune might one day restore him to his throne ; *Monsieur le Duc* offered no opposition ; Stanislaus gave thanks to Heaven that his daughter's hand was sought by so powerful a prince ; Marie had no other wish than that of her father ; and the affair was almost concluded, when events occurred which decided the Government that the marriage of the King to a princess capable of bearing him children was a question which admitted of no delay.

On 30 August, 1724, the young King of Spain died, and Philip V. resumed the crown which he had resigned a few months before. Early in 1725, a despatch from Philip to his Ambassador at the Court of Versailles was intercepted by the agents of *Monsieur le Duc*, which showed that it was his intention to demand "the public declaration of the nuptial arrangements" between Louis XV. and the Infanta. And, almost immediately after this discovery, the young King fell so ill that for several days he was believed to be in serious danger.

This last event precipitated matters, and the French Govern-

Infanta." ¹

When the news was known in Madrid, the indignation of the populace knew no bounds ; excited crowds paraded the streets ; the King of France was burned in effigy, and the French residents trembled for their safety. Philip V. even talked of imprisoning his widowed daughter-in-law and her sister, Mlle. de Beaujolais, in some remote corner of the kingdom, where they should remain as hostages. But afterwards he changed his mind, and at the end of March they were sent back to France, the want of courtesy shown them being in striking contrast to the infinite formalities which marked the journey of the Infanta from Versailles to Bayonne. That little princess departed under the impression that she was merely going to pay a visit to her family.

Meanwhile, the search for the future Queen of France was being busily prosecuted. The claims of over one hundred

¹ Président Hénault, "Mémoires." But, according to Coxe ("History of the House of Austria"), Isabella Farnese was anything but composed : "In the first paroxysms of rage, the Queen tore off a bracelet ornamented with a portrait of the King'of France and trampled it under her foot ; and Philip declared that Spain could never shed enough blood to avenge the indignity offered to his family."

princesses were discussed by the Council, and one after another eliminated from the list, on the score that they were too old or too young or too poor or too delicate, until the number was reduced to three ; the two youngest sisters of *Monsieur le Duc*, Mlle. de Vermandois and Mlle. de Sens, and the Princess Anne of England.

The idea of a marriage between Louis XV. and one of the Condés displeased Fleury, while *Monsieur le Duc* feared that it might expose him to the charge of having sent away the Infanta in order to elevate his own family ; and it was therefore decided to demand the hand of the English princess. It seems astonishing that *Monsieur le Duc* and his advisers should not have understood that the question of religion would prove an insuperable obstacle to the proposed alliance. They made it conditional on the Princess Anne's conversion to Catholicism, although the Hanoverian dynasty occupied the throne of England in virtue of its Protestant professions. As every one but themselves must have foreseen, George I.'s answer was a courteous but firm refusal.

Monsieur le Duc appeared to find himself thrown back upon his sisters. Both possessed all the physical and mental qualifications that could be desired in a queen ; but the younger, Mlle. de Sens, was very much under the domination of her mother, and Madame de Prie feared that *Madame la Duchesse* might exercise through her an influence hostile to her own. The same objection did not apply to her elder sister, and there is a tradition that the favourite went, under an assumed name, to the Abbey of Fontevrault, of which Mlle de Vermandois was a *pensionnaire*, to inform her, on behalf of *Monsieur le Duc*, of the honour in store for her ; that, in the course of their conversation, she inquired if she had ever heard of Madame de Prie, to which the young princess replied, in a horrified tone, that the said lady was a "*méchante créature*," whom no one ever mentioned in the convent without making the sign of the Cross ; that it was deplorable that her brother should have fallen under the influence of a person who was detested by all France, and that he would be well advised to get rid of her as soon as possible.

Whereupon, we are told, Madame de Prie abruptly quitted the room, exclaiming furiously : " *Va ! tu ne seras pas reine de France.*"

In a monotonous age it seems a pity to spoil so striking a story, but, in the interests of truth, we feel bound to mention that, some three months after the date at which this incident is supposed to have occurred, Mlle. de Vermandois wrote to the favourite a letter couched in the most cordial terms, and concluding thus : " I cannot too often repeat to you, Madame, what are the sentiments of confidence, friendship, and consideration that I entertain for you." [1]

The fact of the matter is that Mlle. de Vermandois did not become the bride of Louis XV., because she preferred to become the bride of Heaven, in which she perhaps showed a wise discretion.

The refusal of Mlle. de Vermandois was probably a relief to *Monsieur le Duc*, who was aware that the bitterness and jealousy aroused by the elevation of his sister would go far to outweigh the advantages which he would gain from his close connexion with the King. At the same time, it threatened to prolong a situation the dangers of which had been brought home to him very forcibly by the recent serious illness of his young Sovereign.

It was at this moment that he received, from the Empress Catherine of Russia, an offer which contributed indirectly to give to the great affair of the marriage of Louis XV. the most unexpected *dénoûment*. Catherine proposed that her daughter Elizabeth should wed the King of France, and that *Monsieur le Duc* himself should marry Marie Leczinska—with whom she was no doubt aware that he had already opened matrimonial negotiations—and become the Russian candidate for the throne of Poland, in succession to Augustus III.

This gave Madame de Prie an opening of which she was not slow to take advantage. The Russian alliance, she declared, to *Monsieur le Duc*, was quite out of the question, for the

---

[1] This letter has been published in full by M. Thirion, in his interesting monograph on Madame de Prie.

Princess Elizabeth was reported to be a true child of her mother, and would be certain to acquire a great influence over the young King, which would, of course, be directed by Catherine. But let the prince resign his own pretensions to the hand of Marie Leczinska in favour of his Sovereign, and not only would he escape a marriage which only a sense of the duty he owed his family was impelling him to contract, but he would secure a Queen who would owe everything to him, who had no support either in France or abroad, and whose character promised obedience and docility.

The name of Marie Leczinska had already been erased from the list of marriageable princesses, on the ground that she belonged to a poor and dispossessed family ; but, urged on by his mistress and Pâris-Duverney, *Monsieur le Duc* immediately proceeded to advocate her claims. His proposal met with the most violent opposition from the Duc d'Orléans, who presented himself before Louis XV., with tears coursing down his cheeks, and endeavoured to persuade him from a marriage contrary, he declared, to the wishes of the nation ; while the King of Sardinia, his Majesty's grandfather, indignant at not having been consulted, addressed the most reproachful letters to the young monarch concerning the *mésalliance* which he was about to commit. But Fleury, a word from whom would have had more weight with Louis XV. than the expostulations of all the kings and princes in Europe, excused himself from expressing an opinion, and on 27 May, 1725, his Majesty announced publicly, after dinner, his approaching marriage with Marie Leczinska.

It was a great triumph for *Monsieur le Duc* and his mistress. At one blow, so to speak, they had got rid of the Infanta and the dreaded influence of Philip V. ; affianced the King to a princess who might before a year had elapsed bear him a son to stand between the Duc d'Orléans and the throne, and secured a Queen of France from whose influence they had nothing to fear and everything to hope.

The exiles of Weissembourg were not allowed to remain in doubt as to whom they were indebted for their amazing good fortune, and they displayed a gratitude proportioned to their joy. "In his correspondence with the Maréchal de Bourg," writes M. Thirion, "the dethroned King returned constantly to the gratitude which he, his wife, and his daughter had vowed to the Marquise de Prie, to the admiration which she had inspired in them, to the affection which they all three bore her, to the respectful gratitude which they professed for *Monsieur le Duc.* It was to Madame de Prie that they addressed themselves, when they desired to know what they were expected to do, of this or that custom of the Court. And the day when, in a scene which has remained celebrated, the ex-King of Poland threw himself on his knees to return thanks to Heaven for having called his daughter to such high destinies, he thought still of the favourite. He mentioned her in his thanksgivings."

But great triumphs, whether military or political, are seldom cheaply obtained, and in the present instance the cost was very considerable. Spain had been exasperated to the last degree by the almost brutal repudiation of the Infanta and had thrown herself into the arms of Austria ; the Orléans were furious at being outwitted and at the treatment to which *Monsieur le Duc's* action had exposed their relatives in Spain, and were more than ever determined to compass his disgrace ; while a great part both of the Court and the nation was indignant at the selection of ,a princess without alliance, without fortune, and without credit.

However, when all things were taken into account, the Prime Minister and his favourite felt that they had good cause for rejoicing, and they awaited with impatience the coming of Marie Leczinska and the consummation of their hopes.

On 15 August, 1725, the Duc d'Orléans, in the name of the King of France, espoused Marie Leczinska, at Strasbourg. For obvious reasons, the duty could not have been an altogether pleasant one for his Royal Highness to perform, nor was it rendered any the more agreeable by the fact that his enemy, Madame de Prie, in her capacity as one of the twelve *dames du palais* of the Queen of France, was a witness of his discomfiture. The favourite might have aspired to the more exalted post of *dame d'atours* (mistress of the robes), but this she had prudently decided to forgo, lest she should be accused of wishing to dominate her Majesty too ostensibly. But the successful candidate, the Comtesse de Mailly, mother-in-law of the future mistress of Louis XV., was her selection, as were all the ladies-in-waiting.

Two days later, Marie Leczinska set out to join the King, who had just established himself at Fontainebleau. It was remarked that both at Strasbourg and during the journey her Majesty showed an extreme graciousness towards Madame de Prie, and conversed with her longer and more frequently than with any of her colleagues. At Moret, the Queen was met by Louis XV., accompanied by all the Princesses. Marie descended from her coach, and was preparing to kneel on a cushion hastily thrown, but the King prevented her, kissed her on both cheeks, "with a vivacity which astonished those who were aware of his timidity where women were concerned," and did not conceal his pleasure. On 5 September, the marriage was celebrated, in the chapel at Fontainebleau, with the utmost magnificence, and the next day *Monsieur le Duc* wrote to Stanislaus Leczinski that his Majesty's attitude towards his wife "had surpassed his hopes, and, if possible, his desires," adding certain intimate details, upon which, however, we dare not venture.

The Court remained at Fontainebleau until the first days of December, when it returned to Versailles, where the young Queen was installed in the apartments formerly occupied by Marie Thérèse of Austria and the Duchesse de Bourgogne. No cloud had as yet troubled the royal honeymoon. The King was quite a devoted husband; he passed every night with his wife; compared her to Queen Blanche, the mother of Saint-Louis, and said to those who drew his attention to the beauty of some lady of the Court : "I find the Queen still more beautiful."

Monsieur le Duc and Madame de Prie were delighted, believing that from this passion would spring true friendship and confidence; that gradually Marie Leczinska would acquire ascendency over the mind of this young King, half-man, half-child, and that they would be able to govern him through her.

suppressed ; satires and pamphlets against the Government poured from the printing-presses of the capital ; more than one Minister talked of resigning his office. Unless *Monsieur le Duc* could secure the favour and confidence of the King, his Ministry was doomed.

But between *Monsieur le Duc* and the King stood the figure of Fleury. The prince had now been Prime Minister for two years, yet never had he succeeded in obtaining a single hour's private conversation with Louis XV. on affairs of State. A score of times when he imagined that he had found a favourable occasion to speak to him on business, the King had immediately turned the conversation to the chase, the play or some kindred subject, on which he continued to talk until Fleury, whom he never failed to summon, entered his cabinet. The previous year, when Louis XV. was at Chantilly and the Bishop of Fréjus had gone to spend a week at the country-house of the Duc de Liancourt, *Monsieur le Duc* had endeavoured to take advantage of his absence ; but the King intimated to him that he would do nothing until the return of his preceptor, and even refused to sign some papers of trifling importance which were

awaiting his signature. All his efforts to secure the confidence
of the young monarch remained without result; the Bishop of
Fréjus perpetually barred the way.

And he could not disguise from himself the fact that
Fleury was no longer content to remain neutral. He had
become, if not the opponent of *Monsieur le Duc* himself, at
least that of his chief advisers. One day, in the spring of 1626,
he drew the prince aside, denounced in the strongest terms the
conduct of Madame de Prie and Duverney, whom he stigmatized as enemies of the State, and declared that "the reputation
of his Highness imperiously demanded that he should no
longer submit to the domination of such unworthy counsellors."
It was practically an ultimatum, or, at any rate, *Monsieur le Duc*
regarded it in that light. If he were willing to dismiss his
mistress and Duverney and govern on the advice of Fleury, the
latter would graciously permit him to retain the simulacrum
of power. If not, the bishop intended to procure the disgrace
of all three.

The Prime Minister warmly defended his friends, asserting
that they were the victims of envy and prejudice, and ended
by declaring that, since he well knew that they were ready to
hazard everything for him, even their lives, if they were to fall,
he would fall with them. Then, after high words on both sides,
the prince and the bishop parted.

When this conversation was reported to Madame de Prie,
she at once perceived that there could be no safety for the
Ministry of *Monsieur le Duc* so long as Fleury remained at
Court, and she represented to her lover that all their efforts
must henceforth be directed to separating him from the
King. It was, of course, too much to hope that Louis XV.
would ever consent to banish his former preceptor, but the
latter might be induced to believe that he had forfeited his
Majesty's confidence and retire of his own accord.

But how was this to be accomplished? Obviously, by
means of the Queen. Marie Leczinska, thanks to the efforts
of Madame de Prie and the ladies whom the favourite had
placed about her, who insinuated that Fleury was jealous of the

affection the King entertained for her, was already prejudiced against the bishop ; while she naturally felt herself under great obligations to those who had placed the crown matrimonial upon her head.

On 18 December, 1725, it was decided to make an attempt to accustom the King to work with the Prime Minister without the presence of his preceptor. The Queen, after a good deal of hesitation, had consented to lend herself to this intrigue, certain indiscreet words which Fleury had uttered in her presence having dissipated her last scruples.

In accordance with the plan agreed upon, when Louis XV. returned from the chase, she sent to ask him to join her in her cabinet. It was then about an hour before that which he invariably spent in conversation with his preceptor.

On entering his wife's apartments, the King found her with *Monsieur le Duc.* With her most ingratiating smile, the Queen told him that she had a favour to ask of him. Would he not consent to work in her cabinet that evening with the Prime Minister only ?

The King refused, though she continued to press him until the time arrived for him to join Fleury. Before he left, however, she succeeded in extracting a promise from him that he would return shortly. Proceeding to his own apartments, where his preceptor was awaiting him, the King gave him an exact account of all that had passed, at the same time assuring him that, he was resolved never to work alone with *Monsieur le Duc* and not to return to the Queen. Fleury, however, begged him to go back, as he had given his promise to the Queen, adding that, if he were determined not to discuss affairs of State alone with *Monsieur le Duc*, he had better send for him, " No, no ! " replied the King ; " remain here ; I shall return in a moment."

Louis XV. went out, and did not return, the Queen and *Monsieur le Duc* having detained him on various pretexts. Fleury waited an hour, and then, believing or, more probably, feigning to believe, that the King had yielded to the persuasions of the Queen, retired, and on the following morning wrote to the King, begging him, since his services were no longer of any

From that hour it was clear that the Ministry was doomed, unless it could come to terms with the bishop. The outcry against it redoubled in intensity; its more lukewarm friends began to fall away and to pay their court openly to Fleury; while the King's manner towards his wife plainly showed the irritation which he felt at her conduct.

It is probable that Fleury would have been prepared to leave the nominal direction of affairs in the hands of *Monsieur le Duc*, at any rate until the situation both at home and abroad had become less embarrassing, if the prince had consented to the dismissal of Madame de Prie and Duverney, the two particular objects of public hatred. Several times he urged this step upon the prince, only to be met with an assurance that both of them had practically ceased to exercise any political influence. More wise than her lover, Madame de Prie sought to conciliate the bishop by temporarily renouncing public life, and, when her duties as *dame du palais* did not require her presence at the Court, passing the greater part of her time in Paris. At the beginning of March, 1726, she withdrew to an estate which she had acquired near Lisieux, whence she wrote begging the Queen to accord her permission to remain there for ascendency over the Prime Minister that he would never consent to part with them.

Henceforth, the only question with him was the choice of a convenient moment for the disgrace of *Monsieur le Duc*. Both he and the King, however, found it difficult to take the decisive step, and they were still hesitating when, on 8 June, the Prime Minister, exasperated by a fresh outburst against Madame de Prie, who had just returned to Versailles from a visit to Paris, came to Louis XV. and tendered his resignation. But it was not *Monsieur le Duc's* resignation that the bishop required, but his dismissal, and, on his advice, Louis XV., with that dissimulation which was one of the least edifying traits in his character, not only begged the Prime Minister to retain his office, but gave him " marks of his friendship and satisfaction."

Monsieur le Duc had no choice but to withdraw his resignation, and left the royal presence under the comforting impression that he stood in no immediate danger. He was speedily undeceived.

On Tuesday, 11 June, at three o'clock in the afternoon, *Monsieur le Duc*, Madame de Prie and Duverney being all three still at Versailles, Louis XV. set out for Rambouillet. At dinner the King had shown himself particularly gracious to the Prime Minister. He had given him to taste some bread which had been kneaded specially for him at the Ménagerie; had thrown a little loaf into his hat, and had said, as he rose from

table: "Monsieur, despatch your affairs and come early to
Rambouillet, because I shall sup at half-past eight," a
recommendation which he repeated at the moment of entering
his carriage.

After the King had driven away, *Monsieur le Duc* went to
his cabinet, where he passed the rest of the afternoon working
with the Minister for War, Breteuil, and the Comptroller-
General, Dodun.   Shortly before eight o'clock, the other
Ministers left the château, and the prince was about to follow
them, when he was informed that the Duc de Charost, Captain
of the Guards, had been waiting for three-quarters of an hour in
order to speak to him.

But let us allow Mathieu Marais to relate what followed in
his own words:

"The prince went out and told the Duc de Charost that he
was going to join the King at Rambouillet, and was pressed for
time, and asked him to defer until the morrow what he had to
say to him.   The Captain of the Guards answered in a low tone
that what he had to say to him was from the King ; upon which
they re-entered the cabinet.   The Duc de Charost handed him
an order from the King, which was to the effect that, as he
wished to govern himself in the future, he was suppressing the
office of Prime Minister ; that he thanked him for his services,
and ordered him to retire to Chantilly, until further orders.
This order was in the King's own hand.   The prince's first
movement was one of anger, after which he said that he
would obey.   He asked: 'And my papers?' and was told
that there were no orders concerning them.   He sorted
them, burned some, placed some in his pocket, and filled
a despatch-box with others, observing: 'These are the King's
papers, and all the others that remain are his.'   He wrote to
Madame la Duchesse almost, it is said, in these terms: 'Every
day follows another, and does not resemble it.   Yesterday, I
was Cæsar ; to-day, I am Pompey.   I am going to Chantilly.
I count, *belle maman*, on your still preserving for me your good
graces.'   He was asked for his parole, which he gave, and then
entered his carriage, which had been waiting for a long time to

take him to Rambouillet. He thanked all the courtiers who accompanied him to his carriage, and when he was outside the gates, he was heard to say to his postilion : ' To Chantilly!' M. de Saint-Pol, exempt of the Guards, accompanied him as far as the château."

While Charost was communicating the wishes of the King to the Prime Minister, Fleury, who was about to replace him, proceeded to the Queen's apartments, armed with a letter which he had dictated that morning to his former pupil. It was as follows : "I beg you, Madame, and, if need be, I order you, to do everything that the former Bishop of Fréjus will tell you on my behalf, as if it were myself."[1] The selection of Fleury to inform the Queen of the disgrace of her friends and to signify to her his orders was a refinement of cruelty, and the poor woman wept bitterly. After a while, however, she recovered her composure and wrote to the King : "Gratitude towards *Monsieur le Duc* has made me shed tears, but your commands dry them."

As soon as the bishop had departed, the Queen sent for Madame de Prie and the fallen Minister's favourite sister, Mlle. de Clermont, whom she informed of what had occurred. Both ladies started that same night for Chantilly, where they arrived at daybreak. In the evening, *Madame la Duchesse*, who had received the news of her son's disgrace at the Château of Saint-Maur, appeared upon the scene, with the faithful Lassay in her train.[2] *Madame la Duchesse* had always detested Madame de Prie, and regarding her, as she now did, as the cause of her son's disgrace, her indignation against her knew no bounds. " She was very surprised to learn that Madame de Prie was there, and manifested it in terms which marked her contempt and hatred. After having embraced her son, she told him that she hoped that the lady would not be so indiscreet as to present

---

[1] Maréchal de Villars, "Mémoires." These orders were not to receive *Monsieur le Duc*, in case he should present himself at her apartments, and, on no considera-tion, to make any allusion in the presence of the King to that prince, Madame de Prie, or Pâris-Duverney.

[2] See page 280, supra.

"On the Thursday, on descending to dinner, *Madame la Duchesse* perceived that a place had been laid for Madame de Prie next to her own. She stopped and manifested her surprise. Madame de Prie approached and said to her: 'Is it your wish that I retire?' She replied: 'No, you may sit down to table!' But she called the Prince di Carignano to sit by her, and Madame de Prie took the prince's place.

"As this was done in a manner sufficiently humiliating, there were, after dinner, a great many comings and goings, in order to persuade *Madame la Duchesse* to permit Madame de Prie to sup with her. Finally, *Madame la Duchesse* consented, out of complaisance for *Monsieur le Duc*, in the state in which he was." [1]

For nearly two days after the disgrace of *Monsieur le Duc* no steps were taken against his mistress. But no one at Chantilly doubted that her respite would be but a brief one. Duverney had been exiled forty leagues from Paris; all the Ministers most attached to *Monsieur le Duc* had been relieved of their functions; Le Blanc and the Belle-Isles had been recalled, and the man who, if he had received his deserts, would have been decorating a gibbet had actually been reinstated in his old post of Secretary of State for War, in place of the honest Breteuil. In such a revolution of the palace, it was impossible for her to escape, and on the Thursday evening the blow fell, in the shape of a *lettre de cachet* exiling her to her husband's estate of Courbépine, in Normandy.

Her parting with *Monsieur le Duc* on the morrow was a most touching one. "She kept up the comedy to the last," writes the author of the manuscript we have just cited. "Twice after entering her carriage she returned, not being able, she said, to depart without again embracing *Monsieur le Duc*. She appeared in despair at leaving him, and gave him all the tokens of a

[1] "MS. of the Bastille," published in "la Nouvelle Révue rétrospective."

her, and had told the Maréchal de Villars that "he himself was the cause of all her misfortunes and that she did not deserve them; that she had always been disinterested, and that the unsatisfactory condition of her affairs would in time prove this," people began to think that, in view of a possible return of the prince to power, it would be imprudent to ignore the woman who still retained his affections. From that time it became quite the fashion to go and spend a day or two with the proscribed, and the latter never had any cause to complain of lack of company. Nevertheless, she felt bitterly the change in her position, and could not disguise from herself the fact that, notwithstanding the chivalrous endeavours of *Monsieur le Duc* to saddle himself with the responsibility for their common misfortune, she had largely contributed to it. She saw, too, her relatives and *protégés* deprived of their charges and reduced in some instances to poverty; and this troubled her sorely. There can be no doubt that, in time, she would have been permitted to return, if not to the Court, at least to Paris and Chantilly; but her health, always delicate, had begun to give way beneath the stress of so many agitations. She demanded and obtained authorization to visit the waters of Forges, but the relief they afforded her was only temporary. In the early autumn of 1727 she met with a carriage accident, and though the injuries she received were not in themselves very serious, they hastened her death, which took place on 7 October, 1727, in her thirtieth year.

Her enemies attributed her death to poison administered by her own hand, and the Marquis d'Argenson has published, in his " Mémoires," a highly-coloured version of this hypothesis, upon which we need not dwell here, since its absurdity has now been clearly established.

Monsieur le Duc survived his mistress nearly fourteen years. In 1830, he was pardoned and returned to Court, but he never reappeared again on the political stage, and consecrated the last years of his life to the study of chemistry and natural history. In 1728, he took unto himself a second wife, in the person of the Princess Charlotte of Hesse-Rheinfels, who is described as " *blonde et d'un enbonpoint agréable*," with whom he seems to have lived very contentedly, notwithstanding the fact that she is said to have been erased from the list of eligible princesses at the time of the marriage of Louis XV. on account of her bad temper. By her he left one son, Louis Joseph de Bourbon, Prince de Condé, the organizer and leader of the "Army of Condé," which played so gallant a part in the Wars of the French Revolution. *Monsieur le Duc* died on the 27 January, 1740, in his forty-ninth year.

PRINTED BY
WILLIAM CLOWES AND SONS, LIMITED,
LONDON AND BECCLES

Lightning Source UK Ltd.
Milton Keynes UK
UKOW06f2351071015

260060UK00017B/547/P